MW00387257

THE WALL STREET JOURNAL.

Guide to the

TOP BUSINESS SCHOOLS

2006

Ronald J. Alsop
with Harris Interactive

Random House Reference
New York Toronto London Sydney Auckland

Copyright © 2005 by Dow Jones & Co., Inc.

All rights reserved. No part of this book may be reproduced in any form or by any means, electronic or mechanical, including photo-copying, recording, or by any information storage and retrieval system, without the written permission of the publisher. Published in the United States by Random House Reference, an imprint of The Random House Information Group, a division of Random House, Inc., New York, and simultaneously in Canada by Random House of Canada Limited, Toronto.

RANDOM HOUSE is a registered trademark of Random House, Inc.

Please address inquiries about electronic licensing of any products for use on a network, in software or on CD-ROM to the Subsidiary Rights Department, Random House Information Group, fax 212-572-6003.

This book is available for special discounts for bulk purchases for sales promotions or premiums. Special editions, including personal-ized covers, excerpts of existing books, and corporate imprints, can be created in large quantities for special needs. For more informa-tion, write to Random House, Inc., Special Markets/Premium Sales, 1745 Broadway, MD 6-2, New York, NY, 10019 or e-mail *specialmar-kets@randomhouse.com*.

Visit the Random House Reference Web site: www.randomwords.com

ISBN: 0-375-72098-7

Printed in the United States of America

10 9 8 7 6 5 4 3 2 1

CONTENTS

INTRODUCTION

For prospective M.B.A. students, it's a buyer's market these days. More than ever, business schools are practicing what they preach in their marketing classes. Faced with a decline in applications to M.B.A. programs, they are offering more product selection than ever. Want to complete the degree in 12 months, 15 months, 17 months? All of those fast-track options are readily available. Would you like to spend your first year on campus and complete the degree online from your home or office computer? No problem. Indiana University has created that hybrid. Any executive-M.B.A. programs for health-care professionals? You bet—at Yale University.

"We are asking ourselves if we should be doing things differently and becoming more flexible," Julia Tyler, M.B.A. program director at London Business School, told me recently. "Now, for example, we allow student to waive certain core courses, such as accounting and microeconomics. They can either increase their electives or complete the M.B.A. degree in 15 months rather than 21."

But greater choice also means greater confusion about which school and which type of program best suit prospective students' career aspirations and lifestyles. With the cost of an M.B.A. degree running well over $100,000 at some of the most selective schools, picking the right program is critical.

That's why this book was designed to give you the facts you'll need to guide you in making that important decision. Much of the book is based on *The Wall Street Journal*/Harris Interactive recruiter survey and rankings, which focus on full-time M.B.A. programs. But there is plenty of information in the book about part-time, executive, and online options as well. Schools also are offering students a growing array of specialized master's of science degrees, particularly in finance, which we highlight in individual school profiles.

The book's most distinctive feature is its strong focus on corporate recruiters and the job market, which is finally on the rebound after a very long slump. Recruiters are the people who rate the M.B.A. programs in the Journal survey and determine their ranking among the top national and regional schools in North America and the top international schools. As the buyers of M.B.A. talent, recruiters have strong opinions about the schools they know best. And those opinions should be of utmost importance to prospective students, who after all hope to graduate into a better job with more lucrative compensation. How well students achieve those goals depends on how positively companies view the schools they attend.

The three No. 1 schools this year—Dartmouth College in New Hampshire, Purdue University in Indiana, and IMD in Switzerland—all offer relatively small M.B.A. programs and produce graduates whom recruiters find attractive both for their knowledge and their appealing attitudes. More prestigious schools like Harvard and Stanford receive kudos for their academic excellence but also criticism for students' arrogance and lofty expectations.

The universe of schools in the Journal rankings includes more than 60 U.S. M.B.A. programs and more than a dozen in Canada, Latin America, and Europe. Only people making recruiting decisions rated specific schools—and only schools they know from firsthand experience. We don't want the ratings to be based on the schools' past reputations. We interview the men and women who are out in the field doing the actual recruiting—heads of business units, line managers, small-business owners, and others—and not just human-resource executives stationed at corporate headquarters. We also include a broad array of recruiters from large companies like Ford Motor Co. and Goldman Sachs Group Inc., small consulting and high-tech firms, and non-profit and government agencies.

In addition to our overall rankings, we provide lists of the schools rated highest by recruiters in specific industries, such as financial services and consumer products, and those considered tops in certain academic disciplines, such as accounting and information technology.

The book also provides detailed information about each of the 76 schools that qualified for one or more of the three *Journal* rankings in 2005. We cut through the schools' marketing spiels and provide only the most essential facts, including application information, placement rates, graduates' compensation packages, and the recruiters they attract.

Beyond the school rankings, the book includes essays on some of the major issues in business education today. We analyze the pros and cons of the various M.B.A. degree formats and tell you how much recruiters value full-time vs. part-time vs. executive vs. online degrees. Their opinions may surprise you.

We also provide insights into what corporate recruiters seek most when they hire M.B.A.s—and which attributes they too often find lacking. For one thing, they'd like to see more literate graduates who can communicate well, whether in writing or public speaking. Recruiters also are in pursuit of students who demonstrate personal integrity and have accumulated plenty of work experience, especially involving leadership and teamwork. Recruiters also tell us how weary they are of M.B.A. attitude. Too often, students come off as arrogant with inflated opinions of their worth in the marketplace.

Business schools continue to strive for greater diversity in both the student body and the faculty, but the number of women and minorities remains stubbornly low. Several of the essays examine the issues that are impeding progress, the experiences of women and minorities in business schools, and the most encouraging new diversity programs. In addition, we look at the ways some international M.B.A. students are overcoming the odds and finding good jobs in the U.S. after graduation. In short, it's all about networking.

Our M.B.A. rankings are distinctive from other B-school surveys because Harris Interactive Inc., a highly regarded market-research firm, brings its expertise to the project, from the development of the survey methodology to the analysis of the results. Brenda Roberts of Harris deserves special recognition for her tireless and meticulous work on the survey. Harris's Robert Fronk and Beth Strackbein also provided valuable insight and support on the project.

At *The Wall Street Journal*, Raymund Flandez was of great assistance in gathering and compiling data for the book. Thanks also to Roe D'Angelo at the *Journal* and Jena Pincott at Random House for expertly guiding the editorial process. And most of all, we want to express our gratitude to the many business-school officials and corporate recruiters who helped to make our survey, now in its fifth year, such a success once again.

—Ron Alsop

PART I

AND THE WINNERS ARE. . . .

THE SURVEY RESULTS: HOW RECRUITERS RANKED THE WORLD'S M.B.A. PROGRAMS

And the B-school winners are . . .

Yes, *The Wall Street Journal*/Harris Interactive survey of corporate recruiters produces not one but three No. 1-ranked M.B.A. programs. The three rankings all measure how appealing the schools are to recruiters—the buyers of M.B.A. talent—but the methodology also reflects differences in M.B.A. recruiting patterns among the schools, resulting in separate rankings of:

—19 National schools in North America, led by the Tuck School of Business at Dartmouth College. These M.B.A. programs share many of the same recruiters, primarily national and multinational companies that hire students from a broad range of the most prominent business schools.

—47 Regional schools in North America, with Purdue University's Krannert School of Management in the No. 1 spot for the second consecutive year. These M.B.A. programs tend to be smaller and attract many recruiters from their local regions.

—20 International schools, with IMD, the International Institute for Management Development in Switzerland, on top for the second straight year. This group, a combination of European, North American, and Latin American schools, includes only programs that attract a global mix of recruiters from a variety of countries.

The survey of 3,267 recruiters was conducted online between Dec. 6, 2004, and March 9, 2005, with respondents rating only schools where they said they had recent recruiting experience. To qualify for any of the three rankings, a school had to receive at least 20 recruiter ratings. The M.B.A. rankings are based on recruiters' perceptions of the schools and their graduates on 20 key attributes, such as students' leadership potential, teamwork abilities, and communication and interpersonal skills; the faculty and curriculum; and the career-services office. They also reflect "supportive behavior," defined as the recruiters' intention to return to a particular school and the likelihood that they will offer jobs to its graduates in the next two years. Finally, the rankings include "mass appeal": for National and Regional schools, this is the number of recruiters that the schools attract, and for the International ranking, the number of countries from which schools draw recruiters. The rankings calculation gives equal weight to perception, supportive behavior, and mass appeal.

NATIONAL RANKING

Which factors distinguish the National ranking from the Regional? National recruiters tend to hire from more schools; the programs are often private, located in the eastern U.S., and larger in enrollment. All six Ivy League universities with business schools are in the National ranking.

Recruiters rating the National schools also hire primarily M.B.A. students and offer the highest compensation—25% of National-school recruiters said they paid $100,000 or more in starting salary, compared with only 8% of Regional-school recruiters.

Although Dartmouth doesn't attract as many recruiters as some of the larger National schools, it handily outscores all the rest on perception and supportive behavior. Recruiters rated it most highly for students' personal ethics and integrity, ability to work well in teams, and their well-rounded qualities. Many recruiters praised Tuck graduates for their collegial spirit and interpersonal skills. "Larger class size has helped increase the depth of the talent pool," one survey respondent commented, "but it's still small enough to continue to foster the all-important Tuck culture."

Another school that receives recruiters' praise for its collegiality is the University of California at Berkeley, which showed the biggest rankings jump of all the National schools, up eight spots to No. 7. Berkeley's Haas School of Business received its highest ratings for students' ability to work well in teams, analytical and problem-solving skills, and personal ethics and integrity.

"My impression of the Berkeley M.B.A. candidates is that they are more seasoned—with more real-life experience—than past classes," says John Pollard, who works in corporate finance at Cisco Systems Inc. "There were also more people from different parts of the world than I have seen in the past. It's not a regional or even a national school anymore. They've gone worldwide."

The University of Chicago fell the furthest in the National ranking—eight spots to No. 13. Many recruiters criticize Chicago students as too "geeky" and quantitative. "I've often found that Chicago grads are good within functions but seem to lack the skills and/or experience to drive toward a general management position," says Hal Nelson, a director of strategic planning and analysis at Corning Inc.

Commenting on Chicago, another survey respondent says, "The attitude of students seems to have become more like my experiences at Harvard and Wharton. The students have tremendous academic abilities but sink in an interpersonal and team-oriented culture."

Some of the most elite schools like Stanford University and Harvard University do indeed suffer in the ranking because of students who project the wrong attitude to recruiters. In the survey, recruiters repeatedly used words like "sense of entitlement," "ego problems," and "arrogant" to describe the chief shortcoming of Harvard Business School and its students.

Stanford's Graduate School of Business also received low scores, particularly for students' willingness to relocate for a job, value for the money invested in the recruiting effort, and the school's career-services office. "Stanford has a great name, so the people there feel they can be arrogant to recruiters," one survey respondent says.

Cornell University's Johnson Graduate School of Management places lowest of the Ivies and just one notch above the lowest-ranked University of California at Los Angeles. The big drawbacks for recruiters: location, location, location. Many recruiters complain about the difficulty of reaching Cornell's remote campus in Ithaca, N.Y., which has little direct air service. They advise the Johnson School to reach out to companies more effectively and stage more recruiting events in Manhattan.

The Marshall School of Business at the University of Southern California is the only new nationally ranked school. It moved from the Regional list because the recruiters rating USC in 2005 were more likely to also recruit at such National schools as UCLA, Berkeley, and Stanford.

REGIONAL RANKING

Regional schools are smaller than National schools for the most part, with a fairly even representation of private and public universities and a broad geographic spread across the U.S., Canada, and Mexico. Regional recruiters are more apt to visit a single business school, pay lower salaries, and recruit more non-M.B.A. graduates than National recruiters.

Recruiters classify many of the Regional schools as team-focused and give their students high scores for personal ethics and integrity and being down-to-earth and well-rounded. Those are particularly strong characteristics of the top three Regional schools, all public universities in the Midwest.

No. 1 Purdue is repeatedly praised for students' strong work ethic and technical skills. "The students who have joined us from Purdue tend to fit the strong work ethic of my company," says Russell Flugel, a financial manager at Air Products & Chemicals Inc. "They are often successful in joining a part of our finance function called 'Decision Support,' where much of the work is focused on helping to make business decisions based on risk/reward and data analysis."

Rick Rosler, a financial analyst at Ford Motor Co., believes the caliber of students has risen in recent years because Purdue's Krannert School of Management has steadily improved the quality of its faculty and opened a new building "with the high-tech facilities that top-quality students demand."

Wake Forest University rose the most in the Regional ranking, up 10 places to No. 7. Keith Harman, a managing director at Banc of America Securities, says that recent Wake Forest hires "brought broad work experience, an outstanding work ethic, and a well-rounded understanding of finance and business fundamentals to the table. They stood out in their ability and willingness to dive into projects and take a leadership role in their assignments."

Michigan State University and Thunderbird's Garvin School of International Management both showed impressive gains too, jumping into the Top 5 of the Regional ranking. Recruiters consistently praise Thunderbird for global expertise and cross-cultural richness. As for Michigan State, one recruiter says, the school provides "continually better students and a first-class supply chain program that continues to improve."

Vanderbilt University and the University of Pittsburgh showed the biggest ranking declines. Both received low scores for faculty expertise and students' international knowledge and experience. Recruiters also commented on the uneven quality of graduates.

The McCombs School of Business at the University of Texas at Austin shifted to the Regional ranking from the National list, because it was rated more by survey respondents who also recruited at other schools in Texas. It also placed in the bottom third of the Regional schools, with several recruiters noting a decline in the quality of Texas and its graduates. An investment manager at Goldman Sachs Group Inc. says that although "résumés looked good, when you spoke with the students, they just were not as energetic, not as polished, and not as informed as previous classes we have interviewed."

INTERNATIONAL RANKING

The International Institute for Management Development in Switzerland, known as IMD, took top honors in the ranking of corporate recruiters' favorite global M.B.A. programs. The International list ranks schools that have a global reach in their job-placement activities, attracting recruiters from a mix of countries. Respondents from at least four countries must say they have recruited from a school in order for it to qualify for the International ranking.

The list includes 10 schools from the two North American rankings, along with nine European M.B.A. programs and one Central American school.

Although M.B.A. programs are an American phenomenon dating back more than 100 years, universities throughout the world are formidable rivals these days. Many foreign business schools, particularly those in Europe, offer condensed one-year

M.B.A. programs, a format many students find appealing. They're out of the workplace for a shorter period, so opportunity costs are much lower than for America's traditional two-year programs.

Three European schools really shine in this ranking. IMD in Lausanne, ESADE in Barcelona, Spain, and London Business School scored best among the European schools, with recruiters especially praising their students' international knowledge and experience. London Business School and Insead in Fontainebleau, France, attracted the broadest mix of recruiters, from 20 countries, while IMD drew recruiters from 15 countries.

IMD clearly has many fans in the corporate world, who give it especially high ratings for students' leadership abilities, strategic thinking, and personal ethics and integrity. Roberto Mauro, a global strategist at Samsung, finds that IMD graduates "provide a continuous stream of fresh perspectives to everyday business problems because of their global mindset." The students bring their international diversity to bear on team projects, he adds. "Most participants have lived and gained significant work experience in a different geography than their country of origin. As a consequence, very few things are taken for granted; all assumptions are challenged on the basis of personal experiences."

HEC School of Management in Paris and Stanford University declined the most in the latest International ranking, with both receiving very low perception and supportive-behavior ratings. Specifically, both schools scored poorly for their career-services offices and value for the money invested in the recruiting effort.

Instituto de Empresa in Madrid had the biggest gain, rising eight places to No. 12. Christoph Bug, a manager for Johnson & Johnson in Dusseldorf, Germany, finds the international mix of students and their extensive work experience impressive at Instituto de Empresa. "Hiring IE graduates is especially positive for big global companies," he says, "because these high potentials prove their international focus by being willing to relocate even to remote locations."

Among the U.S. schools in the International ranking, Carnegie Mellon University and Thunderbird fared best at Nos. 3 and 7, respectively. Neither school attracted recruiters from very many countries, but both scored quite well on perception and supportive behavior.

Carnegie Mellon, which also placed third in the National ranking, entered the International ranking for the first time by increasing its recruiter reach to six countries. Thunderbird enjoys the strongest reputation for teaching international business of any school in the survey. Yet it ranked only seventh because its "mass appeal" score was relatively low, with survey respondents from only five countries saying they recruit at Thunderbird.

"I was impressed by the quality of students at Thunderbird, especially the European people that I saw in 2005," one survey respondent says. "They were extremely smart, mature, focused, and expressed themselves very well."

NATIONAL SCHOOLS RANKING

The National ranking is based on how recruiters rated each school on 20 different attributes, their future plans to recruit at the school, and the number of survey respondents who said they had recruited recently at the school. These schools tend to draw recruiters from many of the same companies, usually large national or multinational firms that pay high starting salaries.

2005 Rank	2004 Rank	University (Business School)
1	3	Dartmouth College (Tuck)
2	1	University of Michigan (Ross)
3	2	Carnegie Mellon University (Tepper)
4	7	Northwestern University (Kellogg)
5	6	Yale University
6	4	University of Pennsylvania (Wharton)
7	15	University of California, Berkeley (Haas)
8	8	Columbia University
9	11	University of North Carolina, Chapel Hill (Kenan-Flagler)
10	—	University of Southern California (Marshall)
11	12	University of Virginia (Darden)
12	9	Massachusetts Institute of Technology (Sloan)
13	5	University of Chicago
14	13	Harvard University
15	10	Stanford University
16	17	New York University (Stern)
17	14	Duke University (Fuqua)
18	18	Cornell University (Johnson)
19	19	University of California, Los Angeles (Anderson)

REGIONAL SCHOOLS RANKING

The Regional ranking is based on how recruiters rated each school on 20 different attributes, their future plans to recruit at the school, and the number of survey respondents who said they had recruited recently at the school. These schools tend to draw recruiters from their local regions.

2005 Rank	2004 Rank	University (Business School)
1	1	Purdue University (Krannert)
2	8	Michigan State University (Broad)
3	3	Ohio State University (Fisher)
4	10	Thunderbird (Garvin)
5	11	IPADE
6	5	Brigham Young University (Marriott)
7	17	Wake Forest University (Babcock)
8	9	University of Denver (Daniels)
9	7	Tecnologico de Monterrey
10	16	University of Miami
11	13	Indiana University (Kelley)
12	19	Emory University (Goizueta)
13	15	University at Buffalo/SUNY
14	—	Fordham University
15	4	University of Maryland (Smith)
16	—	University of Iowa (Tippie)
17	20	University of Rochester (Simon)
18	6	Texas Christian University (Neeley)
19	25	College of William and Mary
20	14	Southern Methodist University (Cox)

21	2	Vanderbilt University (Owen)
22	24	Rice University (Jones)
23	12	University of Tennessee, Knoxville
24	—	University of Arizona (Eller)
25	18	Washington University (John M. Olin)
26	30	University of Utah (Eccles)
27	21	University of Florida (Warrington)
28	31	Texas A&M University (Mays)
29	27	University of Notre Dame (Mendoza)
30	38	University of Georgia (Terry)
31	37	George Washington University
32	32	University of Minnesota (Carlson)
33	26	Pennsylvania State University (Smeal)
34	33	University of Wisconsin, Madison
35	—	University of Texas, Austin (McCombs)
36	29	University of Washington
37	22	University of Pittsburgh (Katz)
38	36	Georgetown University (McDonough)
39	34	University of California, Irvine (Merage)
40	41	Arizona State University (Carey)
41	39	Boston University
42	40	University of Illinois, Urbana-Champaign
43	35	University of Western Ontario (Ivey)
44	—	University of California, Davis
45	—	Georgia Institute of Technology
46	43	York University (Schulich)
47	—	University of Colorado, Boulder (Leeds)

INTERNATIONAL SCHOOLS RANKING

This ranking includes European, North American, and Central American schools that have a global pool of recruiters. It is based on how recruiters rated each school on 20 different attributes, their future plans to recruit students from the school, and the number of countries from which a school draws recruiters. To be eligible for this ranking, a school needed respondents from at least four countries.

2005 Rank	2004 Rank	University (Business School)	Number of Countries Recruiters Come From
1	1	IMD, International Institute for Management Development	15
2	3	ESADE	12
3	—	Carnegie Mellon University (Tepper)	6
4	—	IPADE	4
5	2	London Business School	20
6	—	University of Western Ontario (Ivey)	8
7	8	Thunderbird (Garvin)	5
8	5	Massachusetts Institute of Technology (Sloan)	7
9	12	Insead	20
10	—	INCAE	6
11	4	HEC, Paris	7
12	20	Instituto de Empresa	13
13	13	Columbia University	5
14	15	Erasmus University (Rotterdam)	8
15	14	York University (Schulich)	5
16	11	University of Chicago	5
17	16	Harvard University	7
18	10	Stanford University	5
19	18	IESE	13
20	—	Bocconi University	6

RANKING THE ATTRIBUTES

Recruiters in *The Wall Street Journal*/Harris Interactive survey rated each business school on these 20 student and school attributes. Here is how recruiters rated the attributes themselves in terms of importance. The attributes are ranked in order of the percentage of recruiters who rated them as "very important."

	Communication and interpersonal skills	Ability to work well within a team	Personal ethics and integrity	Analytical and problem-solving skills	Success with past hires
Very important	88%	87%	85%	83%	74%
Somewhat important	12%	12%	14%	16%	23%
Not very important		1%	1%		2%
Not at all important					1%

	Fit with the corporate culture	Leadership potential	Strategic thinking	Likelihood of recruiting stars	Well-rounded
Very important	73%	72%	67%	63%	54%
Somewhat important	25%	26%	31%	30%	40%
Not very important	2%	2%	2%	6%	5%
Not at all important				1%	

	Willingness of the school's students to relocate to the job location	Student chemistry	Students' average number of years of work experience	Content of the core curriculum	Overall value for the money invested in the recruiting effort
Very important	52%	46%	36%	36%	31%
Somewhat important	31%	43%	50%	48%	45%
Not very important	13%	9%	13%	14%	19%
Not at all important	4%	1%	2%	2%	5%

	School chemistry	Faculty expertise	Career-services office	Awareness of corporate citizenship issues	Students' international knowledge and experience
Very important	31%	27%	25%	22%	21%
Somewhat important	42%	51%	51%	50%	35%
Not very important	22%	20%	21%	25%	31%
Not at all important	5%	3%	3%	3%	13%

INDUSTRY RANKINGS OF TOP SCHOOLS

Recruiters in the following industries gave these schools the highest ratings in *The Wall Street Journal*/Harris Interactive survey.

Management Consulting

1 Dartmouth College (Tuck)
2 University of California, Berkeley (Haas)
3 Northwestern University (Kellogg)
3 Massachusetts Institute of Technology (Sloan)
5 University of Pennsylvania (Wharton)
6 Harvard University
6 Insead
8 University of North Carolina (Kenan-Flagler)
9 Carnegie Mellon University (Tepper)
10 University of Chicago
10 London Business School

Financial Services

1 Dartmouth College (Tuck)
2 Yale University
3 Thunderbird (Garvin)
3 Massachusetts Institute of Technology (Sloan)
5 London Business School
5 University of North Carolina (Kenan-Flagler)
7 University of Denver (Daniels)
8 IPADE
9 George Washington University
9 Wake Forest University (Babcock)
9 University of Western Ontario (Ivey)

Consumer Products

1 Indiana University (Kelley)
2 Columbia University
2 Northwestern University (Kellogg)
4 Duke University (Fuqua)
5 University of Southern California (Marshall)
5 Dartmouth College (Tuck)
7 University of Michigan (Ross)
8 INCAE
9 Ohio State University (Fisher)
10 University of Chicago

Technology

1 University of California, Berkeley (Haas)
2 Carnegie Mellon University (Tepper)
3 University of Denver (Daniels)
3 Duke University (Fuqua)
5 University of Maryland (Smith)
6 Insead
6 University of North Carolina (Kenan-Flagler)
8 Northwestern University (Kellogg)
9 Pennsylvania State University (Smeal)
9 University of Pennsylvania (Wharton)
9 Massachusetts Institute of Technology (Sloan)

Health Care

1 Northwestern University (Kellogg)
2 University of North Carolina (Kenan-Flagler)
3 University of California, Berkeley (Haas)
3 Duke University (Fuqua)
5 Dartmouth College (Tuck)
5 University of Michigan (Ross)
7 Carnegie Mellon University (Tepper)

Energy and Industrial Products

1 Carnegie Mellon University (Tepper)
2 Northwestern University (Kellogg)
3 Purdue University (Krannert)
4 University of Michigan (Ross)
5 Michigan State University (Broad)

6 Indiana University (Kelley)
7 University of Texas, Austin (McCombs)
8 IMD, the International Institute for Management Development
9 Rice University (Jones)
10 Massachusetts Institute of Technology (Sloan)

HONOR ROLL OF SCHOOLS BY ACADEMIC DISCIPLINE

Recruiters named these schools most often when asked which M.B.A. programs excel in the following academic disciplines. Based on total nominations by recruiters in *The Wall Street Journal/Harris* Interactive survey in 2004 and 2005.

Accounting		Number of Nominations
1	University of Chicago	200
2	University of Pennsylvania (Wharton)	197
3	University of Texas (McCombs)	133
4	Brigham Young University (Marriott)	92
5	University of Illinois, Urbana-Champaign	82
6	University of Denver (Daniels)	65
7	New York University (Stern)	63
8	University of Michigan (Ross)	62
9	Columbia University	61
9	University of Southern California (Marshall)	61

Entrepreneurship		Number of Nominations
1	Stanford University	430
2	Babson College (F. W. Olin)	229
3	Harvard University	172
4	University of California, Berkeley (Haas)	116
5	Massachusetts Institute of Technology (Sloan)	105
6	Carnegie Mellon University (Tepper)	92
7	Northwestern University (Kellogg)	90
8	University of Pennsylvania (Wharton)	82
9	University of Southern California (Marshall)	71
10	University of Virginia (Darden)	63

Finance		Number of Nominations
1	University of Pennsylvania (Wharton)	722
2	University of Chicago	472
3	Columbia University	182
4	New York University (Stern)	139
5	Carnegie Mellon University (Tepper)	133
6	Harvard University	106
7	London Business School	103
8	Yale University	98
9	Massachusetts Institute of Technology (Sloan)	82
10	University of Rochester (Simon)	79

Information Technology		Number of Nominations
1	Massachusetts Institute of Technology (Sloan)	637
2	Carnegie Mellon University (Tepper)	365
3	Stanford University	168
4	University of California, Irvine (Merage)	80
5	University of California, Berkeley (Haas)	77
6	University of Texas (McCombs)	61
7	University of Maryland (Smith)	55
8	Purdue University (Krannert)	47
9	University of Denver (Daniels)	34
10	Boston University	31
10	Georgia Institute of Technology	31

International Business		Number of Nominations
1	Thunderbird (Garvin)	649
2	Insead	265
3	Harvard University	196
4	Columbia University	139
5	University of Pennsylvania (Wharton)	107
6	London Business School	103
7	IMD	82
8	Georgetown University (McDonough)	76
9	University of South Carolina (Moore)	75
10	York University (Schulich)	60

Marketing		Number of Nominations
1	Northwestern University (Kellogg)	1,304
2	University of Michigan (Ross)	123
3	Duke University (Fuqua)	94
4	Indiana University (Kelley)	93
5	Harvard University	89
6	University of Pennsylvania (Wharton)	66
7	ESADE	60
8	Dartmouth College (Tuck)	54
9	University of Chicago	53
10	University of North Carolina, Chapel Hill (Kenan-Flagler)	43

Operations Management		Number of Nominations
1	Massachusetts Institute of Technology (Sloan)	324
2	Carnegie Mellon University (Tepper)	314
3	Purdue University (Krannert)	160
4	University of Michigan (Ross)	129
5	Michigan State University (Broad)	88
6	Ohio State University (Fisher)	53
7	Harvard University	48
8	Pennsylvania State University (Smeal)	46
8	Stanford University	46
10	Dartmouth College (Tuck)	43

Strategy		Number of Nominations
1	Harvard University	996
2	Stanford University	190
3	Dartmouth College (Tuck)	136
4	University of Pennsylvania (Wharton)	134
5	Northwestern University (Kellogg)	112
6	Yale University	109
7	University of Michigan (Ross)	98
8	University of Virginia (Darden)	76
9	University of Chicago	63
10	Insead	61

PART II

SCHOOL PROFILES

UNIVERSITY OF ARIZONA (ELLER COLLEGE OF MANAGEMENT)

More than a half-century after it was founded, the Eller M.B.A. program has grown considerably but still remains relatively intimate: Full-time M.B.A. students number about 130, and part-timers slightly more than 100.

Because of students' varied backgrounds, Eller tries to ensure that all M.B.A.s understand how companies operate through its Business Intelligence Quotient project. Students closely follow a single company, such as Coca-Cola or Wal-Mart, throughout their first year of studies. They become intimately familiar with their companies' finances and business strategy and make executive presentations to the class.

The school also emphasizes action-learning projects, particularly ones with social and environmental themes and international reach. Some Eller students, for example, recently developed market-entry strategies for a grain product from Bolivia and an organic shrimp from Ecuador. Students also perform consulting assignments for such clients as Intuit, Canyon Ranch Health Resort & Spa, and the Tucson Urban League.

M.B.A.s can major in finance, management and policy, management information systems, marketing, public and nonprofit management, accounting, human-resources management, and operations management. There's also the McGuire Entrepreneurship Program, which includes courses, summer internships at start-up businesses and venture-capital firms, and a support network of alumni and local executives to nurture students' business plans.

Eller offers a variety of degree combinations for full-time M.B.A. students, including agriculture and life sciences, engineering, optics, pharmacy, and law. It also has designed a new 14-month executive M.B.A. for experienced managers.

In *The Wall Street Journal*/Harris Interactive survey, recruiters gave Arizona top marks for its career-services office, their success with past hires from the school, and students' analytical and problem-solving skills. But it scored lower for students' international knowledge and experience, communication and interpersonal skills, and awareness of corporate citizenship issues.

School Rankings
- Regional ranking in the recruiter survey: 24 of 47 schools ranked

FALL 2004 INCOMING M.B.A. CLASS

	Total	Full-Time Only
Number of applicants	327	220
Number of offers extended	194	138
Number of students who accepted offer	132	75
Number of students who enrolled	127	70

GMAT score: 639 (mean); 630 (median)
Years of full-time work experience: 3.6 (mean); 3 (median)
Undergraduate GPA: 3.5 (mean); 3.5 (median)

Demographic Profile of Full-Time Students
Male: 68%
Female: 32%
Minorities: 20%

U.S. citizens/residents: 59%
Foreign nationals: 41%

Class of 2004 Most Popular Academic Concentrations (% of Students)

Entrepreneurship 20%
Finance 19%
Marketing 14%

CLASS OF 2004 EMPLOYMENT DATA

Industries Hiring Full-Time Graduates (% Hired)

Financial services/investment banking: 4.8%
Government: 2.4%
Management consulting: 4.8%
Manufacturing: 50%
Nonprofit: 2.4%
Other: 35.6%

Position/Job Function (% Hired)

Consulting: 2.2%
Finance/accounting: 37.8%
General Management: 4.4%
Human Resources: 6.7%
Information Technology/Management Information Systems: 15.6%
Marketing/Sales: 15.6%
Operations/Production/Logistics: 4.4%
Other: 13.3%

ARIZONA ON ARIZONA

(Data provided by Eller College of Management at the University of Arizona)

Business school website: http://www.ellermba.arizona.edu
Business school e-mail: mba_admissions@eller.arizona.edu
Public institution
M.B.A. enrollment: 242
Full-time: 133
Part-time: 109

ADMISSIONS DIRECTOR:
Natacha Keramidas
Director, M.B.A. Admissions
McClelland Hall 210
P.O. Box 210108
Tucson, AZ 85721
520-621-4528 (voice)
520-621-2606 (fax)
E-mail:
natacha@eller.arizona.edu

APPLICATION DEADLINE:
Fall 2006: 11/15/2005, 2/15/2006, 4/15/2006
Annual tuition: $14,451 (in-state); $23,431 (out-of-state)
Annual room and board: $8,000

THE RECRUITERS SPEAK

Arizona's most impressive features

"Great entrepreneurial program"

"Technology savvy"

"Information-management program"

Arizona's major shortcomings

"Looking for the home-run job right off the bat"

"No superstar students"

"Cannot apply learning to real work-world experiences"

How Arizona can increase its appeal

"More pre-M.B.A. experience"

"Improve communication skills"

"Recruit students with proven work experience"

Top Recruiters *(Number of Full-Time Class of 2004 Graduates Hired)*

Raytheon: 3
Honeywell: 3
Clear Blue Ventures: 2
Intel: 2
America West Airlines: 1
E&J Gallo Winery: 1
Ernst & Young: 1
Leapfrog Enterprises: 1
Schreiber Foods: 1
Walbro Engine Management: 1

Percentage of Job-Seeking Full-Time Graduates Who:	All Students	Citizens/Residents	Foreign Nationals
Received offers prior to or within 3 months of graduation	90%	93%	82%
Accepted offers prior to or within 3 months of graduation	87%	89%	82%

	MEAN			MEDIAN		
Overall Compensation	All Students	Citizens/ Residents	Foreign Nationals	All Students	Citizens/ Residents	Foreign Nationals
Annual base salary	$64,609	$66,216	$56,114	$65,500	$68,000	$55,000
Signing bonus	$5,869	$6,171	N/A	$4,000	$4,000	N/A
Other guaranteed compensation	$13,900	$13,900	N/A	$7,750	$7,750	N/A

Three of the Most Famous Graduates of M.B.A. Program

Rodger Ford (class of 1967) Founder, Alphagraphics; President, Anthem Equity Group

Thomas Kalinske (class of 1968) Chairman, Leapfrog Enterprises

Stephen Forte (class of 1983) Senior Vice President and Chief Pilot, United Airlines

ARIZONA STATE UNIVERSITY (CAREY SCHOOL OF BUSINESS)

The Arizona State M.B.A. program is best known for its supply-chain management specialization, in which students learn about such subjects as e-commerce, cost management, relationships with buyers and suppliers, and logistics design and management.

Arizona State recognized early on the growing importance of two areas of business and has achieved some distinction for its specializations in services marketing and management and in sports business. The services concentration teaches students how to manage customers' expectations and the delivery of products and services to build customer relationships and loyalty. In the sports-business concentration, students learn about collecting data to measure fan loyalty and sponsorship effectiveness, laws and political issues affecting the sports industry, and skills in negotiation and relationship management.

Beyond the full-time M.B.A. degree, Arizona State offers an evening part-time option and an executive-M.B.A. program, as well as a special part-time technology M.B.A. in conjunction with the engineering school. Arizona State is also one of only a few major accredited business schools offering an online-M.B.A. degree. Except for a brief on-campus orientation, students complete the degree through an Internet-based curriculum.

In 2003, the university named its business school for William Polk Carey, founder and chairman of W.P. Carey & Co. LLC, a

New York-based investment firm, in recognition of his $50 million gift. It was the largest donation in Arizona State's history and one of the biggest ever to any business school.

In *The Wall Street Journal*/Harris Interactive survey, recruiters were most impressed with Arizona State graduates' ability to work well in teams and their personal ethics and integrity. Arizona State received its lowest ratings for students' international knowledge and experience, their willingness to relocate, and their previous years of work experience.

School Rankings

■ Regional ranking in the recruiter survey: 40 of 47 schools ranked

FALL 2004 INCOMING M.B.A. CLASS

	Total	Full-Time Only
Number of applicants	1,009	428
Number of offers extended	623	195
Number of students who accepted offer	N/A	N/A
Number of students who enrolled	434	82

GMAT score: 649 (mean); 650 (median)
Years of full-time work experience: 4.5 (mean); N/A (median)
Undergraduate GPA: 3.4 (mean); 3.5 (median)

Demographic Profile of Full-Time Students

Male: 82%
Female: 18%
Minorities: 16%
U.S. citizens/residents: 74%
Foreign nationals: 26%

Class of 2004 Most Popular Academic Concentrations (% of Students)

Supply-chain management 29%
Financial management and markets 20%
Services marketing and management 19%

ARIZONA STATE ON ARIZONA STATE

(Data provided by the Carey School of Business at Arizona State University)

Business school website:
http://wpcarey.asu.edu
Business school e-mail:
wpcareymba@asu.edu
Public institution
M.B.A. enrollment: 765
Full-time: 204
Part-time: 476
Executive program: 85

ADMISSIONS DIRECTOR:
Nancy Stephens
Director, Recruiting and
Admissions
P.O. Box 874906
Tempe, AZ 85287
480-965-3332 (voice)
480-965-8569 (fax)
E-mail: wpcareymba@asu.edu

APPLICATION DEADLINE:
Fall 2006: 1/15/2006
Annual tuition: $14,966 (in-state);
$25,230 (out-of-state)
Annual room and board: $8,354

CLASS OF 2004 EMPLOYMENT DATA

Industries Hiring Full-Time Graduates (% Hired)

Financial services/investment banking: 10%
Government: 2%
Management consulting: 11%
Manufacturing: 35%
Nonprofit: 1%
Other: 41%

Position/Job Function (% Hired)

Consulting: 11%
Finance/accounting: 25%
General management: 9%
Information technology/management information systems: 7%
Marketing/sales: 17%
Operations/production/logistics: 26%
Other: 5%

Top Recruiters (Number of Full-Time Class of 2004 Graduates Hired)

Intel: 9
Cisco Systems: 5
Hewlett-Packard: 5
Honeywell: 5
Integrated Information Systems: 4
Citigroup: 2
IBM: 2
J.P. Morgan Chase: 2
MRSI Consulting: 2
Raytheon: 2

THE RECRUITERS SPEAK

Arizona State's most impressive features

"Supply-chain management, operations and logistics"

"Strong understanding of services marketing"

"Students' maturity and integrity"

Arizona State's major shortcomings

"Regional perspective"

"Analytical ability is sub-par"

"Nobody wants to leave Phoenix"

How Arizona State can increase its appeal

"More rigorous admissions"

"Increase diversity and years of experience"

"Provide some practical experience"

Percentage of Job-Seeking Full-Time Graduates Who:	All Students	Citizens/Residents	Foreign Nationals
Received offers prior to or within 3 months of graduation	96%	77%	93%
Accepted offers prior to or within 3 months of graduation	94%	77%	91%

Overall Compensation	MEAN			MEDIAN		
	All Students	Citizens/ Residents	Foreign Nationals	All Students	Citizens/ Residents	Foreign Nationals
Annual base salary	$70,843	$70,668	$72,262	$73,000	$72,995	$76,500
Signing bonus	$8,575	$8,760	$6,667	$7,083	$7,500	$5,000
Other guaranteed compensation	$10,312	$10,485	$9,333	$9,950	$9,900	$10,000

Three of the Most Famous Graduates of M.B.A. Program

Stephen Marriott (class of 1985) Vice President of Marketing, Marriott Hotels

George Schreiber (class of 1971) President and CEO, Semco Energy

Steven Knappenberger (class of 1975) President, United Auto Group West

BOCCONI UNIVERSITY

The SDA Bocconi School of Management offers four M.B.A. programs to try to satisfy a variety of interests and lifestyles. Its traditional full-time program provides a complete 14-month "immersion" at the Milan school. For students who want to keep working, there are both a two-year program of evening classes and a two-year part-time program that alternates between classroom work and distance learning. Bocconi's fourth option is a specialized, 13-month M.B.A. in international economics and management.

The standard full-time M.B.A., which is taught in both English and Italian, combines case studies, group projects, practical experiences, and distance learning. Students also can spend part of the program at a business school abroad.

M.B.A. students specialize in such areas as merchant and investment banking, accounting, risk management, marketing, privatization and management of public-sector companies, technology and production, and business and competitiveness. After graduation, Bocconi students gravitate most often to jobs in management consulting and sales and marketing.

Maurizio Dallocchio, dean of the SDA Bocconi School of Management, believes its Italian heritage provides "one more ace in our hand." In addition to teaching business skills, he says, Bocconi provides students with lessons in "thinking, Italian style" or adding a dash of creativity to solving problems.

In addition to its M.B.A. programs, Bocconi offers an array of specialized master's degrees in such fields as sports management, corporate finance, health care, the entertainment industry, human resources, and fashion and design. Given its location in Milan, Bocconi maintains close ties to the fashion industry. And recently, it formed an alliance with ESSEC Business School in Paris and Fudan University in Shanghai to work together to strengthen their teaching of fashion management.

In *The Wall Street Journal*/Harris Interactive survey, recruiters gave Bocconi its top scores for students' ability to work well in teams, their analytical and problem-solving skills, faculty expertise, and the career-services office. The schools' lowest scores were for students' prior work experience, their fit with the corporate culture, and the value for the money invested in the recruiting effort.

School Rankings

- International ranking in the recruiter survey: 20 of 20 schools ranked

FALL 2004 INCOMING M.B.A. CLASS

	Full-Time Only
Number of applicants	560
Number of offers extended	152
Number of students who accepted offer	130
Number of students who enrolled	129

BOCCONI ON BOCCONI

(Data provided by the SDA Bocconi School of Management)

Business school website:
http://www.sdabocconi.it
Business school e-mail:
antonella.carpani@sdabocconi.it
Private institution
M.B.A. enrollment: 247
Full-time: 130
Part-time: 117

ADMISSIONS DIRECTOR:
Rossana Camera
Via Balilla 18
Milan, Italy 20136
39-02-5836-3297 (voice)
39-02-5836-3293 (fax)
E-mail:
admissions@sdabocconi.it

APPLICATION DEADLINES:
Fall 2006: May 2006
Annual tuition: $41,580
Annual room and board: $21,250

GMAT score: 670 (mean); 660 (median)
Years of full-time work experience: 5 (mean); 5 (median)
Undergraduate GPA: N/A

Demographic Profile of Full-Time Students

Male: 74%
Female: 26%
Italian citizens/residents: 59%
Foreign nationals: 41%

Class of 2004 Most Popular Academic Concentration (% of Students)

Finance 31%
Marketing 20%
Strategy 20%

CLASS OF 2004 EMPLOYMENT DATA

Industries Hiring Full-Time Graduates (% Hired)

Computer/technology/Internet/dot.com: 7%
Consumer products and services: 5%
Energy and utilities: 2%
Financial services/investment banking: 14%
Industrial products and services: 16%
Management consulting: 25%
Manufacturing: 2%
Pharmaceutical/biotechnology/health-care products
and services: 9%
Telecommunications: 7%
Other: 13%

THE RECRUITERS SPEAK

Bocconi's most impressive features

"Global focus"

"Strategic thinking"

"Faculty organization"

Bocconi's major shortcomings

"A bit too young and inexperienced"

"Students don't speak very good English"

"Too Italian"

How Bocconi can increase its appeal

"Align students' expectations with their experience"

"Be more connected with big companies"

"Longer training periods in companies"

Position/Job Function *(% Hired)*

Consulting: 31%
Finance/accounting: 15%
General management: 2%
Marketing/sales: 29%
Operations/production/logistics: 4%
Other: 19%

Top Recruiters *(Number of Full-Time Class of 2004 Graduates Hired)*

Johnson & Johnson: 4
Bain Italy: 4
Boston Consulting Group: 4
Merloni Elettrodomestici: 3
Booz Allen Hamilton: 3
Pirelli Real Estate: 3
Eli Lilly: 3
EL.FI.COLD: 3
Value Partners: 2
Vodafone: 2

Percentage of Job-Seeking Full-Time Graduates Who:	All Students	Citizens/Residents	Foreign Nationals
Received offers prior to or within 3 months of graduation	90%	90%	90%
Accepted offers prior to or within 3 months of graduation	80%	85%	73%

	MEAN			MEDIAN		
Overall Compensation	All Students	Citizens/Residents	Foreign Nationals	All Students	Citizens/Residents	Foreign Nationals
Annual base salary	$77,400	$75,600	$82,300	$75,000	$71,300	$87,000
Signing bonus	$11,300	$10,200	$14,000	$13,200	$11,550	$13,200
Other guaranteed compensation	$26,200	$28,150	$19,000	$23,000	$25,600	$13,200

Three of the Most Famous Graduates of M.B.A. Program

Alessandro Lamanna (class of 1996) CEO, Nokia Italy

Marco Saltalamacchia (class of 1987) Chairman and CEO, BMW Italy

Milan Perovic (class of 1999) CEO, Telecom Montenegro

BOSTON UNIVERSITY

Boston University's management school heavily promotes its combined M.B.A. and master's of science in information systems, which can be completed in the same time—21 months—as a regular M.B.A. The university designed the dual degree because it believes that in today's technology-driven economy, graduates must be "fluent in the language of your company's chief information officer." The school also offers special M.B.A.s in health-care management and public and nonprofit management, as well as international programs that include study in Kobe, Japan, and Shanghai, China.

For the standard M.B.A., students can attend on a full-time basis or opt for a part-time arrangement, either the more structured evening program or a "self paced" format that can take as long as six years to complete. For more experienced managers, there is a 17-month executive-M.B.A. program, as well as an accelerated Asia-Pacific version that includes three months in Japan, Korea, and China, and nine months in Boston.

Among Boston University's special programs is an E-Business Center and Hatchery to help students bring new-venture plans to fruition. With funding from the General Electric Fund, the

BOSTON ON BOSTON

(Data provided by the School of Management at Boston University)

Business school website:
http://management.bu.edu/
Business school e-mail:
mba@bu.edu
Private institution
M.B.A. enrollment: 754
Full-time: 308
Part-time: 385
Executive program: 61

ADMISSIONS DIRECTOR:
Evelyn Tate
Director of Graduate Admissions
Graduate Admissions Office
595 Commonwealth Ave.
Boston, MA 02215
617-353-2670 (voice)
617-353-7368 (fax)
E-mail: etate@bu.edu

APPLICATION DEADLINES:
Fall 2006: 12/1/2005, 1/5/2006,
2/15/2006 (final international),
4/1/2006
Annual tuition: $31,530
Annual room and board: $10,782

school also established a Center for Team Learning that works with students and faculty to instill critical teamwork skills.

While most business schools devote considerable time to prepping students for their internship and full-time job searches, Boston University has made it a formal requirement. First-year M.B.A. students must take a semester-long career course and receive coaching in résumé preparation, networking, interview techniques, and negotiating skills.

In *The Wall Street Journal*/Harris Interactive survey, recruiters gave students their highest scores for teamwork abilities, personal ethics and integrity, their well-rounded qualities, and analytical and problem-solving skills. But recruiters gave the school lower grades for students' previous work experience and faculty expertise.

School Rankings

- Regional ranking in the recruiter survey: 41 of 47 schools ranked

Recognition for Excellence in an Academic Concentration

- With 31 nominations, Boston ranked No. 10 among business schools that recruiters in *The Wall Street Journal*/Harris Interactive survey cited for excellence in information technology.

THE RECRUITERS SPEAK

Boston's most impressive features

"Hard-working students with no attitude"

"Team skills, well-rounded leadership"

"Technically strong"

Boston's major shortcomings

"Soft on experience"

"Implementers, not strategists"

"Too focused on salary and not opportunities"

How Boston can increase its appeal

"Extend reach of M.B.A. corporate-relations department"

"Continue strengthening admissions requirements"

"More and better work experience"

FALL 2004 INCOMING M.B.A. CLASS

	Total	Full-Time Only
Number of applicants	925	703
Number of offers extended	522	355
Number of students who accepted offer	N/A	N/A
Number of students who enrolled	266	156

GMAT score: 637 (mean); 630 (median)
Years of prior full-time work experience: 4.1 (mean); 4 (median)
Undergraduate GPA: 3.21 (mean); 3.21 (median)

Demographic Profile of Full-Time Students

Male: 63%
Female: 37%
Minorities: 14%
U.S. citizens/residents: 68%
Foreign nationals: 32%

Class of 2004 Most Popular Academic Concentrations (% of Students)

Finance 42%
Marketing 16%

CLASS OF 2004 EMPLOYMENT DATA

Industries Hiring Full-Time Graduates (% Hired)

Computer/technology/Internet/dot.com: 20%
Consumer products and services: 8%
Energy and utilities: 1%
Financial services/investment banking: 13%
Government: 3%
Management consulting: 10%
Manufacturing: 4%
Media/entertainment: 3%
Nonprofit: 2%
Pharmaceutical/biotechnology/health-care products and services: 12%
Real estate: 5%
Travel and transportation: 2%

Other professional services (accounting, advertising, etc.): 12%
Other: 5%

Position/Job Function (% Hired)

Consulting: 14%
Finance/accounting: 31%
General management: 12%
Information technology/management information systems: 13%
Marketing/sales: 23%
Operations/production/logistics: 6%
Other: 1%

Top Recruiters (Number of Full-Time Class of 2004 Graduates Hired)

Bearing Point: 3
Novartis: 3
Athenahealth: 2
Bristol-Myers Squibb: 2
Citigroup: 2
Ernst & Young: 2
Fidelity: 2
Google: 2

Percentage of Job-Seeking Full-Time Graduates Who:	All Students	Citizens/Residents	Foreign Nationals
Received offers prior to or within 3 months of graduation	N/A	N/A	N/A
Accepted offers prior to or within 3 months of graduation	89%	92%	83%

	MEAN			MEDIAN		
Overall Compensation	All Students	Citizens/ Residents	Foreign Nationals	All Students	Citizens/ Residents	Foreign Nationals
Annual base salary	$78,299	$78,570	$77,308	$76,500	$79,000	$70,000
Signing bonus	$11,605	$11,594	$11,667	$10,000	$7,000	$10,000
Other guaranteed compensation	$12,329	$12,133	$13,500	$10,000	$10,000	$12,000

Intel: 2
J.P. Morgan Chase: 2

Three of the Most Famous Graduates of M.B.A. Program

Ed Zander (class of 1975) Chairman and CEO, Motorola

Christine Poon (class of 1983) Vice Chairman, Johnson & Johnson

Millard (Mickey) Drexler (class of 1968) Chairman and CEO, J. Crew Group

BRIGHAM YOUNG UNIVERSITY (MARRIOTT SCHOOL OF MANAGEMENT)

Sponsored by the Church of Jesus Christ of Latter-day Saints, Brigham Young's business school declares that its mission is to "attract, develop, and place men and women of faith, character, and professional ability who will become outstanding leaders capable of dealing with change in a global environment." Partly because of this religious focus, corporate recruiters say they find strong personal values and a solid work ethic among the school's graduates.

The Marriott School's M.B.A. academic tracks include finance, marketing, supply-chain management, organizational behavior, and interdisciplinary product development. The school also stresses the international nature of business today, and many students come with some global credentials already in hand. Most have performed missionary work abroad and speak multiple languages.

In addition to the full-time M.B.A., the Marriott School offers an executive M.B.A. in both Provo and Salt Lake City, as well as master's degrees in accountancy, information-systems management, and public administration.

One of recruiters' chief complaints about the Marriott School is its lack of diversity. With women representing only 18% of its student body, minorities at 6%, and international students at 13%, it is one of the least diverse of the business schools in *The Wall Street Journal*/Harris Interactive rankings. In response, Brigham Young has developed an "extended reach" program that aims to recruit more female and minority students and faculty members. It has organized a steering committee to lead the diversity initiative and is offering scholarships to minorities.

In the *Journal* survey, recruiters gave Brigham Young very high marks for students' personal ethics and integrity and their ability to work well in teams. Students received much lower scores for their previous work experience.

School Rankings
- Regional ranking in the recruiter survey: 6 of 47 schools ranked

Recognition for Excellence in an Academic Concentration
- With 92 nominations, Brigham Young ranked No. 4 among business schools that recruiters in *The Wall Street Journal*/Harris Interactive survey cited for excellence in accounting.

Special Recognition
- Good source for recruiting graduates with high ethical standards: 2nd most nominated school, 127 nominations.

FALL 2004 INCOMING M.B.A. CLASS

	Total	Full-Time Only
Number of applicants	455	346
Number of offers extended	259	187
Number of students who accepted offer	197	134
Number of students who enrolled	182	123

BRIGHAM YOUNG ON BRIGHAM YOUNG

(Data provided by the Marriott School of Management at Brigham Young University)

Business school website:
http://marriottschool.byu.edu
Business school e-mail:
marriottschool@byu.edu
Private institution
M.B.A. enrollment: 380
Full-time: 253
Executive Program: 127

ADMISSIONS DIRECTOR:
Carol Thornton
M.B.A. Admissions Coordinator
640 Tanner Building
Provo, UT 84602
801-422-3500 (voice)
801-422-0513 (fax)
E-mail: mba@byu.edu

APPLICATION DEADLINES:
Fall 2006: 1/15/2006
Annual tuition: $7,450 (members of the Church of Jesus Christ of Latter-day Saints); $11,176 (non-members)
Annual room and board: $4,725

GMAT score: 653 (mean); 660 (median)
Years of full-time work experience: 2.3 (mean); 2.8 (median)
Undergraduate GPA: 3.5 (mean); 3.6 (median)

Demographic Profile of Full-Time Students

Male: 82%
Female: 18%
Minorities: 6%
U.S. citizens/residents: 87%
Foreign nationals: 13%

Class of 2004 Most Popular Academic Concentrations (% of Students)

Finance 39%
Marketing 23%
Organizational behavior/human-resource management 14%

CLASS OF 2004 EMPLOYMENT DATA

Industries Hiring Full-Time Graduates (% Hired)

Computer/technology/Internet/dot.com: 14%
Consumer products and services: 19%
Energy and utilities: 1%
Financial services/investment banking: 19%
Industrial products and services: 3%
Manufacturing: 22%
Media/entertainment: 2%
Pharmaceutical/biotechnology/health-care products and services: 8%
Real estate: 9%
Telecommunications: 2%
Travel and transportation: 1%

THE RECRUITERS SPEAK

Brigham Young's most impressive features

"Integrity and maturity of the students"

"Best value for our recruiting dollars"

"Technical accounting skills"

Brigham Young's major shortcomings

"Students lack creativity"

"Regional orientation to the western U.S."

"Students are too humble and conflict-averse"

How Brigham Young can increase its appeal

"More minorities and women—need more selection"

"Seek out recruiters, sell school and students"

"Press for more work experience"

Position/Job Function (% Hired)

Finance/accounting: 46%
General management: 16%
Human resources: 13%
Marketing/sales: 11%
Operations/production/logistics: 6%
Other: 8%

Top Recruiters (Number of Full-Time Class of 2004 Graduates Hired)

Ford Motor: 5
Ensign Group: 5
American Express: 3
Honeywell: 3
Kmart: 3
Zions Bank: 3
Dell: 1
Citigroup: 1
General Mills: 1
Intel: 1

Percentage of Job-Seeking Full-Time Graduates Who:	All Students	Citizens/Residents	Foreign Nationals
Received offers prior to or within 3 months of graduation	84%	83%	85%
Accepted offers prior to or within 3 months of graduation	82%	82%	85%

Overall Compensation	MEAN			MEDIAN		
	All Students	Citizens/Residents	Foreign Nationals	All Students	Citizens/Residents	Foreign Nationals
Annual base salary	$69,402	$70,943	$59,000	$70,860	$72,000	$60,000
Signing bonus	$9,970	$9,889	$10,942	$10,000	$10,000	$5,000
Other guaranteed compensation	$13,290	$11,977	N/A	$11,625	$11,250	N/A

Three of the Most Famous Graduates of M.B.A. Program

Kevin Rollins (class of 1984) CEO, Dell

E. Jeffrey Smith (class of 1974) Partner, Studeo Interactive Direct

D. Fraser Bullock (class of 1980) President and CEO, Salt Lake Organizing Committee of the 2002 Winter Olympic Games, and Co-Founder and Managing Director, Sorenson Capital

UNIVERSITY AT BUFFALO/SUNY

Part of the State University of New York system, the University at Buffalo enjoys a reputation as a solid regional M.B.A. program, producing management talent for companies in the western New York region.

But the school's reach actually extends much farther—all the way to China, in fact. In 1984, Buffalo established the first U.S.-style M.B.A. program in China. It also offers executive-M.B.A. programs in collaboration with Renmin University in Beijing and was selected to create an executive-M.B.A. program at Motorola University, also in Beijing. Buffalo offers a third executive M.B.A. at the Singapore Management Institute. The M.B.A. student body at Buffalo is also quite international, with foreign nationals representing more than 40% of the class.

Established in 1931, the M.B.A. program today offers specialized tracks in accounting, finance, international management, consulting, supply chains and operations management, information systems and e-business, and marketing management. Reflecting 21st-century trends, Buffalo recently added two new specialties: biotechnology management and information assurance. The information assurance track deals with security issues raised by the Internet and other new information channels. Buffalo also focuses on entrepreneurship, including new programs for technology-based companies and for women and minority entrepreneurs.

BUFFALO ON BUFFALO

(Data provided by the School of Management at University at Buffalo/SUNY)

Business school website:
http://www.mgt.buffalo.edu
Business school e-mail:
som-mba@buffalo.edu
Public institution
M.B.A. enrollment: 618
Full-time: 314
Part-time: 170
Executive program: 134

ADMISSIONS DIRECTOR:
David W. Frasier
Assistant Dean
203 Alfiero Center
Buffalo, NY 14260
716-645-3204 (voice)
716-645-2341 (fax)
E-mail: davidf@buffalo.edu

APPLICATION DEADLINE:
Fall 2006: 6/1/2006
Annual tuition: $7,100 (in-state);
$11,340 (out-of-state)
Annual room and board: $9,300

Working professionals in the Buffalo area have the choice of a part-time evening or an executive-M.B.A. program. Specialized master's degrees and combination graduate degrees also are widely available at Buffalo. Beyond the common dual M.D./M.B.A. and J.D./M.B.A. degrees, students can combine their M.B.A. with advanced degrees in geography, architecture, audiology, and pharmacy studies.

In *The Wall Street Journal/Harris Interactive* ranking, recruiters rated Buffalo highest for students' analytical and problem-solving skills and personal ethics and integrity, as well as value for the money invested in the recruiting effort. Students received lower grades for their previous work experience, international knowledge and experience, and willingness to relocate.

School Rankings

- Regional ranking in the recruiter survey: 13 of 47 schools ranked

FALL 2004 INCOMING M.B.A. CLASS

	Total	Full-Time Only
Number of applicants	948	567
Number of offers extended	495	320
Number of students who accepted offer	391	289
Number of students who enrolled	278	148

THE RECRUITERS SPEAK

Buffalo's most impressive features

"Students are excellent team players"

"Blue-collar school—students are willing to work hard"

"Career-resource center is very responsive"

Buffalo's major shortcomings

"Many have very poor work experience"

"Language barriers with international students"

"Regional focus"

How Buffalo can increase its appeal

"Recruit students with more professional work experience"

"Improve polish and soft skills of some applicants"

"Increase awareness beyond Buffalo"

GMAT score: 595 (mean); 600 (median)
Years of full-time work experience: 2.6 (mean); 1.7 (median)
Undergraduate GPA: 3.2 (mean); 3.2 (median)

Demographic Profile of Full-Time Students

Male: 61%
Female: 39%
Minorities: 5%
U.S. citizens/residents: 57%
Foreign nationals: 43%

Class of 2004 Most Popular Academic Concentrations (% of Students)

Finance 38%
Marketing 18%
Management information systems 16%

CLASS OF 2004 EMPLOYMENT DATA

Industries Hiring Full-Time Graduates (% Hired)

Computer/technology/Internet/dot.com: 6%
Consumer products and services: 6%
Financial services/investment banking: 21%
Government: 4%
Management consulting: 17%
Manufacturing: 28%
Media/entertainment: 2%
Pharmaceutical/biotechnology/health-care products and services:
10%
Other professional services (accounting, advertising, etc.): 6%

Position/Job Function (% Hired)

Consulting: 8%
Finance/accounting: 35%
General management: 10%
Human resources: 4%
Information technology/management information systems: 10%
Marketing/sales: 15%
Operations/production/logistics: 18%

Top Recruiters *(Number of Full-Time Class of 2004 Graduates Hired)*

Deloitte: 3
Harris Interactive: 3
M&T Bank: 3
HSBC: 2
General Motors: 2
BearingPoint Consulting: 1
Black Rock Investments: 1
Ernst & Young: 1
IBM: 1
General Electric: 1

Percentage of Job-Seeking Full-Time Graduates Who:	All Students	Citizens/Residents	Foreign Nationals
Received offers prior to or within 3 months of graduation	66%	58%	42%
Accepted offers prior to or within 3 months of graduation	66%	58%	42%

	MEAN			MEDIAN		
Overall Compensation	**All Students**	**Citizens/ Residents**	**Foreign Nationals**	**All Students**	**Citizens/ Residents**	**Foreign Nationals**
Annual base salary	$51,997	$49,048	$56,342	$50,000	$45,880	$55,000
Signing bonus	$12,062	$17,500	$10,250	$12,500	$17,500	$9,250
Other guaranteed compensation	N/A	N/A	N/A	N/A	N/A	N/A

Three of the Most Famous Graduates of M.B.A. Program

Ajit Pendse (class of 1985) President and CEO, eFusion

James M. Ringler (class of 1969) Vice Chairman, Illinois Tool Works

William H. Lichtenberger (class of 1966) Former Chairman and CEO, Praxair

UNIVERSITY OF CALIFORNIA, BERKELEY
(HAAS SCHOOL OF BUSINESS)

University of California
Berkeley
Haas School of Business

Berkeley's Haas School is itching to grow to compete more effectively with such titans of the business-school world as Wharton and Stanford. Rich Lyons, the new acting dean who replaced Tom Campbell when Campbell became California's chief budget officer, has proposed that Haas increase private fundraising and boost the number of full-time faculty members to 90 from 70. He also believes that the school must expand the size of the full-time M.B.A. program as more space becomes available in a new building and enhance its career services, including the addition of a part-time employee in New York to promote students to Wall Street and East Coast companies.

The oldest business school at a public university (founded in 1898), Haas very much reflects its location near Silicon Valley. Named for a former president of Levi Strauss & Co., the school emphasizes entrepreneurship and technology. Many of its graduates start their own ventures or are drawn to the technology companies in San Francisco and Silicon Valley. About 20% of students typically land jobs at computer, Internet and other technology companies.

The Haas School, which offers both full-time and part-time M.B.A. degrees, revamped its curriculum a few years ago, giving students greater freedom to customize their studies. Students who want to specialize can earn certificates in corporate environmental management, entrepreneurship, global man-

UC BERKELEY ON UC BERKELEY

(Data provided by the Haas School of Business at the University of California, Berkeley)

Business school website: http://www.haas.berkeley.edu
Business school e-mail: N/A
Public institution
M.B.A. enrollment: 1,281
Full-time: 495
Part-time: 657
Executive program: 129

ADMISSIONS DIRECTORS:
Peter Johnson and Jett Pihakis
Co-Directors of M.B.A. Admissions
S420 Student Services Building #1902
Berkeley, CA 94720
510-642-1405 (voice)
510-643-6659 (fax)
E-mail: N/A

APPLICATION DEADLINES:
Fall 2006: 3/1/2006
Annual tuition: $21,512 (in-state); $33,758 (out-of-state)
Annual room and board: $19,978

agement, health management, real estate, and technology management.

Berkeley has forged two links with Columbia Business School in New York City in recent years. It has developed a bicoastal executive-M.B.A. degree that capitalizes on Berkeley's strengths in technology and entrepreneurship and Columbia's expertise in finance and international business, as well the schools' ties to Silicon Valley and Wall Street.

In addition, Columbia, along with London Business School and the Goldman Sachs Foundation, have become partners with Berkeley in its social-venture competition to promote new businesses that will produce both "financial and social returns on investment." The business-plan competition began in 1999 at Berkeley, and winners have included a venture to convert ocean wave energy into electricity, a charter elementary school in the South Bronx section of New York City, and a fashion company that employs women in Afghanistan.

Berkeley jumped eight spots in the latest *Wall Street Journal*/Harris Interactive National ranking and can call itself "the best in the West." Berkeley graduates received their highest ratings for their ability to work well in teams, analytical and problem-solving skills, and personal ethics and integrity. Recruiters gave Berkeley its lowest ratings for students' international knowledge and experience, the career-services office, and the willingness of students to relocate for their job.

THE RECRUITERS SPEAK

Berkeley's most impressive features

"Effective leaders in team-oriented environments"

"Strong social consciousness and business savvy"

"Great potential hires at a generally lower cost"

Berkeley's major shortcomings

"Not quite yet sold on capitalism"

"Lack of finance experience or interest"

"Too many with West Coast preferences and relocation issues"

How Berkeley can increase its appeal

"Do research about companies before interviewing"

"Be more outgoing and friendly to recruiters"

"Teach students how to sell themselves"

School Rankings

- National ranking in the recruiter survey: 7 of 19 schools ranked

- Ranking by technology-industry recruiters: 1st place

- Ranking by management-consulting-industry recruiters: 2nd place

- Ranking by health-care-industry recruiters: 3rd place

Recognition for Excellence in Academic Concentrations

- With 116 nominations, Berkeley ranked No. 4 among business schools that recruiters in *The Wall Street Journal*/Harris Interactive survey cited for excellence in entrepreneurship.

- With 77 nominations, Berkeley ranked No. 5 for excellence in information technology.

Special Recognition

- Good source for recruiting women: 5th most nominated school, 64 nominations.

- Good source for recruiting minorities: 5th most nominated school, 52 nominations.

- Good source for recruiting graduates with high ethical standards: 6th most nominated school, 72 nominations.

FALL 2004 INCOMING M.B.A. CLASS

	Total	Full-Time Only
Number of applicants	3,580	2,858
Number of offers extended	780	486
Number of students who accepted offer	N/A	264
Number of students who enrolled	470	230

GMAT score: 701 (mean); 700 (median)
Years of full-time work experience: 5.4 (mean); 5 (median)
Undergraduate GPA: 3.5 (mean); 3.5 (median)

Demographic Profile of Full-Time Students

Male: 74%
Female: 26%
Minorities: 25%
U.S. citizens/residents: 68%
Foreign nationals: 32%

Class of 2004 Most Popular Academic Concentrations (% of Students)

Management of technology 25%
Entrepreneurship 25%
International 25%

CLASS OF 2004 EMPLOYMENT DATA

Industries Hiring Full-Time Graduates (% Hired)

Computer/technology/Internet/dot.com: 20.2%
Consumer products and services: 13.9%
Financial services/investment banking: 20.7%
Government: 1%
Management consulting: 15.4%
Media/entertainment: 1.9%
Nonprofit: 2.4%
Petroleum/energy: 2.4%
Pharmaceutical/biotechnology/health-care products and services: 9.2%
Real estate: 6.7%
Telecommunications: 3.4%
Other professional services (accounting, advertising, etc.): 1%
Other: 1.8%

Position/Job Function (% Hired)

Consulting: 17.2%
Finance/accounting: 34.5%
General management: 19.1%
Information technology/management information systems: 1.9%
Marketing/sales: 23.9%
Operations/production/logistics: 3.4%

Top Recruiters (Number of Full-Time Class of 2004 Graduates Hired)

McKinsey: 11
Gap: 8
Wells Fargo Bank: 5
Microsoft: 5
Yahoo!: 5
Lehman Brothers: 4
Boston Consulting Group: 4
ChevronTexaco: 4
Citigroup: 4
Genentech: 4

Percentage of Job-Seeking Full-Time Graduates Who:	All Students	Citizens/Residents	Foreign Nationals
Received offers prior to or within 3 months of graduation	92%	93%	91%
Accepted offers prior to or within 3 months of graduation	90%	91%	88%

Overall Compensation	MEAN			MEDIAN		
	All Students	Citizens/Residents	Foreign Nationals	All Students	Citizens/Residents	Foreign Nationals
Annual base salary	$88,234	$89,842	$85,440	$87,500	$88,000	$85,000
Signing bonus	$12,824	$12,350	$13,546	$10,000	$10,000	$13,500
Other guaranteed compensation	$24,465	$25,547	$22,713	$18,000	$19,250	$17,250

Three of the Most Famous Graduates of M.B.A. Program

Arun Sarin (class of 1978) CEO, Vodafone

Paul Otellini (class of 1974) CEO, Intel

Rodrigo Rato (class of 1974) Managing Director, International Monetary Fund

Graduate School of Management

UCDAVIS

Davis • Sacramento
San Francisco Bay Area

UNIVERSITY OF CALIFORNIA, DAVIS

The University of California at Davis started its management school nearly 25 years ago to provide talent to the growing Sacramento Valley region. Today, it remains a small school with about 125 full-time and nearly 300 part-time M.B.A. students, and it boasts that its 10-to-1 student/faculty ratio allows for more individual attention.

In fall 2005, UC Davis is taking a major step by expanding into the Bay Area, with a weekend executive-M.B.A. program at a conference center 35 miles east of San Francisco. The school acknowledges that the environment will be quite competitive, with a total of about 10 executive offerings in the San Francisco area, including such major players as the University of Pennsylvania's Wharton West and the University of California at Berkeley.

At UC Davis, M.B.A. students can focus on technology management and entrepreneurship, finance, marketing, accounting, information technology, corporate environmental management, or management of organizations. They also can design their own area of concentration.

Located near the wineries of California, the management school offers special programs for vintners. In a four-day executive-development program, the management school and department of viticulture and enology present such classes as "Stay Out of the Red: Financial Management of Wineries and Vineyards," "Got Wine? Strategic Image Management in Good

Times and Bad," "Where Buyers Meet Cellars: Exploring Brand Loyalty," and "Crushing the Competition: Marketing for the Wine Industry."

UC Davis also has joined three other business schools in a program that leads to a Wine M.B.A. awarded by the Bordeaux Business School in France. In addition to France and the U.S., students in the part-time program visit Chile and Australia, studying such subjects as merchandising, e-business, and supply-chain management in the wine industry.

In *The Wall Street Journal*/Harris Interactive survey, recruiters gave students the highest scores for personal ethics and integrity, fit with the corporate culture, and their ability to work effectively in teams. The lowest scores for UC Davis: students' international knowledge and experience, the career-services office, and faculty expertise.

School Rankings

- Regional ranking in the recruiter survey: 44 of 47 schools ranked

FALL 2004 INCOMING M.B.A. CLASS

	Total	Full-Time Only
Number of applicants	491	329
Number of offers extended	202	93
Number of students who accepted offer	155	69
Number of students who enrolled	143	60

GMAT score: 678 (mean); 680 (median)
Years of full-time work experience: 5.3 (mean); 4 (median)
Undergraduate GPA: 3.3 (mean); 3.3 (median)

Demographic Profile of Full-Time Students

Male: 70%
Female: 30%

UC DAVIS ON UC DAVIS

(Provided by the Graduate School
of Management at the University
of California, Davis)

Business school website:
http://www.gsm.ucdavis.edu
Business school e-mail:
admissions@gsm.ucdavis.edu
Public institution
M.B.A. enrollment: 412
Full-time: 122
Part-time: 290

ADMISSIONS DIRECTOR:
Kathy Gleed
Director of Admissions and
Student Services
One Shields Ave, AOB IV
Davis, CA 95616
530-752-7658 (voice)
530-754-9355 (fax)
E-mail: krgleed@ucdavis.edu

APPLICATION DEADLINES:
Fall 2006: March 2006
Annual tuition: $21,462 (in-state);
$33,707 (out-of-state)
Annual room and board: $13,846

Minorities: 23%
U.S. citizens/residents: 90%
Foreign nationals: 10%

Class of 2004 Most Popular Academic Concentrations (% of Students)

Finance 28%
Marketing 22%
Strategic management 14%

CLASS OF 2004 EMPLOYMENT DATA

Industries Hiring Full-Time Graduates (% Hired)

Computer/technology/Internet/dot.com: 20%
Consumer products and services: 14%
Financial services/investment banking: 14%
Government: 7%
Management consulting: 13%
Media/entertainment: 10%
Pharmaceutical/biotechnology/health-care products and services: 11%
Telecommunications: 2%
Other professional services (accounting, advertising, etc.): 9%

Position/Job Function (% Hired)

Consulting: 11%
Finance/accounting: 30%
General management: 11%
Information technology/management information systems: 7%
Marketing/sales: 34%
Other: 7%

THE RECRUITERS SPEAK

UC Davis's most impressive features

"Good team players"

"Leadership capabilities"

"Down to earth"

UC Davis's major shortcomings

"Too many techies and greenies"

"Too little practical experience"

"Needs more stars"

How UC Davis can increase its appeal

"Higher-quality instructors"

"Strong proactive career center"

"Attract students with more real-world experience"

Top Recruiters *(Number of Full-Time Class of 2004 Graduates Hired)*

Hewlett-Packard: 3
BearingPoint: 2
Gartner Consulting: 2
Mervyns: 2
UC Davis: 2
E & J Gallo Winery: 1
SBC Communication: 1
Wells Fargo: 1
Bristol-Myers Squibb: 1
National Park Service: 1

Percentage of Job-Seeking Full-Time Graduates Who:	All Students	Citizens/Residents	Foreign Nationals
Received offers prior to or within 3 months of graduation	86%	91%	50%
Accepted offers prior to or within 3 months of graduation	83%	87%	50%

	MEAN			MEDIAN		
Overall Compensation	All Students	Citizens/ Residents	Foreign Nationals	All Students	Citizens/ Residents	Foreign Nationals
Annual base salary	$73,396	$74,820	$63,033	$74,000	$75,000	$70,000
Signing bonus	$6,750	$6,344	$10,000	$5,000	$5,000	$10,000
Other guaranteed compensation	N/A	N/A	N/A	N/A	N/A	N/A

Three of the Most Famous Graduates of M.B.A. Program

David H. Russ (class of 1986) University of California Treasurer and Vice President of Investments

Christine Smith (class of 1996) Founder of two nanotechnology start-ups, UltraDots and Christalis

Eric Robison (class of 1983) Founder and President, IdeaTrek

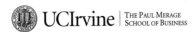

UNIVERSITY OF CALIFORNIA, IRVINE
(MERAGE SCHOOL OF BUSINESS)

The University of California at Irvine calls its focus "information technology for management" and integrates IT throughout its curriculum and its wired classrooms. Its intranet system, called Catalyst, allows students to turn in homework, use the electronic library, check grades, and even take quizzes that are graded instantly.

The full-time M.B.A. program doesn't designate specific academic majors, but students can specialize through their choice of electives. There is also an intercampus program in corporate environmental management with the University of California at Santa Barbara.

In addition to the full-time M.B.A., UC Irvine offers a part-time program and both general executive-M.B.A. and health-care executive-M.B.A. degrees.

In line with its technology focus, UC Irvine runs a Center for Entrepreneurship and Innovation, a central clearinghouse for the many offerings available to budding entrepreneurs. One project is the Irvine Innovation Initiative, or "I cubed," a "24/7 operation" to develop new-business plans. Student ventures range from making personalized mountain bikes to providing environmental-compliance management solutions.

The management school also operates a leadership development center that pairs students with mentors who are senior executives at local companies; helps them strengthen writing, presentation, and other leadership skills; and encourages them to develop a social conscience by doing consulting work for nonprofit community groups.

In 2005, UC Irvine named its business school after Paul Merage, after receiving a $30 million gift from the philanthropist and entrepreneur who created the Hot Pockets sandwich brand.

In *The Wall Street Journal*/Harris Interactive survey, recruiters gave the highest ratings to UC Irvine graduates for their ability to work well in teams and their analytical and problem-solving skills. UC Irvine received its lowest scores for faculty expertise, students' international knowledge and experience, and their previous work experience.

School Rankings
■ Regional ranking in recruiter survey: 39 of 47 schools ranked

Recognition for Excellence in an Academic Concentration
■ With 80 nominations, UC Irvine ranked No. 4 among business schools that recruiters in *The Wall Street Journal*/Harris Interactive survey cited for excellence in information technology.

FALL 2004 INCOMING M.B.A. CLASS

	Total	Full-Time Only
Number of applicants	988	527
Number of offers extended	578	226
Number of students who accepted offer	397	118
Number of students who enrolled	374	103

GMAT scores: 658 (mean); 650 (median)
Years of full-time work experience: 4.4 (mean); 3.9 (median)
Undergraduate GPA: 3.3 (mean); 3.3 (median)

UC IRVINE ON UC IRVINE

(Data provided by the Paul Merage School of Business at the University of California, Irvine)

Business school website: http://www.gsm.uci.edu
Business school e-mail: gsm-mba@uci.edu
Public institution
M.B.A. enrollment: 888
Full-time: 207
Part-time: 476
Executive program: 205

ADMISSIONS DIRECTOR:
Marty Bell
Director, Full-Time M.B.A. Program
University of California, Irvine
110 MPAA
Irvine, CA 92697
949-824-4622 (voice)
949-824-2235 (fax)
E-mail: cmbell@gsm.uci.edu

APPLICATION DEADLINES:
Fall 2006: 3/1/2006 (full-time international); 5/1/2006 (full-time domestic); 7/10/2006 (part-time and executive)
Annual tuition: $24,923 (in-state); $36,198 (out-of-state)
Annual room and board: $14,796

Demographic Profile of Full-Time Students

Male: 68%
Female: 32%
Minorities: 24%
U.S. citizens/residents: 72%
Foreign nationals: 28%

Class of 2004 Most Popular Academic Concentrations (% of Students)

Finance 41%
Marketing 35%
Management information systems 10%

CLASS OF 2004 EMPLOYMENT DATA

Industries Hiring Full-Time Graduates (% Hired)

Computer/technology/Internet/dot.com: 16%
Consumer products and services: 5%
Energy and utilities: 1%
Financial services/investment banking: 27%
Government: 1%
Management consulting: 14%
Manufacturing: 10%
Media/entertainment: 5%
Nonprofit: 1%
Pharmaceutical/biotechnology/health-care products and services: 5%
Real estate: 6%
Telecommunications: 4%
Travel and transportation: 1%
Other professional services (accounting, advertising, etc.): 4%

THE RECRUITERS SPEAK

UC Irvine's most impressive features

"Analytical skills and expertise in statistical software"

"Detail orientation"

"Technology focus"

UC Irvine's major shortcomings

"Lack of star-quality candidates"

"Followers, not doers"

"Career-placement office"

How UC Irvine can increase its appeal

"Continue polishing students for poise and presentation"

"Campus recruiting should be more professional"

"Increase the size of the program"

Position/Job Function *(% Hired)*

Consulting: 20%
Finance/accounting: 33%
General management: 6%
Information technology/management information systems: 4%
Marketing/sales: 27%
Operations/production/logistics: 3%
Other: 7%

Top Recruiters *(Number of Full-Time Class of 2004 Graduates Hired)*

KPMG: 5
PricewaterhouseCoopers: 4
Countrywide Securities: 2
SAP America: 2
IBM: 2
Far East National Bank: 2
Deloitte: 2
Moss Adams: 2
Mattel: 1
Verizon: 1

Percentage of Job-Seeking Full-Time Graduates Who:	All Students	Citizens/Residents	Foreign Nationals
Received offers prior to or within 3 months of graduation	85%	84%	88%
Accepted offers prior to or within 3 months of graduation	84%	84%	83%

	MEAN			MEDIAN		
Overall Compensation	All Students	Citizens/ Residents	Foreign Nationals	All Students	Citizens/ Residents	Foreign Nationals
Annual base salary	$69,016	$69,858	$64,929	$68,000	$70,000	$65,000
Signing bonus	$8,125	$7,481	$11,600	$5,000	$5,000	$5,000
Other guaranteed compensation	$15,529	$15,115	$19,250	$13,000	$13,000	$19,250

Three of the Most Famous Graduates of M.B.A. Program

Phyllis Factor Scheinberg (class of 1979) Deputy Assistant Secretary, U.S. Department of Transportation

George Kessinger (class of 1987) President and CEO, Goodwill Industries International

Gary Toyama (class of 1978) Deputy Vice President, IDS Operations, Boeing

UNIVERSITY OF CALIFORNIA, LOS ANGELES
(ANDERSON SCHOOL)

The M.B.A. program at the 70-year-old Anderson School emphasizes "global perspective, entrepreneurship, and teamwork" and sends the largest share of its graduates into the financial-services industry. The school offers full-time, part-time, and executive-M.B.A. degrees, including a 15-month dual executive-degree program with the National University of Singapore.

Students take required courses in leadership and business fundamentals in their first year of the full-time program. In the second year, a major part of the M.B.A. program is the applied management research project. Students spend two quarters in small teams working on strategic consulting plans for client firms, developing a new business plan, or devising their own special project.

Reflecting its location near the Hollywood movie studios, UCLA has established a Center for Communication Policy and Entertainment/Media and an Entertainment and Media Management Institute for both research and teaching. Students with a movie or television career in mind can take courses both in the business school and through UCLA's theater, film, and television school. The Anderson School notes that more than 160 of its alumni hold the title of vice president or higher at such major entertainment companies as Time Warner, Walt Disney, and Viacom.

UCLA ON UCLA

(Data provided by the Anderson School at the University of California, Los Angeles)

Business school website: http://www.anderson.ucla.edu
Business school e-mail: mba.admissions@anderson.ucla.edu
Public institution
M.B.A. enrollment: 1,423
Full-time: 668
Part-time: 594
Executive program: 161

ADMISSIONS DIRECTOR:
Linda Baldwin
Director of M.B.A. Admissions
110 Westwood Plaza
Gold Hall, Suite B201
Los Angeles, CA 90095
310-825-6944 (voice)
310-825-8582 (fax)
E-mail: linda.baldwin@anderson.ucla.edu

APPLICATION DEADLINE:
Fall 2006: April 2006
Annual tuition: $23,516 (in-state);
$33,829 (out-of-state)
Annual room and board: $12,000

Real estate is another strong focus at the Anderson School, which offers a special concentration that has included such courses as "Entrepreneurial Real-Estate Development" and "Urban Real-Estate Financing." Richard Ziman, a southern California real-estate executive, provided half of the $10 million needed to launch a center for real-estate research and education that bears his name.

Among the Anderson School's international offerings: an advanced international management program and a student-exchange arrangement with other business schools throughout the world. Other special programs cover corporate environmental management and the effect on business of political and economic issues in Washington.

The Anderson School has produced many accomplished alumni. But Donald Trump made the school especially proud at the end of 2004, when he picked M.B.A. alumnus Kelly Perdew as the winner of his "Apprentice" competition.

UCLA placed last among the 19 schools in the National ranking in *The Wall Street Journal*/Harris Interactive recruiter survey. Recruiters rated the school most positively for students' communication and interpersonal skills and leadership potential. UCLA received lower scores for students' international knowledge and experience, the career-services office, and faculty expertise.

THE RECRUITERS SPEAK

UCLA's most impressive features

"Confident students"

"Extremely well-rounded, fit well in all cultures"

"Collegial atmosphere"

UCLA's major shortcomings

"Some students unwilling to get their hands dirty"

"Some have 'pay your fee, get a B' mentality"

"Too entertainment-focused"

How UCLA can increase its appeal

"More recruiter-friendly policies"

"Send more graduates East"

"Temper salary expectations"

School Rankings

- National ranking in the recruiter survey: 19 of 19 schools ranked

FALL 2004 INCOMING M.B.A. CLASS

	Full-Time Only
Number of applicants	2,941
Number of offers extended	N/A
Number of students who accepted offer	328
Number of students who enrolled	328

GMAT score: 705 (mean); 710 (median)
Years of full-time work experience: 4.7 (mean); 4.8 (median)
Undergraduate GPA: 3.6 (mean); 3.6 (median)

Demographic Profile of Full-Time Students

Male: 67%
Female: 33%
Minorities: 26%
U.S. citizens/residents: 73%
Foreign nationals: 27%

Class of 2004 Most Popular Academic Concentrations (% of Students)

Finance N/A
Marketing N/A
Entrepreneurship N/A

CLASS OF 2004 EMPLOYMENT DATA

Industries Hiring Full-Time Graduates (% Hired)

Computer/technology/Internet/dot.com: 8.7%
Consumer products and services: 5.5%
Financial services/investment banking: 32.7%
Industrial products and services: 4.1%
Management consulting: 11.9%
Manufacturing: 2.3%
Media/entertainment: 9.7%

Petroleum/energy: 1%
Pharmaceutical/biotechnology/health-care products and services: 5.5%
Real estate: 9.6%
Telecommunications: 1%
Travel and transportation: 1.9%
Other professional services (accounting, advertising, etc.): 2.3%
Other: 3.8%

Position/Job Function (% Hired)

Consulting: 14.7%
Finance/accounting: 42.9%
General management: 11.1%
Marketing/sales: 20.7%
Operations/production/logistics: 2.8%
Other: 7.8%

Top Recruiters (Number of Full-Time Class of 2004 Graduates Hired)

Lehman Brothers: 8
Citigroup: 7
Amgen: 6

Percentage of Job-Seeking Full-Time Graduates Who:	All Students	Citizens/Residents	Foreign Nationals
Received offers prior to or within 3 months of graduation	91%	92%	84%
Accepted offers prior to or within 3 months of graduation	88%	89%	81%

Overall Compensation	MEAN			MEDIAN		
	All Students	Citizens/ Residents	Foreign Nationals	All Students	Citizens/ Residents	Foreign Nationals
Annual base salary	$87,022	$86,612	$89,534	$85,000	$85,000	$85,000
Signing bonus	$15,621	$15,507	$16,312	$15,000	$15,000	$15,000
Other guaranteed compensation	$24,829	$24,699	$25,818	$15,000	$12,500	$20,000

Mattel: 6
McKinsey: 5
Deloitte Consulting: 5
Countrywide Financial: 5
NBC-Universal: 4
Toyota Financial Services: 4
Bain: 3
General Mills: 3
Houlihan Lokey: 3
J.P. Morgan Chase: 3

Three of the Most Famous Graduates of M.B.A. Program

Bill Gross (class of 1971) Founder and Chief Investment Officer, Pacific Investment Management

Laurence Fink (class of 1976) Chairman and CEO, BlackRock

Jeff Henley (class of 1967) Chairman, Oracle

CARNEGIE MELLON UNIVERSITY
(TEPPER SCHOOL OF BUSINESS)

With the longtime motto "bringing science to the study of business," Carnegie Mellon's M.B.A. program continues to focus on quantitative decision-making skills and enjoys a sterling reputation for teaching information technology and operations management. Founded in 1949, it says it was the first business school to use computers for research and teaching—an IBM 650 in 1955—the first to successfully replicate the live data feeds and sophisticated software of Wall Street's major trading firms, and the first to create a wireless computing environment.

Carnegie Mellon calls itself the "borderless business school." It recently created a series of "depth tracks for a customized academic experience" that reach beyond the business school and include courses taught by professors in computer science, engineering, industrial design, and robotics. Among the tracks: wealth and asset management, biotechnology, computational marketing, e-business, integrated product development, operations management, international management, and entrepreneurship.

Full-time M.B.A. students can consider the early graduation option after 16 months of classes and without a summer internship. The school doesn't recommend that most students skip the internship, but it does see merit in early graduation for company-sponsored students who plan to return to the same employer.

Other alternative programs include a three-year part-time M.B.A. in Pittsburgh and a three-year corporate-sponsored distance-learning M.B.A. Since 1996, such companies as General Electric, United Technologies, and Lockheed Martin have sponsored students who take courses via interactive televised instruction. Now, the school is opening the distance-learning program to the public at its Moffett Field campus in California.

Carnegie Mellon joined the growing list of business schools adopting donor names in 2004. It became the David A. Tepper School of Business after receiving a $55 million donation from Mr. Tepper, an alumnus and founder of Appaloosa Management, a hedge-fund investment firm in Chatham, N.J.

In *The Wall Street Journal*/Harris Interactive recruiter survey, Carnegie Mellon received its highest ratings for students' analytical and problem-solving skills, their personal ethics and integrity, and the school's core curriculum. Carnegie Mellon's lowest scores: students' international knowledge and experience, awareness of corporate citizenship issues, and communication and interpersonal skills.

School Rankings

- National ranking in the recruiter survey: 3 of 19 schools ranked
- International ranking: 3 of 20 schools ranked
- Ranking by energy and industrial-products-industry recruiters: 1st place
- Ranking by technology-industry recruiters: 2nd place
- Ranking by health-care-industry recruiters: 7th place
- Ranking by management-consulting-industry recruiters: 9th place

Recognition for Excellence in Academic Concentrations

- With 314 nominations, Carnegie Mellon ranked No. 2 among business schools that recruiters in *The Wall Street Journal*/Harris Interactive survey cited for excellence in operations management.

CARNEGIE MELLON ON CARNEGIE MELLON

(Data provided by the Tepper School of Business at Carnegie Mellon University)

Business school website: http://www.tepper.cmu.edu
Business school e-mail: mba-admissions@andrew.cmu.edu
Private institution
M.B.A. enrollment: 661
Full-time: 387
Part-time: 274

ADMISSIONS DIRECTOR:
Laurie Stewart
Executive Director, Masters Admissions
5000 Forbes Avenue
Pittsburgh, PA 15213
412-268-2273 (voice)
412-268-4209 (fax)
E-mail: lstewart@andrew.cmu.edu

APPLICATION DEADLINE:
Fall 2006: March 2006
Annual tuition: $38,800
Annual room and board: $12,755

- With 365 nominations, Carnegie Mellon ranked No. 2 for excellence in information technology.

- With 133 nominations, Carnegie Mellon ranked No. 5 for excellence in finance.

- With 92 nominations, Carnegie Mellon ranked No. 6 for excellence in entrepreneurship.

Special Recognition

- Good source for recruiting graduates with high ethical standards: 10th most nominated school, 51 nominations.

- Good source for recruiting minorities: 10th most nominated school, 33 nominations.

FALL 2004 INCOMING M.B.A. CLASS

	Total	Full-Time Only
Number of applicants	1,348	1,194
Number of offers extended	432	337
Number of students who accepted offer	232	151
Number of students who enrolled	232	151

GMAT score: 691 (mean); 690 (median)
Years of full-time work experience: 4.3 (mean); 4 (median)
Undergraduate GPA: 3.3 (mean); 3.3 (median)

THE RECRUITERS SPEAK

Carnegie Mellon's most impressive features

"Teamwork"

"Analytical skills and technical background"

"Finance skills"

Carnegie Mellon's major shortcomings

"Not big-picture people"

"Often too introverted"

"Small size of class"

How Carnegie Mellon can increase its appeal

"Focus more on general management and corporate strategy"

"Emphasize leadership development"

"Continue building soft skills and promote creativity"

Demographic Profile of Full-Time Students

Male: 79%
Female: 21%
Minorities: 5%
U.S. citizens/residents: 74%
Foreign nationals: 26%

Class of 2004 Most Popular Academic Concentrations (% of Students)

Finance 50%
Strategy 40%
Marketing 30%

CLASS OF 2004 EMPLOYMENT DATA

Industries Hiring Full-Time Graduates (% Hired)

Computer/technology/Internet/dot.com: 15%
Consumer products and services: 5%
Energy and utilities: 3%
Financial services/investment banking: 23%
Industrial products and services: 3%
Management consulting: 21%
Manufacturing: 12%
Pharmaceutical/biotechnology/health-care products and services: 6%
Telecommunications: 3%
Travel and transportation: 2%
Other professional services (accounting, advertising, etc.): 6%
Other: 1%

Position/Job Function (% Hired)

Consulting: 22%
Finance/accounting: 35%
General management: 11%
Information technology/management information systems: 4%
Marketing/sales: 16%
Operations/production/logistics: 7%
Other: 5%

Top Recruiters *(Number of Full-Time Class of 2004 Graduates Hired)*

IBM Consulting: 8
Deloitte: 8
Citigroup: 6
McKinsey: 5
Intel: 5
Honeywell: 5
DiamondCluster: 5
Fisher Scientific: 4
Merck: 4
United Technologies: 4

Percentage of Job-Seeking Full-Time Graduates Who:	All Students	Citizens/Residents	Foreign Nationals
Received offers prior to or within 3 months of graduation	93%	94%	93%
Accepted offers prior to or within 3 months of graduation	92%	93%	89%

	MEAN			MEDIAN		
Overall Compensation	All Students	Citizens/Residents	Foreign Nationals	All Students	Citizens/Residents	Foreign Nationals
Annual base salary	$82,185	$83,029	$79,558	$85,000	$85,000	$80,000
Signing bonus	$12,550	$12,839	$11,536	$10,000	$10,000	$10,000
Other guaranteed compensation	$13,346	$13,420	$13,050	$10,000	$10,000	$10,000

Three of the Most Famous Graduates of M.B.A. Program

David Coulter (class of 1971) Vice Chairman, J.P. Morgan Chase

Yoshiaki Fujimori (class of 1981) President and CEO, GE Asia

David Tepper (class of 1982) Founder and President, Appaloosa Management

UNIVERSITY OF CHICAGO

The University of Chicago Graduate School of Business

Boasting a strong reputation for its rigorous analytical and quantitative approach, the University of Chicago's Graduate School of Business offers a full portfolio of M.B.A. programs. The full-time program, the school's cornerstone, is housed in a brand-new $125 million building in Chicago's Hyde Park neighborhood, while its part-time courses are offered at a downtown facility. For experienced managers, Chicago's executive M.B.A. programs span the globe from Chicago to London to Singapore.

As the second-oldest business school in the U.S., Chicago claims a number of pioneering accomplishments, including the first doctoral program in business in 1920, the first scholarly business-school journal in 1928, the first executive-M.B.A. program in 1943, and the first school to boast six Nobel Prize-winning faculty members.

Chicago students can pursue academic concentrations in 13 areas, including econometrics and statistics, analytic finance, entrepreneurship, marketing management, and managerial and organizational behavior. Beyond the regular curriculum, they also must participate in Leadership Effectiveness and Development, a required program for mastering the leadership and interpersonal skills that corporate recruiters value most highly.

Traditionally, more than half of Chicago full-time graduates have taken jobs in finance and accounting, with management

CHICAGO ON CHICAGO

(Data provided by the University of Chicago Graduate School of Business)

Business school website:
http://ChicagoGSB.edu
Business school e-mail:
admissions@ChicagoGSB.edu
Private institution
M.B.A. enrollment: 3,001
Full-time: 1,087
Part-time: 1,433
Executive program: 481

ADMISSIONS DIRECTOR:
Rosemarie Martinelli
Associate Dean for Student Recruitment and Admissions
5807 S. Woodlawn Ave.
Chicago, IL 60637
773-702-7369 (voice)
773-702-9085 (fax)
E-mail:
admissions@Chicago.GSB.edu

APPLICATION DEADLINES:
Fall 2006: November 2005, January 2006, March 2006
Annual tuition: $38,800
Annual room and board: $17,100

consulting the next most popular career choice. Despite its image as a finance-centric school, however, Chicago actually grants its M.B.A. students great flexibility in designing their course of study. There are few requirements, and students can take up to six electives in other university departments. That could mean a course in philosophy or literature.

Full-time students aiming for a multicultural career can enroll in Chicago's international M.B.A. program. It stretches beyond the regular curriculum to require more classes in international business, proficiency in a foreign language, and one term spent abroad as an exchange student at one of Chicago's partner schools.

Soon, Chicago M.B.A.s may start looking younger. The school has established the GSB Scholars program, allowing Chicago undergraduates to apply to the M.B.A. program in their last year of studies. Those who are provisionally admitted must gain two to three years of "substantive" work experience before starting classes. Chicago began the program in response to corporate recruiters' desire for talented, younger M.B.A. graduates. At most top full-time M.B.A. programs, including Chicago's, students typically have four to five years of work experience and are nearly 30 years old when they graduate.

Chicago dropped eight spots to 13th place in the latest *Wall Street Journal*/Harris Interactive National ranking. The business school received its strongest ratings for its faculty's expertise and its graduates' analytical and problem-solving skills and

THE RECRUITERS SPEAK

Chicago's most impressive features	**Chicago's major shortcomings**	**How Chicago can increase its appeal**
"Analytical, thoughtful, deliberate"	"Too quantitative and geeky"	"More heart, passion for people"
"Brainpower, capacity to perform in investment banking"	"Not good general managers"	"Focus on developing CEO-type thinkers"
"Impressive new classroom building"	"Class is very homogenous"	"Build students' collaboration skills"

personal ethics and integrity. Recruiters gave Chicago much lower grades, however, for well-rounded students, their ability to work well in teams, and their awareness of corporate citizenship issues.

School Rankings

■ National ranking in the recruiter survey: 13 of 19 schools ranked

■ International ranking: 16 of 20 schools ranked

■ Ranking by management-consulting-industry recruiters: 10th place

■ Ranking by consumer-products-industry recruiters: 10th place

Recognition for Excellence in Academic Concentrations

■ With 200 nominations, Chicago ranked No. 1 among business schools that recruiters in *The Wall Street Journal*/Harris Interactive survey cited for excellence in accounting.

■ With 472 nominations, Chicago ranked No. 2 for excellence in finance.

■ With 63 nominations, Chicago ranked No. 9 for excellence in strategy.

■ With 53 nominations, Chicago ranked No. 9 for excellence in marketing.

FALL 2004 INCOMING M.B.A. CLASS

	Full-Time Only
Number of applicants	N/A
Number of offers extended	N/A
Number of students who accepted offer	N/A
Number of students who enrolled	520

GMAT score: 695 (mean); 710 (median)
Years of full-time work experience: 4.9 (mean); 4.5 (median)
Undergraduate GPA: 3.4 (mean); 3.4 (median)

Demographic Profile of Full-Time Students

Male: 73%
Female: 27%
Minorities: 25%
U.S. citizens/residents: 70%
Foreign nationals: 30%

Class of 2004 Most Popular Academic Concentrations (% of Students)

Finance 77%
Entrepreneurship 47%
Accounting 35%

CLASS OF 2004 EMPLOYMENT DATA

Industries Hiring Full-Time Graduates (% Hired)

Computer/technology/Internet/dot.com: 5%
Consumer products and services: 5%
Financial services/investment banking: 47%
Management consulting: 23%
Manufacturing: 5%
Petroleum/energy: 1%
Pharmaceutical/biotechnology/health-care products and services: 4%
Real estate: 1%
Travel and transportation: 3%
Other professional services (accounting, advertising, etc.): 2%
Other: 4%

Position/Job Function (% Hired)

Consulting: 22%
Finance/accounting: 59%
General management: 3%
Marketing/sales: 7%
Other: 9%

Top Recruiters (Number of Full-Time Class of 2004 Graduates Hired)

McKinsey: 21
Citigroup: 17
Credit Suisse First Boston: 15
Deutsche Bank: 15

Lehman Brothers: 14
Booz Allen Hamilton: 13
Bain: 10
Boston Consulting Group: 10
J.P. Morgan Chase: 9
Morgan Stanley: 8
UBS Investment Bank: 8

Percentage of Job-Seeking Full-Time Graduates Who:	All Students	Citizens/Residents	Foreign Nationals
Received offers prior to or within 3 months of graduation	90%	90%	90%
Accepted offers prior to or within 3 months of graduation	88%	88%	86%

Overall Compensation	MEAN			MEDIAN		
	All Students	Citizens/ Residents	Foreign Nationals	All Students	Citizens/ Residents	Foreign Nationals
Annual base salary	$90,121	$91,151	$87,202	$85,000	$85,000	$85,000
Signing bonus	$15,832	$15,283	$15,981	$15,000	$15,000	$20,000
Other guaranteed compensation	$33,430	$34,048	$32,011	$25,000	$26,000	$20,000

Three of the Most Famous Graduates of M.B.A. Program

Philip Purcell (class of 1967) Former Chairman and CEO, Morgan Stanley

Karen Katen (class of 1974) Vice Chairman, Pfizer

James Kilts (class of 1974) Chairman, President and CEO, Gillette

University of Colorado at Boulder

Colorado
LEEDS
School of Business

UNIVERSITY OF COLORADO AT BOULDER (LEEDS SCHOOL OF BUSINESS)

The Leeds School defines as its mission the development of "individuals who can adapt to and lead change while building an organization that values, respects, and maintains the world's human and environmental resources."

The school's Center for Business and Society conducts research on business ethics and leadership and social and environmental responsibility, while the Center for Sustainable Tourism examines the economic, environmental, and social impact of travel. M.B.A. students are required to take at least one course that addresses the connection between business and society.

Entrepreneurship is the most popular M.B.A. major. The university offers such courses as entrepreneurial finance, the law for entrepreneurs, and business-plan preparation, and it helps place M.B.A.s in summer internships with new and emerging growth companies. In addition to becoming entrepreneurs, many Colorado M.B.A. graduates are drawn to jobs in accounting and finance.

Besides its full-time M.B.A. degree, the university offers a part-time evening program in Boulder, providing shuttle-bus service from downtown Denver. There's also an executive M.B.A. program in Denver that is a joint offering of the university's three graduate business schools in Boulder, Colorado Springs, and Denver.

Nestled at the foothills of the Rocky Mountains, the business school became the Leeds School in 2001 in recognition of a $35 million commitment from the Leeds family, which founded CMP Media Inc. The gift is not only large, but it also carries some unusual terms. As part of the endowment, for example, the school will offer more courses and special programs on corporate social responsibility and diversity.

Colorado finished at the bottom of *The Wall Street Journal*/Harris Interactive Regional ranking. In the survey, recruiters awarded Colorado its best scores for students' communication and interpersonal skills, personal ethics and integrity, analytical and problem-solving skills, and ability to work well in teams. Colorado's lowest scores: success with past hires from the school, the career-services office, and students' international knowledge and experience.

School Rankings

■ Regional ranking in the recruiter survey: 47 of 47 schools ranked

FALL 2004 INCOMING M.B.A. CLASS

	Total	Full-Time Only
Number of applicants	294	249
Number of offers extended	168	132
Number of students who accepted offer	91	71
Number of students who enrolled	75	55

GMAT score: 648 (mean); 650 (median)
Years of full-time work experience: 4.7 (mean); 4.7 (median)
Undergraduate GPA: 3.3 (mean); 3.3 (median)

Demographic Profile of Full-Time Students

Male: 76%
Female: 24%

COLORADO ON COLORADO

(Data provided by the Leeds School of Business at the University of Colorado at Boulder)

Business school website:
http://leeds.colorado.edu/
Business school e-mail:
leedsmba@colorado.edu
Public institution
M.B.A. enrollment: 256
Full-time: 117
Part-time: 62
Executive program: 77

ADMISSIONS DIRECTOR:
Anne Sandoe-Thorp
Director of M.B.A. Admissions & Marketing
Leeds School of Business, UCB 419
Boulder, CO 80309
303-492-1832 (voice)
303-492-1727 (fax)
E-mail: anne.sandoe-thorp@colorado.edu

APPLICATION DEADLINES:
Fall 2006: December 2005, February 2006, April 2006
Annual tuition: $6,050 (in-state); $21,632 (out-of-state)
Annual room and board: $16,000

Minorities: 9%
U.S. citizens/residents: 87%
Foreign nationals: 13%

Class of 2004 Most Popular Academic Concentrations (% of Students)

Entrepreneurship 46%
Finance 27%
Marketing 20%

CLASS OF 2004 EMPLOYMENT DATA

Industries Hiring Full-Time Graduates (% Hired)

Manufacturing: 19%
Other professional services (accounting, advertising, etc.): 81%

Position/Job Function (% Hired)

Consulting: 13%
Finance/accounting: 39%
General management: 23%
Marketing/sales: 19%
Operations/production/logistics: 6%

Top Recruiters (Number of Full-Time Class of 2004 Graduates Hired)

Hitachi Consulting: 2
Accenture: 2
StorageTek: 2
Pulte Homes: 2
Wall Street On Demand: 1
Madison Group: 1
Kindred Keziah: 1

THE RECRUITERS SPEAK

Colorado's most impressive features

"Students are tenacious"

"Good accounting program"

"Entrepreneurial"

Colorado's major shortcomings

"Clueless about the work world"

"Students believe they don't have to pay their dues"

"Lack international knowledge"

How Colorado can increase its appeal

"Make the program more rigorous"

"Teach candidates how to interview"

"Enhance corporate interaction for image improvement"

Sterling Rice Group: 1
Shawnee Investments: 1
Catlin Properties: 1

Percentage of Job-Seeking Full-Time Graduates Who:	All Students	Citizens/Residents	Foreign Nationals
Received offers prior to or within 3 months of graduation	85%	84%	100%
Accepted offers prior to or within 3 months of graduation	85%	84%	100%

	MEAN			MEDIAN		
Overall Compensation	All Students	Citizens/ Residents	Foreign Nationals	All Students	Citizens/ Residents	Foreign Nationals
Annual base salary	$64,800	$65,300	$50,000	$65,000	$65,000	$50,000
Signing bonus	$6,332	$6,543	N/A	$7,500	$7,500	N/A
Other guaranteed compensation	N/A	N/A	N/A	N/A	N/A	N/A

Three of the Most Famous Graduates of M.B.A. Program

John Puerner (class of 1978) Former Publisher, Los Angeles Times

Mary Reisher (class of 1979) Executive Vice President, First Bank, Colorado

Dick Engretson (class of 1972) Executive Vice President, dmg world media

COLUMBIA BUSINESS SCHOOL

COLUMBIA UNIVERSITY

Columbia University's business school officials pride themselves on being "edgy and aggressive" and reflecting the cultural mix of New York City. The school's diversification drive has resulted in a student body in which women represent more than one-third of its full-time M.B.A. candidates; U.S. minorities, 24%; and foreign nationals, 30%.

Just a subway ride away from Wall Street, Columbia Business School is a major supplier of talent—typically at least half its M.B.A. graduates—to investment banks and financial-services companies. Global management is another key strength at Columbia through its international business academic concentration, as well as the Jerome A. Chazen Institute of International Business and student-exchange programs with more than 20 business schools abroad.

Columbia has responded to the recent wave of corporate scandals with a major new initiative called "The Individual, Business, and Society: Tradeoffs, Choices, and Accountability." The Sanford C. Bernstein & Co. Center for Leadership and Ethics oversees the program, which includes special sessions in which professor and corporate executives debate such topics as the costs and benefits of the Sarbanes-Oxley Act, corporate social responsibility and the bottom line, and the changing role of boards of directors.

In addition, professors now incorporate discussion of conflicts and tradeoffs in courses throughout the curriculum. For example, in corporate finance classes, they question whether maximizing shareholder value should be a company's sole or primary objective, and in the marketing strategy course, they discuss the limits of marketing legal but potentially dangerous products.

M.B.A. students have an unusually large array of 11 dual-degree options with other Columbia schools, including architecture, journalism, nursing, social work, engineering, and dental and oral surgery.

Columbia sees executive-M.B.A. degrees as a significant growth opportunity. In 2001, it began offering a global executive M.B.A. degree with the London Business School. A bicoastal executive M.B.A. program with the University of California at Berkeley was launched a year later. Columbia also has teamed with both Berkeley and London on a social-venture competition to promote new businesses that will produce both "financial and social returns on investment."

In the latest *Wall Street Journal*/Harris Interactive ranking, corporate recruiters gave Columbia graduates high marks for their analytical and problem-solving abilities, strategic thinking, and communication and interpersonal skills. Students received their lowest ratings for awareness of corporate citizenship issues, well-rounded qualities, and willingness to relocate.

School Rankings

- National ranking in the recruiter survey: 8 of 19 schools ranked
- International ranking: 13 of 20 schools ranked
- Ranking by consumer-products-industry recruiters: 2nd place

Recognition for Excellence in Academic Concentrations

- With 182 nominations, Columbia ranked No. 3 among business schools that recruiters in *The Wall Street Journal*/Harris Interactive survey cited for excellence in finance.

COLUMBIA ON COLUMBIA

(Data provided by Columbia Business School)

Business school Web site:
http://www.gsb.columbia.edu
Business school e-mail:
apply@claven.gsb.columbia.edu
Private institution
M.B.A. enrollment: 1,796
Full-time: 1,196
Executive program: 600

ADMISSIONS DIRECTOR:
Linda Meehan
Assistant Dean for Admissions
216 Uris Hall
3022 Broadway
New York, NY 10027
212-854-1961 (voice)
212-662-6754 (fax)
E-mail: apply@claven.gsb.
columbia.edu

APPLICATION DEADLINES:
Fall 2006: 3/1/2006 (international); 4/20/2006 (domestic)
Winter 2007: 10/1/2006 (international); 10/20/2006 (domestic)
Annual tuition and fees: $38,290
Annual room and board: $18,450

- With 139 nominations, Columbia ranked No. 4 for excellence in international business.
- With 61 nominations, Columbia ranked No. 9 for excellence in accounting.

Special Recognition

- Good source for recruiting women: the most nominated school, 123 nominations.
- Good source for recruiting minorities: 3rd most nominated school, 67 nominations.

FALL 2004 INCOMING M.B.A. CLASS

	Full-Time Only
Number of applicants	4,871
Number of offers extended	711
Number of students who accepted offer	502
Number of students who enrolled	502

GMAT score: 709 (mean); 710 (median)
Years of full-time work experience: 5 (mean); 4.6 (median)
Undergraduate GPA: 3.4 (mean); 3.4 (median)

Demographic Profile of Full-Time Students

Male: 64%
Female: 36%
Minorities: 24%
U.S. citizens/residents: 70%
Foreign nationals: 30%

THE RECRUITERS SPEAK

Columbia's most impressive features

"New York energy"

"Urbane, multicultural"

"Analytical mindset of the students"

Columbia's major shortcomings

"Inconsistent—some very good students, others are duds"

"Snooty"

"Herd mentality for careers—investment banking, private equity"

How Columbia can increase its appeal

"Foster a more friendly environment"

"Recruit more students with technology background"

"Increase interaction with companies outside New York"

Class of 2004 Most Popular Academic Concentrations

N/A

CLASS OF 2004 EMPLOYMENT DATA

Industries Hiring Full-Time Graduates (% Hired)

Computer/technology/Internet/dot.com: 3%
Media/entertainment: 2%
Financial services/investment banking: 52%
Management consulting: 23%
Manufacturing: 4%
Nonprofit and government: 2%
Petroleum/energy: 1%
Pharmaceutical/biotechnology/health-care products and services: 3%
Real estate: 4%
Telecommunications: 1%
Other professional services (accounting, advertising, etc.): 5%

Position/Job Function (% Hired)

Consulting: 25%
Finance/accounting: 50%
General management: 4%
Marketing/sales: 9%
Other: 11%

Top Recruiters (Number of Full-Time Class of 2004 Graduates Hired)

McKinsey: 47
Lehman Brothers: 27
Citigroup: 25
Goldman Sachs: 18
Deutsche Bank: 14
American Express: 11
J.P. Morgan Chase: 11
Booz Allen Hamiliton: 10
Morgan Stanley: 10
Bank of America: 9
Boston Consulting Group: 9
Credit Suisse First Boston: 9

Percentage of Job-Seeking Full-Time Graduates Who:	All Students	Citizens/Residents	Foreign Nationals
Received offers prior to or within 3 months of graduation	95%	N/A	N/A
Accepted offers prior to or within 3 months of graduation	90%	N/A	N/A

Overall Compensation	MEAN			MEDIAN		
	All Students	Citizens/ Residents	Foreign Nationals	All Students	Citizens/ Residents	Foreign Nationals
Annual base salary	$90,173	N/A	N/A	$85,000	N/A	N/A
Signing bonus	$17,363	N/A	N/A	$20,000	N/A	N/A
Other guaranteed compensation	$36,146	N/A	N/A	$25,000	N/A	N/A

Three of the Most Famous Graduates of M.B.A. Program

Warren Buffett (class of 1951) Chairman, Berkshire Hathaway

Henry Kravis (class of 1969) Founding Partner, Kohlberg Kravis Roberts

Rochelle Lazarus (class of 1970) Chairman and CEO, Ogilvy & Mather Worldwide

CORNELL UNIVERSITY
(JOHNSON GRADUATE SCHOOL OF MANAGEMENT)

Cornell University
The Johnson School

One of the Johnson School's most distinctive features is its "immersion learning" curriculum, or what its M.B.A. students call "the semester in reality." Students work on real-world problems under real-world pressure, often go on the road to see companies up close, and are evaluated as they would be on an actual job. Cornell's immersions include brand management, investment banking, managerial finance, entrepreneurship and private equity, manufacturing, and research, sales, and trading.

Another distinctive Cornell offering is the 12-month M.B.A. option for applicants with scientific or technical backgrounds. Students' prior analytical training enables them to move at an accelerated pace through the curriculum. Aspiring physician executives also can earn an M.B.A. in just one year through the Johnson School's M.D./M.B.A. partnership with Weill Cornell Medical College. Other dual-degree programs couple an M.B.A. with a master's in law, Asian studies, human resources, real estate, or engineering.

Cornell is expanding its executive-M.B.A. degree options in 2005, with the launch of a 16-month program called the Boardroom Executive M.B.A. Created in partnership with Canada's Queens School of Business, the program will be taught through interactive videoconferencing, unlike Cornell's existing executive M.B.A.

Cornell has long had close ties with members of the business school's namesake family and their company, S.C. Johnson &

CORNELL ON CORNELL

(Data provided by the S.C. Johnson Graduate School of Management at Cornell University)

Business school website:
http://www.johnson.cornell.edu
Business school e-mail:
mba@cornell.edu
Private institution
M.B.A. enrollment: 652
Full-time: 544
Executive Program: 108

ADMISSIONS DIRECTOR:
Natalie Grinblatt
Director of Admissions
112 Sage Hall
Cornell University
Ithaca, NY 14853
607-254-7477 (voice)
607-255-0065 (fax)
E-mail: nmg10@cornell.edu

APPLICATION DEADLINES:
Fall 2006: Two-year program—
10/15/2005, 11/15/2005,
1/15/2006, 3/15/2006
12-month program—10/15/2005,
11/15/2005, 12/15/2005,
1/15/2006, 3/1/2006
Annual tuition: $36,350
Annual room and board: $9,500

Son, the maker of such household product brands as Pledge, Glade, and Ziploc. The Johnson family's most recent contribution is the Center for Sustainable Global Enterprise, endowed with $5 million by the late Samuel Curtis Johnson. He also donated $2.5 million to establish a professorship in global sustainability with the charge to prepare students "to be leaders of ethical, equitable, and economically and environmentally sustainable enterprises."

As the M.B.A. market becomes more crowded, the Johnson School is taking steps to remain competitive. It recently developed a five-year strategic plan that calls for increasing the faculty count to at least 65 from 58, attracting more female and minority students and professors, strengthening alumni relations, and connecting admissions and career services in "a customer-focused supply-chain model."

In *The Wall Street Journal/Harris Interactive* ranking, recruiters gave Cornell its highest grades for students' fit with the corporate culture, ability to work well in teams, and personal ethics and integrity. Cornell received its lowest ratings for students' awareness of corporate citizenship issues, their international knowledge and experience, and the faculty's expertise. Many recruiters also complain about the difficulty of reaching Cornell's remote campus in Ithaca, N.Y., which has little direct air service.

THE RECRUITERS SPEAK

Cornell's most impressive features

"Scrappiness"

"Finance skills"

"Affable and team oriented"

Cornell's major shortcomings

"Quality of the bottom half of the student body"

"Finance students focus too much on Wall Street jobs"

"Isolated location"

How Cornell can increase its appeal

"Better communication with corporate contacts"

"Encourage students to consider various geographic areas for jobs"

"Increase diversity"

School Rankings

■ National ranking in the recruiter survey: 18 of 19 schools ranked

FALL 2004 INCOMING M.B.A. CLASS

	Full-Time Only
Number of applicants	1,827
Number of offers extended	656
Number of students who accepted offer	306
Number of students who enrolled	306

GMAT score: 673 (mean); 680 (median)
Years of full-time work experience: 5 (mean); 5 (median)
Undergraduate GPA: 3.3 (mean); 3.3 (median)

Demographic Profile of Full-Time Students

Male: 72%
Female: 28%
Minorities: 18%
U.S. citizens/residents: 72%
Foreign nationals: 28%

Class of 2004 Most Popular Academic Concentrations (% of Students)

Managerial finance 21%
Brand management 20%
Manufacturing 17%

CLASS OF 2004 EMPLOYMENT DATA

Industries Hiring Full-Time Graduates (% Hired)

Computer/technology/Internet/dot-com: 6%
Consumer products and services: 10.7%
Financial services/investment banking: 29.5%
Management consulting: 17.9%
Manufacturing: 5.6%
Petroleum/energy: 4.7%
Pharmaceutical/biotechnology/health-care products and services: 11.5%

Real estate: 2.1%
Telecommunications: 3%
Travel and transportation: 1%
Other professional services (accounting, advertising, etc.): 3.4%
Other: 4.6%

Position/Job Function (% Hired)

Consulting: 15.4%
Finance/accounting: 35%
General management: 16.2%
Human resources: 1%
Information technology/management information systems: 1.3%
Marketing/sales: 23.9%
Operations/production/logistics: 2.1%
Other: 5.1%

Top Recruiters (Number of Full-Time Class of 2004 Graduates Hired)

Citigroup: 11
Johnson & Johnson: 11
Deloitte Consulting: 8
American Express: 6
General Electric: 6

Percentage of Job-Seeking Full-Time Graduates Who:	All Students	Citizens/Residents	Foreign Nationals
Received offers prior to or within 3 months of graduation	87%	88%	83%
Accepted offers prior to or within 3 months of graduation	83%	82%	83%

Overall Compensation	MEAN			MEDIAN		
	All Students	Citizens/Residents	Foreign Nationals	All Students	Citizens/Residents	Foreign Nationals
Annual base salary	$87,831	$88,636	$82,966	$85,000	$85,000	$85,000
Signing bonus	$15,490	$15,284	$16,417	$15,000	$15,000	$20,000
Other guaranteed compensation	$15,049	$15,088	$14,750	$10,000	$10,000	$15,000

Honeywell: 6
Pfizer: 6
IBM: 5
Unilever: 5
Avaya: 4
Kraft: 4
Lehman Brothers: 4
UBS: 4

Three of the Most Famous Graduates of M.B.A. Program

Richard Marin (class of 1976) Chairman and CEO, Bear Stearns Asset Management

H. Fisk Johnson (class of 1984) Chairman, S.C. Johnson & Son

Jim Morgan (class of 1963) Chairman, Applied Materials

DARTMOUTH COLLEGE
(TUCK SCHOOL OF BUSINESS)

TUCK

America's first graduate school of management, Dartmouth's Tuck School, rose to first place in the latest National ranking in *The Wall Street Journal*/Harris Interactive recruiter survey. The survey respondents repeatedly praised Tuck graduates for their character, collegiality, and strong skills in both finance and consulting.

Tuck is one of the smaller top-rated M.B.A. programs. It also is perhaps the most focused, awarding only one degree—the full-time M.B.A—and offering all its students a general-management curriculum. Tuck does partner with other schools at Dartmouth and with other universities to offer joint and dual programs that combine the M.B.A. with degrees in medicine, diplomacy, public administration, public health, environmental law, and engineering.

Tuck's curriculum was revised in 2000 to put more emphasis on entrepreneurship, technology, and global business. Among the newest programs is the Allwin Initiative for Corporate Citizenship, which features an annual conference on business sustainability with speakers from such companies and organizations as Ford Motor, Ben & Jerry's, and Greenpeace.

Tuck maintains close ties with its 7,800 alumni, many of whom are also recruiters at the school. In fact, it boasts that it enjoys the highest rate of alumni giving of any business school, with 65% making annual contributions. Tuck clearly will be counting on that support for its $110 million fundraising campaign, launched at the start of 2005 in New York.

As for career path, financial services and consulting traditionally have been the top choices of Tuck graduates. But the New England school is as much about teamwork as it is about finance and strategy. Its students thrive on camaraderie—whether in study groups or on the ski slopes. Tuck's program has been dubbed "the happy M.B.A.," and some recruiters wonder whether Tuck goes a bit overboard with its teamwork focus. But clearly most companies like the Tuck combination of "smart and nice," as one recruiter put it.

Tuck's biggest image problem is its remote location, which makes it harder to attract students, new faculty and even corporate recruiters. Indeed, in *The Wall Street Journal*/Harris Interactive survey, travel difficulties were a frequent complaint from recruiters. Tuck received its highest scores in the survey for students' personal ethics and integrity, ability to work well in teams, and well-rounded qualities. Recruiters gave Tuck its lowest scores for students' international knowledge and experience and the faculty's expertise.

School Rankings

- National ranking in the recruiter survey: 1 of 19 schools ranked
- Ranking by financial-services-industry recruiters: 1st place
- Ranking by management-consulting-industry recruiters: 1st place
- Ranking by health-care-industry recruiters: 5th place
- Ranking by consumer-products-industry recruiters: 5th place

Recognition for Excellence in Academic Concentrations

- With 136 nominations, Dartmouth ranked No. 3 among business schools that recruiters in *The Wall Street Journal*/Harris Interactive survey cited for excellence in strategy.
- With 54 nominations, Dartmouth ranked No. 8 for excellence in marketing.

- With 43 nominations, Dartmouth ranked No. 10 for excellence in operations management.

Special Recognition
- Good source for recruiting graduates with high ethical standards: 3rd most nominated school, 122 nominations.

FALL 2004 INCOMING M.B.A. CLASS

	Full-Time Only
Number of applicants	1,716
Number of offers extended	455
Number of students who accepted offer	N/A
Number of students who enrolled	262

GMAT score: 704 (mean); 710 (median)
Years of full-time work experience: 5 (mean); N/A (median)
Undergraduate GPA: 3.4 (mean); N/A (median);

Demographic Profile of Full-Time Students
Male: 75%
Female: 25%
Minorities: 18%
U.S. citizens/residents: 69%
Foreign nationals: 31%

Class of 2004 Most Popular Academic Concentrations
N/A

DARTMOUTH ON DARTMOUTH

(Data provided by the Tuck School of Business at Dartmouth College)

Business school website: http://www.tuck.dartmouth.edu
Business school e-mail: tuck.admissions@dartmouth.edu
Private institution
M.B.A. enrollment: 503
Full-time: 503

ADMISSIONS DIRECTOR:
Kristine Laca
Director of Admissions
Tuck School of Business at Dartmouth
100 Tuck Hall
Hanover, NH 03755
603-646-3162 (voice)
603-646-1308 (fax)
E-mail: tuck.admissions@dartmouth.edu

APPLICATION DEADLINE:
Fall 2006: April 2006
Annual tuition: $38,400
Annual room and board: $9,525

THE RECRUITERS SPEAK

Dartmouth's most impressive features

"Socially responsible students"

"Team spirit"

"Well-rounded, savvy generalists"

Dartmouth's major shortcomings

"Sometimes students lack fire in the belly"

"Students can be conflict-avoidant"

"Far from civilization"

How Dartmouth can increase its appeal

"Globalize the brand"

"Set up alternate interview locations in New York, Boston, and elsewhere"

"More consumer-goods focus"

CLASS OF 2004 EMPLOYMENT DATA

Industries Hiring Full-Time Graduates (% Hired)

Computer/technology/Internet/dot-com: 6%
Consumer products and services: 14%
Financial services/investment banking: 36%
Management consulting: 21%
Manufacturing: 10%
Pharmaceutical/biotechnology/health-care products and services: 8%
Other professional services (accounting, advertising, etc.): 5%

Position/Job Function (% Hired)

Consulting: 21%
Finance/accounting: 35%
General management: 9%
Marketing/sales: 18%
Other: 17%

Percentage of Job-Seeking Full-Time Graduates Who:	All Students	Citizens/Residents	Foreign Nationals
Received offers prior to or within 3 months of graduation	N/A	N/A	N/A
Accepted offers prior to or within 3 months of graduation	95%	94%	94%

Overall Compensation	MEAN			MEDIAN		
	All Students	Citizens/ Residents	Foreign Nationals	All Students	Citizens/ Residents	Foreign Nationals
Annual base salary	$91,900	$91,400	$93,400	$87,300	$86,500	$89,000
Signing bonus	$16,500	$15,700	$18,500	$15,000	$15,000	$17,500
Other guaranteed compensation	$27,900	$28,200	$27,100	$20,000	$20,000	$15,000

Top Recruiters *(Number of Full-Time Class of 2004 Graduates Hired)*

Lehman Brothers: N/A
Citigroup:
Gillette:
Bain:
Boston Consulting Group:
Guidant:
UBS Investment Bank:
McKinsey:
General Mills:
Mercer Management Consulting:

Three of the Most Famous Graduates of M.B.A. Program

John Costas (class of 1981) Chairman, UBS Investment Bank

Peter Dolan (class of 1980) CEO, Bristol-Myers Squibb

Donald Peterson (class of 1973) Chairman and CEO, Avaya

UNIVERSITY OF DENVER
(DANIELS COLLEGE OF BUSINESS)

Established in 1908, the Daniels College of Business declares its mission to be imparting "knowledge and technical ability, interpersonal skills and intercultural understanding, and ethically based leadership and social responsibility." Indeed, the college's namesake, cable-television pioneer Bill Daniels, donated $11 million to ensure that the business-school curriculum incorporated ethics, values, and social responsibility issues.

Students can specialize in such areas as innovation and entrepreneurship, finance, data mining, e-commerce, accounting, integrated marketing strategy, real estate, construction management, and values-based leadership. In addition to the traditional two-year M.B.A. program, students can take the fast track and earn their degree in a single year. And for more experienced managers, Daniels offers an 18-month executive-M.B.A. degree.

The executive program teaches basic M.B.A. skills and also takes students outside the classroom for a weekend of sailing, not for fun but to give them practical experience in leadership and team dynamics. The M.B.A.s travel to San Diego, where they are assigned to nine boats and participate in races and other nautical challenges. During a "silent sail," team members must communicate nonverbally to guide their boats, and in a "blind sail," the student steering the boat is blindfolded and must rely on instinct and verbal instructions from teammates.

DENVER ON DENVER

(Data provided by the Daniels College of Business at the University of Denver)

Business school website:
http://www.daniels.du.edu
Business school e-mail:
daniels@du.edu
Private institution
M.B.A. enrollment: 597
Full-time: 283
Part-time: 224
Executive program: 90

ADMISSIONS DIRECTOR:
Scott Campbell
Director, Admissions and
Financial Aid
2101 S. University Boulevard,
Room 258
Denver, CO 80208
303-871-3416 (voice)
303-871-4466 (fax)
E-mail: daniels@du.edu

APPLICATION DEADLINES:
Fall 2006: 1/15/2006, 3/15/2006,
5/15/2006
Annual tuition: $27,756
Annual room and board: $9,900

Daniels recently joined the still small but growing number of business schools with female deans. Karen Newman was to be appointed dean in summer 2005, moving from the deanship at the Robins School of Business at the University of Richmond.

In *The Wall Street Journal*/Harris Interactive survey, recruiters gave the highest ratings to students' personal ethics and integrity, and teamwork abilities, and to the career-services office. The Daniels College received its lowest marks for students' willingness to relocate for their jobs, their previous work experience, and their international knowledge and experience.

School Rankings

- Regional ranking in the recruiter survey: 8 of 47 schools ranked
- Ranking by technology-industry recruiters: 3rd place
- Ranking by financial-services-industry recruiters: 7th place

Recognition for Excellence in Academic Concentrations

- With 65 nominations, Denver ranked No. 6 among business schools that recruiters in *The Wall Street Journal*/Harris Interactive survey cited for excellence in accounting.
- With 34 nominations, Denver ranked No. 9 for excellence in information technology.

THE RECRUITERS SPEAK

Denver's most impressive features	Denver's major shortcomings	How Denver can increase its appeal
"High integrity, morals"	"Students do not know how to write professionally"	"Toughen the curriculum"
"Ease of using the career center"	"Mediocre interviewing skills"	"Raise the bar for entrance"
"Work ethic"	"Grads are hit or miss"	"Increase focus on soft skills"

Special Recognition

■ Good source for recruiting graduates with high ethical standards: 4th most nominated school, 101 nominations.

FALL 2004 INCOMING M.B.A. CLASS

	Total	Full-Time Only
Number of applicants	465	366
Number of offers extended	344	269
Number of students who accepted offer	197	143
Number of students who enrolled	192	126

GMAT score: 571 (mean); 560 (median)
Years of full-time work experience: 5 (mean); 4 (median)
Undergraduate GPA: 3.2 (mean); 3.3 (median)

Demographic Profile of Full-Time Students

Male: 65%
Female: 35%
Minorities: 11%
U.S. citizens/residents: 78%
Foreign nationals: 22%

Class of 2004 Most Popular Academic Concentrations (% of Students)

Real estate 10%
International 7%

CLASS OF 2004 EMPLOYMENT DATA

Industries Hiring Full-Time Graduates (% Hired)

Computer/technology/Internet/dot-com: 7.3%
Consumer products and services: 2.8%
Energy and utilities: 1%
Media/entertainment: 2.8%
Financial services/investment banking: 14.7%
Government: 3.7%
Industrial products and services: 1.8%
Management consulting: 9.2%

Manufacturing: 6.4%
Nonprofit: 5.5%
Pharmaceutical/biotechnology/health-care products and services: 4.6%
Real estate: 14.7%
Telecommunications: 6.4%
Travel and transportation: 1%
Other professional services (accounting, advertising, etc.): 10%
Other: 8.1%

Position/Job Function (% Hired)

Consulting: 11.9%
Finance/accounting: 40.4%
General management: 9.2%
Human resources: 1.8%
Information technology/management information systems: 2.8%
Marketing/sales: 21.1%
Operations/production/logistics: 6.4%
Other: 6.4%

Percentage of Job-Seeking Full-Time Graduates Who:	All Students	Citizens/Residents	Foreign Nationals
Received offers prior to or within 3 months of graduation	89%	89%	100%
Accepted offers prior to or within 3 months of graduation	89%	89%	100%

	MEAN			MEDIAN		
Overall Compensation	All Students	Citizens/ Residents	Foreign Nationals	All Students	Citizens/ Residents	Foreign Nationals
Annual base salary	$55,756	$55,231	$65,840	$57,500	$57,500	$45,500
Signing bonus	$9,350	$9,833	$5,000	$3,500	$3,500	$5,000
Other guaranteed compensation	$9,582	$9,582	N/A	$8,000	$8,000	N/A

Top Recruiters *(Number of Full-Time Class of 2004 Graduates Hired)*

EchoStar Satellite: 6
Colorado Business Bank: 4
PricewaterhouseCoopers: 4
Coors Brewing: 3
Hitachi Consulting: 3
KPMG: 3
Pulte Homes: 3
Ernst & Young: 2
First Data: 2
IBM: 2

Three of the Most Famous Graduates of M.B.A. Program

Carol Tome (class of 1981) Chief Financial Officer, Home Depot

Peter Coors (class of 1970) Chairman, Coors Brewing

Thomas Marsico (class of 1979) Founder and CEO, Marsico Capital Management

DUKE UNIVERSITY
(FUQUA SCHOOL OF BUSINESS)

One of the youngest of the major M.B.A. programs, Duke's Fuqua School has adopted a strong general-management focus and been dubbed "Southern Ivy League" by corporate recruiters impressed with its academic prowess. The school has grown from 12 students in 1970 to about 800 full-time M.B.A. candidates and about 500 participants in various executive-M.B.A. programs.

Duke's global and cross-continent executive-M.B.A. programs entail foreign study and travel, along with distance learning via the Internet. It also has designed a dual degree called the Duke Goethe Executive M.B.A. with Frankfurt University in Germany. The program, starting in 2005, will draw students primarily from Germany and surrounding countries.

Most Fuqua graduates take jobs in finance and accounting, and marketing and sales. The health-care industry attracts graduates who specialize in health-sector management in either the full-time M.B.A. or weekend executive program. Students also can specialize by combining their M.B.A. with degrees in such areas as medicine, nursing, law, environment and earth science, and public policy.

The business school recently established the Fuqua/Coach K Center of Leadership and Ethics, in collaboration with Duke's ethics institute and athletics department, to support academic research, develop new leadership electives for M.B.A. students, and offer executive-education courses. Duke basketball coach Mike Krzyzewski (Coach K) joined the center and Fuqua's faculty as an executive-in-residence, teaching and writing about ethics and leadership during the off-season.

Duke boasts a higher percentage of minority M.B.A. students than many other leading business schools, due in part to the school's ongoing recruiting efforts. Every November, for example, Fuqua and Ford Motor Co. invite 80 prospective minority students to campus to learn more about management education and career opportunities.

The business school is named for a generous donor—Atlanta industrialist J.B. Fuqua. Duke is very sensitive about how people pronounce the name of its business school and provides help on its Web page. It should be pronounced few-kwa. Whatever you do, Duke officials warn, don't say foo-kwa—or any even worse mispronunciation.

In *The Wall Street Journal*/Harris Interactive ranking, recruiters rated Duke students highest for their analytical and problem-solving abilities, strategic thinking, communication and interpersonal skills, and leadership potential. Duke received lower grades for faculty expertise, the career-services office, and students' international knowledge and experience.

School Rankings

- National ranking in the recruiter survey: 17 of 19 schools ranked
- Ranking by technology-industry recruiters: 3rd place
- Ranking by health-care-industry recruiters: 3rd place
- Ranking by consumer-products-industry recruiters: 4th place

Recognition for Excellence in an Academic Concentration

- With 94 nominations, Duke ranked No. 3 among business schools that recruiters in *The Wall Street Journal*/Harris Interactive survey cited for excellence in marketing.

DUKE ON DUKE

(Data provided by the Fuqua
School of Business at Duke
University)

Business school website:
http://www.fuqua.duke.edu
Business school e-mail:
admissions-info@fuqua.duke.edu
Private institution
M.B.A. enrollment: 1,286
Full-time: 800
Executive program: 486

ADMISSIONS DIRECTOR:
Liz Riley
Assistant Dean and Director of
Admissions
Fuqua School of Business
Duke University
1 Towerview Drive
Durham, NC 27708
919-660-7705 (voice)
919-681-8026 (fax)
E-mail: admissions-
info@fuqua.duke.edu

APPLICATION DEADLINES:
Fall 2006: October 2005, January
2006, February 2006, March 2006
Annual tuition: $37,500
Annual room and board: $9,250

Special Recognition

■ Good source for recruiting women: 7th most nominated school, 58 nominations.

FALL 2004 INCOMING M.B.A. CLASS

	Full-Time Only
Number of applicants	2,367
Number of offers extended	902
Number of students who accepted offer	N/A
Number of students who enrolled	402

GMAT score: 705 (mean); 710 (median)
Years of full-time work experience: 5 (mean); 5.7 (median)
Undergraduate GPA: 3.4 (mean); 3.4 (median)

Demographic Profile of Full-Time Students

Male: 70%
Female: 30%
Minorities: 30%
U.S. citizens: 72%
Foreign nationals: 28%

Class of 2004 Most Popular Academic Concentrations

N/A

THE RECRUITERS SPEAK

Duke's most impressive features

"Health-care sector management program"

"Strategic and analytical students"

"Bright marketers"

Duke's major shortcomings

"Too-high expectations for their first responsibilities"

"Polarized talent pool—very good or very bad"

"Not good team players"

How Duke can increase its appeal

"Teach students importance of adding value"

"Remove chip from shoulder"

"Students could be more versatile— they're very consumer-products- focused"

CLASS OF 2004 EMPLOYMENT DATA

Industries Hiring Full-Time Graduates (% Hired)

Computer/technology/Internet/dot-com: 7%
Consumer products and services: 8%
Energy and utilities: 2%
Financial services/investment banking: 27%
Management consulting: 11%
Manufacturing: 12%
Media/entertainment: 3%
Nonprofit: 3%
Petroleum/energy: 3%
Pharmaceutical/biotechnology/health-care products and services: 9%
Telecommunications: 2%
Travel and transportation: 4%
Other professional services (accounting, advertising, etc.): 7%
Other: 2%

Percentage of Job-Seeking Full-Time Graduates Who:	All Students	Citizens/Residents	Foreign Nationals
Received offers prior to or within 3 months of graduation	94%	94%	95%
Accepted offers prior to or within 3 months of graduation	91%	90%	93%

	MEAN			MEDIAN		
Overall Compensation	All Students	Citizens/ Residents	Foreign Nationals	All Students	Citizens/ Residents	Foreign Nationals
Annual base yearly	$81,284	N/A	N/A	$85,000	N/A	N/A
Signing bonus	$15,121	N/A	N/A	$15,000	N/A	N/A
Other guaranteed compensation	$12,293	N/A	N/A	$8,694	N/A	N/A

Position/Job Function *(% Hired)*

Consulting: 13%
Finance/accounting: 39%
General management: 8%
Marketing/sales: 22%
Operations/production/logistics: 2%
Other: 16%

Top Recruiters *(Number of Full-Time Class of 2004 Graduates Hired)*

Johnson & Johnson: 10
Brunswick: 7
Deloitte Consulting: 6
Eli Lilly: 6
Goldman Sachs: 5
McKinsey: 5
Whirlpool: 5
Lehman Brothers: 4
Merrill Lynch: 4
Citigroup: 4

Three of the Most Famous Graduates of M.B.A. Program

Melinda Gates (class of 1987) Co-founder of the Bill and Melinda Gates Foundation

George Morrow (class of 1981) Executive Vice President, Global Commercial Operations, Amgen

Mary Minnick (class of 1983) Executive Vice President, Coca-Cola

EMORY UNIVERSITY
(GOIZUETA BUSINESS SCHOOL)

Emory's business school, named for Roberto Goizueta, the former CEO of Coca-Cola, believes strongly in the power of branding and positions itself as the M.B.A. program that produces "principled leaders for global enterprise."

The Goizueta School says it stresses "leadership in action" and the importance of courage in facing the uncertainties of business. Indeed, many Emory M.B.A.s demonstrate their courage early on by skydiving during student orientation. Back down to earth, students take such courses as "Strategic Management for Leaders," "Entrepreneurial Leadership," and "Communication Skills for Leaders." They end their first year with the "capstone leadership challenge," in which they put their mental and physical skills to the test. Teams compete in a daylong "survival race" that involves hiking, whitewater rafting, and mountain biking.

For even more training, M.B.A.s can apply to the Goizueta Leadership Institute. In that program, they receive one-on-one coaching, participate in exercises involving creativity, workforce motivation, and diplomacy, and spend a weekend at the Marine Corps University in Virginia.

To gain international experience, students can study abroad at another business school for a semester or spend a week in another country to research a project and meet local business and government officials. In addition, M.B.A.s can consider an international concentration in Russian and East European studies or Latin American/Caribbean studies.

EMORY ON EMORY

(Data provided by the Goizueta
Business School at Emory
University)

Business school website:
http://www.goizueta.emory.edu
Business school e-mail:
admissions@bus.emory.edu
Private institution
M.B.A. Enrollment: 677
Full-time: 354
Part-time: 175
Executive program: 148

ADMISSIONS DIRECTOR:
Julie Barefoot
Associate Dean of M.B.A.
Admissions
1300 Clifton Road
Atlanta, GA 30322
404-727-6311 (voice)
404-727-4612 (fax)
E-mail:
admissions@bus.emory.edu

APPLICATION DEADLINES:
Fall 2006: 2/1/2006, 3/15/2006
Annual tuition: $34,000
Annual room and board: $17,000

Students also can major in decision and information analysis, marketing, organization and management, accounting, finance, ethics and leadership, or global management.

Emory offers a one-year "fast track" M.B.A. designed for full-time students with an undergraduate degree in business or economics or a strong quantitative background from majoring in math or engineering. Students interested in a part-time option can choose the evening M.B.A. or the executive-M.B.A. programs for more-seasoned managers.

Emory rose seven spots to 12th place in the latest *Wall Street Journal*/Harris Interactive Regional ranking. Recruiters gave Emory's graduates top ratings for personal ethics and integrity, and teamwork abilities. They received their lowest scores for international knowledge and experience, and willingness to relocate for their jobs.

School Rankings

- Regional ranking in the recruiter survey: 12 of 47 schools ranked

FALL 2004 INCOMING M.B.A. CLASS

	Total	Full-Time Only
Number of applicants	1,741	1,080
Number of offers extended	691	397
Number of students who accepted offer	N/A	N/A
Number of students who enrolled	385	155

THE RECRUITERS SPEAK

Emory's most impressive features

"Integrity and character"

"Communication and teamwork skills"

"Students seem hungry and well-prepared"

Emory's major shortcomings

"Not enough work experience"

"Regional focus"

"Not enough Wall Street-focused students"

How Emory can increase its appeal

"Broaden curriculum to include technology issues"

"Heighten brand management focus vs. general marketing"

"Recruit more-dynamic leaders into the class"

GMAT score: 680 (mean); 680 (median)
Years of full-time work experience: 5 (mean); 4 (median);
Undergraduate GPA: 3.41 (mean); 3.44 (median)

Demographic Profile of Full-Time Students

Male: 71%
Female: 29%
Minorities: 16%
U.S. citizens/nationals: 68%
Foreign nationals: 32%

Class of 2004 Most Popular Academic Concentrations (% of Students)

Finance 50%
Marketing 28%
General management 12%

CLASS OF 2004 EMPLOYMENT DATA

Industries Hiring Full-Time Graduates (% Hired)

Computer/technology/Internet/dot-com: 4%
Consumer products and services: 11%
Financial services/investment banking: 26%
Industrial products and services: 3%
Management consulting: 16%
Pharmaceutical/biotechnology/health-care products and services:
4%
Real estate: 8%
Telecommunications: 4%
Travel and transportation: 6%
Other professional services (accounting, advertising, etc.): 5%
Other: 13%

Position/Job Function (% Hired)

Consulting: 21%
Finance/accounting: 33%
General management: 5%
Marketing/sales: 24%
Operations/production/logistics: 3%
Other: 14%

Top Recruiters *(Number of Full-Time Class of 2004 Graduates Hired)*

Wachovia: 6
Deloitte: 4
EarthLink: 4
CHEP: 3
Delta Air Lines: 3
Kurt Salmon Associates: 3
Lehman Brothers: 3
Navigant: 3
A.T. Kearney: 2
Bank of America: 2

Percentage of Job-Seeking Full-Time Graduates Who:	All Students	Citizens/Residents	Foreign Nationals
Received offers prior to or within 3 months of graduation	92%	91%	95%
Accepted offers prior to or within 3 months of graduation	85%	86%	83%

Overall Compensation	MEAN			MEDIAN		
	All Students	Citizens/ Residents	Foreign Nationals	All Students	Citizens/ Residents	Foreign Nationals
Annual base salary	$80,163	$81,183	$76,764	$82,000	$82,000	$80,000
Signing bonus	$12,886	$13,770	$9,889	$10,000	$10,000	$7,750
Other guaranteed compensation	$11,545	$12,301	$9,278	$9,800	$9,550	$10,000

Three of the Most Famous Graduates of M.B.A. Program

Alan Lacy (class of 1977) CEO, Sears

Charles Jenkins (class of 1965) CEO, Publix

John Spiegel (class of 1965) Former Vice Chairman and CFO, SunTrust Banks

ERASMUS UNIVERSITY (ROTTERDAM SCHOOL OF MANAGEMENT)

The key selling point for the Rotterdam School of Management in the Netherlands is its international culture. The faculty is internationally diverse and the student body is becoming increasingly global. More than 95% of the students in the full-time M.B.A. program are foreign, the highest percentage ever, and they represent more than 50 nationalities, with the majority from Western Europe and Asia. Because lectures are in English, however, all students need a firm command of the language.

In Rotterdam's 15-month international M.B.A. program, students can go the general-management route or choose a specialized course of study in marketing, finance, or information and communication technology. The school selected those concentrations based partly on corporate demand for M.B.A.s skilled in those areas, and it encourages students to consider one of those concentrations to boost their chances of landing a summer internship and eventually a full-time position. M.B.A.s also can apply for a semester of study abroad at one of more than 30 partner schools.

The school offers a weekend executive M.B.A. in Rotterdam and is part of the OneM.B.A. executive degree program, along with four business schools in the U.S., Brazil, Mexico, and China. OneM.B.A. targets executives with growing international responsibilities, who attend most of the 21-month program in Rotterdam, but also spend a week each in the U.S., Asia, and Latin America.

ROTTERDAM ON ROTTERDAM

(Data provided by the Rotterdam
School of Management at
Erasmus University)

Business school website:
http://www.rsm.nl
Business school e-mail:
info@rsm.nl
Private institution*
M.B.A. enrollment: 475
Full-time: 278
Executive program: 197
(*Erasmus University is a public
institution, but the business
school is privately run)

ADMISSIONS DIRECTOR:
Dianne Bevelander
Director of Degree Programs
Burg. Oudlaan 50
Rotterdam, The Netherlands 3062
PA
31-10-408-2062 (voice)
31-10-452-9509 (fax)
E-mail: dbevelander@rsm.nl

APPLICATION DEADLINE:
Fall 2006: 7/15/2006
Annual tuition: $34,500
Annual room and board: $10,300

In *The Wall Street Journal*/Harris Interactive survey, Rotterdam graduates scored best on teamwork abilities and international knowledge and experience. Recruiters gave Rotterdam its lowest scores for the core curriculum, students' awareness of corporate citizenship issues, faculty expertise, and students' leadership potential.

School Rankings

- International ranking in the recruiter survey: 14 of 20 schools ranked

FALL 2004 INCOMING M.B.A. CLASS

	Total
Number of applicants	486
Number of offers extended	199
Number of students who accepted offer	119
Number of students who enrolled	114

GMAT score: 630 (mean); N/A (median)
Years of full-time work experience: 5.3 (mean); N/A (median)
Undergraduate GPA: N/A

Demographic Profile of Full-Time Students

Male: 73%
Female: 27%
Dutch citizens/residents: 4%
Foreign nationals: 96%

THE RECRUITERS SPEAK

Rotterdam's most impressive features

"International outlook"

"Ethics"

"No-nonsense approach, team spirit"

Rotterdam's major shortcomings

"Lack of strategic approach and vision"

"Less self-confident than students from U.S. schools"

"Low profile; not active enough in advocating the school"

How Rotterdam can increase its appeal

"Rigorous screening for English-language skills"

"Reduce friction between students and recruiters"

"Increase leadership qualities of students"

Class of 2004 Most Popular Academic Concentrations (% of Students)

Finance 30%
Marketing and strategy 25%
Information technology 20%

CLASS OF 2004 EMPLOYMENT DATA

Industries Hiring Full-Time Graduates (% Hired)

Computer/technology/Internet/dot-com: 5%
Consumer products and services: 14%
Energy and utilities: 1%
Financial services/investment banking: 20%
Government: 1%
Industrial products and services: 7%
Management consulting: 16%
Manufacturing: 3%
Media/entertainment: 2%
Petroleum/energy: 1%
Pharmaceutical/biotechnology/health-care products and services: 8%
Real estate: 3%
Telecommunications: 6%
Travel and transportation: 4%
Other professional services (accounting, advertising, etc.): 5%
Other: 4%

Position/Job Function (% Hired)

Consulting: 34%
Finance/accounting: 26%
General management: 9%
Human resources: 1%
Information technology/management information systems: 18%
Marketing/sales: 2%
Operations/production/logistics: 5%
Other: 5%

Top Recruiters (Number of Full-Time Class of 2004 Graduates Hired)

Siemens Business Services: 4
Novartis: 3
General Electric: 3
ABN AMRO: 3

McKinsey: 2
Philips: 2
L'Oréal: 2
Banco de Credito: 2
Reckitt Benckiser: 2
Shell Oil Products: 1

Percentage of Job-Seeking Full-Time Graduates Who:	All Students	Citizens/Residents	Foreign Nationals
Received offers prior to or within 3 months of graduation	86%	N/A	N/A
Accepted offers prior to or within 3 months of graduation	77%	N/A	N/A

	MEAN			MEDIAN		
Overall Compensation	All Students	Citizens/Residents	Foreign Nationals	All Students	Citizens/Residents	Foreign Nationals
Annual base salary	$72,500	N/A	N/A	$72,000	N/A	N/A
Signing bonus	$15,000	N/A	N/A	$10,000	N/A	N/A
Other guaranteed compensation	N/A	N/A	N/A	N/A	N/A	N/A

Three of the Most Famous Graduates of M.B.A. Program

Boudewijn Beerkens (class of 1991) Executive Board Member and CFO, Wolters Kluwer

Michael Wunderbaldinger (class of 1996) CFO, GE Real Estate, Central Europe

Jan van den Berg (class of 1989) Chairman, AXA, Netherlands

ESCUELA SUPERIOR DE ADMINISTRACION Y DIRECCION DE EMPRESAS (ESADE)

ESADE Business School

ESADE, a Jesuit business school, was established in 1958 in Barcelona by a group of business people in collaboration with the Society of Jesus. It began life with only undergraduate and doctorate programs but quickly added the M.B.A. in 1964. Today, it has campuses in both Barcelona and Madrid and offers four varieties of M.B.A. degrees: one-year, 18-month, part-time, and executive.

ESADE's general-management M.B.A. program is bilingual; by the time they graduate, students are expected to be fluent in both English and Spanish. ESADE students also can participate in exchange programs at some 60 business schools throughout the world.

After a month of basic business principles, students in the 18-month program follow three stages of study: general management and the business environment, integrating strategy with business functions, and global management. In the second year, they can major in such areas as health-care management, corporate taxation, public-sector management, finance, marketing, business policy, operations and innovation, human resources, and information systems. Students also create a business plan to hone their entrepreneurial skills.

Given its religious roots, ESADE emphasizes personal values and corporate social and environmental responsibility through both the M.B.A. curriculum and research at its Institute for the Individual, Corporations, and Society.

ESADE ON ESADE

(Data provided by the ESADE Business School)

Business school website:
http://www.esade.edu
Business school e-mail:
mba@esade.edu
Private institution
M.B.A. enrollment: 604
Full-time: 195
Part-time: 239
Executive program: 170

ADMISSIONS DIRECTOR:
Núria Guilera
Admissions and Marketing
Director, M.B.A. Programs
Avenida Esplugues, 92-96
Barcelona, Spain 08034
34-93-280-6162 (voice)
34-93-204-8105 (fax)
E-mail: guilera@esade.edu

APPLICATION DEADLINE:
Fall 2006: 6/30/2006
Annual tuition: $29,295
Annual room and board: $15,296

One of ESADE's newest offerings is an international master's degree in tourism and leisure. The degree was created as part of an agreement with the Spanish government and tourism companies to improve training of industry managers.

In the latest *Wall Street Journal*/Harris Interactive survey, recruiters gave ESADE graduates their highest marks for communication and interpersonal skills and the ability to work well in teams. ESADE received its lowest ratings for faculty expertise and the likelihood of hiring stars.

School Rankings

- International ranking in the recruiter survey: 2 of 20 schools ranked

Recognition for Excellence in an Academic Concentration

- With 60 nominations, ESADE ranked No. 7 among business schools that recruiters in *The Wall Street Journal*/Harris Interactive survey cited for excellence in marketing.

Special Recognition

- Good source for recruiting graduates with high ethical standards: 10th most nominated school, 51 nominations.

THE RECRUITERS SPEAK

ESADE's most impressive features

"Working with emotional intelligence"

"Capacity for adapting to any circumstance"

"Social/humanistic profile"

ESADE's major shortcomings

"Lack of international experience"

"Less visionary"

"Lack of self-confidence"

How ESADE can increase its appeal

"Increase marketing efforts to promote the school"

"Improve finance curriculum"

"Enhance experience before getting into M.B.A. program"

FALL 2004 INCOMING M.B.A. CLASS

	Total	Full-Time Only
Number of applicants	621	281
Number of offers extended	387	177
Number of students who accepted offer	287	82
Number of students who enrolled	285	80

GMAT score: 630 (mean); N/A (median)
Years of full-time work experience: 4.5 (mean); N/A (median)
Undergraduate GPA: N/A

Demographic Profile of Full-Time Students

Male: 80%
Female: 20%
Spanish citizens/residents: 28%
Foreign nationals: 72%

Class of 2004 Most Popular Academic Concentrations (% of Students)

General management and entrepreneurship 33%
Finance 30%
Marketing 15%

CLASS OF 2004 EMPLOYMENT DATA

Industries Hiring Full-Time Graduates (% Hired)

Computer/technology/Internet/dot-com: 7%
Consumer products and services: 13%
Financial services/investment banking: 13%
Government: 2%
Management consulting: 12%
Manufacturing: 10%
Media/entertainment: 4%
Petroleum/energy: 4%
Pharmaceutical/biotechnology/health-care products and services:
6%
Real estate: 6%
Telecommunications: 6%
Travel and transportation: 2%

Other professional services (accounting, advertising, etc.): 7%
Other: 8%

Position/Job Function *(% Hired)*

Consulting: 23%
Finance/accounting: 16%
General management: 34%
Marketing/sales: 23%
Other: 4%

Top Recruiters *(Number of Full-Time Class of 2004 Graduates Hired)*

L'Oréal: 3
Lear: 3
McKinsey: 2
Boston Consulting Group: 1
General Electric: 1
Hewlett-Packard: 1
Novartis: 1
Eli Lilly: 1
Philips International: 1
Roca Group: 1

Percentage of Job-Seeking Full-Time Graduates Who:	All Students	Citizens/Residents	Foreign Nationals
Received offers prior to or within 3 months of graduation	89%	95%	88%
Accepted offers prior to or within 3 months of graduation	89%	95%	88%

	MEAN			MEDIAN		
Overall Compensation	All Students	Citizens/ Residents	Foreign Nationals	All Students	Citizens/ Residents	Foreign Nationals
Annual base salary	$72,093	$69,328	$72,837	$68,910	$69,782	$65,837
Signing bonus	$11,790	$5,966	$12,686	$13,258	$5,966	$13,258
Other guaranteed compensation	$18,822	$7,292	$20,058	$13,258	$7,955	$15,114

Three of the Most Famous Graduates of M.B.A. Program

Enrique Rueda (class of 1979) Senior Manager and Director of Corporate Strategy, World Bank

Ignacio Fonts (class of 1982) Vice President and General Manager, Hewlett-Packard Inkjet Division

Ferran Soriano (class of 1990) Vice President, Finance and Operations, and board member, FC Barcelona

UNIVERSITY OF FLORIDA (WARRINGTON COLLEGE OF BUSINESS)

The University of Florida, which established its business college in 1927 and awarded its first M.B.A. degrees in 1946, offers one of the broadest arrays of M.B.A. delivery options of any school. There's the traditional two-year M.B.A. degree; accelerated one-year options; part-time and executive programs; a specialized M.B.A. for engineers and scientists; and an Internet program for people who can't attend classes regularly at the Gainesville campus.

In fact, Florida was one of the first accredited business schools to offer an online-degree program. The courses are taught through e-mail, online bulletin boards, group-discussion and class-presentation software, and interactive CD-ROM technology. Students also meet once each term in Gainesville to take finals and participate in case presentations.

The Warrington College recently established an M.B.A. program outpost in Fort Lauderdale. It stresses that the courses will not be "watered down," but will be taught by the same faculty as the M.B.A. programs in Gainesville.

In the two-year M.B.A. program, students can tailor their course work to focus on such areas as finance, real estate and urban analysis, Latin American business, security analysis, sports administration, decision and information sciences, global management, marketing, competitive strategy, and entrepreneurship. More than half of the full-time M.B.A. graduates land jobs in accounting and finance.

Students with global business ambitions can participate in exchange programs with foreign business schools, as well as earn a dual M.B.A. and master's of international management from Florida and Thunderbird's Garvin School in Arizona.

In *The Wall Street Journal*/Harris Interactive survey, recruiters gave top ratings for students' fit with the corporate culture, ability to work well in teams, and leadership potential. Florida received its lowest scores for students' international knowledge and past work experience.

School Rankings

- Regional ranking in the recruiter survey: 27 of 47 schools ranked

FALL 2004 INCOMING M.B.A. CLASS

	Total	Full-Time Only
Number of applicants	707	408
Number of offers extended	379	168
Number of students who accepted offer	273	84
Number of students who enrolled	273	84

GMAT score: 666 (mean); 660 (median)
Years of full-time work experience: 5 (mean); 5 (median)
Undergraduate GPA: 3.3 (mean); 3.3 (median)

Demographic Profile of Full-Time Students

Male: 80%
Female: 20%
Minorities: 16%
U.S. citizens/residents: 72%
Foreign nationals: 28%

Class of 2004 Most Popular Academic Concentrations (% of Students)

Finance 47%
Marketing 26%
Decision and information sciences 21%

FLORIDA ON FLORIDA

(Data provided by the Warrington College of Business at the University of Florida)

Business school website:
http://www.floridamba.ufl.edu
Business school e-mail:
floridamba@cba.ufl.edu
Public institution
M.B.A. enrollment: 768
Full-time: 137
Part-time: 576
Executive program: 55

ADMISSIONS DIRECTOR:
Alex Sevilla
Director of Executive and
Working Professional Admissions
134 Bryan Hall
P.O. Box 117152
Gainesville, FL 32611
877-435-2622 (voice)
352-392-8791 (fax)
E-mail: floridamba@cba.ufl.edu

APPLICATION DEADLINES:
Fall 2006: April 2006
Annual tuition: $5,484 (in-state);
$21,359 (out-of-state)
Annual room and board: $7,500

CLASS OF 2004 EMPLOYMENT DATA

Industries Hiring Full-Time Graduates (% Hired)

Computer/technology/Internet/dot-com: 8%
Consumer products and services: 5%
Financial services/investment banking: 24%
Management consulting: 5%
Manufacturing: 8%
Pharmaceutical/biotechnology/health-care products and services: 8%
Real estate: 26%
Telecommunications: 3%
Other professional services (accounting, advertising, etc.): 5%
Other: 8%

Position/Job Function (% Hired)

Consulting: 11%
Finance/accounting: 55%
General management: 13%
Marketing/sales: 8%
Operations/Production/Logistics: 5%
Other: 8%

Top Recruiters (Number of Full-Time Class of 2004 Graduates Hired)

Pulte Homes: 6
Accenture: 2
IBM: 2
Bank of America: 1
Wachovia Securities: 1
Nextel: 1
Jabil Circuit: 1

THE RECRUITERS SPEAK

Florida's most impressive features

"Broad spectrum of academic concentrations"

"Very good career-services staff"

"Strong business-school fundamentals"

Florida's major shortcomings

"Small school, not enough candidates"

"Lack of big-business understanding"

"Students not interested in relocating"

How Florida can increase its appeal

"Increased experience and willingness to relocate from the South"

"Work on technical skills and applying what students learn"

"Increase number of graduates"

Cintas: 1
Lennar Homes: 1
United Health Care: 1

Percentage of Job-Seeking Full-Time Graduates Who:	All Students	Citizens/Residents	Foreign Nationals
Received offers prior to or within 3 months of graduation	83%	83%	83%
Accepted offers prior to or within 3 months of graduation	80%	80%	83%

| | MEAN | | | MEDIAN | | |
Overall Compensation	All Students	Citizens/Residents	Foreign Nationals	All Students	Citizens/Residents	Foreign Nationals
Annual base salary	$61,380	$65,530	$34,500	$60,000	$60,000	$34,500
Signing bonus	$5,400	$5,410	N/A	$5,000	$5,000	N/A
Other guaranteed compensation	$8,817	$8,817	N/A	$8,000	$8,000	N/A

Three of the Most Famous Graduates of M.B.A. Program

John Dasburg (class of 1970) Chairman and CEO, ASTAR Air Cargo

Hal Steinbrenner (class of 1994) General Partner, New York Yankees

Laurie Burns (class of 1986) President, Bahama Breeze Restaurants

FORDHAM UNIVERSITY

Founded more than 30 years ago, Fordham's business school campus is adjacent to Lincoln Center in the hub of culture, commerce, and communication in Manhattan. The school's motto: *urbi et orbi*, which means "for the city and the world." Fordham offers a full-range of M.B.A.s, including full-time, part-time, and executive options. It has branded its program "the portfolio-based M.B.A." and encourages students to view the degree like an investment portfolio, managing courses, their network of alumni and business connections, internships, and other practical experiences to get the maximum return on their investment.

M.B.A. candidates can concentrate in as many as two areas, including accounting and taxation, communications and media management, entrepreneurship, finance and business economics, information and communications systems, management systems, and marketing. In addition, students can take courses to earn a special designation on their transcripts in the areas of electronic business, personal financial planning, and international business. And for a select group, Fordham offers the Deming Scholars M.B.A. program, which teaches the management theories of W. Edwards Deming, the well-known consultant to business on quality and statistical methods.

In the international arena, Fordham awards a global professional M.B.A., which can be completed on a full-time or part-time basis. There's also a dual-degree program with Thunderbird's Garvin School of International Management in

Arizona, which leads to both an M.B.A. and master's degree in international management. In addition, Fordham is the degree-granting institution for the Beijing International M.B.A., the first foreign M.B.A. degree in Beijing to be approved by the Chinese government. A consortium of Jesuit business schools, including Fordham, provides the faculty for the program. With the courses taught in English, Fordham students can attend Beijing International and earn some of the credits toward their M.B.A.

In *The Wall Street Journal*/Harris Interactive survey, recruiters gave Fordham its highest scores for students' ability to work well in teams and their analytical and problem-solving skills. Fordham's lowest scores: students' willingness to relocate, their international knowledge and experience, and faculty expertise.

School Rankings
- Regional ranking in the recruiter survey: 14 of 47 schools ranked

FALL 2004 INCOMING M.B.A. CLASS

	Total	Full-Time Only
Number of applicants	988	346
Number of offers extended	413	136
Number of students who accepted offer	377	104
Number of students who enrolled	340	95

GMAT score: 596 (mean); 590 (median)
Years of full-time work experience: 5.3 (mean); 5 (median)
Undergraduate GPA: 3.21 (mean); 3.17 (median)

Demographic Profile of Full-Time Students

Male: 59%
Female: 41%
Minorities: 15%
U.S. citizens/residents: 83%
Foreign nationals: 17%

FORDHAM ON FORDHAM

(Data provided by Fordham Business School)

Business school website:
http://www.fordham.edu/
business
Business school e-mail:
admissionsgb@fordham.edu
Private institution
M.B.A. enrollment: 1,675
Full-time: 379
Part-time: 1,249
Executive program: 47

ADMISSIONS DIRECTOR:
Frank Fletcher
Director of M.B.A. Admissions
33 West 60th Street, 4th Floor
New York, NY 10023
212-636-6200 (voice)
212-636-7076 (fax)
E-mail: ffletcher@fordham.edu

APPLICATION DEADLINES:
Fall 2006: 6/1/2006
Annual tuition: $24,750
Annual room and board: $12,800

Class of 2004 Most Popular Academic Concentrations (% of Students)

Finance 37%
Management 9%

CLASS OF 2004 EMPLOYMENT DATA

Industries Hiring Full-Time Graduates (% Hired)

Computer/technology/Internet/dot-com: 3%
Consumer products and services: 14%
Energy and utilities: 1%
Financial services/investment banking: 40%
Government: 1%
Industrial products and services: 1%
Management consulting: 3%
Manufacturing: 2%
Media/entertainment: 16%
Nonprofit: 2%
Pharmaceutical/biotechnology/health-care products and services: 5%
Travel and transportation: 1%
Other professional services (accounting, advertising, etc.): 11%

Position/Job Function (% Hired)

Consulting: 7%
Finance/accounting: 52%
General management: 4%
Information technology/management information systems: 9%
Marketing/sales: 25%
Operations/production/logistics: 1%
Other: 2%

THE RECRUITERS SPEAK

Fordham's most impressive features

"Good mix of practice and theory"

"Generally great work ethic"

"Strong foreign students"

Fordham's major shortcomings

"Students are less strategic compared to other schools"

"Very regional focus in terms of recruiting"

"Students are rough around the edges"

How Fordham can increase its appeal

"Provide more in-depth, analytical students"

"Increase visibility and reach out to corporations"

"Improve students' interviewing skills"

Top Recruiters *(Number of Full-Time Class of 2004 Graduates Hired)*

Ernst & Young: 7
American Express: 2
Bank of New York: 2
Citigroup: 2
GE Capital: 2
Goldman Sachs: 2
PricewaterhouseCoopers: 2
Reckitt Benckiser: 2
Bloomberg: 1
CNBC: 1

Percentage of Job-Seeking Full-Time Graduates Who:	All Students	Citizens/Residents	Foreign Nationals
Received offers prior to or within 3 months of graduation	N/A	N/A	N/A
Accepted offers prior to or within 3 months of graduation	89%	89%	90%

Overall Compensation	MEAN			MEDIAN		
	All Students	Citizens/Residents	Foreign Nationals	All Students	Citizens/Residents	Foreign Nationals
Base yearly salary of graduates hired	$75,101	$79,354	$67,113	$75,000	$79,500	$70,000
Signing bonus	$9,543	$10,657	$5,833	$12,350	$15,000	$7,210
Value of guaranteed year-end bonus	$15,245	$15,245	N/A	$15,000	$15,000	N/A

Three of the Most Famous Graduates of M.B.A. Program

Nemir Kirdar (class of 1972) President and CEO, Investcorp Bank

Patricia Fili-Krushel (class of 1982) Executive Vice President, Administration, Time Warner

Frank J. Petrilli (class of 1974) President and CEO, TD Waterhouse USA

GEORGE WASHINGTON UNIVERSITY

George Washington's M.B.A. program has its roots in the university's schools of government and international affairs, and it still maintains close ties with those programs. The School of Government introduced the M.B.A. some 50 years ago; it wasn't until 1990 that a separate School of Business was established.

Today, one of the school's most distinctive assets is its location in downtown Washington, D.C., near federal agencies, the World Bank, the International Monetary Fund, and many corporate and nonprofit headquarters.

In the full-time M.B.A. program, students have a choice of more than 15 concentrations, including finance and investments; international business; nonprofit-organization management; tourism, hospitality, event, and sports management; health-services administration; real-estate and urban development; and environmental policy and management.

M.B.A. students also take summer study-abroad courses on such topics as "Corporate Social Impact: Comparing U.K. and U.S. Policies and Practices" and "Sustainable Tourism Strategies for Panama." In fact, the Aspen Institute and World Resources Institute have honored George Washington as one of the world's top business schools for teaching social and environmental responsibility.

In addition to the full-time M.B.A. program, students can choose from specialized master's degrees in information-systems technology, tourism administration, project management, finance, and accountancy. There are also part-time and executive-M.B.A. programs.

The business school's new $56 million building, which brings together various departments that had been spread among eight locations across campus, features the newest technologies and team study rooms. "Students will no longer have to sit on the floor in the hallway to do team projects," says Dean Susan Phillips.

In *The Wall Street Journal*/Harris Interactive survey, recruiters were most positive about students' ability to work well in teams and their personal ethics and integrity. They gave the lowest scores for students' previous work experience and strategic thinking.

School Rankings
- Regional ranking in the recruiter survey: 31 of 47 schools ranked
- Ranking by financial-services-industry recruiters: 9th place

FALL 2004 INCOMING M.B.A. CLASS

	Total	Full-Time Only
Number of applicants	997	625
Number of offers extended	581	303
Number of students who accepted offer	277	102
Number of students who enrolled	260	85

GMAT score: 631 (mean); 630 (median)
Years of full-time work experience: 4.5 (mean); 4.3 (median)
Undergraduate GPA: 3.3 (mean); 3.1 (median)

Demographic Profile of Full-Time Students
Male: 64%
Female: 36%

GEORGE WASHINGTON ON GEORGE WASHINGTON

(Data provided by the School of Business at George Washington University)

Business school website:
http://www.mba.gwu.edu
Business school e-mail:
gwmba@gwu.edu
Private institution
M.B.A. enrollment: 831
Full-time: 168
Part-time: 638
Executive program: 25

ADMISSIONS DIRECTOR:
Kathleen A. Rogan
Director, Global M.B.A. Program
710 21st Street, N.W., Suite 301
Washington, D.C. 20052
202-994-5536 (voice)
202-994-3571 (fax)
E-mail: gwmba@gwu.edu

APPLICATION DEADLINES:
Fall 2006: 12/1/2005, 1/15/2006, 4/1/2006
Annual tuition: $24,948
Annual room and board: $15,600

Minorities: 15%
U.S. citizens/residents: 67%
Foreign nationals: 33%

Class of 2004 Most Popular Academic Concentrations (% of Students)

International business 28%
Finance and investments 22%
Marketing/sales 9%

CLASS OF 2004 EMPLOYMENT DATA

Industries Hiring Full-Time Graduates (% Hired)

Computer/technology/Internet/dot-com: 3%
Consumer products and services: 3%
Financial services/investment banking: 20%
Government: 9%
Industrial products and services: 1%
Management consulting: 30%
Manufacturing: 6%
Nonprofit: 9%
Pharmaceutical/biotechnology/health-care products and services: 3%
Real estate: 3%
Telecommunications: 7%
Other professional services (accounting, advertising, etc.): 6%

Position/Job Function (% Hired)

Consulting: 34%
Finance/accounting: 29%
General management: 7%
Human resources: 4%

THE RECRUITERS SPEAK

George Washington's most impressive features

"Sophisticated and global-thinking"

"Unpretentious"

"Interest in and skills needed for federal government jobs"

George Washington's major shortcomings

"Too little real-life experience"

"Not enough name recognition with U.S. corporations"

"Poor interview training"

How George Washington can increase its appeal

"Create a stronger analytics component in the curriculum"

"Develop strong written and verbal communication skills"

"Better outreach efforts to companies"

Marketing/sales: 13%
Operations/production/logistics: 7%
Other: 6%

Top Recruiters *(Number of Full-Time Class of 2004 Graduates Hired)*

BearingPoint: 13
U.S. Government: 7
Nextel Communications: 3
Freddie Mac: 2
World Bank: 2
Samsung: 2
International Finance Corp.: 2
Friedman, Billings, Ramsey: 1
IBM Business Consulting: 1
America Online: 1

Percentage of Job-Seeking Full-Time Graduates Who:	All Students	Citizens/Residents	Foreign Nationals
Received offers prior to or within 3 months of graduation	86%	83%	95%
Accepted offers prior to or within 3 months of graduation	78%	80%	71%

Overall Compensation	MEAN			MEDIAN		
	All Students	Citizens/Residents	Foreign Nationals	All Students	Citizens/Residents	Foreign Nationals
Annual base salary	$67,251	$69,357	$61,429	$65,000	$65,000	$60,000
Signing bonus	$4,575	$4,036	$5,833	$4,250	$2,500	$5,000
Other guaranteed compensation	$11,575	$13,767	$5,000	$5,650	$6,300	$5,000

Three of the Most Famous Graduates of M.B.A. Program

Colin L. Powell (class of 1971) Former U.S. Secretary of State

Henry ("Ric") Duques (class of 1969) Former Chairman, First Data

Edward M. Liddy, (class of 1972) Chairman and CEO, Allstate Insurance

GEORGETOWN UNIVERSITY (MCDONOUGH SCHOOL OF BUSINESS)

Georgetown University, the oldest Catholic university in the U.S., was founded in 1789, but the business school dates to only 1957 and is an outgrowth of the business administration division of the School of Foreign Service.

Given its roots in foreign relations and its location in the nation's capital, the McDonough School's M.B.A. program provides a general-management education with a global and political spin. Throughout the curriculum, the emphasis is on international management strategies, along with ethical decision-making and interpersonal, teamwork, and presentation skills.

The "Global Integrative Experience" course in the second year of the M.B.A. program, for example, requires students to spend nine days in such cities as São Paulo, Shanghai, and Prague, working in teams on consulting projects, visiting a local factory, and participating in a corporate-responsibility or community-service event. What's more, Georgetown's M.B.A. program still retains ties to its School of Foreign Service by offering students the opportunity to earn a special certificate in international business diplomacy.

Another option for more experienced managers is Georgetown's 18-month international executive-M.B.A. degree, which requires students to conduct consulting projects in both Asia and Latin America. Past M.B.A. projects have evaluated the potential for a secondary mortgage market in Southeast

Asia countries for an international bank, determined the feasibility of an extended-stay facility in Manila for a hotel chain, and identified opportunities for a Mexican telecommunications company to expand its market share in Central America.

The McDonough School's newest degree programs are an evening M.B.A. and a weekend executive master's in leadership, both for working professionals. The curriculum for the one-year executive program will include strategic and ethical lessons drawn from the Battle of Gettysburg and an exploration of spirituality and moral leadership.

In *The Wall Street Journal*/Harris Interactive survey, recruiters were most impressed with Georgetown students' personal ethics and integrity and their well-rounded qualities. The school received its lowest scores for students' previous work experience, the career-services office, and faculty expertise.

School Rankings

■ Regional ranking in the recruiter survey: 38 of 47 schools ranked

Recognition for Excellence in an Academic Concentration

■ With 76 nominations, Georgetown ranked No. 8 among business schools that recruiters in *The Wall Street Journal*/Harris Interactive survey cited for excellence in international business.

FALL 2004 INCOMING M.B.A. CLASS

	Full-Time Only
Number of applicants	1,582
Number of offers extended	648
Number of students who accepted offer	296
Number of students who enrolled	258

GMAT score: 662 (mean); 660 (median)
Years of full-time work experience: 5 (mean); 5 (median)
Undergraduate GPA: 3.3 (mean); 3.3 (median)

GEORGETOWN ON GEORGETOWN

(Data provided by the
McDonough School of Business
at Georgetown University)

Business school website:
http://msb.georgetown.edu
Business school e-mail:
mba@georgetown.edu
Private institution
M.B.A. enrollment: 605
Full-time: 509
Executive program: 96

ADMISSIONS DIRECTOR:
Monica Gray
Director of Admissions
Box 571148
Georgetown University
Washington, D.C. 20057
202-687-4200 (voice)
202-687-7809 (fax)
E-mail: mba@georgetown.edu

APPLICATION DEADLINE:
Fall 2006: 12/2/2005, 2/10/2006,
4/21/2006
Annual tuition: $33,960
Annual room and board: $12,750

Demographic Profile of Full-Time Students

Male: 69%
Female: 31%
Minorities: 18%
U.S. citizens/residents: 62%
Foreign nationals: 38%

Class of 2004 Most Popular Academic Concentrations

N/A

CLASS OF 2004 EMPLOYMENT DATA

Industries Hiring Full-Time Graduates (% Hired)

Financial services/investment banking: 36%
Government: 7%
Management consulting: 14%
Manufacturing: 12%
Nonprofit: 2%
Other: 29%

Position/Job Function (% Hired)

Consulting: 20%
Finance/accounting: 34%
General management: 7%
Marketing/sales: 25%
Operations/production/logistics: 4%
Other: 10%

THE RECRUITERS SPEAK

Georgetown's most impressive features

"The international focus"

"Students more cosmopolitan than most"

"Tenacious and well-rounded students"

Georgetown's major shortcomings

"Lack of practical experience"

"Not enough passion"

"Small portion of star students"

How Georgetown can increase its appeal

"Better customer service"

"Stiffer admissions criteria"

"Develop more innovative, risk-taking individuals"

Top Recruiters *(Number of Full-Time Class of 2004 Graduates Hired)*

Booz Allen Hamilton: 8
Corporate Executive Board: 7
Citigroup: 6
American Express: 4
IBM: 4
Lehman Brothers: 4
Ernst & Young: 3
Nextel: 3
Samsung Electronics: 3
Sirva: 3

Percentage of Job-Seeking Full-Time Graduates Who:	All Students	Citizens/Residents	Foreign Nationals
Received offers prior to or within 3 months of graduation	88%	89%	82%
Accepted offers prior to or within 3 months of graduation	85%	88%	79%

Overall Compensation	MEAN			MEDIAN		
	All Students	Citizens/ Residents	Foreign Nationals	All Students	Citizens/ Residents	Foreign Nationals
Annual base salary	$77,861	$79,832	$70,790	$80,000	$80,000	$75,000
Signing bonus	$12,638	$12,417	$13,688	$11,500	$10,000	$14,500
Other guaranteed compensation	$16,151	$17,172	$12,825	$10,000	$10,000	$10,000

Three of the Most Famous Graduates of M.B.A. Program

Lisa M. Cregan (class of 1983) Regional Director and Senior Vice President, UBS

Michael L. Chasen (class of 1996) CEO, Blackboard

Timothy Tassopoulos (class of 1983) Senior Vice President, Chick-Fil-A

Georgia Tech | College of Management
The Business School at Georgia Tech

GEORGIA INSTITUTE OF TECHNOLOGY

As part of a technically oriented university, the management school naturally emphasizes technology and innovation and takes a strong quantitative approach in its M.B.A. program. In fact, Georgia Tech called its degree a master's of science in management until 2002, when its name was officially changed to an M.B.A.

Georgia Tech students come well-equipped with quantitative skills. The business school stipulates that students must have received a satisfactory grade in a college-level calculus course and must be familiar with probability concepts.

Beyond technology management, students can major in a range of other subjects, including accounting, finance, international business, marketing, operations management, organizational behavior, and strategic management. M.B.A.s also can earn special certificates in entrepreneurship, international management, management of technology, and engineering entrepreneurship.

In addition to its full-time program, Georgia Tech offers an executive master's in technology, along with a new global executive M.B.A. created in partnership with two other technology-oriented universities in France and Argentina.

Georgia Tech boasts a new $57 million business-school building, which is part of the school's Technology Square complex in midtown Atlanta. Besides providing the latest in high-tech facilities, the building will enable the school to boost the size of both its M.B.A. and executive-education programs. At a time when most business schools are adopting the names of wealthy donors, Georgia Tech has moved in the opposite direction. It "reluctantly" removed the name of alumnus Tom DuPree from the management school in 2004 because he couldn't fulfill his $25 million pledge.

In *The Wall Street Journal*/Harris Interactive survey, Georgia Tech students received their highest ratings for analytical and problem-solving skills and fit with the corporate culture. Georgia Tech was rated lowest for students' international knowledge and previous work experience.

School Rankings
- Regional ranking in the recruiter survey: 45 of 47 schools ranked

Recognition for Excellence in an Academic Concentration
- With 31 nominations, Georgia Tech ranked No. 10 among business schools that recruiters in *The Wall Street Journal*/Harris Interactive survey cited for excellence in information technology.

FALL 2004 INCOMING M.B.A. CLASS

	Full-Time Only
Number of applicants	317
Number of offers extended	107
Number of students who accepted offer	64
Number of students who enrolled	64

GMAT score: 655 (mean); 660 (median);
Years of full-time work experience: 3.8 (mean); 2.9 (median)
Undergraduate GPA: N/A (mean); 3.5 (median)

Demographic Profile of Full-Time Students
Male: 75%
Female: 25%

GEORGIA TECH ON GEORGIA TECH

(Data provided by the College of Management at the Georgia Institute of Technology)

Business school website:
http://www.mgt.gatech.edu/mba
Business school e-mail:
mba@mgt.gatech.edu
Public institution
M.B.A. enrollment: 235
Full-time: 167
Executive program: 68

ADMISSIONS DIRECTOR:
Paula C. Wilson
Director, M.B.A. Admissions
800 W. Peachtree St. N.W., Suite 302
Atlanta, GA 30308
404-385-2354
404-894-4199
E-mail: paula.wilson@mgt.gatech.edu

APPLICATION DEADLINES:
Fall 2006: 11/15/2005, 1/15/2006, 3/15/2006, 5/1/2006
Annual tuition: $6,960 (in-state); $24,814 (out-of-state)
Annual room and board: $10,000

Minorities: 19%
U.S. citizens/residents: 68%
Foreign nationals: 32%

Class of 2004 Most Popular Academic Concentrations (% of Students)

Operations management 24%
Finance 18%
Consulting 18%

CLASS OF 2004 EMPLOYMENT DATA

Industries Hiring Full-Time Graduates (% Hired)

Computer/technology/Internet/dot-com: 14.3%
Consumer products and services: 7.8%
Energy and utilities: 2.6%
Financial services/investment banking: 13%
Government: 2.6%
Industrial products and services: 2.6%
Management consulting: 11.7%
Manufacturing: 13%
Media/entertainment: 1.3%
Nonprofit: 1.3%
Petroleum/energy: 1.3%
Pharmaceutical/biotechnology/health-care products and services: 7.8%
Real estate: 1.3%
Telecommunications: 5.2%
Travel and transportation: 2.6%
Other professional services (accounting, advertising, etc.): 11.7%

THE RECRUITERS SPEAK

Georgia Tech's most impressive features	Georgia Tech's major shortcomings	How Georgia Tech can increase its appeal
"Analytical, quantitative prowess"	"Students have poor communication skills"	"Promote soft skills"
"Logistics/supply-chain program"	"Limited work experience"	"Increase diversity"
"Raw smarts, ability to learn quickly"	"Too many engineers"	"Work to polish students"

Position/Job Function *(% Hired)*

Consulting: 17.6%
Finance/accounting: 26.4%
General management: 7.4%
Information technology/management information systems: 13.2%
Marketing/sales: 11.8%
Operations/production/logistics: 23.5%

Top Recruiters *(Number of Full-Time Class of 2004 Graduates Hired)*

Honeywell: 5
PricewaterhouseCoopers: 3
BearingPoint: 2
General Electric: 2
Grant Thornton: 2
IBM: 2
Johnson & Johnson: 2
Standard & Poor's: 2
Accenture: 1
Bank of America: 1

Percentage of Job-Seeking Full-Time Graduates Who:	All Students	Citizens/Residents	Foreign Nationals
Received offers prior to or within 3 months of graduation	92%	91%	95%
Accepted offers prior to or within 3 months of graduation	92%	91%	95%

	MEAN			MEDIAN		
Overall Compensation	All Students	Citizens/ Residents	Foreign Nationals	All Students	Citizens/ Residents	Foreign Nationals
Annual base salary	$68,731	$68,630	$69,094	$70,860	$70,430	$72,000
Signing bonus	$7,336	$7,275	$7,538	$8,113	$7,500	$8,113
Other guaranteed compensation	$9,253	$8,163	$12,630	$7,400	$9,000	$6,000

Three of the Most Famous Graduates of M.B.A. Program

Robert A. Anclien (class of 1970) Former Global Managing Partner, Accenture

Jack Guynn (class of 1970) President and CEO, Federal Reserve Bank of Atlanta

Thomas Fanning (class of 1980) Executive Vice President and CFO, Southern Co.

UNIVERSITY OF GEORGIA (TERRY COLLEGE OF BUSINESS)

Georgia's M.B.A. program begins with a basic curriculum teaching analytical, functional, and managerial skills, followed by a second year of specializations. Students can choose from about 15 majors, including accounting, brand management, international business, Internet technology, entrepreneurship, investments, real-estate analysis, and risk management and insurance.

Leadership development has become a higher priority at the Terry College since the creation of the Institute for Leadership Advancement in 2000, which offers M.B.A. students a variety of self-assessment tools. During the first year, each M.B.A. also is assigned to a leadership coach to help create a personal development plan.

At the end of each semester, students are challenged to "integrate" what they've learned in various classes through a case or business-plan competition, debate, or business simulation. And to gain international experience, M.B.A.s can take one- or two-week trips abroad during spring break or at the end of the spring semester.

GEORGIA ON GEORGIA

(Data provided by the Terry College of Business at the University of Georgia)

Business school website:
http://www.terry.uga.edu
Business school e-mail:
terrymba@terry.uga.edu
Public institution
M.B.A. enrollment: 387
Full-time: 148
Part-time: 202
Executive program: 37

ADMISSIONS DIRECTOR:
Anne Cooper
Director of Admissions
350 Brooks Hall
Terry College of Business
University of Georgia
Athens, GA 30602
706-542-5671 (voice)
706-542-5351 (fax)
E-mail: acooper@terry.uga.edu

APPLICATION DEADLINES:
Fall 2006: 4/1/2006 (international); 6/1/2006 (domestic)
Annual tuition: $7,294 (in-state); $24,126 (out-of-state)
Annual room and board: $16,000

Besides the traditional two-year full-time degree, the Terry College offers an 11-month full-time M.B.A. to people who majored in business as undergraduates, as well as executive-M.B.A. and part-time evening programs in the Atlanta area. There also are master's degrees in accounting, Internet technology, and marketing research.

Terry has forged close ties with regional companies through student projects, internships, and recruiting. Indeed, Atlanta-based Coca-Cola's influence is especially apparent through its sponsorship of centers for both international business and marketing studies.

In *The Wall Street Journal*/Harris Interactive survey, recruiters gave students the highest ratings for communication and interpersonal skills and the ability to work well in teams. Georgia's lowest ratings: students' international knowledge and experience and the faculty's expertise.

School Rankings

- Regional ranking in the recruiter survey: 30 of 47 schools ranked

THE RECRUITERS SPEAK

Georgia's most impressive features

"Practicality"

"Good communicators"

"Students' willingness to relocate"

Georgia's major shortcomings

"International students lacking English skills"

"Strategic thinking"

"School's reputation outside Georgia"

How Georgia can increase its appeal

"Network more aggressively, interact with alums"

"More rigor"

"Promote the school more"

FALL 2004 INCOMING M.B.A. CLASS

	Full-Time Only
Number of applicants	249
Number of offers extended	89
Number of students who accepted offer	49
Number of students who enrolled	49

GMAT score: 663 (mean); 670 (median)
Years of full-time work experience: 4.67 (mean); 4.17 (median)
Undergraduate GPA: 3.34 (mean); 3.33 (median)

Demographic Profile of Full-Time Students

Male: 75%
Female: 25%
Minorities: 18%
U.S. citizens/residents: 69%
Foreign nationals: 31%

Class of 2004 Most Popular Academic Concentrations (% of Students)

Finance 49%
Marketing 33%
Entrepreneurship 21%

CLASS OF 2004 EMPLOYMENT DATA

Industries Hiring Full-Time Graduates (% Hired)

Computer/technology/Internet/dot-com: 8%
Consumer products and services: 7%
Financial services/investment banking: 19%
Government: 2%
Management consulting: 5%
Manufacturing: 8%
Nonprofit: 2%
Pharmaceutical/biotechnology/health-care products and services:
2%
Real estate: 23%
Telecommunications: 3%
Travel and transportation: 8%

Other professional services (accounting, advertising, etc.): 8%
Other: 5%

Position/Job Function (% Hired)

Consulting: 17%
Finance/accounting: 34%
General management: 2%
Human resources: 3%
Information technology/management information systems: 3%
Marketing/sales: 16%
Other: 25%

Top Recruiters (Number of Full-Time Class of 2004 Graduates Hired)

Pulte Homes: 4
FedEx: 3
Liberty Mutual: 2
Bank of America: 2
Ernst & Young: 2
American Express: 1
Kimberly-Clark: 1
PricewaterhouseCoopers: 1

Percentage of Job-Seeking Full-Time Graduates Who:	All Students	Citizens/Residents	Foreign Nationals
Received offers prior to or within 3 months of graduation	89%	90%	65%
Accepted offers prior to or within 3 months of graduation	84%	88%	65%

	MEAN			MEDIAN		
Overall Compensation	All Students	Citizens/ Residents	Foreign Nationals	All Students	Citizens/ Residents	Foreign Nationals
Annual base salary	$65,476	$65,826	$64,000	$65,000	$67,992	$60,000
Signing bonus	$7,833	$8,474	$5,750	$5,000	$5,000	$5,000
Other guaranteed compensation	$15,015	$16,388	N/A	$7,000	$12,000	N/A

KPMG: 1
Deloitte & Touche: 1

Three of the Most Famous Graduates of M.B.A. Program

Mason Hawkins (class of 1972) Chairman and CEO, Southeastern Asset Management

George Slusser (class of 1979) President, Caldwell Banker Commercial

Sheila Taoramina (class of 1996) 2004 World Triathlon Champion and U.S. Olympic team member

HARVARD UNIVERSITY

Founded in 1908, Harvard Business School was a "delicate experiment" in the new field of professional management training. Its first class included 33 regular students and 47 special students taking only certain courses. The experiment, of course, proved to be a huge success, and the prestigious business school now enrolls about 1,800 full-time M.B.A. candidates.

Nearly a century later, Harvard continues its general management tradition and case-method approach to teaching. Harvard says that more than 80% of the business cases sold in the world are written by its professors, meaning there's a good chance Harvard students will be taught by the authors of the cases they analyze. Some of the protagonists in the cases also visit classes and discuss their experiences.

The business school enjoys a strong research tradition, with the faculty writing or co-authoring as many as three dozen books a year, along with their many academic papers, articles, and case studies. Harvard notes that its annual research budget of more than $70 million is entirely self-funded to help ensure objectivity.

Recent academic changes include the creation of a new first-year course—"Leadership and Corporate Accountability"—to prepare students for the inevitable ethical challenges they will face in the business world. The business school also has just inaugurated a five-year joint M.B.A./M.D. degree with Harvard Medical School to produce physicians skilled in both medicine and management.

While many Harvard M.B.A. graduates join management-consulting and investment-banking firms, entrepreneurship has been part of the school for more than 50 years. "The Entrepreneurial Manager" has become a first-year required course, and more than 25 faculty members teach nearly 20 elective courses on entrepreneurship in the second year.

Harvard also has been a pioneer among business schools in the field of corporate citizenship through its Social Enterprise Initiative. M.B.A. students can join the social enterprise club, attend guest lectures by speakers from the public and nonprofit sectors, compete in a social-enterprise business-plan contest, perform community service in the Boston area, take courses on such topics as strategic social responsibility and nonprofit leadership, and secure public-service internships.

Like other elite business schools, Harvard can claim many CEOs as alumni. But it has the distinction of producing the world's most powerful graduate: George W. Bush, class of 1975 and the first U.S. president with an M.B.A. degree.

Despite its distinguished faculty and reputation, recruiters have a big problem with Harvard that can be summed up in one word: arrogance. Recruiters repeatedly complain about students' inflated egos and expectations. In the latest *Wall Street Journal*/Harris Interactive recruiter survey, Harvard received its highest scores for students' strategic thinking, leadership potential, and communication and interpersonal skills, as well as the faculty's expertise. Survey respondents gave the lowest ratings for the career-services office and the value for the money invested in the recruiting effort.

HARVARD ON HARVARD

(Data provided by Harvard
Business School)

Business School website:
http://www.hbs.edu
Business School e-mail:
admissions@hbs.edu
Private institution
M.B.A. enrollment: 1,786
Full-time: 1,786

ADMISSIONS DIRECTOR:
Brit Dewey
Managing Director, Admissions
and Financial Aid
Dillon House
Soldiers Field
Boston, MA 02163
617-495-6127 (voice)
617-496-9272 (fax)
E-mail: admissions@hbs.edu

APPLICATION DEADLINE:
Fall 2006: 3/2006
Annual tuition: $37,500
Annual room and board: $22,432

School Rankings

- National ranking in the recruiter survey: 14 of 19 schools ranked
- International ranking: 17 of 20 schools ranked
- Ranking by management-consulting-industry recruiters: 6th place

Recognition for Excellence in Academic Concentrations

- With 996 nominations, Harvard ranked No. 1 among business schools that recruiters in *The Wall Street Journal*/Harris Interactive survey cited for excellence in strategy.
- With 172 nominations, Harvard ranked No. 3 for excellence in entrepreneurship.
- With 196 nominations, Harvard ranked No. 3 for excellence in international business.
- With 89 nominations, Harvard ranked No. 5 for excellence in marketing.
- With 106 nominations, Harvard ranked No. 6 for excellence in finance.
- With 48 nominations, Harvard ranked No. 7 for excellence in operations management.

Special Recognition

- Good source for recruiting minorities: 4th most nominated school, 55 nominations.
- Good source for recruiting women: 8th most nominated school, 55 nominations.

THE RECRUITERS SPEAK

Harvard's most impressive features

"Gold standard—extremely smart people"

"Talent, achievement, and worldliness"

"Strategic, intuitive thinking"

Harvard's major shortcomings

"Students seem to think the world owes them a living"

"Institutional crustiness"

"Cutthroat competition creates leaders, not team players"

How Harvard can increase its appeal

"Realize the companies are the customer"

"Reduce 'better than thou' attitude"

"Increase flexibility, openness to new companies"

FALL 2004 INCOMING M.B.A. CLASS

	Full-Time Only
Number of applicants	7,139
Number of offers extended	1,026
Number of students who accepted offer	893
Number of students who enrolled	893

GMAT score: 707 (mean); N/A (median)
Years of full-time work experience: 4 (mean); N/A (median)
Undergraduate GPA: 3.6 (mean); N/A (median)

Demographic Profile of Full-Time Students

Male: 66%
Female: 34%
Minorities: 21%
U.S. citizens/residents: 68%
Foreign nationals: 32%

Class of 2004 Most Popular Academic Concentrations

N/A

CLASS OF 2004 EMPLOYMENT DATA

Industries Hiring Full-Time Graduates (% Hired)

Computer/technology/Internet/dot-com: 7%
Consumer products and services: 6%
Financial services/investment banking: 31%
Government: 1%
Management consulting: 26%
Manufacturing: 5%
Media/entertainment: 5%
Nonprofit: 3%
Pharmaceutical/biotechnology/health-care products and services:
7%
Real estate: 2%
Telecommunications: 2%
Other professional services (accounting, advertising, etc.): 5%

Position/Job Function (% Hired)

Consulting: 29%
Finance/accounting: 31%
General management: 10%
Marketing/sales: 21%
Other: 9%

Top Recruiters

N/A

Percentage of Job-Seeking Full-Time Graduates Who:	All Students	All Citizens/Residents	All Foreign Nationals
Received offers prior to or within 3 months of graduation	96%	N/A	N/A
Accepted offers prior to or within 3 months of graduation	90%	N/A	N/A

	MEAN			MEDIAN	
Overall Compensation	All Students	Citizens/ Residents	Foreign Nationals	All Students	Citizens/ Residents
Annual base salary	$99,848	N/A	N/A	$100,000	N/A
Signing bonus	$17,358	N/A	N/A	$15,000	N/A
Other guaranteed compensation	$39,711	N/A	N/A	$20,000	N/A

Three of the Most Famous Graduates of M.B.A. Program

George W. Bush (class of 1975) President of the United States

A.G. Lafley (class of 1977) Chairman, President and CEO, Procter & Gamble

Meg Whitman (class of 1979) President and CEO, eBay

HEC SCHOOL OF MANAGEMENT, PARIS

Created by the Paris Chamber of Commerce in 1881, the HEC School of Management is still closely tied to the local business community. But it also has evolved from its local roots into a highly international institution.

More than three-quarters of the M.B.A. students come from 45 countries, and two-thirds of the professors hired in the last four years have been foreign. HEC offers student-exchange programs with more than 40 other business schools, as well as double-degree programs with some foreign schools. It also has established an executive-M.B.A. program in partnership with New York University and the London School of Economics and Political Science.

M.B.A. students start the 16-month HEC program with core management courses taught either entirely in English or in both English and French. Eventually, students are expected to master both languages. The second part of the M.B.A. curriculum gives students several options: a company consulting project, a foreign-exchange program, and academic specialization. Specialties include entrepreneurship, international finance, marketing, and strategies for growth.

HEC also offers a dozen specialized master's degrees that are awarded after eight months of courses, a four-month internship, and a professional thesis project. Among the areas of study: marketing intelligence, sustainable development management, digital business strategy, and international risk management.

HEC ON HEC

(Data provided by the HEC
M.B.A. Program at the HEC
School of Management, Paris)

Business school website:
http://www.hec.edu
Business school e-mail:
perrin@hec.fr
Public institution
M.B.A. enrollment: 404
Full-time: 197
Executive program: 207

ADMISSIONS DIRECTOR:
Isabelle Cota
Admissions and Student Affairs
Director
1 Rue de la Libération
Jouy-en-Josas, France 78351
33-1-3967-9516 (voice)
33-1-3967-7465 (fax)
E-mail: cota@hec.fr

APPLICATION DEADLINES:
Fall 2006: April 2006
Annual tuition: $36,975
Annual room and board: $20,200

HEC slipped seven places to No. 11 in the latest *Wall Street Journal*/Harris Interactive International ranking. HEC received especially weak ratings for overall perception and for recruiters' intentions to return to the school over the next few years. HEC's lowest scores were for fit with the corporate culture, value for the money invested in the recruiting effort, and the career-services office. Recruiters also complained that the school isn't international enough in its focus. They gave HEC its strongest ratings for students' analytical and problem-solving skills, strategic thinking, and personal ethics and integrity, as well as for the core curriculum.

School Rankings

■ International ranking in the recruiter survey: 11 of 20 schools ranked

FALL 2004 INCOMING M.B.A. CLASS

	Full-Time Only
Number of applicants	888
Number of offers extended	184
Number of students who accepted offer	109
Number of students who enrolled	107

GMAT score: 656 (mean); 650 (median)
Years of full-time work experience: 5.7 (mean); 5 (median)
Undergraduate GPA: N/A

THE RECRUITERS SPEAK

HEC's most impressive features	HEC's major shortcomings	How HEC can increase its appeal
"In-depth curriculum"	"Not world-class students"	"Be more rigorous"
"Integration with the local business community"	"Too French"	"Be more humble about compensation and benefits"
"Good in finance"	"Need to work more on international recognition"	"Increase international publicity"

Demographic Profile of Full-Time Students

Male: 75%
Female: 25%
French citizens/residents: 22%
Foreign nationals: 78%

Class of 2004 Most Popular Academic Concentration (% of Students)

Entrepreneurship 35%
International finance 23%
Strategies for growth 21%

CLASS OF 2004 EMPLOYMENT DATA

Industries Hiring Full-Time Graduates (% Hired)

Computer/technology/Internet/dot-com: 5%
Consumer products and services: 4%
Energy and utilities: 7%
Financial services/investment banking: 17%
Government: 0.5%
Industrial products and services: 10%
Management consulting: 15%
Manufacturing: 6%
Media/entertainment: 1%
Nonprofit: 0.5%
Petroleum/energy: 7%
Pharmaceutical/biotechnology/health-care products and services: 7%
Telecommunications: 7%
Travel and transportation: 3%
Other professional services (accounting, advertising, etc.): 10%

Position/Job Function (% Hired)

Consulting: 20%
Finance/accounting: 20%
General management: 33%
Human resources: 1%
Marketing/sales: 19%
Operations/production/logistics: 4%
Other: 3%

Top Recruiters *(Number of Full-Time Class of 2004 Graduates Hired)*

Johnson & Johnson: 6
Renault: 5
General Electric: 4
Hilti: 3
Michelin: 3
L'Oréal: 2
Boston Consulting Group: 2
Merrill Lynch: 2
BNP Paribas: 2
Cap Gemini: 2

Percentage of Job-Seeking Full-Time Graduates Who:	All Students	Citizens/Residents	Foreign Nationals
Received offers prior to or within 3 months of graduation	59%	61%	50%
Accepted offers prior to or within 3 months of graduation	57%	54%	49%

	MEAN			MEDIAN		
Overall Compensation	All Students	Citizens/Residents	Foreign Nationals	All Students	Citizens/Residents	Foreign Nationals
Annual base salary	$91,534	$94,018	$88,593	$86,112	$92,736	$80,813
Signing bonus	$16,482	$13,910	$16,685	$16,560	$14,573	$16,560
Other guaranteed compensation	$22,851	$24,684	$21,663	$19,872	$21,197	$18,878

Three of the Most Famous Graduates of M.B.A. Program

Gilles Dard (class of 1995) CEO, Merrill Lynch, Pierce, Fenner & Smith SAF

Pascal Cagni (Class of 1986) Vice President and Managing Director, Apple Europe

Jean-Louis Borloo (Class of 1976) French Minister Delegate for Urban Affairs

IESE BUSINESS SCHOOL AT THE UNIVERSITY OF NAVARRA

Universidad de Navarra

Established in Barcelona in 1958 as the graduate business school of the University of Navarra, IESE began life as an executive-education program for the Spanish-speaking market. It continues to be a major player in that market and in recent years has earned a reputation for customized executive-education programs for such companies as Sun Microsystems, Boeing, Volkswagen, and Philips.

After forging an alliance with Harvard Business School, IESE offered Europe's first two-year M.B.A. program in 1964. The Harvard connection continues today through collaboration on executive-education programs and the annual meeting of the IESE-Harvard Business School Advisory Committee.

In 1974, IESE branched out from its main campus in Barcelona to open an outpost in Madrid because of high demand for executive education in the Spanish capital. Today, it also offers an executive-M.B.A. program in Madrid. IESE's newest degree is a global-executive M.B.A., which features residential sessions in Spain, California, and Shanghai, along with online instruction.

The full-time M.B.A. program attracts an international mix of students representing some 55 countries. The number of Asian students, in particular, has been growing, with most coming from India, Taiwan, Japan, and South Korea. Only about a quarter of students are Spanish.

IESE ON IESE

(Data provided by IESE Business School)

Business school website:
http://www.iese.edu
Business school e-mail:
mbainfo@iese.edu
Private institution
M.B.A. enrollment: 623
Full-time: 401
Executive program: 222

ADMISSIONS DIRECTOR:
Mireia Rius
Director of Admissions
Avenida Pearson, 21
Barcelona, Spain 08034
34-93-253-4317 (voice)
34-93-253-4343 (fax)
E-mail: mrius@iese.edu

APPLICATION DEADLINE:
Fall 2006: November 2005
Annual tuition: $37,200
Annual room and board: $19,000

Students must be fluent in English to be admitted to IESE's bilingual M.B.A. program. But they also are expected to learn Spanish while at IESE and take some business courses that are taught in Spanish. Nearly a third of the M.B.A. students spend one semester abroad at one of the 22 international schools that are partners with IESE.

IESE is distinctive in its humanistic approach, which emphasizes the personal, social, and ethical consequences of business leadership and decision-making. IESE maintains ties to the Roman Catholic lay organization Opus Dei, whose members founded the University of Navarra. But IESE notes that its recruiting of students is nondenominational.

In *The Wall Street Journal*/Harris Interactive recruiter survey, IESE's students received their highest ratings for international knowledge and experience and analytical and problem-solving skills. IESE's lowest scores: success with past hires from the school, value for the money invested in the recruiting effort, and students' fit with the corporate culture.

School Rankings

- International ranking in the recruiter survey: 19 of 20 schools ranked

THE RECRUITERS SPEAK

IESE's most impressive features	IESE's major shortcomings	How IESE can increase its appeal
"International program"	"Some of the students are very Spanish-centric"	"Increase standards for bottom third of students"
"Moral values"	"Too much religious zeal"	"Suggest students be more modest in interviews"
"Strategic thinking"	"Students want to become general managers immediately"	"Market the school better"

FALL 2004 INCOMING M.B.A. CLASS

	Full-Time Only
Number of applicants	935
Number of offers extended	374
Number of students who accepted offer	226
Number of students who enrolled	205

GMAT score: 673 (mean); 670 (median)
Years of full-time work experience: 4.6 (mean); 4.1 (median)
Undergraduate GPA: N/A

Demographic Profile of Full-Time Students

Male: 75%
Female: 25%
Spanish citizens/residents: 27%
Foreign nationals: 73%

Class of 2004 Most Popular Academic Concentrations

N/A

CLASS OF 2004 EMPLOYMENT DATA

Industries Hiring Full-Time Graduates (% Hired)

Consumer products and services: 8%
Energy and utilities: 2%
Financial services/investment banking: 32%
Industrial products and services: 10%
Management consulting: 36%
Pharmaceutical/biotechnology/health-care products and services: 4%
Travel and transportation: 1%
Other professional services (accounting, advertising, etc.): 5%
Other: 2%

Position/Job Function (% Hired)

Consulting: 30%
Finance/accounting: 21%
General management: 20%
Human resources: 1%
Information technology/management information systems: 2%

Marketing/sales: 19%
Operations/production/logistics: 6%
Other: 1%

Top Recruiters *(Number of Full-Time Class of 2004 Graduates Hired)*

McKinsey: 11
Celsa: 9
Bain: 5
Johnson & Johnson: 4
Morgan Stanley: 3
A.T. Kearney: 3
Lehman Brothers: 3
Grupo Santander: 3
Affinity Petcare: 3
Booz Allen Hamilton: 3

Percentage of Job-Seeking Full-Time Graduates Who:	All Students	Citizens/Residents	Foreign Nationals
Received offers prior to or within 3 months of graduation	96%	N/A	N/A
Accepted offers prior to or within 3 months of graduation	90%	N/A	N/A

Overall Compensation	MEAN			MEDIAN		
	All Students	Citizens/Residents	Foreign Nationals	All Students	Citizens/Residents	Foreign Nationals
Annual base salary	$84,758	$65,980	$110,764	$74,566	$63,200	$98,720
Signing bonus	$23,920	$9,800	$25,400	$21,600	$8,510	$23,350
Other guaranteed compensation	N/A	N/A	N/A	N/A	N/A	N/A

Three of the Most Famous Graduates of M.B.A. Program

Aloise Linder (class of 1973), Vice President, Henkel KGAA

Harri Andersson (class of 1995) Vice President, Boston Consulting Group, Helsinki

Luis Enrique Yarur (class of 1975) President, Banco de Crédito e Inversiones, Chile

UNIVERSITY OF ILLINOIS AT URBANA-CHAMPAIGN

I COLLEGE *of* BUSINESS
UNIVERSITY OF ILLINOIS AT URBANA-CHAMPAIGN

The College of Business at the University of Illinois stresses real-world experience for its students. OSBI Consulting (formerly known as the Office for Strategic Business Initiatives), for example, is a bona fide management-consulting service run by M.B.A. students who advise major corporations, start-ups, nonprofit organizations, and university departments. Among OSBI's clients: Dow Chemical, the Mayo Clinic, McDonald's, and Nissan.

There's also the new Center for Entrepreneurial Development, where students provide business-plan reviews, market feasibility studies, and financial modeling to start-up ventures. Students also can gain experience at the university's Food and Brand Lab, which conducts research into why consumers buy what they buy and eat what they eat.

Illinois M.B.A.s major in marketing, finance, operations, information technology, or general management. More than a quarter of recent graduates landed jobs in consulting, while about 20% chose finance or accounting careers.

M.B.A. students can receive joint graduate degrees from a number of other Illinois schools, including architecture, engineering, computer science, medicine, law, journalism, and labor and industrial relations.

Illinois also offers an executive-M.B.A. program in Chicago and recently created an evening part-time degree at the main

ILLINOIS ON ILLINOIS

(Data provided by the College of
Business at the University of
Illinois at Urbana-Champaign)

Business school website:
http://www.mba.uiuc.edu
Business school e-mail:
mba@uiuc.edu
Public institution
M.B.A. enrollment: 330
Full-time: 276
Executive program: 54

ADMISSIONS DIRECTOR:
Victor C. Mullins
Assistant Dean
405 DKH, MC-706
1407 W. Gregory Drive
Urbana, IL 61801
217-244-7602 (voice)
217-333-1156 (fax)
E-mail: mba@uiuc.edu

APPLICATION DEADLINE:
Fall 2006: 3/15/2006
Annual tuition: $16,400 (in-state);
$23,500 (out-of-state)
Annual room and board: $15,168

campus in Urbana. The school also has formed a partnership with Warsaw University in Poland to offer an executive M.B.A.

In the latest *Wall Street Journal/Harris* Interactive survey, recruiters gave Illinois its strongest ratings for students' teamwork abilities and fit with the corporate culture. The school received its lowest ratings for students' previous work experience and their international knowledge and experience, as well as for the core curriculum.

School Rankings
- Regional ranking in the recruiter survey: 42 of 47 schools ranked

Recognition for Excellence in an Academic Concentration
- With 82 nominations, Illinois ranked No. 5 among business schools that recruiters in *The Wall Street Journal/*Harris Interactive survey cited for excellence in accounting.

FALL 2004 INCOMING M.B.A. CLASS

	Full-Time Only
Number of applicants	643
Number of offers extended	247
Number of students who accepted offer	117
Number of students who enrolled	94

THE RECRUITERS SPEAK

Illinois' most impressive features

"Strong accounting skills"

"Doers"

"Down-to-earth students"

Illinois' major shortcomings

"Finance students too trained to be auditors"

"Too many foreign nationals in the M.B.A. program"

"Inexperienced students; little significant leadership"

How Illinois can increase its appeal

"Expand its professional outreach beyond major accounting firms"

"Higher-profile faculty"

"More marketing of the school"

GMAT score: 649 (mean); 660 (median)
Years of full-time work experience: 4.4 (mean); 4 (median);
Undergraduate GPA: 3.4 (mean); 3.5 (median)

Demographic Profile of Full-Time Students

Male: 73%
Female: 27%
Minorities: 10%
U.S. citizens/residents: 46%
Foreign nationals: 54%

Class of 2004 Most Popular Academic Concentrations (% of Students)

Finance 38%
Marketing 29%
General management 14%

CLASS OF 2004 EMPLOYMENT DATA

Industries Hiring Full-Time Graduates (% Hired)

Computer/technology/Internet/dot-com: 5.8%
Consumer products and services: 11.8%
Financial services/investment banking: 8.8%
Management consulting: 26.5%
Nonprofit: 2.9%
Petroleum/energy: 2.9%
Real estate: 2.9%
Telecommunications: 14.7%
Other: 23.7%

Position/Job Function (% Hired)

Consulting: 29.4%
Finance/accounting: 20.6%
General management: 17.6%
Human resources: 5.9%
Information technology/management information systems: 2.9%
Marketing/sales: 17.6%
Operations/production/logistics: 5.9%

Top Recruiters (Number of Full-Time Class of 2004 Graduates Hired)

Samsung: 5
SBC Communications: 4

Deloitte & Touche: 3
Procter & Gamble: 3
IBM: 2
International Truck & Engine: 2
Walgreen: 2
Whirlpool: 2
Discover: 1
Goldman Sachs: 1

Percentage of Job-Seeking Full-Time Graduates Who:	All Students	Citizens/Residents	Foreign Nationals
Received offers prior to or within 3 months of graduation	95%	98%	94%
Accepted offers prior to or within 3 months of graduation	95%	98%	94%

Overall Compensation	MEAN			MEDIAN		
	All Students	Citizens/ Residents	Foreign Nationals	All Students	Citizens/ Residents	Foreign Nationals
Annual base salary	$68,997	$67,811	$73,571	$70,000	$69,900	$80,000
Signing bonus	$11,230	$10,225	$20,000	$8,750	$6,750	$20,000
Other guaranteed compensation	$11,000	$10,857	$12,000	$11,000	$10,000	$12,000

Three of the Most Famous Graduates of M.B.A. Program

Tom Siebel (class of 1983) Founder and Chairman, Siebel Systems

Mike Tokarz (class of 1973) President, Tokarz Group

Alan Feldman (class of 1976) President and CEO, Midas

IMD, THE INTERNATIONAL INSTITUTE FOR MANAGEMENT DEVELOPMENT

Real World. Real Learning®

For the second straight year, IMD topped the International ranking in *The Wall Street Journal*/Harris Interactive recruiter survey.

A management institute in Switzerland and not a traditional university, IMD was established in 1990 as the successor to two business schools: IMI, founded in Geneva by Alcan, and IMEDE, founded in Lausanne by Nestlé. With only about 90 students in its full-time program, IMD offers a 10-month general-management M.B.A. degree in an intimate international setting. Just a fraction of the students are Swiss citizens; the rest represent about 40 other countries and include a diverse mix of people, from an Icelandic computer engineer to a Malaysian lawyer. Throughout the M.B.A. program, students work in small teams and learn to cope with the cultural and personality differences that arise in a diverse, multinational group.

IMD attracts older, more experienced students than many M.B.A. programs. The average age tends to be about 30, and the average work experience seven years. The school seeks applicants with excellent interpersonal and leadership skills and managers whose responsibilities increased as their career progressed. The program moves at a demanding pace, and students participate in a variety of programs in a very short time. There's little time for slacking off and enjoying the school's stunning location in Lausanne.

IMD ON IMD

(Data provided by the International Institute for Management Development)

Business school website:
http://www.imd.ch/mba
Business school e-mail:
mbainfo@imd.ch
Private institution
M.B.A. enrollment: 149
Full-time: 89
Executive program: 60

ADMISSIONS DIRECTOR:
Katty Ooms Suter
Director, M.B.A. Admissions and
Career Services
IMD
Ch. de Bellerive 23, P.O. Box 915
Lausanne, Switzerland 1001
41-21-618-0298 (voice)
41-21-618-0615 (fax)
E-mail: mbainfo@imd.ch

APPLICATION DEADLINES:
Winter 2007: 2/1/2006, 4/1/2006,
6/1/2006, 8/1/2006, 9/1/2006
Annual tuition: $45,600
Annual room and board: $19,100

Some recruiters question whether an IMD degree is truly the equal of the more typical two-year program with summer internship. But IMD defends its abbreviated course of study, noting that its students already have extensive work experience and don't need an internship.

Applying to IMD requires a visit to the campus that includes a five-minute impromptu presentation and a case-study discussion so the admission committee can screen applicants for their ability to interact and communicate well.

In addition to the full-time M.B.A., IMD offers an executive-M.B.A. degree to a class of 60 to 70 students with even more experience, about 14 years on average. Participants spend 17½ weeks outside their offices—at IMD and on trips to Ireland, China, and California's Silicon Valley—and devote more than 40 weeks to online "distance learning."

In the full-time program, M.B.A. teams gain practical experience by working with start-up companies to develop business plans. They also participate in international consulting projects that have included developing a strategy for General Motors to enter the "secondhand-car market" in France and for Guinness to make its Irish pub concept more female-friendly. And for the past few years, IMD students have provided advice to Bosnia-Herzegovina on rebuilding its economy. In 2004, students worked on a plan for promoting the winter tourism industry to European consumers.

THE RECRUITERS SPEAK

IMD's most impressive features

"Global mindset"

"Very mature group, extensive work experience"

"Excellent general-management skills"

IMD's major shortcomings

"High expectations of salary and pace of promotions"

"Too few female faculty members and M.B.A.s"

"Acts too much like a business"

How IMD can increase its appeal

"Younger and larger class of students"

"Raise international visibility"

"Connect better with smaller recruiters"

In the *Journal* survey, recruiters gave IMD its highest scores for students' previous work experience, international knowledge and experience, and leadership potential. IMD's lowest scores: faculty expertise, value for the money invested in the recruiting effort, and students' awareness of corporate citizenship issues.

School Rankings

- International ranking in the recruiter survey: 1 of 20 schools ranked
- Ranking by energy and industrial-products-industry recruiters: 8th place

Recognition for Excellence in an Academic Concentration

- With 82 nominations, IMD ranked No. 7 among business schools that recruiters in *The Wall Street Journal*/Harris Interactive survey cited for excellence in international business.

2004 INCOMING M.B.A. CLASS

	Full-Time Only
Number of applicants	600
Number of offers extended	107
Number of students who accepted offer	91
Number of students who enrolled	89

GMAT score: 680 (mean); 670 (median)
Years of full-time work experience: 7 (mean); 7.5 (median)
Undergraduate GPA: N/A

Demographic Profile of Full-Time Students

Male: 80%
Female: 20%
Swiss citizens/residents: 2%
Foreign nationals: 98%

Class of 2004 Most Popular Academic Concentrations (% of Students)

General management 100%
Leadership 100%
Entrepreneurship 100%

CLASS OF 2004 EMPLOYMENT DATA

Industries Hiring Full-Time Graduates (% Hired)

Computer/technology/Internet/dot-com: 7%
Consumer products and services: 19%
Energy and utilities: 4%
Financial services/investment banking: 6%
Industrial products and services: 13%
Management consulting: 21%
Manufacturing: 1%
Media/entertainment: 1%
Pharmaceutical/biotechnology/health-care products and services: 9%
Real estate: 1%
Telecommunications: 4%
Travel and transportation: 4%
Other: 10%

Position/Job Function (% Hired)

Consulting: 22%
Finance/accounting: 9%
General management: 18%
Human resources: 3%
Information technology/management information systems: 1%
Marketing/sales: 44%
Operations/production/logistics: 3%

Top Recruiters (Number of Full-Time Class of 2004 Graduates Hired)

McKinsey: 5
Merloni: 4
Samsung Global Strategy Group: 3
Hilti: 2
Novartis International: 2
Shell International: 2
Nokia: 2

GE Capital Bank: 2
Argentina Microfinance: 2
J.M. Huber: 1

Percentage of Job-Seeking Full-Time Graduates Who:	All Students	Citizens/Residents	Foreign Nationals
Received offers prior to or within 3 months of graduation	95%	N/A	N/A
Accepted offers prior to or within 3 months of graduation	89%	N/A	N/A

Overall Compensation	MEAN			MEDIAN		
	All Students	Citizens/ Residents	Foreign Nationals	All Students	Citizens/ Residents	Foreign Nationals
Annual base salary fix	$123,000	N/A	N/A	$120,500	N/A	N/A
Signing bonus	$23,000	N/A	N/A	$20,250	N/A	N/A
Other guaranteed compensation	$29,903	N/A	N/A	$25,500	N/A	N/A

Three of the Most Famous Graduates of M.B.A. Program

Nick Shreiber (class of 1975) President & CEO, Tetra Pak Group

K. Y. Lee (class of 1990) Chairman, BenQ Corp.

Jürgen Fischer (class of 1988) President, Commercial Operations Group, Hilton International

INCAE

Founded in 1964 by the business communities and governments of Central America, INCAE Business School offers both master's degree programs and executive education and conducts research on business issues affecting the region. INCAE maintains close ties with Harvard Business School, which has provided technical supervision and educational support through the years.

INCAE operates two campuses in Costa Rica and Nicaragua and attracts students from throughout Latin America, with no single nationality representing more than 20% of the student body. Most courses are taught in Spanish, with some in English. INCAE also offers student-exchange programs with about 20 business schools in the U.S., Spain, and Germany.

M.B.A. students can concentrate in business economics, sustainable development, or industry and technology. INCAE has been recognized as a leader in the area of sustainable development by the Aspen Institute and World Resources Institute.

INCAE also offers a master's of medical management in an alliance with Tulane University's School of Public Health and Tropical Medicine. The program is designed in an executive format for practicing physicians and is taught by faculty from both schools.

Beyond the classroom, the INCAE Research Center explores topics that are most relevant to Latin American managers and in recent years has produced an average of 80 case studies annually. The school's other research arm—the Latin American Center for Competitiveness and Sustainable Development—is devoted to promoting economic growth along with social equity and environmental balance.

In *The Wall Street Journal*/Harris Interactive recruiter survey, INCAE received its highest scores for its core curriculum and students' ability to work well in teams. Recruiters rated it lowest for students' previous work experience, their international knowledge and experience, and the likelihood of recruiting stars.

School Rankings

- International ranking in the recruiter survey: 10 of 20 schools ranked
- Ranking by consumer-products-industry recruiters: 8th place

FALL 2004 INCOMING M.B.A. CLASS

	Full-Time Only
Number of applicants	193
Number of offers extended	169
Number of students who accepted offer	169
Number of students who enrolled	92

GMAT score: N/A (mean); N/A (median)
Years of full-time work experience: 4.5 (mean); 3.8 (median)
Undergraduate GPA: N/A

Demographic Profile of Full-Time Students

Male: 66%
Female: 34%
Costa Rican citizens/residents: 26%
Foreign nationals: 74%

INCAE ON INCAE

(Data provided by INCAE
Business School)

Business school website:
http://www.incae.edu
Business school e-mail: Roderick.
MacGregor@incae.edu
Private institution
M.B.A. enrollment: 487
Full-time: 217
Executive program: 270

ADMISSIONS DIRECTOR:
Roderick MacGregor
M.B.A. Administrative Director
P.O. Box 960
Alajuela, Costa Rica 4050
506-437-2357 (voice)
506-433-9101 (fax)
E-mail:
Roderick.MacGregor@incae.edu

APPLICATION DEADLINES:
Fall 2006: 8/1/2006
Annual tuition: $13,625
Annual room and board: $2,905

Class of 2004 Most Popular Academic Concentrations (% of Students)

Finance and economics: N/A
Industry and technology: N/A
Sustainable development: N/A

CLASS OF 2004 EMPLOYMENT DATA

Industries Hiring Full-Time Graduates (% Hired)

Consumer products and services: 34%
Financial services/investment banking: 26%
Government: 4%
Industrial products and services: 2%
Management consulting: 2%
Manufacturing: 9%
Nonprofit: 4%
Pharmaceutical/biotechnology/health-care products and services: 2%
Real estate: 2%
Telecommunications: 1%
Travel and transportation: 6%
Other: 8%

Position/Job Function (% Hired)

Consulting: 6%
Finance/accounting: 24%
General management: 8%
Marketing/sales: 35%
Operations/production/logistics: 7%
Other: 20%

THE RECRUITERS SPEAK

INCAE's most impressive features

"Good 'real life' academic program"

"Professional, hard workers"

"Strategy focus"

INCAE's major shortcomings

"Too high expectations for Latin American market"

"Communications, English fluency"

"Students seemed immature"

How INCAE can increase its appeal

"More international students from outside Central America"

"Résumé preparation and interview training"

"Visit company recruiters in major U.S. cities"

Top Recruiters *(Number of Full-Time Class of 2004 Graduates Hired)*

SAB Miller/Cerveceria Hondurena: 4
EPA Venezuela: 4
Banistmo: 3
Procter & Gamble: 2
Central American Bank for Economic Integration: 2
Taca Airlines: 2
Cargill: 1
Kerns Guatemala: 1
Johnson & Johnson: 1
Coca-Cola Interamerican: 1

Percentage of Job-Seeking Full-Time Graduates Who:	All Students	Citizens/Residents	Foreign Nationals
Received offers prior to or within 3 months of graduation	71%	96%	65%
Accepted offers prior to or within 3 months of graduation	71%	96%	65%

	MEAN			MEDIAN		
Overall Compensation	All Students	Citizens/ Residents	Foreign Nationals	All Students	Citizens/ Residents	Foreign Nationals
Annual base salary	$84,741	$88,770	$82,317	$81,891	$88,443	$81,891
Signing bonus	N/A	N/A	N/A	N/A	N/A	N/A
Other guaranteed compensation	N/A	N/A	N/A	N/A	N/A	N/A

Three of the Most Famous Graduates of M.B.A. Program

Rodrigo Uribe (class of 1975) President, Corporacion Supermercados Unidos

Gilberto Perezalonso (class of 1974) President, Fundacion Perezalonso

Roberto Mollison Jimenez (class of 1989) President, Agricola Industrial Tropical

INDIANA UNIVERSITY

KELLEY

School of Business

INDIANA UNIVERSITY
(KELLEY SCHOOL OF BUSINESS)

Indiana University offers M.B.A. students unusual flexibility in how they complete their degree. The full-time program in Bloomington allows students to spend the first year on campus, then complete the degree online. The school figures students might choose that alternative should their summer internship turn into an immediate full-time job.

Students also can complete the entire degree online, an uncommon option at a top-ranked business school. In 1999, Indiana saw an opportunity for an online-M.B.A. program that would appeal to the corporate clients of its executive-education program. Soon Kelley Direct Online was opened to the public, and it has been growing fast ever since.

For working students who prefer the classroom to the Internet, Kelley also offers a part-time evening program in Indianapolis.

The Kelley School encourages specialization early on in the M.B.A. program. Full-time students join "academies," where they immerse themselves in a particular industry or job function, such as consulting, investment banking, supply-chain management, consumer and business marketing, and sports and entertainment. Students learn about the industry, do consulting work and other projects, and travel to meet corporate executives in the field. The sports and entertainment group, for example, ventures to New York, Nashville and Las Vegas.

Indiana students are discovering more real-world opportunities for learning. For example, marketing students can manage an actual consumer brand on an ongoing basis, not just as part of a short-term consulting project. The program, Bloomington Brands, is the brainchild of alumnus Bob Stohler, who proposed that six M.B.A. students try to boost sales of a neglected fertilizer product for Scotts, his former employer. Graduate students and faculty from the Kelley School also will staff and provide product development, marketing, and other business expertise to a new life-sciences company that's part of a consortium between Eli Lilly, Indiana University, and Purdue University.

In *The Wall Street Journal*/Harris Interactive ranking, recruiters awarded Indiana top ratings for its students' ability to work well in teams, analytical and problem-solving skills, personal ethics and integrity, and fit with the corporate culture. The lowest scores were for students' international knowledge and experience and their awareness of corporate citizenship issues.

School Rankings

- Regional ranking in the recruiter survey: 11 of 47 schools ranked
- Ranking by consumer-products-industry recruiters: 1st place
- Ranking by energy- and industrial-products-industry recruiters: 6th place

Recognition for Excellence in an Academic Concentration

- With 93 nominations, Indiana ranked No. 4 among business schools that recruiters in *The Wall Street Journal*/Harris Interactive survey cited for excellence in marketing.

INDIANA ON INDIANA

(Data provided by the Kelley School of Business at Indiana University)

Business school website: http://kelley.iu.edu/mba
Business school e-mail: mbaoffice@indiana.edu
Public institution
M.B.A. enrollment: 771
Full-time: 450
Part-time: 321

ADMISSIONS DIRECTOR:
James Holmen
Director of Admissions and Financial Aid
Graduate and Executive Education Center
Bloomington, IN 47405
812-855-8006 (voice)
812-855-9039 (fax)
E-mail: mbaoffice@indiana.edu

APPLICATION DEADLINES:
Fall 2006: 11/15/2005, 1/15/2006, 3/1/2006, 4/15/2006
Annual tuition: $12,584 (in-state); $25,652 (out-of-state)
Annual room and board: $11,300

FALL 2004 INCOMING M.B.A. CLASS

	Total	Full-Time Only
Number of applicants	1,340	1,221
Number of offers extended	475	405
Number of students who accepted offer	N/A	N/A
Number of students who enrolled	258	196

GMAT score: 644 (mean); 640 (median)
Years of full-time work experience: 5 (mean); 5 (median)
Undergraduate GPA: 3.3 (mean); 3.3 (median)

Demographic Profile of Full-Time Students

Male: 74%
Female: 26%
Minorities: 15%
U.S. citizens/residents: 71%
Foreign nationals: 29%

Class of 2004 Most Popular Academic Concentrations (% of Students)

Finance 61%
Marketing 48%
Strategic management consulting 16%

CLASS OF 2004 EMPLOYMENT DATA

Industries Hiring Full-Time Graduates (% Hired)

Computer/technology/Internet/dot-com: 4%
Consumer products and services: 16.2%

THE RECRUITERS SPEAK

Indiana's most impressive features

"Work ethic and interpersonal skills"

"Faculty's passion for students' success"

"Good values instilled"

Indiana's major shortcomings

"Not driven enough"

"Limited previous achievements"

"Breadth of talent"

How Indiana can increase its appeal

"Leadership development"

"More geographically diverse student population"

"More diversity—women and people of color"

Energy and utilities: 1.1%
Financial services/investment banking: 18%
Industrial products and services: 9.3%
Management consulting: 11.6%
Manufacturing: 9.3%
Media/entertainment: 1.1%
Petroleum/energy: 1.1%
Pharmaceutical/biotechnology/health-care products and services:
11.6%
Telecommunications: 2.3%
Travel and transportation: 4%
Other professional services (accounting, advertising, etc.): 1.1%
Other: 9.3%

Position/Job Function (% Hired)

Consulting: 14%
Finance/accounting: 36%
General management: 5.5%
Human resources: 3.5%
Information technology/management information systems: 1%
Marketing/sales: 38%
Operations/production/logistics: 2%

Percentage of Job-Seeking Full-Time Graduates Who:	All Students	Citizens/Residents	Foreign Nationals
Received offers prior to or within 3 months of graduation	85%	88%	74%
Accepted offers prior to or within 3 months of graduation	74%	83%	54%

Overall Compensation	MEAN			MEDIAN		
	All Students	Citizens/ Residents	Foreign Nationals	All Students	Citizens/ Residents	Foreign Nationals
Annual base salary	$76,866	$77,981	$74,031	$80,000	$80,000	$80,000
Signing bonus	$12,394	$12,068	$12,195	$10,500	$10,000	$15,000
Other guaranteed compensation	$14,565	$15,173	$13,290	$10,000	$10,000	$10,000

Top Recruiters *(Number of Full-Time Class of 2004 Graduates Hired)*

Deloitte Consulting: 6
General Electric: 5
Cummins: 4
Guidant: 4
Target: 4
Eli Lilly: 3
3M: 3
Mead Johnson Nutritionals: 3
Intel: 3
Sabre: 3

Three of the Most Famous Graduates of M.B.A. Program

John Chambers (class of 1976) President and CEO, Cisco Systems

Jeff Fettig (class of 1981) Chairman and CEO, Whirlpool

Phillip Francis (class of 1971) Chairman and CEO, PetsMart

INSEAD

Founded in 1957, Insead qualifies as one of the most multicultural business schools, with nearly 90% of its students coming from other countries and taking their M.B.A. courses on as many as three continents.

Insead operates a second campus in Singapore so students can split their time between that location and Fontainebleau, France. What's more, Insead has created an exchange program with the University of Pennsylvania's Wharton School that allows students to take some classes in Philadelphia and San Francisco. The alliance features a faculty-exchange program and research collaboration between the two schools. Looking ahead, Insead said it and Wharton may work together to expand in new markets such as Latin America, India, China, and Japan.

Insead offers a general-management education in its one-year full-time M.B.A. program. Language skills are critical: The school requires applicants to be bilingual and especially fluent in English, which is used to teach the courses. To qualify for graduation, students must acquire a working knowledge of a third "commercially useful" language.

In 2003, Insead launched a 14-month executive-M.B.A. program on both of its campuses for students with at least seven years of work experience. Its newest program is a certificate in entrepreneurship that requires its M.B.A. graduates to devote an additional 11 weeks to an internship and more coursework at the Singapore campus.

INSEAD ON INSEAD

(Data provided by the Insead
M.B.A. program)

Business school website:
http://www.insead.edu/MBA
Business school e-mail:
mba.info@Insead.edu
Private institution
M.B.A. enrollment: 891
Full-time: 839
Executive program: 52

ADMISSIONS DIRECTOR:
Johanna Hellborg
Associate Admissions Director
Insead
Boulevard de Constance
Fontainebleau, France 77305
33-1-6072-4005 (voice)
33-1-6074-5530 (fax)
E-mail: mba.info@Insead.edu

APPLICATION DEADLINES:
Fall 2006: 10/5/2005, 12/7/2005,
2/1/2006
Annual tuition: $56,115
Annual room and board: $15,000

Insead's full-time graduates are particularly drawn to the management-consulting industry. In fact, the top four recruiters of Insead's 2004 graduates were all consulting firms, with McKinsey hiring nearly 100 students.

In *The Wall Street Journal*/Harris Interactive survey, graduates of Insead received their highest ratings for their international knowledge and experience, analytical and problem-solving skills, and strategic thinking. Recruiters gave Insead its lowest scores for the career-services office, value for the money invested in the recruiting effort, and students' prior work experience. Many recruiters also complain that Insead's one-year program is too short and lacks depth.

School Rankings

- International ranking in the recruiter survey: 9 of 20 schools ranked
- Ranking by management-consulting-industry recruiters: 6th place
- Ranking by technology-industry recruiters: 6th place

Recognition for Excellence in Academic Concentrations

- With 265 nominations, Insead ranked No. 2 among business schools that recruiters in *The Wall Street Journal*/Harris Interactive survey cited for excellence in international business.
- With 61 nominations, Insead ranked No. 10 for excellence in strategy.

THE RECRUITERS SPEAK

Insead's most impressive features

"Strong language skills"

"Assertiveness, initiative, international mindset"

"Work-hard, play-hard mentality"

Insead's major shortcomings

"Getting too big—M.B.A. factory"

"The one-year program lacks depth"

"Students' overinflated sense of self-worth"

How Insead can increase its appeal

"Provide reality check on salary expectations"

"Strengthen alumni network"

"Refocus school to smaller, high-quality group of students"

FALL 2004 INCOMING M.B.A. CLASS

	Full-Time Only
Number of applicants	N/A
Number of offers extended	N/A
Number of students who accepted offer	N/A
Number of students who enrolled	N/A

GMAT score: 707 (mean); N/A (median)
Years of full-time work experience: 5 (mean); N/A (median)
Undergraduate GPA: N/A

Demographic Profile of Full-Time Students

Male: 81%
Female: 19%
French citizens/residents: 13%
Foreign nationals: 87%

Class of 2004 Most Popular Academic Concentrations

N/A

CLASS OF 2004 EMPLOYMENT DATA

Industries Hiring Full-Time Graduates (% Hired)

Computer/technology/Internet/dot-com: 3.7%
Consumer products and services: 11.5%
Media/entertainment: 2.5%
Financial services/investment banking: 20.5%
Industrial products and services: 3.5%
Management consulting: 36.8%
Manufacturing: 1.5%
Petroleum/energy: 2.8%
Pharmaceutical/biotechnology/health-care products and services:
5.1%
Telecommunications: 3.7%
Travel and transportation: 3.7%
Other professional services (accounting, advertising, etc.): 2.5%
Other: 2.2%

Position/Job Function (% Hired)

Consulting: 38%
Finance/accounting: 22%
General management: 10%
Human resources: 1%
Marketing/sales: 11.6%
Corporate planning/business development: 10.3%
Operations/production/logistics: 3.4%
Other: 3.7%

Top Recruiters (Number of Full-Time Class of 2004 Graduates Hired)

McKinsey: 91
Bain: 25
Boston Consulting Group: 22
Booz Allen Hamilton: 17
General Electric: 11
Barclays Capital: 10
CHEP: 7
Cap Gemini Ernst & Young: 6
Eli Lilly: 6
Novartis: 6

Percentage of Job-Seeking Full-Time Graduates Who:	All Students	Citizens/Residents	Foreign Nationals
Received offers prior to or within 3 months of graduation	74%	N/A	N/A
Accepted offers prior to or within 3 months of graduation	65%	N/A	N/A

	MEAN			MEDIAN		
Overall Compensation	All Students	Citizens/ Residents	Foreign Nationals	All Students	Citizens/ Residents	Foreign Nationals
Annual base salary	$103,300	N/A	N/A	$102,600	N/A	N/A
Signing bonus	$20,000	N/A	N/A	$10,900	N/A	N/A
Other guaranteed compensation	N/A	N/A	N/A	N/A	N/A	N/A

Philip Morris: 6
Royal Dutch/Shell: 6

Three of the Most Famous Graduates of the M.B.A. Program

Lindsay Owen-Jones (class of 1969) CEO, L'Oréal

Kevin Ryan (class of 1990) CEO, Doubleclick

Helen Alexander (class of 1984) CEO, the Economist Group

INSTITUTO DE EMPRESA (IE)

Located in the heart of Madrid, Instituto de Empresa is an independent business school that dates back to 1973. Entrepreneurship is by far the most popular academic major, followed by finance and information technology. IE estimates that more than 15% of its graduates go on to start their own businesses.

In addition to its standard 10-month M.B.A. degree, IE students who hope to work at a multinational company can enroll in the International M.B.A. program. IE also offers several executive-M.B.A. programs, including an online degree, as well as a portfolio of other master's degrees in tourism management, financial management and control, human resources, sales and marketing, operations management, information systems and technologies, tax law, and legal practice.

Even before the recent wave of corporate scandals, IE focused on ethics and social-responsibility issues in its curriculum and research. It created a professorship in corporate social responsibility and established research centers for corporate governance, "eco-intelligent" management, and diversity in global management. The school even drafted an oath for M.B.A. students to pledge their commitment to ethics and social responsibility in their careers.

IE has announced a number of recent collaborations with universities in other countries. It has partnered with Tecnologico de Monterrey in Mexico to offer academic training and research for family businesses in Latin America, and is working with Babson College in Massachusetts on teaching and research in entrepreneurship and family enterprises. In addition, IE said that it and the law school at Northwestern University in Illinois have developed the first executive master's of laws degree in Europe.

In the latest *Wall Street Journal*/Harris Interactive survey, IE received its highest scores for the career-services office and value for the money invested in the recruiting effort. Recruiters gave IE its lowest scores for graduates' fit with the corporate culture, their previous work experience, and the likelihood of recruiting stars.

School Rankings

■ International ranking in the recruiter survey: 12 of 20 schools ranked

FALL 2004 INCOMING M.B.A. CLASS

	Total	Full-Time Only
Number of applicants	3,132	1,400
Number of offers extended	1,012	461
Number of students who accepted offer	852	416
Number of students who enrolled	795	383

GMAT score: 676 (mean); 680 (median)
Years of full-time work experience: 3.7 (mean); 4 (median)
Undergraduate GPA: N/A

Demographic Profile of Full-Time Students

Male: 64%
Female: 36%
Spanish citizens/residents: 26%
Foreign nationals: 74%

INSTITUTO DE EMPRESA

INSTITUTO DE EMPRESA ON INSTITUTO DE EMPRESA

(Data provided by Instituto de Empresa)

Business school website:
http://www.ie.edu
Business school e-mail:
admissions@ie.edu
Private institution
M.B.A. enrollment: 770
Full-time: 383
Part-time: 101
Executive program: 286

ADMISSIONS DIRECTOR:
Julian Trigo
Admissions Director
María de Molina 11-13-15
Madrid, Spain 28006
34-91-568-9610 (voice)
34-91-568-9710 (fax)
E-mail: admissions@ie.edu

APPLICATION DEADLINES:
Fall 2006: Rolling admissions
Annual tuition: $48,640
Annual room and board: $30,000

Class of 2004 Most Popular Academic Concentrations (% of Students)

Entrepreneurship 100%

Finance 45%

Information technology 35%

CLASS OF 2004 EMPLOYMENT DATA

Industries Hiring Full-Time Graduates (% Hired)

Computer/technology/Internet/dot-com: 6%

Consumer products and services: 7%

Energy and utilities: 4%

Media/entertainment: 8%

Financial services/investment banking: 19%

Government: 1%

Industrial products and services: 5%

Management consulting: 18%

Manufacturing: 3%

Nonprofit: 1%

Petroleum/energy: 2%

Pharmaceutical/biotechnology/health-care products and services: 3%

Telecommunications: 4%

Travel and transportation: 4%

Other professional services (accounting, advertising, etc.): 5%

Other: 10%

Position/Job Function (% Hired)

Consulting: 17%

Finance/accounting: 14%

General management: 17%

Human resources: 8%

Information technology/management information systems: 6%

THE RECRUITERS SPEAK

IE's most impressive features

"Integrity"

"Student ambition"

"Focus on entrepreneurship"

IE's major shortcomings

"Too Spanish"

"Years of relevant work experience vs. salary expectations"

"Less academic rigor"

How IE can increase its appeal

"Build their brand"

"Admit more students from Asia and other European countries"

"Increase contacts in the international corporate world"

Marketing/sales: 19%
Operations/production/logistics: 11%
Other: 8%

Top Recruiters

Telefónica
BBVA
Accenture
Pfizer
KPMG
Endesa
Ernest & Young
Bayer
Eli Lilly
Grupo Santander

Percentage of Job-Seeking Full-Time Graduates Who:	All Students	Citizens/Residents	Foreign Nationals
Received offers prior to or within 3 months of graduation	89%	83%	90%
Accepted offers prior to or within 3 months of graduation	85%	81%	86%

Overall Compensation	MEAN			MEDIAN		
	All Students	Citizens/ Residents	Foreign Nationals	All Students	Citizens/ Residents	Foreign Nationals
Annual base salary	$76,110	$65,800	$79,550	N/A	N/A	N/A
Signing bonus	$12,600	$9,300	$13,700	N/A	N/A	N/A
Other guaranteed compensation	N/A	N/A	N/A	N/A	N/A	N/A

Three of the Most Famous Graduates of M.B.A. Program

Pilar de Zulueta (class of 1987) Vice President and General Manager, Warner Brothers Consumer Products

Gerhard Gross Rojas (class of 1985) President and Managing Director, DaimlerChrysler, Mexico

Clodoaldo Valdecantos (class of 1984) President, Esso Espanola

IPADE

UNIVERSIDAD
PANAMERICANA

INSTITUTO PANAMERICANO DE ALTA DIRECCION DE EMPRESA—IPADE

Established in 1967 by a group of prominent businessmen who wanted to make Mexican management more professional, IPADE received early support and guidance from the IESE business school in Spain and Harvard Business School in the U.S. Since then, IPADE has expanded its links to many more business schools worldwide for management-education programs. With its main campus in Mexico City, IPADE has branched out and opened satellite facilities in Guadalajara and Monterrey.

The school, which offers a two-year M.B.A. program for recent college graduates and a two-year executive M.B.A. for more seasoned managers, teaches general-management skills through the analysis of business cases. IPADE faculty members generate many cases that focus on the Mexican business community, while the rest are derived from Harvard and other schools.

IPADE views management as "a people affair," emphasizing the human and ethical implications of any business decision. In addition to traditional areas like marketing and finance, IPADE's academic departments include the political and social environment of organizations, philosophy and business, business and family, and human behavior. The human behavior courses delve beyond traditional leadership and organization matters and focus on such issues as management of insecurity and human problems at work and at home. In the area of business and family, IPADE says it aims to "provide managers, as parents, a perspective that can enrich the upbringing of their children."

In the latest *Wall Street Journal/Harris* Interactive ranking, recruiters gave IPADE its highest ratings for students' strategic thinking and their personal ethics and integrity. IPADE received its lowest scores for students' past work experience and international knowledge and experience.

School Rankings

- Regional ranking in the recruiter survey: 5 of 47 schools ranked
- International ranking: 4 of 20 schools ranked
- Financial-services-industry ranking: 8th place

Special Recognition

- Good source for recruiting graduates with high ethical standards: 7th most nominated school, 70 nominations.

FALL 2004 INCOMING M.B.A. CLASS

	Total	Full-Time Only
Number of applicants	1,461	652
Number of offers extended	387	110
Number of students who accepted offer	268	74
Number of students who enrolled	232	70

GMAT score: 615 (mean); 610 (median)
Years of full-time work experience: 3 (mean); 2.5 (median)
Undergraduate GPA: N/A

Demographic Profile of Full-Time Students

Male: 79%
Female: 21%
Mexican citizens/residents: 92%
Foreign nationals: 8%

IPADE ON IPADE

(Data provided by the Instituto Panamericano de Alta Dirección de Empresa—IPADE)

Business school website:
http://www.ipade.com.mx
Business school e-mail: N/A
Private institution
M.B.A. enrollment: 507
Full-time: 137
Executive program: 370

ADMISSIONS DIRECTOR:
Oscar Carbonell
Admissions Director
Floresta 20
Col. Claveria
Mexico City
Mexico 02080
55-5354-1800 (voice)
55-5354-1852 (fax)
E-mail: ocarbonell@ipade.mx

APPLICATION DEADLINE:
Fall 2006: June 2006
Annual tuition: $16,000
Annual room and board: $9,250

Class of 2004 Most Popular Academic Concentrations

N/A

CLASS OF 2004 EMPLOYMENT DATA

Industries Hiring Full-Time Graduates (% Hired)

Computer/technology/Internet/dot-com: 3%
Consumer products and services: 14%
Financial services/investment banking: 16%
Industrial products and services: 30%
Management consulting: 6%
Manufacturing: 6%
Media/entertainment: 5%
Pharmaceutical/biotechnology/health-care products and services: 11%
Travel and transportation: 1%
Other: 8%

Position/Job Function (% Hired)

Consulting: 7%
Finance/accounting: 28%
General management: 18%
Human resources: 2%
Information technology/management information systems: 2%
Marketing/sales: 30%
Operations/production/logistics: 9%
Other: 4%

THE RECRUITERS SPEAK

IPADE's most impressive features

"Ethics and personal development"

"Mexican business knowledge"

"Entrepreneurship"

IPADE's major shortcomings

"Communications and interview skills"

"Lack of work experience"

"Creativity"

How IPADE can increase its appeal

"Increase students' technical skills"

"More international students"

"Demand more from students, make them more competitive"

Top Recruiters *(Number of Full-Time Class of 2004 Graduates Hired)*

HSBC: 6
Mattel: 3
Homex: 3
Novartis: 2
Janssen Cilag: 2
Banamex: 2
Mexxsub: 2
G. Acción: 2
Zermat: 2
Nestlé: 1

Percentage of Job-Seeking Full-Time Graduates Who:	All Students	Citizens/Residents	Foreign Nationals
Received offers prior to or within 3 months of graduation	93%	92%	100%
Accepted offers prior to or within 3 months of graduation	90%	89%	100%

Overall Compensation	MEAN			MEDIAN		
	All Students	Citizens/Residents	Foreign Nationals	All Students	Citizens/Residents	Foreign Nationals
Annual base salary	$42,968	$43,347	$35,668	$41,419	$42,727	$35,966
Signing bonus	$1,087	$1,176	N/A	N/A	N/A	N/A
Other guaranteed compensation	$933	$844	$2,007	N/A	N/A	$1,672

Three of the Most Famous Graduates of M.B.A. Program

Ronald Gurdián (class of 1979) Costa Rican Ambassador to Mexico

Federico Toussaint (class of 1979) Director General, Grupo Lamosa

Jorge A. Lozano (class of 1979) General Director, Prolec-GE

UNIVERSITY OF IOWA
(TIPPIE SCHOOL OF MANAGEMENT)

The University of Iowa's full-time M.B.A. students begin with the core curriculum of basic management skills and can later specialize in accounting, entrepreneurship, finance, marketing, management-information systems, operations management, or strategic management and consulting. They also can design their own concentrations.

In addition, Iowa offers a part-time evening M.B.A. and an executive M.B.A. at various locations in the state. Iowa also has teamed up with Iowa State University to create an executive engineer program that awards both an executive M.B.A. and a master's in engineering. There are combined M.B.A. degree programs at Iowa in nursing, hospital administration, medicine, law, and library science as well.

The Tippie School enjoys a global presence through its international executive-M.B.A. programs in Shanghai and Hong Kong, and an M.B.A. venture with Purdue University in Beijing that focuses on agribusiness and the food market.

The University of Iowa has become well-known for its Iowa Electronic Markets, in which students can invest real money ($5 to $500) and trade in a variety of futures contracts. Faculty members at the business school operate the futures market as a teaching and research tool, but some of the contracts have entertainment as well as educational value. Contract payoffs have been determined by the outcome of presidential elections and by the box-office receipts for such movies as *Harry Potter and the Sorcerer's Stone.*

In *The Wall Street Journal*/Harris Interactive survey, recruiters gave Iowa graduates high marks for their willingness to relocate, ability to work well in teams, and fit with the corporate culture. The school was also rated a good value for the money invested in the recruiting effort. Iowa received its lowest ratings for students' international knowledge and experience, prior work experience, and awareness of corporate citizenship issues.

School Rankings

■ Regional ranking in the recruiter survey: 16 of 47 schools ranked

FALL 2004 INCOMING M.B.A. CLASS

	Total	Full-Time Only
Number of applicants	571	273
Number of offers extended	396	128
Number of students who accepted offer	297	62
Number of students who enrolled	295	62

GMAT score: 645 (mean); 640 (median)
Years of full-time work experience: 4 (mean); 3.5 (median)
Undergraduate GPA: 3.36 (mean); 3.32 (median)

Demographic Profile of Full-Time Students

Male: 72%
Female: 28%
Minorities: 10%
U.S. citizens/residents: 61%
Foreign nationals: 39%

IOWA ON IOWA

(Data provided by the Henry B. Tippie School of Management at the University of Iowa)

Business school website: http://www.biz.uiowa.edu
Business school e-mail: tippiemba@uiowa.edu
Public institution
M.B.A. enrollment: 1,017
Full-time: 150
Part-time: 746
Executive program: 121

ADMISSIONS DIRECTOR:
Mary Spreen
Director, Full-Time M.B.A. Admissions and Financial Aid
108 John Pappajohn Business Building, Suite C140
University of Iowa
Iowa City, IA 52242
319-335-1039 (voice)
319-335-3604 (fax)
E-mail: mary-spreen@uiowa.edu

APPLICATION DEADLINES:
Fall 2006: 4/15/2006 (international), 7/15/2006 (U.S.)
Annual tuition: $11,970 (in-state); $21,960 (out-of-state)
Annual room and board: $10,000

Class of 2004 Most Popular Academic Concentrations (% of Students)

Finance 53%
Marketing 29%
Strategy 6%

CLASS OF 2004 EMPLOYMENT DATA

Industries Hiring Full-Time Graduates (% Hired)

Computer/technology/Internet/dot-com: 6%
Consumer products and services: 23%
Financial services/investment banking: 29%
Management consulting: 3%
Manufacturing: 3%
Media/entertainment: 3%
Pharmaceutical/biotechnology/health-care products and services: 9%
Travel and transportation: 12%
Other: 12%

Position/Job Function (% Hired)

Consulting: 3%
Finance/accounting: 34%
General management: 16%
Human resources: 3%
Marketing/sales: 31%
Operations/production/logistics: 13%

Top Recruiters (Number of Full-Time Class of 2004 Graduates Hired)

Aegon USA: 4
Allsteel: 2

THE RECRUITERS SPEAK

Iowa's most impressive features

"Professionalism of students and career services"

"Hungry, hard-working"

"MBAs are quick studies and good team players"

Iowa's major shortcomings

"Conservative"

"Too much academia, not enough practical experience"

"Domestic students lack international exposure"

How Iowa can increase its appeal

"Practice interviewing and communication skills"

"Establish realistic first-job expectations"

"More geographic representation in student body"

AC Nielsen: 2
General Electric: 1
John Deere Credit: 1
Johnson & Johnson: 1
Meredith: 1
Olsen Engineering: 1
Pearson Education: 1
Procter & Gamble: 1

Percentage of Job-Seeking Full-Time Graduates Who:	All Students	Citizens/Residents	Foreign Nationals
Received offers prior to or within 3 months of graduation	96%	96%	94%
Accepted offers prior to or within 3 months of graduation	91%	89%	94%

	MEAN			MEDIAN		
Overall Compensation	All Students	Citizens/ Residents	Foreign Nationals	All Students	Citizens/ Residents	Foreign Nationals
Annual base salary	$71,416	$70,721	$73,360	$72,020	$70,510	$72,800
Signing bonus	$14,082	$11,863	$20,000	$11,000	$9,250	$20,000
Other guaranteed compensation	$8,277	$2,820	$13,733	$3,830	$3,000	$6,000

Three of the Most Famous Graduates of M.B.A. Program

Dr. Michael D. Maves (class of 1988) CEO, American Medical Association

Kerry K. Killinger (class of 1971) Chairman, President and CEO, Washington Mutual Savings Bank

Kathleen A. Dore (class of 1984) President, TV & Radio CanWest Mediaworks

London Business School

UNIVERSITY OF LONDON (LONDON BUSINESS SCHOOL)

Founded in 1965, London Business School offers one of the leading M.B.A. programs in Europe and attracts a very international faculty and student body, with 85% of its full-time graduates from outside the U.K. and its professors representing 23 countries. More than two-thirds of its graduates typically take jobs in financial services and management consulting.

Students can choose academic concentrations in finance, marketing, entrepreneurial management, technology management, strategy, or international business. About one-third of second-year students spend a term abroad at one of more than 30 business school partners.

As part of the leadership focus, London Business School assigns students to a "shadowing project" that requires them to observe a manager on the job for up to five days and then submit a report on their observations. More than a third of the managers shadowed have been from outside the U.K., and about 15% have been CEOs. Many managers say they believe they learn as much or more than the students from the exercise.

The full-time program culminates with the second-year project. Working in small teams on a paid consulting basis, students negotiate the terms and timetable of the project with clients such as IBM and Nike.

Most students seek an internship during the summer between the program's first and second years. But London Business

School offers another option: Entrepreneurship Summer School. It is designed for students who have business ideas they want to pursue immediately or who simply want to sharpen their entrepreneurial skills for the future.

Some full-time students choose to accelerate the program, finishing in as little as 15 months. Course waivers are granted to students already highly competent in economics or accounting.

In addition to the full-time M.B.A., London Business School offers two executive-M.B.A. programs, one a partnership with Columbia Business School in New York. The 20-month trans-Atlantic M.B.A. emphasizes teamwork, as students alternate their studies between the two schools.

In the latest *Wall Street Journal*/Harris Interactive survey, recruiters gave the school its highest ratings for students' analytical and problem-solving abilities, international knowledge and experience, and communication and interpersonal skills. The school received its lowest scores for the career-services office, value for the money invested in the recruiting effort, and students' awareness of corporate citizenship issues.

School Rankings

- International ranking in the recruiter survey: 5 of 20 schools ranked
- Ranking by financial-services-industry recruiters: 5th place
- Ranking by management-consulting-industry recruiters: 10th place

Recognition for Excellence in Academic Concentrations

- With 103 nominations, London Business School ranked No. 6 among business schools that recruiters in *The Wall Street Journal*/Harris Interactive survey cited for excellence in international business.
- With 103 nominations, London Business School ranked No. 7 for excellence in finance.

LONDON BUSINESS SCHOOL ON LONDON BUSINESS SCHOOL

(Data provided by London Business School)

Business school website:
http://www.london.edu
Business school e-mail:
mbainfo@london.edu
Public institution
M.B.A. enrollment: 905
Full-time: 607
Executive program: 298

ADMISSIONS DIRECTOR:
David Simpson
Senior Manager, Marketing and Admissions
London Business School
Regent's Park
London, UK NW1 4SA
44-20-7706-6774 (voice)
44-20-7724-7875 (fax)
E-mail: dsimpson@london.edu

APPLICATION DEADLINES:
Fall 2006: October 2005, January 2006, February 2006, April 2006
Annual tuition: $38,000
Annual room and board:
$18,000–$36,000

FALL 2004 INCOMING M.B.A. CLASS

	Full-Time Only
Number of applicants	1,467
Number of offers extended	N/A
Number of students who accepted offer	N/A
Number of students who enrolled	304

GMAT score: 680 (mean); 680 (median)
Years of full-time work experience: 5.5 (mean); 5.5 (median)
Undergraduate GPA: N/A

Demographic Profile of Full-Time Students

Male: 77%
Female: 23%
British citizens/residents: 14%
Foreign nationals: 86%

Class of 2004 Most Popular Academic Concentrations (% of Students)

Finance 24%
Marketing 5%
Entrepreneurial management 4%

CLASS OF 2004 EMPLOYMENT DATA

Industries Hiring Full-Time Graduates (% Hired)

Financial services/investment banking: 38%
Management consulting: 30%
Other: 32%

THE RECRUITERS SPEAK

London Business School's most impressive features

"World-class faculty"

"International focus"

"Financially savvy"

London Business School's major shortcomings

"Too focused on banking"

"Lack of concern about business ethics and corporate social responsibility"

"Too ambitious"

How London Business School can increase its appeal

"More emphasis on general management"

"Treat recruiting companies from outside the U.K. well"

"Strengthen entrepreneurship and leadership programs"

Position/Job Function

N/A

Top Recruiters *(Number of Full-Time Class of 2004 Graduates Hired)*

Barclays Capital: 10
McKinsey: 10
Deloitte Consulting: 9
CSFB: 8
Boston Consulting Group: 8
Booz Allen Hamilton: 5
Lehman Brothers: 5
Roland Berger Strategy Consultants: 5
American Express: 4
CHEP: 4

Percentage of Job-Seeking Full-Time Graduates Who:	All Students	Citizens/Residents	Foreign Nationals
Received offers prior to or within 3 months of graduation	85%	85%	85%
Accepted offers prior to or within 3 months of graduation	85%	85%	85%

	MEAN			MEDIAN		
Overall Compensation	All Students	Citizens/ Residents	Foreign Nationals	All Students	Citizens/ Residents	Foreign Nationals
Annual base salary	$101,831	N/A	N/A	N/A	N/A	N/A
Signing bonus	$23,765	N/A	N/A	N/A	N/A	N/A
Other guaranteed compensation	$27,410	N/A	N/A	N/A	N/A	N/A

Three of the Most Famous Graduates of M.B.A. Program

Tony Wheeler (class of 1972) Managing Director, Lonely Planet Publications

Nigel Morris (class of 1985) President, Ffestiniog

Kumar Birla (class of 1992) Chairman, Aditya Birla Group

ROBERT H. SMITH
SCHOOL OF BUSINESS

Leaders for the Digital Economy

UNIVERSITY OF MARYLAND (SMITH SCHOOL OF BUSINESS)

The University of Maryland's business school embraced the Internet in the late 1990s, offering some 50 courses related to e-business. Today, it talks more broadly about information technology and the digital economy and has adopted the slogan: Leaders for the Digital Economy. To produce such leaders, the school has designed its core courses to explore how information technology and the Internet are changing business practices and creating new markets and careers.

Maryland also offers academic concentrations in information systems, management of technology, e-service and electronic commerce and conducts research at its Center for Electronic Markets and Enterprises and its Netcentricity Laboratory.

Like many business schools in this post-Enron era, Maryland is emphasizing ethics more than ever in its courses. But Maryland goes an extra step, taking students on an expedition to a federal prison to speak with executives-turned-inmates about their ethical lapses.

In recent years, the Smith School has expanded both regionally and internationally. It has taken its part-time M.B.A. program—both evening and weekend—to Washington, D.C., to tap a large pool of potential applicants. In 2004, it awarded 67 degrees to its first executive-M.B.A. class in Beijing through a joint program with China's University of International Business and Economics. And, most recently, it created an executive-M.B.A. program in conjunction with the Graduate School of Business Administration Zurich.

Maryland dropped 11 spots to No. 15 in the latest *Wall Street Journal*/Harris Interactive Regional ranking. It received relatively low ratings for overall perception and for recruiters' intentions to return to the school over the next few years. On specific attributes, recruiters gave the lowest ratings for students' international knowledge and experience and the career-services office. They also complained about students' lack of experience and weak communication skills. Recruiters gave the school its highest ratings for students' personal ethics and integrity, success with past hires, and value for the money invested in the recruiting effort.

School Rankings

- Regional ranking in the recruiter survey: 15 of 47 schools ranked
- Ranking by technology-industry recruiters: 5th place

Recognition for Excellence in an Academic Concentration

- With 55 nominations, Maryland ranked No. 7 among business schools that recruiters in *The Wall Street Journal*/Harris Interactive survey cited for excellence in information technology.

FALL 2004 INCOMING M.B.A. CLASS

	Total	Full-Time Only
Number of applicants	1,369	851
Number of offers extended	708	302
Number of students who accepted offer	537	183
Number of students who enrolled	481	151

GMAT score: 651 (mean); 650 (median)
Years of full-time work experience: 5.25 (mean); 4 (median)
Undergraduate GPA: 3.3 (mean); 3.4 (median)

MARYLAND ON MARYLAND

(Data provided by the Robert H. Smith School of Business at the University of Maryland)

Business school website:
http://www.rhsmith.umd.edu
Business school e-mail:
mba_info@rhsmith.umd.edu
Public institution
M.B.A. enrollment: 1,441
Full-time: 317
Part-time: 1,019
Executive program: 105

ADMISSIONS DIRECTOR:
Sabrina White
Director of M.B.A. and M.S. Admissions
Smith School of Business
2308 Van Munching Hall
University of Maryland
College Park, MD 20742
301-405-2559 (voice)
301-314-9862 (fax)
E-mail: swhite@rhsmith.umd.edu

APPLICATION DEADLINES:
Fall 2006: 5/1/2006
Annual tuition: $14,454 (in-state); $23,814 (out-of-state)
Annual room and board: $11,500

Demographic Profile of Full-Time Students

Male: 66%
Female: 34%
Minorities: 19%
U.S. citizens/residents: 61%
Foreign nationals: 39%

Class of 2004 Most Popular Academic Concentrations

N/A

CLASS OF 2004 EMPLOYMENT DATA

Industries Hiring Full-Time Graduates (% Hired)

Financial services/investment banking: 31.5%
Government: 1%
Management consulting: 16.1%
Manufacturing: 23.4%
Nonprofit: 2.4%
Other professional services (accounting, advertising, etc.): 25.8%

Position/Job Function (% Hired)

Consulting: 16.1%
Finance/accounting: 43.5%
General management: 9.7%
Human resources: 1%
Information technology/management information systems: 7.3%
Marketing/sales: 19.4%
Operations/production/logistics: 2.4%

THE RECRUITERS SPEAK

Maryland's most impressive features

"Motivated, creative thinkers"

"Analytical and information-technology skills"

"Entrepreneurial spirit"

Maryland's major shortcomings

"Students' communication and presentation skills"

"Career-services center"

"Lack of rigor"

How Maryland can increase its appeal

"Focus on finance acumen"

"Develop greater leadership skills"

"Train students for the interviewing process"

Top Recruiters *(Number of Full-Time Class of 2004 Graduates Hired)*

Avaya: 5
PricewaterhouseCoopers: 4
Constellation Power Source: 4
Intel: 4
General Electric: 2
UBS: 2
Deloitte: 2
Delta: 2
Johnson & Johnson: 2
IBM: 2

Percentage of Job-Seeking Full-Time Graduates Who:	All Students	Citizens/Residents	Foreign Nationals
Received offers prior to or within 3 months of graduation	91%	90%	95%
Accepted offers prior to or within 3 months of graduation	89%	89%	89%

Overall Compensation	MEAN			MEDIAN		
	All Students	Citizens/ Residents	Foreign Nationals	All Students	Citizens/ Residents	Foreign Nationals
Annual base salary	$75,090	$75,658	$73,348	$75,000	$75,000	$75,000
Signing bonus	$11,261	$11,689	$9,643	$10,000	$10,000	$10,000
Other guaranteed compensation	$12,811	$13,493	$7,325	$10,000	$10,000	$7,000

Three of the Most Famous Graduates of M.B.A. Program

Carly Fiorina (class of 1980) Former CEO, Hewlett-Packard

Paul Norris (class of 1971) Chairman and CEO, W. R. Grace

Paul Mullan (class of 1970) Strategic Partner, Charterhouse Group

MASSACHUSETTS INSTITUTE OF TECHNOLOGY (SLOAN SCHOOL OF MANAGEMENT)

Mens et manus. **Latin for "mind and hand,"** the motto for the Massachusetts Institute of Technology is also the guiding philosophy for its Sloan School of Management, which aims to attract "visionary pragmatists" and "hands-on thinkers." From its beginnings, the school has emphasized the importance of linking academic research with management practice.

In 2002, the Sloan School celebrated its 50th anniversary, but M.I.T.'s role in management education dates back much further—to the development of an engineering administration curriculum in 1914. A master's degree in management and the world's first university-based executive-education program soon followed. Then, in 1952, an M.I.T. Sloan Foundation grant established the School of Industrial Management to help strengthen the connection between science and industry and educate "the ideal manager."

Sloan still attracts engineers, but its scope has broadened considerably. The majority of graduates aim for the two most popular M.B.A. fields—financial services and management consulting—but Sloan boasts that its alumni also have founded more than 650 companies.

M.I.T. recently redesigned its M.B.A. program, breaking the traditional 13-week semester into two six-week sections of classes with an "innovation week" in the middle. Courses cease during that week, and students participate in seminars, workshops, and other activities.

The Sloan School tries to keep its curriculum in tune with the latest business issues. For example, it put a student-proposed course on outsourcing on the fast track in 2004. Prof. Amar Gupta said such a course is important for M.B.A.s who will not only have to deal with outsourcing as managers, but also could potentially be outsourced themselves.

In addition to the traditional M.B.A., Sloan also offers joint and dual degrees through M.I.T. and nearby Harvard University in such fields as biomedicine, government, manufacturing, and system design. There's also the M.I.T. Sloan Fellows Program, in which midcareer managers can earn an M.B.A. or a master's of science degree in either management or management of technology over one or two years.

In *The Wall Street Journal*/Harris Interactive ranking, recruiters rated M.I.T. highest for faculty expertise, students' analytical and problem-solving skills, and their strategic thinking. M.I.T. received its lowest ratings for the career-services office, value for the money invested in the recruiting effort, and students' awareness of corporate citizenship issues.

School Rankings

- National ranking in the recruiter survey: 12 of 19 schools ranked
- International ranking: 8 of 20 schools ranked
- Ranking by management-consulting-industry recruiters: 3rd place
- Ranking by financial-services-industry recruiters: 3rd place
- Ranking by technology-industry recruiters: 9th place
- Ranking by energy- and industrial-products-industry recruiters: 10th place

Recognition for Excellence in Academic Concentrations

- With 637 nominations, M.I.T. ranked No. 1 among business schools that recruiters in *The Wall Street Journal*/Harris Interactive survey cited for excellence in information technology.
- With 324 nominations, M.I.T. ranked No. 1 for excellence in operations management.

M.I.T. ON M.I.T.

(Data provided by the Sloan School of Management at the Massachusetts Institute of Technology)

Business school website:
http://mitsloan.mit.edu
Business school e-mail:
mbaadmissions@sloan.mit.edu
Private institution
M.B.A. enrollment: 776
Full-time: 776

ADMISSIONS DIRECTOR:
Rod Garcia
Director of Admissions
50 Memorial Drive
E52-101
Cambridge, MA 02142
617-258-5434 (voice)
617-253-6405 (fax)
E-mail: rgarcia@mit.edu

APPLICATION DEADLINES:
Fall 2006: October 2005, January 2006
Annual tuition: $36,850
Annual room and board: $25,000

- With 105 nominations, M.I.T. ranked No. 5 for excellence in entrepreneurship.
- With 82 nominations, M.I.T. ranked No. 9 for excellence in finance.

FALL 2004 INCOMING M.B.A. CLASS

	Full-Time Only
Number of applicants	2,730
Number of offers extended	568
Number of students who accepted offer	374
Number of students who enrolled	374

GMAT score: 697 (mean); 700 (median)
Years of full-time work experience: 5.4 (mean); 5 (median)
Undergraduate GPA: 3.4 (mean); 3.4 (median)

Demographic Profile of Full-Time Students

Male: 70%
Female: 30%
Minorities: 8%
U.S. citizens/residents: 68%
Foreign nationals: 32%

Class of 2004 Most Popular Academic Concentrations (% of Students)

Financial management 24%
New-product and venture development 8%
Strategic management and consulting 5%

THE RECRUITERS SPEAK

M.I.T.'s most impressive features

"Analytical horsepower"

"High technology capability"

"Super smart and entrepreneurial"

M.I.T.'s major shortcomings

"Some students lack a mature, polished persona"

"Technology overwhelms their business sense"

"A little ivory tower sometimes and East Coast-centric"

How M.I.T. can increase its appeal

"Recruit and develop more well-rounded talent"

"Work with recruiters to get a better sense of our needs"

"Temper salary prospects of students"

CLASS OF 2004 EMPLOYMENT DATA

Industries Hiring Full-Time Graduates (% Hired)

Computer/technology/Internet/dot-com: 16.8%
Consumer products and services: 1.9%
Financial services/investment banking: 23.3%
Management consulting: 30.3%
Media/entertainment: 3.1%
Nonprofit: 1%
Petroleum/energy: 1.8%
Pharmaceutical/biotechnology/health-care products and services:
4.6%
Real estate: 1.5%
Telecommunications: 1.9%
Travel and transportation: 8.4%
Other professional services (accounting, advertising, etc.): 1.8%
Other: 3%

Position/Job Function (% Hired)

Consulting: 35%
Finance/accounting: 23.6%
General management: 10.6%
Information technology/management information systems: 1%
Marketing/sales: 9.5%
Operations/production/logistics: 11%
Other: 8.7%

Top Recruiters (Number of Full-Time Class of 2004 Graduates Hired)

McKinsey: 26
Boston Consulting Group: 11
Bain: 10
IBM: 8
Citigroup: 6
Raytheon: 5
Intel: 4
Monitor Group: 4
Thompson Corp.: 4
Morgan Stanley: 3

Percentage of Job-Seeking Full-Time Graduates Who:	All Students	Citizens/Residents	All Foreign Nationals
Received offers prior to or within 3 months of graduation	96%	N/A	N/A
Accepted offers prior to or within 3 months of graduation	91%	N/A	N/A

	MEAN			MEDIAN		
Overall Compensation	All Students	Citizens/ Residents	Foreign Nationals	All Students	Citizens/ Residents	Foreign Nationals
Annual base salary	$94,131	N/A	N/A	$95,000	N/A	N/A
Signing bonus	$14,451	N/A	N/A	$10,000	N/A	N/A
Other guaranteed compensation	$24,261	N/A	N/A	$15,000	N/A	N/A

Three of the Most Famous Graduates of M.B.A. Program

Richard Carrion (class of 1977) President and CEO, Banco Popular

John S. Reed (class of 1965) Former Chairman, New York Stock Exchange

Bradley Peterson (class of 1989) Chief Information Officer, eBay

UNIVERSITY OF MIAMI

The University of Miami established its business school in 1929 and first offered the M.B.A. degree in 1948. Today, its full-time program includes more than 250 students who attend small classes of 30 to 35 and major in such subjects as computer information systems, international business, marketing, finance, accounting, and management science.

Beyond those areas of specialization, Dean Paul Sugrue says, the business school aims to produce "creative thinkers with strong communication and negotiation skills." The business school also promotes the diversity of cultures and international business climate at the university and throughout the Miami area.

The school has developed a part-time M.B.A. program for executives and professionals, which is offered at the Miami campus and at several satellite locations, including Orlando, Tampa, and Delray Beach. There's even an outpost in the Bahamas.

More specialized programs include part-time and executive M.B.A.s designed for health-care professionals and students interested in international business, as well as a joint M.B.A. and master's in industrial engineering and an M.B.A. and law-degree combination.

More than a third of Miami's M.B.A. graduates pursue careers in finance and accounting, with the rest spread across a variety of job functions and industries.

MIAMI ON MIAMI

(Data provided by the School of Business Administration at the University of Miami)

Business school website: http://www.bus.miami.edu/grad
Business school e-mail: mba@miami.edu
Private institution
M.B.A. enrollment: 810
Full-time: 266
Part-time: 36
Executive program: 508

ADMISSIONS DIRECTOR:
Ania Nozewnik Green
Assistant Dean, Graduate
Business Programs
P.O. Box 248505
Coral Gables, FL 33133
305-284-4607 (voice)
305-284-1878 (fax)
E-mail: mba@miami.edu

APPLICATION DEADLINES:
Fall 2006: 7/15/2006
Annual tuition: $28,992
Annual room and board: $11,826

In *The Wall Street Journal/Harris* Interactive survey, recruiters graded Miami highest for its career-services office, students' ability to work well in teams, and their communication and interpersonal skills. The school received its lowest ratings for students' prior work experience, their willingness to relocate for a job, and their awareness of corporate citizenship issues.

School Rankings

■ Regional ranking in the recruiter survey: 10 of 47 schools ranked

FALL 2004 INCOMING M.B.A. CLASS

	Full-Time Only
Number of applicants	494
Number of offers extended	323
Number of students who accepted offer	137
Number of students who enrolled	123

GMAT score: 605 (mean); 590 (median)
Years of full-time work experience: 3 (mean); 3 (median)
Undergraduate GPA: 3.2 (mean); 3.1 (median)

Demographic Profile of Full-Time Students

Male: 73%
Female: 27%
Minorities: 26%
U.S. citizens/residents: 74%
Foreign nationals: 26%

THE RECRUITERS SPEAK

Miami's most impressive features

"Diverse backgrounds of students"

"International perspective and training"

"Eager students hungry for the job"

Miami's major shortcomings

"Many students do not have English as a first language"

"Not recognized nationally"

"Unrealistic salary expectations"

How Miami can increase its appeal

"Identify students who will relocate for recruiters"

"Increase entry standards"

"Encourage students to gain work experience"

Class of 2004 Most Popular Academic Concentrations *(% of Students)*

Finance 59%
Marketing 28%
International business 23%

CLASS OF 2004 EMPLOYMENT DATA

Industries Hiring Full-Time Graduates *(% Hired)*

Computer/technology/Internet/dot-com: 6%
Consumer products and services: 9%
Financial services/investment banking: 14%
Government: 5%
Industrial products and services: 5%
Management consulting: 7%
Manufacturing: 4%
Media/entertainment: 5%
Nonprofit: 7%
Petroleum/energy: 1%
Pharmaceutical/biotechnology/health-care products and services: 2%
Real estate: 7%
Telecommunications: 1%
Travel and transportation: 6%
Other professional services (accounting, advertising, etc.): 8%
Other: 13%

Position/Job Function *(% Hired)*

Consulting: 8%
Finance/accounting: 35%
General management: 7%
Human resources: 1%
Information technology/management information systems: 7%
Marketing/sales: 18%
Operations/production/logistics: 8%
Other: 16%

Top Recruiters *(Number of Full-Time Class of 2004 Graduates Hired)*

PricewaterhouseCoopers: 3
AOL Latin America: 2
Citigroup: 2
Ernst & Young: 2
IBM: 2

Royal Caribbean International: 2
Walt Disney: 2
Bacardi: 1
Accenture: 1
FedEx: 1

Percentage of Job-Seeking Full-Time Graduates Who:	All Students	Citizens/Residents	Foreign Nationals
Received offers prior to or within 3 months of graduation	81%	79%	90%
Accepted offers prior to or within 3 months of graduation	81%	79%	90%

	MEAN			MEDIAN		
Overall Compensation	All Students	Citizens/ Residents	Foreign Nationals	All Students	Citizens/ Residents	Foreign Nationals
Annual base salary	$61,902	$61,909	$61,857	$55,000	$55,000	$60,000
Signing bonus	$7,650	$2,643	$19,333	$3,000	$2,500	$15,000
Other guaranteed compensation	N/A	N/A	N/A	N/A	N/A	N/A

Three of the Most Famous Graduates of M.B.A. Program

Jack Creighton (class of 1966) Retired CEO, Weyerhaeuser and United Airlines

Martin Zweig (class of 1967) Chairman and President, Zweig Consulting

Betty Amos (class of 1976) President and Owner, Abkey Cos.

UNIVERSITY OF MICHIGAN (ROSS SCHOOL OF BUSINESS)

MICHIGAN ☒
ROSS SCHOOL OF BUSINESS

Michigan's marketing slogan—"leading in thought and action"—sums up well what sets it apart from other top-ranked schools. More than most schools, Michigan emphasizes the value of real-world experiences and tries to connect theory with practice. For example, all first-year students participate in teams on some 80 "multidisciplinary action projects," which may involve a corporate assignment, an entrepreneurial venture, an international opportunity, or something more experimental. They might work with Northwest Airlines, the Detroit public-school system, or the Landmine Survivors Network in Bosnia. Some students also manage the $3 million Wolverine Venture Fund, while others apply for "dare to dream" grants to refine their own new-business concepts.

Another distinctive feature is the Ross School's focus on corporate citizenship. The Aspen Institute and World Resources Institute cited Michigan as one of six business schools "on the cutting edge" of incorporating social and environmental responsibility into their M.B.A. programs.

Michigan also enjoys a reputation with recruiters for producing outstanding minority M.B.A. graduates and has been at the forefront of business schools in trying to attract more women to M.B.A. programs. It was a driving force behind the formation of the Forte Foundation, a group of corporations and business schools that aims to increase the number of women business leaders and boost women's awareness of the merits of a business degree.

MICHIGAN ON MICHIGAN

(Data provided by the Stephen M. Ross School of Business at the University of Michigan)

Business school website: http://www.bus.umich.edu
Business school e-mail: rossmba@umich.edu
Public institution
M.B.A. enrollment: 1,873
Full-time: 841
Part-time: 914
Executive program: 118

ADMISSIONS DIRECTOR:
James P. Hayes
Director of Admissions and Financial Aid
701 Tappan, Room D2260
Ann Arbor, MI 48109
734-936-4830 (voice)
734-647-5348 (fax)
E-mail: jphayes@umich.edu

APPLICATION DEADLINES:
Fall 2006: November 2005, January 2006, March 2006
Annual tuition: $33,076 (in-state); $38,326 (out-of-state)
Annual room and board: $9,752

Michigan's business school adopted the name of New York real-estate developer Stephen M. Ross in 2004 in recognition of his pledge to donate $100 million to his alma mater. The money will help fund a $145 million facilities expansion plan that will provide plenty of group study rooms and other space for the school's many team projects.

In addition to the full-time M.B.A., Michigan offers an evening program in both Ann Arbor and Dearborn and an executive-M.B.A. degree that's a combination of classroom and online learning. The M.B.A. program also teams up with such schools and departments as education, engineering, medicine, music, Asian studies, and natural resources and environment for dual degrees or other joint ventures.

Among Michigan's academic strengths are marketing and operations management. But some recruiters consider Michigan too closely focused on manufacturing operations and the state's automotive industry. Ross School officials, however, contend that's an outdated perception and note Michigan's growing recognition in such fields as organizational behavior and international business.

Michigan lost its first-place spot in the latest *Wall Street Journal*/Harris Interactive National ranking, dropping to second place behind Dartmouth College. Recruiters rated Michigan's M.B.A. graduates strongest on analytical and problem-solving abilities, communication and interpersonal skills, leadership potential, and personal ethics and integrity. The school re-

THE RECRUITERS SPEAK

Michigan's most impressive features

"Midwestern attitude with bicoastal credibility"

"Related experience and interest in the auto industry"

"Leadership potential, team players"

Michigan's major shortcomings

"Overrepresentation of engineering backgrounds"

"Lack of global view"

"Sometimes too humble"

How Michigan can increase its appeal

"Target Wall Street with greater fervor"

"Don't take recruiters for granted"

"Improve their facilities"

ceived its lowest scores for students' international knowledge and experience and the faculty's expertise.

School Rankings

- National ranking in the recruiter survey: 2 of 19 schools ranked
- Ranking by energy- and industrial-products-industry recruiters: 4th place
- Ranking by health-care industry recruiters: 5th place
- Ranking by consumer-products-industry recruiters: 7th place

Recognition for Excellence in Academic Concentrations

- With 123 nominations, Michigan ranked No. 2 among business schools that recruiters in *The Wall Street Journal*/Harris Interactive survey cited for excellence in marketing.
- With 129 nominations, Michigan ranked No. 4 for excellence in operations management.
- With 98 nominations, Michigan ranked No. 7 for excellence in strategy.
- With 62 nominations, Michigan ranked No. 8 for excellence in accounting.

Special Recognition

- Good source for recruiting minorities: the most nominated school, 113 nominations.
- Good source for recruiting women: 4th most nominated school, 67 nominations.
- Good source for recruiting graduates with high ethical standards: 10th most nominated school, 51 nominations.

FALL 2004 INCOMING M.B.A. CLASS

	Total	Full-Time Only
Number of applicants	2,223	2,039
Number of offers extended	867	725
Number of students who accepted offer	621	483
Number of students who enrolled	567	434

GMAT score: 690 (mean); 690 (median)
Years of full-time work experience: 5.8 (mean); 6 (median)
Undergraduate GPA: 3.3 (mean); 3.3 (median)

Demographic Profile of Full-time Students

Male: 73%
Female: 27%
Minorities: 26%
U.S. citizens/residents: 69%
Foreign nationals: 31%

Class of 2004 Most Popular Academic Concentrations (% of Students)

Marketing 30%
Finance 30%
Corporate strategy 5%

CLASS OF 2004 EMPLOYMENT DATA

Industries Hiring Full-Time Graduates (% Hired)

Computer/technology/Internet/dot-com: 14%
Consumer products and services: 9%
Financial services/investment banking: 22%
Management consulting: 17%
Manufacturing: 6%
Petroleum/energy: 5%
Pharmaceutical/biotechnology/health-care products and services: 10%
Real estate: 1%
Travel and transportation: 2%
Other professional services (accounting, advertising, etc.): 4%
Other: 10%

Position/Job Function (% Hired)

Consulting: 21%
Finance/accounting: 30%
General management: 4%
Human resources: 1%
Marketing/sales: 30%
Operations/production/logistics: 4%
Other: 10%

Top Recruiters *(Number of Full-Time Class of 2004 Graduates Hired)*

Citigroup: 14
Booz Allen Hamilton: 13
Dell: 13
McKinsey: 10
Deloitte Consulting: 9
Johnson & Johnson: 8
American Express: 8
J.P. Morgan Chase: 8
A.T. Kearney: 6
Eli Lily: 6

Percentage of Job-Seeking Full-Time Graduates Who:	All Students	Citizens/Residents	Foreign Nationals
Received offers prior to or within 3 months of graduation	91%	93%	84%
Accepted offers prior to or within 3 months of graduation	87%	89%	84%

	MEAN			MEDIAN		
Overall Compensation	All Students	Citizens/ Residents	Foreign Nationals	All Students	Citizens/ Residents	Foreign Nationals
Annual base salary	$85,734	$86,994	$82,456	$85,000	$85,000	$85,000
Signing bonus	$16,466	$16,047	$17,663	$15,000	$15,000	$15,000
Other guaranteed compensation	$20,252	$20,917	$19,149	$10,000	$10,750	$10,000

Three of the Most Famous Graduates of M.B.A. Program

Bharat Desai (class of 1981) Chairman and CEO, Syntel

Don Leclair (class of 1976) Executive VP and CFO, Ford Motor

Stephen W. Sanger (class of 1970) Chairman and CEO, General Mills

MICHIGAN STATE UNIVERSITY (BROAD GRADUATE SCHOOL OF MANAGEMENT)

Michigan State's M.B.A. program is best known for its supply-chain management specialization, with about one-third of its graduates taking jobs in operations and production management. The Broad School's other primary concentrations include marketing, finance, and human-resources management.

In 2003, Michigan State revised the M.B.A. program to be more flexible and make students more marketable. Now, students can take electives during their first year and specialize earlier so they're better prepared for their all-important summer internships.

Above all, Michigan State stresses its "team-intensive environment" and has developed a core course on leadership and teamwork. M.B.A. students participate in simulation exercises in the Team Leadership Lab, where they use unclassified military scenarios and learn how to manage conflicts, develop trusting relationships, and motivate teammates.

The Broad School believes strongly in laboratory simulations in other areas, as well. There's the Financial Analysis Lab, where students can develop trading and hedging strategies. In the IBM On-Demand Supply Chain Lab, hardware and software replicate IBM's supply-chain platform. To prepare students to expect the unexpected, supply-chain simulations always include a few surprises, such as a glitch in the transportation system or a surge in product demand.

Some students go beyond simulations to run a firm called Spartan Consulting, which has worked for such diverse clients as United Technologies, Delta Dental, and CyberPunk Entertainment Group on strategy, marketing plans, and distribution channels.

To expose students to international business issues, the Broad School offers study-abroad trips every May that include visits with government officials, cultural tours, and meetings with alumni. There are also semester-long exchange programs with schools in Europe, Mexico, and Japan. And students can seek a dual degree with Thunderbird's Garvin School of International Management in Arizona that includes course work at both schools.

Michigan State jumped six spots to second place in the latest *Wall Street Journal*/Harris Interactive Regional ranking. Recruiters gave the school its top scores for students' fit with the corporate culture, their teamwork skills, success with past hires, and value for the money invested in the recruiting effort. Students were rated lowest for international knowledge and past work experience.

School Rankings

- Regional ranking in the recruiter survey: 2 of 47 schools ranked
- Ranking by energy- and industrial-products-industry recruiters: 5th place

Recognition for Excellence in an Academic Concentration

- With 88 nominations, Michigan State ranked No. 5 among business schools that recruiters in *The Wall Street Journal*/Harris Interactive survey cited for excellence in operations management.

MICHIGAN STATE ON MICHIGAN STATE

(Data provided by the Broad Graduate School of Management at Michigan State University)

Business school website:
http://www.mba.msu.edu
Business school e-mail:
mba@msu.edu
Public institution
M.B.A. enrollment: 526
Full-time: 204
Part-time: 219
Executive program: 103

ADMISSIONS DIRECTOR:
Esmeralda Cardenal
Director, M.B.A. Admissions
215 Eppley Center
East Lansing, MI 48824
517-355-7604 (voice)
517-353-1649 (fax)
E-mail: cardenal@msu.edu

APPLICATION DEADLINE:
Fall 2006: 5/2/2006
Annual tuition: $17,000 (in-state);
$23,800 (out-of-state)
Annual room and board: $7,314

FALL 2004 INCOMING M.B.A. CLASS

	Total	Full-Time Only
Number of applicants	863	648
Number of offers extended	381	202
Number of students who accepted offer	270	107
Number of students who enrolled	254	107

GMAT score: 637 (mean); 640 (median)
Years of full-time work experience: 5 (mean); 4 (median)
Undergraduate GPA: 3.4 (mean); 3.3 (median)

Demographic Profile of Full-Time Students

Male: 70%
Female: 30%
Minorities: 22%
U.S. citizens/residents: 68%
Foreign nationals: 32%

Class of 2004 Most Popular Academic Concentrations (% of Students)

Finance 39%
Supply-chain management 35%
Marketing 16%

CLASS OF 2004 EMPLOYMENT DATA

Industries Hiring Full-Time Graduates (% Hired)

Computer/technology/Internet/dot-com: 10.2%
Consumer products and services: 12.7%

THE RECRUITERS SPEAK

Michigan State's most impressive features

"Excellent manufacturing basics"

"Practical curriculum"

"Supply-chain knowledge"

Michigan State's major shortcomings

"Too focused on numbers rather than the big picture"

"Lack of true global experience"

"Small class size"

How Michigan State can increase its appeal

"Raise the age and experience requirements"

"Make networking with companies a priority"

"Teach strategy more"

Energy and utilities: 3.8%
Financial services/investment banking: 3.8%
Government: 2.5%
Industrial products and services: 13.9%
Management consulting: 15.2%
Manufacturing: 20.2%
Nonprofit: 2.5%
Pharmaceutical/biotechnology/health-care products and services: 5.1%
Telecommunications: 2.5%
Travel and transportation: 2.5%
Other: 5.1%

Position/Job Function (% Hired)

Consulting: 15%
Finance/accounting: 23%
General management: 10%
Human resources: 5%
Marketing/sales: 10%
Operations/production/logistics: 34%
Other: 3%

Percentage of Job-Seeking Full-Time Graduates Who:	All Students	Citizens/Residents	Foreign Nationals
Received offers prior to or within 3 months of graduation	85%	84%	85%
Accepted offers prior to or within 3 months of graduation	81%	81%	82%

	MEAN			MEDIAN		
Overall Compensation fix	All Students	Citizens/ Residents	Foreign Nationals	All Students	Citizens/ Residents	Foreign Nationals
Annual base salary	$76,313	$76,228	$76,504	$77,000	$78,000	$75,000
Signing bonus	$9,732	$90,187	$11,269	$8,000	$7,500	$10,000
Other guaranteed compensation	N/A	N/A	N/A	$4,469	N/A	N/A

Top Recruiters *(Number of Full-Time Class of 2004 Graduates Hired)*

IBM: 5
Cummins: 3
Deloitte Consulting: 3
Delphi: 3
Ford Motor: 3
Intel: 3
Steelcase: 3
Avaya: 2
Microsoft: 2
Procter & Gamble: 2

Three of the Most Famous Graduates of M.B.A. Program

David P. Cosper (class of 1977) Chief Financial Officer, Ford Motor Credit

Toichi Takenaka (class of 1968) President and CEO, Takenaka

James M. Cornelius (class of 1967) Chairman, Guidant

UNIVERSITY OF MINNESOTA (CARLSON SCHOOL OF MANAGEMENT)

The Carlson School, primarily a part-time M.B.A. program, retains close ties to the Twin Cities business community, sending many graduates to such local companies as General Mills, Target, and Medtronic. Students tend to focus most on finance and marketing.

In addition to the full-time and part-time M.B.A., Carlson offers an 18-month executive-M.B.A. program, plus specialized master's degrees in health-care administration and business taxation.

The full-time M.B.A. program features several "enterprise programs" that give students real-world experience. Students can manage $15 million in growth and fixed-income funds, work with high-tech start-ups with products ranging from artificial livers to LCD television screens, perform consulting work for clients, or tackle brand and marketing challenges for companies.

Students interested in global business issues can participate in semester-long exchange programs with foreign schools. A shorter alternative is the global enrichment elective abroad, which can last from 10 days to six weeks. Students focus on such topics as environmental business strategy, off-shoring and outsourcing, the ethical environment of international business, and marketing strategies in Central and Eastern Europe.

MINNESOTA ON MINNESOTA

(Data provided by the Carlson School of Management at the University of Minnesota)

Business school website:
http://www.carlsonschool.umn.edu
Business school e-mail: full-timeMBAinfo@csom.umn.edu
Public institution
M.B.A. enrollment: 1,948
Full-time: 217
Part-time: 1,623
Executive program: 108

ADMISSIONS DIRECTOR:
Dustin Cornwell
Director of Admissions and Recruiting
Carlson School of Management
321 19th Avenue South,
Suite 2-210
Minneapolis, MN 55455
612-625-5555 (voice)
612-626-7785 (fax)
E-mail: full-timeMBAinfo@csom.umn.edu

APPLICATION DEADLINES:
Fall 2006: 12/15/2005, 2/15/2006, 4/15/2006 (domestic); 12/1/2005, 2/15/2006 (international)
Annual tuition: $19,820 (in-state); $28,200 (out-of-state)
Annual room and board: $13,200

Beyond the regular curriculum, Carlson students participate in the Leadership Edge, a program that begins with thorough testing and self-assessment and proceeds to working with coaches to develop a self-improvement plan. Among the areas of focus are building relationships, thinking globally, managing disagreements, influencing others, and championing change.

In the latest *Wall Street Journal*/Harris Interactive survey, Minnesota was rated highest for students' personal ethics and integrity, and their ability to work well in teams. Minnesota received the lowest scores for students' international knowledge and experience and their prior work experience, as well as for faculty expertise.

School Rankings
- Regional ranking in the recruiter survey: 32 of 47 schools ranked

FALL 2004 INCOMING M.B.A. CLASS

	Total	Full-Time Only
Number of applicants	1,019	509
Number of offers extended	625	225
Number of students who accepted offer	465	110
Number of students who enrolled	465	110

THE RECRUITERS SPEAK

Minnesota's most impressive features

"Strong Midwestern work ethic"

"Nice and informal"

"Good financial experience"

Minnesota's major shortcomings

"Inconsistent—mix of stars and dogs"

"Little student diversity"

"More theoretical than practical"

How Minnesota can increase its appeal

"Take the quality of the student body up a notch"

"Increase students' willingness to relocate"

"Seek out recruiters, sell the school and students"

GMAT score: 655 (mean); 650 (median)
Years of full-time work experience: 5.1 (mean); 5 (median)
Undergraduate GPA: 3.3 (mean); 3.2 (median)

Demographic Profile of Full-Time Students

Male: 80%
Female: 20%
Minorities: 8%
U.S. citizens/residents: 66%
Foreign nationals: 34%

Class of 2004 Most Popular Academic Concentrations (% of Students)

Finance 47%
Marketing 28%
Management information systems 15%

CLASS OF 2004 EMPLOYMENT DATA

Industries Hiring Full-Time Graduates (% Hired)

Computer/technology/Internet/dot-com: 3%
Consumer products and services: 22%
Financial services/investment banking: 19%
Industrial products and services: 13%
Management consulting: 6%
Pharmaceutical/biotechnology/health-care products and services: 14%
Real estate: 1%
Telecommunications: 1%
Travel and transportation: 9%
Other professional services (accounting, advertising, etc.): 7%
Other: 5%

Position/Job Function (% Hired)

Consulting: 16%
Finance/accounting: 29%
General management: 5%
Information technology/management information systems: 8%
Marketing/sales: 28%
Operations/production/logistics: 12%
Other: 2%

Top Recruiters *(Number of Full-Time Class of 2004 Graduates Hired)*

General Mills: 5
Medtronic: 5
Piper Jaffray: 4
Target: 3
Best Buy: 3
3M: 3
Guidant: 2
Northwest Airlines: 2
Kimberly-Clark: 2
Samsung Electronics: 2

Percentage of Job-Seeking Full-Time Graduates Who:	All Students	Citizens/Residents	Foreign Nationals
Received offers prior to or within 3 months of graduation	93%	92%	96%
Accepted offers prior to or within 3 months of graduation	92%	90%	96%

Overall Compensation	MEAN			MEDIAN		
	All Students	Citizens/ Residents	Foreign Nationals	All Students	Citizens/ Residents	Foreign Nationals
Annual base salary	$77,821	$79,181	$71,700	$78,000	$79,200	$70,000
Signing bonus	$11,330	$11,699	$9,625	$10,000	$10,000	$6,000
Other guaranteed compensation	$13,870	$16,058	$7,964	$11,000	$12,600	$7,650

Three of the Most Famous Graduates of M.B.A. Program

Curtis C. Nelson (class of 1994) President and COO, Carlson Cos.

Charles W. Mooty (class of 1984) President and CEO, International Dairy Queen

Robert A. Kierlin (class of 1964) Chairman, Fastenal

NEW YORK UNIVERSITY
(STERN SCHOOL OF BUSINESS)

NEW YORK UNIVERSITY

NYU
STERN

LEONARD N. STERN
SCHOOL OF BUSINESS

Given its location in the heart of America's largest city, the Stern School attracts many of New York's working professionals in the evening and on weekends. Uptown rival Columbia Business School doesn't offer a part-time M.B.A. program, so NYU's program of about 1,700 students has grown to more than double the size of its full-time class.

Manhattan clearly is a driving force behind many of NYU's courses and its students' career plans. The Stern School's primary focus has long been finance and accounting, grooming many of its graduates for Wall Street. NYU also capitalizes on its proximity to Broadway, cultural institutions, and media conglomerates with its Entertainment, Media, and Technology Initiative. Popular electives include the new Models of Leadership in the Communications Industry, which has featured Donald Trump as a guest speaker, and the Craft and Commerce of Cinema, which included a trip to the annual film festival in Cannes.

The Stern School also reaches far beyond Manhattan to strongly emphasize international business. It has established an extensive network of semester-long exchange programs with foreign schools. A shorter option is a "Doing Business In . . ." course that focuses on a single country or region and includes two weeks of intensive study abroad.

NYU also offers an international executive-M.B.A. program called Trium in partnership with the HEC School of Manage-

NYU ON NYU

(Data provided by the Leonard N. Stern School of Business at New York University)

Business school website:
http://www.stern.nyu.edu
Business school e-mail:
sternmba@stern.nyu.edu
Private institution
M.B.A. enrollment: 2,661
Full-time: 756
Part-time: 1,689
Executive program: 216

ADMISSIONS DIRECTOR:
Dina Dommett
Assistant Dean for M.B.A. Admissions
44 W. 4th Street, Suite 6-70
New York, NY 10012
212-998-0600 (voice)
212-995-4231 (fax)
E-mail: sternmba@stern.nyu.edu

APPLICATION DEADLINES:
Fall 2006: 12/1/2005, 1/15/2006, 3/15/2006 (full-time); 5/15/2006 (part-time)
Annual tuition: $35,900
Annual room and board: $18,040

ment in Paris and the London School of Economics and Political Science. For full-time M.B.A.s, Stern plans to start a dual degree with HEC in fall 2005 that will entail a year of study at each school.

One of the Stern School's newest courses is "Social Enterprise Development," which teaches students how to generate capital and start ventures that can help solve social problems. Stern recruited the founder of the anti-hunger organization Share Our Strength to teach the class, with guest lecturers from companies and organizations like Timberland and Housing Works. The school also has created a social entrepreneurship fund that awards grants to Stern-affiliated social ventures in such fields as health care and philanthropy.

In the latest *Wall Street Journal*/Harris Interactive ranking, the Stern School was given its highest scores for students' analytical and problem-solving abilities, communication and interpersonal skills, and fit with the corporate culture. Recruiters rated NYU lowest for students' awareness of corporate citizenship issues, their previous work experience, and well-rounded qualities.

School Rankings

- National ranking in the recruiter survey: 16 of 19 schools ranked

THE RECRUITERS SPEAK

NYU's most impressive features	NYU's major shortcomings	How NYU can increase its appeal
"Ready to play in investment banking"	"Quality of students varies widely"	"Improve students' manners"
"Bright, often with a broad world view"	"Students have a sense of entitlement but haven't earned it"	"More leadership training"
"Street-smart"	"Not team-focused"	"Recruit well-rounded students willing to leave New York City"

Recognition for Excellence in Academic Concentrations

- With 139 nominations, NYU ranked No. 4 among business schools that recruiters in *The Wall Street Journal*/Harris Interactive survey cited for excellence in finance.

- With 63 nominations, NYU ranked No. 7 for excellence in accounting.

Special Recognition

- Good source for recruiting minorities: 7th most nominated school, 41 nominations.

- Good source for recruiting women: 9th most nominated school, 47 nominations.

FALL 2004 INCOMING M.B.A. CLASS

	Total	Full-Time Only
Number of applicants	4,572	3,403
Number of offers extended	1,296	762
Number of students who accepted offer	884	438
Number of students who enrolled	805	364

GMAT score: 700 (mean); 700 (median)
Years of full-time work experience: 5 (mean); 5 (median)
Undergraduate GPA: 3.4 (mean); 3.4 (median)

Demographic Profile of Full-Time Students

Male: 67%
Female: 33%
Minorities: 26%
U.S. citizens: 72%
Foreign nationals: 28%

Class of 2004 Most Popular Academic Concentrations (% of Students)

Finance 82%
Marketing 25%
Management 21%

CLASS OF 2004 EMPLOYMENT DATA

Industries Hiring Full-Time Graduates (% Hired)

Computer/technology/Internet/dot-com: 2%
Consumer products and services: 8%
Financial services/investment banking: 55%
Government: 1%
Management consulting: 11%
Manufacturing: 2%
Media/entertainment: 7%
Nonprofit: 1%
Pharmaceutical/biotechnology/health-care products and services: 3%
Real estate: 2%
Telecommunications: 2%
Travel and transportation: 1%
Other: 5%

Position/Job Function (% Hired)

Consulting: 15%
Finance/accounting: 56%

Percentage of Job-Seeking Full-Time Graduates Who:	All Students	Citizens/Residents	Foreign Nationals
Received offers prior to or within 3 months of graduation	81%	81%	83%
Accepted offers prior to or within 3 months of graduation	81%	81%	82%

	MEAN			MEDIAN		
Overall Compensation	All Students	Citizens/ Residents	Foreign Nationals	All Students	Citizens/ Residents	Foreign Nationals
Annual base salary	$86,744	$86,462	$87,304	$85,000	$85,000	$85,000
Signing bonus	$19,759	$19,736	$19,807	$20,000	$20,000	$20,000
Other guaranteed compensation	$19,076	$18,812	$19,615	$16,500	$16,000	$16,500

General management: 2%
Marketing/sales: 21%
Operations/production/logistics: 2%
Other: 4%

Top Recruiters *(Number of Full-Time Class of 2004 Graduates Hired)*

Citigroup: N/A
American Express:
J.P. Morgan Chase:
Lehman Brothers:
Goldman Sachs:
Deutsche Bank:
Deloitte:
Credit Suisse First Boston:
Merrill Lynch:
Bear Stearns:

Three of the Most Famous Graduates of M.B.A. Program

Richard Fuld (class of 1972) Chairman and CEO, Lehman Brothers

Thomas E. Freston (class of 1969) Co-President, Viacom

Abby F. Kohnstamm (class of 1979) Senior Vice President of Marketing, IBM

UNIVERSITY OF NORTH CAROLINA AT CHAPEL HILL (KENAN-FLAGLER BUSINESS SCHOOL)

North Carolina's business school, which offers students a general-management education, lists teamwork, leadership, community, and integrity among its core values.

But students can specialize as well, choosing from 10 career and enrichment concentrations. The seven career concentrations are corporate finance, customer and product management, investment management, global supply-chain management, consulting, real estate, and entrepreneurship.

One of the school's most distinctive features is its enrichment concentration in sustainable enterprise, which teaches students about the need to balance profitability with environmental and social responsibility. The Aspen Institute and the World Resources Institute have honored North Carolina as one of the top business schools in the world teaching about social and environmental responsibility. The two other enrichment programs deal with international business and electronic business and digital commerce.

Students can participate in independent study and practicum projects as well. Team-based, faculty-led projects have ranged from designing a capital structure and dividend policy for a pharmaceutical company to crafting a marketing plan for a symphony orchestra. Kenan-Flagler also allows students to earn dual degrees, combining their M.B.A. with advanced degrees in law, information and library science, public health, and city and regional planning.

North Carolina emphasizes communication skills in the full-time M.B.A. program, recognizing how important they are to corporate recruiters. Students are required to take a 14-week management communications class to polish their writing and public speaking and become more effective at persuasion.

In addition to the full-time degree, Kenan-Flagler offers three executive-M.B.A. degrees, including both evening and week-end programs at Chapel Hill. It also joined with four business schools in China, Brazil, Mexico, and the Netherlands in 2002 to offer a third executive M.B.A., an example of just how global the business community and the M.B.A. degree have become. North Carolina students spend most of their time in the U.S., but live abroad for three weeks in Europe, Asia, and Latin America.

In *The Wall Street Journal*/Harris Interactive ranking, recruiters said the chemistry is strong with North Carolina, meaning they have generally good feelings about the school and its students. They gave students the highest marks for their teamwork orientation, communication and interpersonal skills, and personal ethics and integrity. North Carolina received its lowest scores for students' international knowledge and experience and for faculty expertise.

School Rankings

- National ranking in the recruiter survey: 9 of 19 schools ranked
- Ranking by health-care-industry recruiters: 2nd place
- Ranking by financial-services-industry recruiters: 5th place
- Ranking by technology-industry recruiters: 6th place
- Ranking by management-consulting-industry recruiters: 8th place

Recognition for Excellence in an Academic Concentration

- With 43 nominations, North Carolina ranked No. 10 among business schools that recruiters in *The Wall Street Journal*/Harris Interactive survey cited for excellence in marketing.

NORTH CAROLINA ON NORTH CAROLINA

(Data provided by the Kenan-Flagler Business School at the University of North Carolina at Chapel Hill)

Business school website:
http://www.kenan-flagler.unc.edu
Business school e-mail:
mba_info@unc.edu
Public institution
M.B.A. enrollment: 855
Full-time: 541
Executive program: 314

ADMISSIONS DIRECTOR:
Sherry Wallace
Director of M.B.A. Admissions
CB 3490, McColl Building
University of North Carolina at
Chapel Hill
Chapel Hill, NC 27599
919-962-3236 (voice)
919-962-0898 (fax)
E-mail: mba_info@unc.edu

APPLICATION DEADLINES:
Fall 2006: October 2005,
December 2005, January 2006,
March 2006
Annual tuition: $16,375 (in-state);
$32,749 (out-of-state)
Annual room and board: $15,032

FALL 2004 INCOMING M.B.A. CLASS

	Full-Time Only
Number of applicants	1,500
Number of offers extended	701
Number of students who accepted offer	327
Number of students who enrolled	277

GMAT score: 652 (mean); 660 (median)
Years of full-time work experience: 5 (mean); 5 (median)
Undergraduate GPA: 3.3 (mean); 3.3 (median)

Demographic Profile of Full-Time Students

Male: 71%
Female: 29%
Minorities: 14%
U.S. citizens/residents: 72%
Foreign nationals: 28%

Class of 2004 Most Popular Academic Concentrations (% of Students)

Customer and product management 25%
Corporate finance 22%
Global supply-chain management 13%

CLASS OF 2004 EMPLOYMENT DATA

Industries Hiring Full-Time Graduates (% Hired)

Computer/technology/Internet/dot-com: 10%
Consumer products and services: 10%

THE RECRUITERS SPEAK

North Carolina's most impressive features

"Team players"

"Friendly, easygoing students"

"Integrity, values-driven"

North Carolina's major shortcomings

"Ability to thing strategically"

"Need richer business experience"

"Lack of aggressiveness"

How North Carolina can increase its appeal

"Improve diversity of students"

"Increase international perspective"

"Better analytical and quant skills"

Financial services/investment banking: 34%
Management consulting: 11%
Manufacturing: 4%
Nonprofit: 2%
Pharmaceutical/biotechnology/health-care products and services:
10%
Real estate: 9%
Travel and transportation: 3%
Other professional services (accounting, advertising, etc.): 2%
Other: 5%

Position/Job Function (% Hired)

Consulting: 10%
Finance/accounting: 37%
General management: 7%
Marketing/sales: 21%
Operations/production/logistics: 3%
Other: 22%

Top Recruiters (Number of Full-Time Class of 2004 Graduates Hired)

Bank of America: 11
Citigroup: 9

Percentage of Job-Seeking Full-Time Graduates Who:	All Students	Citizens/Residents	Foreign Nationals
Received offers prior to or within 3 months of graduation	86%	86%	85%
Accepted offers prior to or within 3 months of graduation	81%	81%	81%

	MEAN			MEDIAN		
Overall Compensation	All Students	Citizens/Residents	Foreign Nationals	All Students	Citizens/Residents	Foreign Nationals
Annual base salary	$78,751	$79,628	$74,898	$82,900	$83,000	$75,000
Signing bonus	$14,163	$14,420	$12,810	$12,500	$13,150	$10,500
Other guaranteed compensation	$13,814	$15,339	$8,020	$10,000	$10,000	$8,500

Wachovia: 8
McKinsey: 6
Deloitte Consulting: 6
Johnson & Johnson: 5
Pulte Homes: 5
Lehman Brothers: 4
Booz Allen Hamilton: 4
IBM: 4
Credit Suisse First Boston: 4

Three of the Most Famous Graduates of M.B.A. Program

Lee Ainslie (class of 1990) Managing Partner, Maverick Capital Management

Daryl Brewster (class of 1982) Group Vice President, Kraft Foods North America

Brent Callinicos (class of 1989) Corporate VP, Worldwide Licensing/Pricing, Microsoft

NORTHWESTERN UNIVERSITY (KELLOGG SCHOOL OF MANAGEMENT)

Northwestern's Kellogg School, founded in 1908, has become virtually synonymous with marketing. By an overwhelming margin, recruiters in *The Wall Street Journal*/Harris Interactive survey nominate it as the premier M.B.A. program for teaching marketing skills.

But Kellogg is far from a one-note M.B.A. program, with many students also majoring in finance, management, and strategy. In fact, slightly more graduates go to work in management consulting than in marketing and sales.

Kellogg stresses its evolving curriculum, with more than 50 courses added since 1995. A new requirement in 2005, for example, is "Values and Crisis Decision Making," a response to the recent spate of corporate scandals. The class includes case studies and crisis-simulation exercises to teach students the importance of anticipating and preparing for potential business threats.

Corporate citizenship also has become a higher priority at Kellogg, with a major now offered in "business and its social environment." In their courses, students examine the growing role of corporations in social change and the ways in which they are being held accountable for far more than financial performance. Beyond the classroom, Ford Motor awarded $3 million to Kellogg to establish the Center for Global Citizenship, which focuses on the environment, ethics, and social responsibility. There is also the new Center for Business, Government, and

NORTHWESTERN ON NORTHWESTERN

(Data provided by the Kellogg School of Management at Northwestern University)

Business school website:
http://www.kellogg.northwestern
.edu
Business school e-mail:
MBAadmissions@kellogg.
northwestern.edu
Private institution
M.B.A. enrollment: 2,650
Full-time: 1,050
Part-time: 1,200
Executive program: 400

ADMISSIONS DIRECTOR:
Beth Flye
Director of Admissions
Donald P. Jacobs Center
2001 Sheridan Road
Evanston, IL 60208-2001
847-491-3308 (voice)
847-491-4960 (fax)
E-mail: MBAadmissions@
kellogg.northwestern.edu

APPLICATION DEADLINES:
Fall 2006: October 2005, January
2006, March 2006
Annual tuition: $38,844
Annual room and board: $13,515

Society, which will help managers learn to assess political and social risks and opportunities.

Kellogg's standard M.B.A. program lasts two years, but students can take a one-year shortcut if they have completed an undergraduate business degree or compiled a record of extensive business training and work experience. They also can opt for the M.B.A./master's in engineering management, a joint venture of the Kellogg School and Northwestern's School of Engineering and Applied Science, as well as M.B.A. combinations with degrees in law and medicine.

Kellogg offers both a part-time M.B.A. degree and an increasingly international executive-M.B.A. program. Beginning in 1996, Kellogg established executive-M.B.A. partnerships with business schools in Canada, China, Germany, and Israel, and is planning to start a new executive M.B.A. in 2006 in Miami for U.S. and Latin American managers.

In *The Wall Street Journal*/Harris Interactive ranking, the Kellogg School was rated most highly for students' communication and interpersonal skills, ability to work well in teams, and personal ethics and integrity. Its lowest ratings: students' international knowledge and experience, the career-services office, and value for the money invested in the recruiting effort.

School Rankings

- National ranking in recruiter survey: 4 of 19 schools ranked
- Ranking by health-care-industry recruiters: 1st place

THE RECRUITERS SPEAK

Northwestern's most impressive features	Northwestern's major shortcomings	How Northwestern can increase its appeal
"Excellent marketing acumen"	"Light on analytical rigor in the classroom"	"Reach out and be more customer-focused"
"Students tend to have charisma and are good communicators"	"Sometimes students are overconfident for entry-level jobs"	"Rein in cocky students"
"General-management potential"	"Many poets without enough quantitative skills"	"Think beyond the Midwest, think beyond marketing"

- Ranking by consumer-products-industry recruiters: 2nd place
- Ranking by energy- and industrial-products-industry recruiters: 2nd place
- Ranking by management-consulting-industry recruiters: 3rd place
- Ranking by technology-industry recruiters: 8th place

Recognition for Excellence in Academic Concentrations

- With 1,304 nominations, Northwestern ranked No. 1 among business schools that recruiters in *The Wall Street Journal*/Harris Interactive survey cited for excellence in marketing.
- With 112 nominations, Northwestern ranked No. 5 for excellence in strategy.
- With 90 nominations, Northwestern ranked No. 7 for excellence in entrepreneurship.

Special Recognition

- Good source for recruiting women: 2nd most nominated school, 116 nominations.

FALL 2004 INCOMING M.B.A. CLASS

	Full-Time Only
Number of applicants	4,299
Number of offers extended	960
Number of students who accepted offer	534
Number of students who enrolled	534

GMAT score: 700 (mean); N/A (median)
Years of full-time work experience: 5.2 (mean); N/A (median)
Undergraduate GPA: 3.45 (mean); N/A (median)

Demographic Profile of Full-Time Students

Male: 71%
Female: 29%
Minorities: 24%
U.S. citizens: 71%
Foreign nationals: 29%

Class of 2004 Most Popular Academic Concentrations (% of Students)

Marketing 71%
Management and strategy 61%
Finance 58%

CLASS OF 2004 EMPLOYMENT DATA

Industries Hiring Full-Time Graduates (% Hired)

Computer/technology/Internet/dot-com: 10%
Consumer products and services: 11%
Financial services/investment banking: 18%
Management consulting: 28%
Manufacturing: 12%
Pharmaceutical/biotechnology/health-care products and services: 9%
Other professional services (accounting, advertising, etc.): 12%

Position/Job Function (% Hired)

Consulting: 32%
Finance/accounting: 24%

Percentage of Job-Seeking Full-Time Graduates Who:	All Students	Citizens/Residents	Foreign Nationals
Received offers prior to or within 3 months of graduation	94%	N/A	N/A
Accepted offers prior to or within 3 months of graduation	91%	N/A	N/A

	MEAN			MEDIAN		
Overall Compensation	All Students	Citizens/ Residents	Foreign Nationals	All Students	Citizens/ Residents	Foreign Nationals
Annual base salary	$91,390	N/A	N/A	$90,000	N/A	N/A
Signing bonus	$14,380	N/A	N/A	$14,000	N/A	N/A
Other guaranteed compensation	$25,670	N/A	N/A	$27,500	N/A	N/A

General management: 13%
Marketing/sales: 30%
Other: 1%

Top Recruiters *(Number of Full-Time Class of 2004 Graduates Hired)*

McKinsey: 38
Boston Consulting Group: 16
General Electric: 12
Johnson & Johnson: 12
A.T. Kearney: 8
Microsoft: 6
Morgan Stanley: 6
United Airlines: 6
American Airlines: 5
Goldman Sachs: 5

Three of the Most Famous Graduates of M.B.A. Program

Robert A. Eckert (class of 1977) Chairman and CEO, Mattel

Craig Donohue (class of 1995) CEO, Chicago Mercantile Exchange

Philip A. Marineau (class of 1970) President and CEO, Levi Strauss

UNIVERSITY OF NOTRE DAME (MENDOZA COLLEGE OF BUSINESS)

Long before many people ever heard of Enron and Tyco, Notre Dame made business ethics the foundation of its M.B.A. program. Now, many schools have jumped on the ethics bandwagon, but it's hard to match Notre Dame.

The Mendoza College infuses ethics-related issues throughout its curriculum, including the traditional two-year M.B.A. program, an accelerated one-year M.B.A. option for undergraduate business majors, and executive-M.B.A. programs in South Bend, Ind., and Chicago. It also operates the Center for Ethics and Religious Values in Business and the Institute for Ethical Business Worldwide, and promotes its annual Ethics Week, a lecture series on such topics as ethics and earnings management and ethics and the media.

In 2005, the school revised its M.B.A. curriculum to give students greater flexibility. Two seven-week modules, separated by a one-week interim session and a break week, will replace the regular semester design. Students can take electives or study abroad during the break and interim session. In addition, Notre Dame is adding new courses in such subject areas as cost accounting, leadership, values in decision-making, and strategic information technology.

The Roman Catholic university also deals increasingly with spirituality in the workplace. Joseph Holt, who teaches the new class "Spirituality and Religion in the Workplace," challenges students to look beyond prestige and salary and ask whether a potential employer is a good fit morally and spiritually. The course addresses such concerns as treating fellow employees with respect, the role of prayer in blending one's faith and work, and the ways that e-mail, cell phones, and other modern technology threaten spiritual time.

Notre Dame graduates please many recruiters because of their interpersonal skills. Through the Fanning Center for Business Communication, students take courses on public speaking and writing and presenting a business plan. There's also a class on the art of listening and responding that teaches students how to listen to criticism nondefensively and how to provide feedback properly to speakers.

Recruiters in *The Wall Street Journal*/Harris Interactive survey gave Notre Dame its highest ratings for students' personal ethics and integrity, teamwork orientation, and awareness of corporate citizenship issues. Notre Dame students received the lowest marks for their international knowledge and previous work experience.

School Rankings

- Regional ranking in the recruiter survey: 29 of 47 schools ranked

Special Recognition

- Good source for recruiting graduates with high ethical standards: 8th most nominated school, 67 nominations.

FALL 2004 INCOMING M.B.A. CLASS

	Full-Time Only
Number of applicants	679
Number of offers extended	335
Number of students who accepted offer	159
Number of students who enrolled	129

NOTRE DAME ON NOTRE DAME

(Data provided by the Mendoza College of Business at Notre Dame)

Business school website:
http://www.nd.edu/~cba
Business school e-mail:
MBA.1@nd.edu
Private institution
M.B.A. enrollment: 564
Full-time: 324
Executive program: 240

ADMISSIONS DIRECTOR:
Mary Goss
Senior Director of Admissions
and Student Services
276 Mendoza College of Business
Notre Dame, IN 46556
574-631-8488 (voice)
574-631-8800 (fax)
E-mail: Mary.Goss.6@nd.edu

APPLICATION DEADLINES:
Fall 2006: 11/15/2005, 1/15/2006,
3/15/2006
Annual tuition: $31,820
Annual room and board: $6,915

GMAT score: 657 (mean); 660 (median)
Years of full-time work experience: 4.3 (mean); 4 (median)
Undergraduate GPA: 3.3 (mean); 3.3 (median)

Demographic Profile of Full-Time Students

Male: 79%
Female: 21%
Minorities: 15%
U.S. citizens/residents: 75%
Foreign nationals: 25%

Class of 2004 Most Popular Academic Concentrations (% of Students)

Corporate finance and investment 58%
Marketing 20%
General management 14%

CLASS OF 2004 EMPLOYMENT DATA

Industries Hiring Full-Time Graduates (% Hired)

Computer/technology/Internet/dot-com: 5%
Consumer products and services: 8%
Energy and utilities: 1%
Financial services/investment banking: 16%
Government: 2%
Industrial products and services: 7%
Management consulting: 20%
Manufacturing: 17%
Nonprofit: 2%
Pharmaceutical/biotechnology/health-care products and services: 7%
Real estate: 3%

THE RECRUITERS SPEAK

Notre Dame's most impressive features

"Ethics, commitment"

"Social responsibility"

"Great team players"

Notre Dame's major shortcomings

"Students can be too nice—need to show they can be tough"

"Average writing skills"

"School thinks it is more elite than it is"

How Notre Dame can increase its appeal

"Improve diversity recruitment of students"

"Be more visible to a national and international audience"

"Add more top-flight finance students"

Telecommunications: 5%
Travel and transportation: 1%
Other professional services (accounting, advertising, etc.): 4%
Other: 2%

Position/Job Function (% Hired)

Consulting: 22%
Finance/accounting: 37%
General management: 17%
Information technology/management information systems: 2%
Marketing/sales: 15%
Operations/production/logistics: 2%
Other: 5%

Top Recruiters (Number of Full-Time Class of 2004 Graduates Hired)

Johnson & Johnson: 5
IBM: 5
FTI Consulting: 4
PricewaterhouseCoopers: 4
Avaya: 3
Bank of America: 3
General Electric: 3

Percentage of Job-Seeking Full-Time Graduates Who:	All Students	Citizens/Residents	Foreign Nationals
Received offers prior to or within 3 months of graduation	84%	86%	74%
Accepted offers prior to or within 3 months of graduation	84%	86%	74%

Overall Compensation	MEAN			MEDIAN		
	All Students	Citizens/ Residents	Foreign Nationals	All Students	Citizens/ Residents	Foreign Nationals
Annual base salary	$79,331	$78,856	$80,650	$80,000	$80,000	$80,000
Signing bonus	$10,081	$10,071	$11,800	$10,000	$10,000	$13,000
Other guaranteed compensation	$9,070	$10,067	$5,100	$6,000	$6,875	$5,000

Kraft Foods: 3
Ford Motor: 2
Deloitte & Touche: 2

Three of the Most Famous Graduates of M.B.A. Program

Bob Reilly (class of 1979) Chairman, Reilly Partners

Jim Corgel (class of 1975) General Manager, IBM Global Services

Don Casey (class of 1983) President, Vistakon

OHIO STATE UNIVERSITY
(FISHER COLLEGE OF BUSINESS)

Ohio State's Fisher College of Business has earned a solid reputation for its emphasis on operations management and logistics in its full-time, part-time, and executive-M.B.A. degrees. And starting in fall 2005, Fisher is partnering with the College of Engineering to offer a special master's of business logistics engineering degree.

Despite that focus, however, Fisher M.B.A.s are more likely to take finance, accounting, marketing, and sales jobs after graduation.

The Fisher College also offers a variety of opportunities for international experience. For example, students in an "Emerging Markets" course have visited multinational companies, such as Hewlett-Packard, IBM, and Wal-Mart, in about a dozen countries, including Hungary, China, Singapore, South Africa, Mexico, and Argentina. On their return to school, they write case studies based on their study of a country's business, economic, and cultural conditions.

Students have another opportunity to gain international experience through a partnership with the Peace Corps, including a two-year Peace Corps stint between the first and second year of M.B.A. studies.

Founded in 1916, Fisher College has grown to become a campus within a campus. It includes a $120 million complex of five academic buildings that are linked to an upscale hotel that

OHIO STATE ON OHIO STATE

(Data provided by the Fisher College of Business at Ohio State University)

Business school website:
http://fisher.osu.edu
Business school e-mail:
fishergrad@.cob.osu.edu
Public institution
M.B.A. enrollment: 633
Full-time: 260
Part-time: 284
Executive program: 89

ADMISSIONS DIRECTOR:
Eric Chambers
Director of Admissions
100 Gerlach Hall
2100 Neil Ave.
Columbus, OH 43210
614-292-2249 (voice)
614-292-9006 (fax)
E-mail: fishergrad@cob.osu.edu

APPLICATION DEADLINE:
Fall 2006: 4/28/2006
Annual tuition: $16,806 (in-state);
$29,403 (out-of-state)
Annual room and board: $6,300

serves as the residence center for the school's executive-education program.

In *The Wall Street Journal*/Harris Interactive survey, recruiters were most impressed with the students' personal ethics and integrity, fit with the corporate culture, and well-rounded qualities. The recruiters gave Ohio State its lowest grades for students' international knowledge and their past work experience.

School Rankings

- Regional ranking in the recruiter survey: 3 of 47 schools ranked
- Ranking by consumer-products-industry recruiters: 9th place

Recognition for Excellence in an Academic Concentration

- With 53 nominations, Ohio State ranked No. 6 among business schools that recruiters in *The Wall Street Journal*/Harris Interactive survey cited for excellence in operations management.

FALL 2004 INCOMING M.B.A. CLASS

	Full-Time Only
Number of applicants	609
Number of offers extended	335
Number of students who accepted offer	157
Number of students who enrolled	137

THE RECRUITERS SPEAK

Ohio State's most impressive features

"Supply-chain program"

"Good project-management skills"

"Down-to-earth candidates"

Ohio State's major shortcomings

"Quality of work experiences prior to M.B.A."

"Small size makes broad recruiting effort difficult"

"Lack of passion"

How Ohio State can increase its appeal

"More leadership classes"

"More personal involvement from the career-services office"

"Develop structured strategic thinking"

GMAT score: 665 (mean); 670 (median)
Years of full-time work experience: 4.6 (mean); 4 (median)
Undergraduate GPA: 3.4 (mean); 3.5 (median)

Demographic Profile of Full-Time Students

Male: 75%
Female: 25%
Minorities: 26%
U.S. citizens/residents: 66%
Foreign nationals: 34%

Class of 2004 Most Popular Academic Concentrations (% of Students)

Corporate finance 30%
Marketing 26%
Operations and logistics 23%

CLASS OF 2004 EMPLOYMENT DATA

Industries Hiring Full-Time Graduates (% Hired)

Computer/technology/Internet/dot-com: 10%
Consumer products and services: 26%
Energy and utilities: 1%
Financial services/investment banking: 18%
Government: 3%
Industrial products and services: 2%
Management consulting: 13%
Manufacturing: 13%
Media/entertainment: 3%
Nonprofit: 2%
Pharmaceutical/biotechnology/health-care products and services:
2%
Real estate: 2%
Telecommunications: 1%
Travel and transportation: 1%
Other: 3%

Position/Job Function (% Hired)

Consulting: 16%
Finance/accounting: 35%
General management: 5%
Marketing/sales: 25%

Operations/production/logistics: 16%
Other: 3%

Top Recruiters *(Number of Full-Time Class of 2004 Graduates Hired)*

Alliance Data Systems: 4
Deloitte Consulting: 3
General Electric: 3
Kimberly-Clark: 3
Ford Motor: 3
Limited Brands: 3
PricewaterhouseCoopers: 2
Time Warner: 2
Procter & Gamble: 2
Abbott/Ross Products: 2

Percentage of Job-Seeking Full-Time Graduates Who:	All Students	Citizens/Residents	All Foreign Nationals
Received offers prior to or within 3 months of graduation	90%	92%	86%
Accepted offers prior to or within 3 months of graduation	90%	92%	86%

	MEAN			MEDIAN		
Overall Compensation	All Students	Citizens/ Residents	Foreign Nationals	All Students	Citizens/ Residents	Foreign Nationals
Annual base salary	$73,422	$73,301	$76,375	$75,000	$75,000	$79,500
Signing bonus	$11,203	$11,262	$10,896	$10,000	$10,000	$10,000
Other guaranteed compensation	$11,360	$9,450	$12,460	$10,000	$10,000	$15,000

Three of the Most Famous Graduates of M.B.A. Program

Clayton Daley (class of 1974) Chief Financial Officer, Procter & Gamble

Mark Johnson (class of 1980) Vice Chairman, Checkfree

James O'Brien (class of 1978) Chairman and CEO, Ashland

UNIVERSITY OF PENNSYLVANIA
(WHARTON SCHOOL)

The Wharton School, established in 1881 as America's first business school, has long enjoyed a stellar reputation for its finance curriculum and sending many of its graduates to the leading Wall Street and management-consulting firms. But Wharton officials bristle at perceptions of it as merely a "finance factory." Among the school's other well-respected academic concentrations: marketing, health-care management, real estate, and insurance.

In recent years, Wharton has significantly broadened its geographic reach beyond the University of Pennsylvania campus. Wharton West opened its doors in San Francisco in 2001 to offer an executive-M.B.A. degree, complementing the school's executive program in Philadelphia. Wharton also has established a partnership with Insead in Fontainebleau, France, that allows students to spend seven weeks at one of Insead's campuses in France or Singapore and take advantage of its career-management and alumni connections in Europe and Asia.

M.B.A. students also can gain international exposure through Wharton's global immersion programs. They recently made the school's first trek to India to meet with local business and government leaders and learn more about the country's growing influence in the global marketplace. The university's Lauder Institute provides a comprehensive preparation for the global economy, with students receiving both an M.B.A. and a master's of international studies, as well as advanced language training.

WHARTON ON WHARTON

Data provided by the Wharton
School at the University of
Pennsylvania

Business school website:
http://www.wharton.upenn.edu
Business school e-mail: mba.
admissions@wharton.upenn.edu
Private institution
M.B.A. enrollment: 1,840
Full-time: 1,639
Executive Program: 201

ADMISSIONS DIRECTOR:
Director of Admissions and
Financial Aid
420 Jon M. Huntsman Hall
3730 Walnut Street
Philadelphia, PA 19104
215-898-6183 (voice)
215-898-0120 (fax)
E-mail: mba.admissions@
wharton.upenn.edu

APPLICATION DEADLINES:
Fall 2006: 10/13/2005, 1/5/2006,
3/2/2006
Annual tuition: $40,458
Annual room and board: $17,700

Wharton is also well regarded for its hands-on leadership training. Students can learn leadership and teamwork skills by mountain climbing in Ecuador, Tanzania, and Nepal; camping on the ice in Antarctica; or visiting the Gettysburg battlefield. Other students focus on the importance of creativity and collaboration by choreographing and performing dance routines with a modern-dance theater company.

Long a leader in academic research, Wharton created its own publishing brand in 2004. Wharton School Publishing will produce business books in conjunction with Pearson's education division, providing high-profile competition for Harvard Business School Press.

Recruiters in *The Wall Street Journal*/Harris Interactive survey gave Wharton its highest scores for students' analytical and problem-solving skills, strategic thinking, and personal ethics and integrity. Wharton received its lowest marks for the career-services office, students' awareness of corporate citizenship issues, and value for the money invested in the recruiting effort.

School Rankings

- National ranking in the recruiter survey: 6 of 19 schools ranked
- Ranking by management-consulting-industry recruiters: 5th place
- Ranking by technology-industry recruiters: 9th place

THE RECRUITERS SPEAK

Wharton's most impressive features

"Problem-solving skills"

"Ambition and drive"

"Critical thinkers"

Wharton's major shortcomings

"Students are programmed to think they are the cat's meow"

"Financially focused, not as well-rounded"

"Pompous attitude of career center"

How Wharton can increase its appeal

"Enhance students' teamwork skills"

"Treat companies as customers"

"More students willing to go somewhere other than Wall Street"

Recognition for Excellence in Academic Concentrations

- With 722 nominations, Wharton ranked No. 1 among business schools that recruiters in *The Wall Street Journal*/Harris Interactive survey cited for excellence in finance.

- With 197 nominations, Wharton ranked No. 2 for excellence in accounting.

- With 134 nominations, Wharton ranked No. 4 for excellence in strategy.

- With 107 nominations, Wharton ranked No. 5 for excellence in international business.

- With 66 nominations, Wharton ranked No. 6 for excellence in marketing.

- With 82 nominations, Wharton ranked No. 8 for excellence in entrepreneurship.

Special Recognition

- Good source for recruiting women: 9th most nominated school, 47 nominations.

- Good source for recruiting minorities: 9th most nominated school, 40 nominations.

FALL 2004 INCOMING M.B.A. CLASS

	Total	Full-Time Only
Number of applicants	6,519	5,622
Number of offers extended	1,441	1,219
Number of students who accepted offer	N/A	N/A
Number of students who enrolled	1,026	825

GMAT score: 716 (mean); 710 (median)
Years of full-time work experience: 6.2 (mean); 6 (median)
Undergraduate GPA: 3.5 (mean); 3.5 (median)

Demographic Profile of Full-Time Students

Male: 67%
Female: 33%
Minorities: 27%

U.S. citizens/residents: 64%
Foreign nationals: 36%

Class of 2002 Most Popular Academic Concentrations (% of Students)

Finance 44%
Marketing 14%
Strategy 11%

CLASS OF 2004 EMPLOYMENT DATA

Industries Hiring Full-Time Graduates (% Hired)

Computer/technology/Internet/dot-com: 6.4%
Consumer products and services: 7.6%
Energy and utilities: 1.8%
Entertainment and media: 1.5%
Financial services/investment banking: 40.6%
Management consulting: 22.5%
Manufacturing: 3.1%
Pharmaceutical/biotechnology/health-care products and services: 9.7%
Real estate: 2.7%

Percentage of Job-Seeking Full-Time Graduates Who:	All Students	Citizens/Residents	Foreign Nationals
Received offers prior to or within 3 months of graduation	92%	93%	90%
Accepted offers prior to or within 3 months of graduation	88%	91%	85%

	MEAN			MEDIAN		
Overall Compensation	All Students	Citizens/ Residents	Foreign Nationals	All Students	Citizens/ Residents	Foreign Nationals
Annual base salary	$92,986	$92,427	$94,061	$90,000	$90,000	$90,000
Signing bonus	$16,803	$16,363	$17,475	$15,000	$15,000	$20,000
Other guaranteed compensation	$24,485	$26,944	$20,334	$20,000	$20,000	$19,700

Telecommunications: 1.5%
Other: 2.6%

Position/Job Function *(% Hired)*

Consulting: 28%
Finance/accounting: 36.5%
General management: 9.8%
Marketing/sales: 11%
Operations/production/logistics: 1.5%
Other: 13.2%

Top Recruiters *(Number of Full-Time Class of 2004 Graduates Hired)*

McKinsey: 48
Goldman Sachs: 29
Boston Consulting Group: 25
Bain: 24
Citigroup: 17
Johnson & Johnson: 15
Lehman Brothers: 14
J.P. Morgan Chase: 13
Credit Suisse First Boston: 12
Banc of America Securities: 10
Booz Allen Hamilton: 10

Three of the Most Famous Graduates of M.B.A. Program

Lewis Platt (class of 1966) Lead Director, Boeing

Peter Lynch (class of 1968) Vice Chairman, Fidelity Management &
Research

James Tisch (class of 1976) President and CEO, Loews

PENNSYLVANIA STATE UNIVERSITY (SMEAL COLLEGE OF BUSINESS)

Penn State's M.B.A. program features six "specialty portfolios" of courses and "immersion weeks" for students to gain experience in actual business settings. Specialties include corporate financial analysis and planning; corporate innovation and entrepreneurship; investment management and portfolio analysis; product and market development; strategic leadership; and supply-chain management.

The Smeal College encourages hands-on learning in its financial trading room, with live data feeds, ticker displays, and 45 trading stations, and through the new $2.2 million Nittany Lion Fund. Both M.B.A. and undergraduate students manage the investment portfolio, which is distinctive because it's structured as a limited liability company with actual investor dollars. At some schools, student-managed funds are created from endowments or donations, but alumni and other "friends of Penn State" have invested their own money in the Nittany Lion Fund.

M.B.A. students can receive joint degrees in law, health-services management, and quality and manufacturing management. In addition to the full-time program, Smeal offers an executive-M.B.A. program that includes a few weeks at Penn State's main University Park campus and alternating weekends at a conference center in suburban Philadelphia. Just before receiving their executive M.B.A., students spend a concluding week abroad in countries such as Belgium, the Czech Republic, and Singapore.

The Smeal College is building a new home, scheduled for completion in 2005, to be financed with $39 million of university funds and $29 million of private donations. The 210,000-square-foot building will be the largest academic facility on campus and will bring various parts of the business school together under one roof.

In *The Wall Street Journal*/Harris Interactive survey, Penn State received its best scores for students' ability to work well in teams, analytical and problem-solving skills, personal ethics and integrity, and fit with the corporate culture. The lowest ratings: students' international knowledge and past work experience.

School Rankings

- Regional ranking in the recruiter survey: 33 of 47 schools ranked
- Ranking by technology-industry recruiters: 9th place

Recognition for Excellence in an Academic Concentration

- With 46 nominations, Penn State ranked No. 8 among business schools that recruiters in *The Wall Street Journal*/Harris Interactive survey cited for excellence in operations management.

FALL 2004 INCOMING M.B.A. CLASS

	Full-Time Only
Number of applicants	439
Number of offers extended	170
Number of students who accepted offer	72
Number of students who enrolled	72

GMAT score: 643 (mean); 650 (median)
Years of full-time work experience: 4.5 (mean); 4 (median)
Undergraduate GPA: 3.2 (mean); 3.3 (median)

Demographic Profile of Full-Time Students

Male: 74%
Female: 26%

PENN STATE ON PENN STATE

(Data provided by the Smeal
College of Business at
Pennsylvania State University)
Business school website:
http://www.smeal.psu.edu
Business school e-mail:
smealmba@psu.edu
Public institution
M.B.A. enrollment: 216
Full-time: 173
Executive program: 43

ADMISSIONS DIRECTOR:
Michele Kirsch
Director, Admissions
M.B.A. Program
Smeal College of Business
Pennsylvania State University
106 Business Administration
Building
University Park, PA 16802
814-863-0474 (voice)
814-863-8072 (fax)
E-mail: msk11@psu.edu

APPLICATION DEADLINES:
Fall 2006: 2/1/2006 (interna-
tional), 4/15/2006 (domestic)
Annual tuition: $14,500 (in-state);
$24,796 (out-of-state)
Annual room and board: $7,650

Minorities: 22%
U.S. citizens/residents: 66%
Foreign nationals: 34%

Class of 2004 Most Popular Academic Concentrations (% of Students)

Corporate finance 34%
Supply-chain management 21%
Product and market development 19%

CLASS OF 2004 EMPLOYMENT DATA

Industries Hiring Full-Time Graduates (% Hired)

Computer/technology/Internet/dot-com: 15%
Consumer products and services: 6%
Financial services/investment banking: 23%
Industrial products and services: 8%
Management consulting: 13%
Manufacturing: 2%
Petroleum/energy: 4%
Pharmaceutical/biotechnology/health-care products and services: 8%
Real estate: 3%
Telecommunications: 1%
Travel and transportation: 3%
Other professional services (accounting, advertising, etc.): 4%
Other: 10%

Position/Job Function (% Hired)

Consulting: 9%
Finance/accounting: 37%
General management: 7%
Information technology/management information systems: 1%
Marketing/sales: 14%

THE RECRUITERS SPEAK

Penn State's most impressive features

"Students have realistic goals and aspirations"

"Knowledge of supply-chain concepts"

"Friendly"

Penn State's major shortcomings

"Solid grads, but few or no real stars"

"Not enough drive and depth"

"Communication skills"

How Penn State can increase its appeal

"Students with more experience"

"Continually work on alumni and corporate outreach"

"Raise visibility"

Operations/production/logistics: 26%
Other: 6%

Top Recruiters *(Number of Full-Time Class of 2004 Graduates Hired)*

IBM: 4
Dell: 4
Bear Stearns: 3
Cigna: 3
Black & Decker: 2
Citigroup: 2
Honeywell: 2
Navigant Consulting: 2
Praxair: 2
Wal-Mart: 2

Percentage of Job-Seeking Full-Time Graduates Who:	All Students	Citizens/Residents	Foreign Nationals
Received offers prior to or within 3 months of graduation	92%	91%	94%
Accepted offers prior to or within 3 months of graduation	92%	91%	94%

Overall Compensation	MEAN			MEDIAN		
	All Students	Citizens/ Residents	Foreign Nationals	All Students	Citizens/ Residents	Foreign Nationals
Annual base salary	$76,096	$77,470	$73,690	$75,000	$75,000	$75,000
Signing bonus	$9,633	$9,000	$10,727	$10,000	$10,000	$10,000
Other guaranteed compensation	$15,739	$17,527	$12,163	$8,700	$12,000	$8,100

Three of the Most Famous Graduates of M.B.A. Program

John M. Arnold, (class of 1987) Chairman and CEO, Petroleum Products

James R. Stengel (class of 1983) Chief Marketing Officer, Procter & Gamble

J. David Rogers (class of 1980) Chairman and CEO, JD Capital Management

JOSEPH M. katz
Graduate School of Business
University of Pittsburgh

UNIVERSITY OF PITTSBURGH (KATZ GRADUATE SCHOOL OF BUSINESS)

The Katz School encourages a speedy education through its one-year M.B.A. program, which was created in 1960 and was the first of its kind in the U.S. Katz promotes the graduates of its one-year program as people with a strong work ethic who can move "at the pace of business." Most of the fast-track students bring an academic background in business or economics, plus substantial work experience.

For students who need more grounding in business fundamentals and the experience of a summer internship, the school established a more traditional full-time two-year M.B.A. as well. Pittsburgh also offers a part-time M.B.A. degree—the most popular choice—and a global executive-M.B.A. program that stretches from Pittsburgh to the U.K., Czech Republic, and Brazil.

With a small full-time program, Pittsburgh touts its personal touch and flexibility as well as students' ability to customize their M.B.A. program. Students can concentrate in such disciplines as finance, marketing, strategy, manufacturing and operations, and human resources. They also can choose one of the three "signature programs," which are a distinctive, multidisciplinary part of the Katz M.B.A. These feature a sequence of classes across academic disciplines and focus on marketing of technology-based products and services, valuation and corporate finance, and process management and integration.

The Katz School has created several dual-degree programs, including the timely combination of an M.B.A. and a master's of science in bioengineering with the schools of medicine and engineering. There are also the "Techno-M.B.A." dual degrees that combine the M.B.A. with a master's in information-systems management or a master's in industrial engineering.

Recruiters in *The Wall Street Journal*/Harris Interactive survey gave Pittsburgh its highest ratings for the career-services office and students' teamwork abilities and personal ethics and integrity. Pittsburgh was rated lowest for faculty expertise, students' international knowledge and experience, awareness of corporate citizenship issues, and previous work experience.

School Rankings
- Regional ranking in the recruiter survey: 37 of 47 schools ranked

FALL 2004 INCOMING M.B.A. CLASS

	Total	Full-Time Only
Number of applicants	809	512
Number of offers extended	507	275
Number of students who accepted offer	323	127
Number of students who enrolled	306	112

GMAT score: 620 (mean); 610 (median)
Years of full-time work experience: 4.1 (mean); 3.1 (median)
Undergraduate GPA: 3.22 (mean); 3.29 (median)

Demographic Profile of Full-Time Students
Male: 71%
Female: 29%
Minorities: 9%
U.S. citizens/residents: 52%
Foreign nationals: 48%

PITTSBURGH ON PITTSBURGH

(Data provided by the Joseph M. Katz Graduate School of Business at the University of Pittsburgh)

Business school website:
http://www.katz.pitt.edu
Business school e-mail:
mba@katz.pitt.edu
Public institution
M.B.A. enrollment: 718
Full-time: 187
Part-time: 466
Executive program: 65

ADMISSIONS DIRECTOR:
Kelly Wilson
Director, M.B.A. Admissions
University of Pittsburgh/Katz School
276 Mervis Hall
Pittsburgh, PA 15260
412-648-1700 (voice)
412-648-1659 (fax)
E-mail: mba@katz.pitt.edu

APPLICATION DEADLINES:
Fall 2006: 12/01/2005, 1/15/2006, 3/1/2006, 4/15/2006
Annual tuition: $27,310 (in-state); $44,079 (out-of-state)
Annual room and board: $11,500

Class of 2004 Most Popular Academic Concentrations (% of Students)

Finance 43%
Marketing 22%
Management information systems 12%

CLASS OF 2004 EMPLOYMENT DATA

Industries Hiring Full-Time Graduates (% Hired)

Computer/technology/Internet/dot-com: 18%
Consumer products and services: 5%
Financial services/investment banking: 5%
Government: 5%
Management consulting: 19%
Manufacturing: 23%
Pharmaceutical/biotechnology/health-care products and services: 7%
Real estate: 2%
Telecommunications: 2%
Travel and transportation: 2%
Other professional services (accounting, advertising, etc.): 7%
Other: 5%

Position/Job Function (% Hired)

Consulting: 5%
Finance/accounting: 43%
Human resources: 3%
Information technology/management information systems: 14%
Marketing/sales: 25%
Operations/production/logistics: 5%
Other: 5%

THE RECRUITERS SPEAK

Pittsburgh's most impressive features	Pittsburgh's major shortcomings	How Pittsburgh can increase its appeal
"Excellent work ethic"	"Light work experience"	"Fewer non-U.S. students"
"Technical backgrounds"	"A little unpolished"	"Strengthen core curriculum"
"Well-rounded students"	"Regional focus"	"Improve leadership skills"

Top Recruiters *(Number of Full-Time Class of 2004 Graduates Hired)*

Johnson & Johnson: 4
Ford Motor: 3
Bayer Chemicals: 3
Alcoa: 2
Ernst & Young: 2
KPMG: 2
Eckerd Health Systems: 2
PNC Bank: 2
Deloitte Consulting: 1
GlaxoSmithKline: 1

Percentage of Job-Seeking Full-Time Graduates Who:	All Students	Citizens/Residents	Foreign Nationals
Received offers prior to or within 3 months of graduation	86%	87%	80%
Accepted offers prior to or within 3 months of graduation	86%	87%	80%

	MEAN			MEDIAN		
Overall Compensation	All Students	Citizens/ Residents	Foreign Nationals	All Students	Citizens/ Residents	Foreign Nationals
Annual base salary	$63,000	$65,000	$54,500	$63,000	$65,000	$50,000
Signing bonus	$5,600	$8,250	$8,250	$5,600	$5,000	$8,250
Other guaranteed compensation	$6,400	$5,300	$12,000	$4,800	$4,200	$12,000

Three of the Most Famous Graduates of M.B.A. Program

Christopher V. Dodds (class of 1983) Executive Vice President and CFO, Charles Schwab

Kevin March (class of 1984) CFO, Texas Instruments

Richard J. Santorum (class of 1981) U.S. Senator from Pennsylvania

KRANNERT
SCHOOL OF MANAGEMENT
PURDUE UNIVERSITY

PURDUE UNIVERSITY
(KRANNERT SCHOOL OF MANAGEMENT)

Purdue maintained its No. 1 spot in *The Wall Street Journal*/Harris Interactive Regional ranking for the second straight year, winning recruiters' praise for its students' analytical skills and dogged work habits.

Established in 1958 as the School of Industrial Management, Purdue's business school grew out of the university's economics department and its engineering school. It has never strayed far from its roots, maintaining its focus on quantitative skills, operations management, manufacturing, and technology. That consistency showed up in the *Journal* survey: Krannert was among the top 10 schools named by recruiters as most outstanding in the fields of operations management and information technology.

Although still closely connected to manufacturing companies, Purdue is moving away from its old industrial image. Taking shape on the outskirts of the Purdue campus is Discovery Park, which will include centers on entrepreneurship, nanotechnology, bioscience, and e-enterprise. Discovery Park will integrate the business school more than ever with other parts of the university, as well as encourage professors and students to think more about applications, not just theory.

The strong connection with operations management and technology overshadows some of Krannert's other strengths, causing frustration among some professors who feel that other academic areas such as finance don't receive their due.

Krannert is expanding at a time when many schools are struggling financially to maintain the status quo. It is in the midst of a faculty expansion that will result in a net increase of 20 professors by 2007. Krannert also opened a $35 million classroom building in 2003 that was designed to incorporate the latest technologies and encourage more interaction among students and faculty in the public areas within its light-drenched atrium.

In addition to the full-time M.B.A., the Krannert School offers an executive-M.B.A. degree and plans to add a weekend-only executive-M.B.A. option in 2007.

In the *Journal* survey, Purdue was rated highest for students' analytical and problem-solving skills and their willingness to relocate, as well as for being a good value for the money invested in the recruiting effort. Purdue received its lowest ratings for students' international knowledge and prior work experience.

School Rankings

- Regional ranking in the recruiter survey: 1 of 47 schools ranked
- Ranking by energy- and industrial-products-industry recruiters: 3rd place

Recognition for Excellence in Academic Concentrations

- With 160 nominations, Purdue ranked No. 3 among business schools that recruiters in *The Wall Street Journal*/Harris Interactive survey cited for excellence in operations management.
- With 47 nominations, Purdue ranked No. 8 for excellence in information technology.

FALL 2004 INCOMING M.B.A. CLASS

	Full-Time Only
Number of applicants	828
Number of offers extended	364
Number of students who accepted offer	178
Number of students who enrolled	122

PURDUE ON PURDUE

(Data provided by the Krannert
School of Management at Purdue
University)

Business school website:
http://www.krannert.purdue.edu
Business school e-mail:
masters@krannert.purdue.edu
Public institution
M.B.A. enrollment: 496
Full-time: 281
Executive program: 215

ADMISSIONS DIRECTOR:
Jamie Hobba
Director of Admissions
2020 Rawls Hall
100 S. Grant St.
West Lafayette, IN 47907
765-494-0773 (voice)
765-494-9841 (fax)
E-mail: masters@krannert.
purdue.edu

APPLICATION DEADLINES:
Fall 2006: 12/1/2005, 1/20/2006
(international); 11/1/2005,
1/1/2006, 3/1/2006, 5/1/2006
(domestic)
Annual tuition: $14,174 (in-state);
$28,076 (out-of-state)
Annual room and board: $7,500

GMAT score: 667 (mean); 670 (median)
Years of full-time work experience: 4.6 (mean); 3.8 (median)
Undergraduate GPA: 3.3 (mean); 3.3 (median)

Demographic Profile of Full-Time Students

Male: 82%
Female: 18%
Minorities: 27%
U.S. citizens/residents: 62%
Foreign nationals: 38%

Class of 2004 Most Popular Academic Concentrations (% of Students)

Finance 44%
Operations 29%
Marketing 24%

CLASS OF 2004 EMPLOYMENT DATA

Industries Hiring Full-Time Graduates (% Hired)

Computer/technology/Internet/dot-com: 14.3%
Consumer products and services: 12%
Energy and utilities: 1.1%
Financial services/investment banking: 9.9%
Government: 2.6%
Industrial products and services: 5.4%
Management consulting: 8.7%
Manufacturing: 26.6%
Pharmaceutical/biotechnology/health-care products and services:
9.9%
Telecommunications: 2.2%
Other: 7.3%

THE RECRUITERS SPEAK

Purdue's most impressive features

"Analytical capabilities are top-notch"

"Friendly, flexible, team-oriented"

"Finding diamonds in the rough"

Purdue's major shortcomings

"Interpersonal skills"

"Inability to look at the big picture"

"Need for meaty leadership experiences"

How Purdue can increase its appeal

"Improve language skills of international students"

"Increase the number of women and minority students"

"Emphasize work experience in admissions"

Position/Job Function *(% Hired)*

Consulting: 5.2%
Finance/accounting: 18.2%
General management: 16.9%
Human resources: 2.6%
Information technology/management information systems: 6.5%
Marketing/sales: 24.7%
Operations/production/logistics: 22%
Other: 3.9%

Top Recruiters *(Number of Full-Time Class of 2004 Graduates Hired)*

Eaton: 3
Ford: 3
IBM: 3
Procter & Gamble: 3
Raytheon: 3
United Technologies: 3
Air Products: 2
Guidant: 2
General Electric: 2
Johnson & Johnson: 2

Percentage of Job-Seeking Full-Time Graduates Who:	All Students	Citizens/Residents	Foreign Nationals
Received offers prior to or within 3 months of graduation	89%	93%	75%
Accepted offers prior to or within 3 months of graduation	87%	90%	75%

	MEAN			MEDIAN		
Overall Compensation	All Students	Citizens/ Residents	Foreign Nationals	All Students	Citizens/ Residents	Foreign Nationals
Annual base salary	$74,915	$76,394	$68,905	$77,125	$78,120	$68,450
Signing bonus	$12,552	$13,054	$10,700	$12,000	$12,000	$10,000
Other guaranteed compensation	$6,532	$4,496	$18,750	$5,000	$5,000	$18,750

Three of the Most Famous Graduates of M.B.A. Program

Joe W. Forehand (class of 1972) Chairman, Accenture

Marjorie Magner (class of 1974) Chairman and CEO, Global Consumer Group, Citigroup

Marshall O. Larsen (class of 1977) Chairman, President and CEO, Goodrich

RICE UNIVERSITY
(JONES GRADUATE SCHOOL OF MANAGEMENT)

Jesse H. Jones Graduate
School of Management
RICE UNIVERSITY

The Jones Graduate School of Management's M.B.A. program takes a general-management approach, giving students flexibility in designing course schedules to suit their career goals without any specific concentrations.

The most significant curriculum development has been the increase in practical experience. The Jones School surveyed CEOs about what they find lacking in M.B.A. graduates and discovered that most named leadership and communication skills. The school's response was its "action-learning curriculum." Now, for example, in the required Action Learning Project, students consult for 10 weeks for such companies as Continental Airlines, IBM, and Exxon Mobil on issues like brand image, e-commerce strategies, new-product development, and mergers and acquisitions.

Full-time students can combine their M.B.A. with engineering or medical degrees. In addition to the full-time program, Rice offers an executive-M.B.A. degree over 22 months. In the second year of the executive program, students can participate in the International Business Briefing, traveling to a foreign country to meet with business and government officials.

Given the school's Houston location, Rice attracts recruiters from such energy companies as ConocoPhillips, but it lost one of its biggest recruiters with Enron's stunning collapse. One of Rice's strongest areas is finance, with its high-tech El Paso Corporation Finance Center that links students to the finance and energy markets, and its M.A. Wright Fund, a student-run equity fund. Not surprisingly, then, more than half of Rice's M.B.A.s take jobs in accounting and finance.

The Jones School recently opened an architecturally striking $60 million, 167,000-square-foot building that is three times as large as Herring Hall, its old facility.

Recruiters in *The Wall Street Journal*/Harris Interactive survey rated Rice students highest for their analytical and problem-solving skills, teamwork abilities, and personal ethics and integrity. Rice received its lowest scores for students' awareness of corporate social responsibility issues, their international knowledge and experience, and the faculty's expertise.

School Rankings

- Regional ranking in the recruiter survey: 22 of 47 schools ranked
- Ranking by energy- and industrial-products-industry recruiters: 9th place

FALL 2004 INCOMING M.B.A. CLASS

	Total	Full-Time Only
Number of applicants	831	695
Number of offers extended	465	361
Number of students who accepted offer	271	175
Number of students who enrolled	251	160

RICE ON RICE

(Data provided by the Jesse H. Jones Graduate School of Management at Rice University)

Business school website: http://www.jonesgsm.rice.edu
Business school e-mail: ricemba@rice.edu
Private institution
M.B.A. enrollment: 503
Full-time: 325
Executive program: 178

ADMISSIONS DIRECTOR:
Lisa Anderson
Director of Admissions
P.O. Box 2932
Rice University
Houston, TX 77252
888-844-4773 (voice)
713-348-6147 (fax)
E-mail: ricemba@rice.edu

APPLICATION DEADLINES:
Fall 2006: October 2005, December 2005, February 2006, April 2006
Annual tuition: $30,900
Annual room and board: $7,500

THE RECRUITERS SPEAK

Rice's most impressive features

"Strong candidates without big heads"

"Awesome facilities"

"Quality students at a reasonable price"

Rice's major shortcomings

"More generalists than specialists"

"Interpersonal communications"

"Too focused on finance"

How Rice can increase its appeal

"Continue to network with firms outside Texas"

"Recruit more students with strategic-thinking abilities"

"Increase diversity, more Hispanics and blacks"

GMAT score: 624 (mean); 640 (median)
Years of full-time work experience: 5 (mean); 5 (median)
Undergraduate GPA: 3.2 (mean); 3.3 (median)

Demographic Profile of Full-Time Students

Male: 73%
Female: 27%
Minorities: 27%
U.S. citizens: 79%
Foreign nationals: 21%

Class of 2004 Most Popular Academic Concentrations N/A

CLASS OF 2004 EMPLOYMENT DATA

Industries Hiring Full-Time Graduates (% Hired)

Government: 3%
Manufacturing: 19%
Nonprofit: 2%
Other: 76%

Position/Job Function (% Hired)

Consulting: 16%
Finance/accounting: 55%
General management: 9%
Marketing/sales: 12%
Operations/production/logistics: 3%
Other: 5%

Top Recruiters (Number of Full-Time Class of 2004 Graduates Hired)

Deloitte: 5
ConocoPhillips: 4
PricewaterhouseCoopers: 3
Continental Airlines: 3
Intel: 3
FMC Technologies: 3
Direct Energy: 3
American Express: 2
Hewlett-Packard: 2
Ernst & Young: 2

Percentage of Job-Seeking Full-Time Graduates Who:	All Students	Citizens/Residents	Foreign Nationals
Received offers prior to or within 3 months of graduation	89%	97%	40%
Accepted offers prior to or within 3 months of graduation	85%	94%	34%

	MEAN			MEDIAN		
Overall Compensation	All Students	Citizens/ Residents	Foreign Nationals	All Students	Citizens/ Residents	Foreign Nationals
Annual base salary	$74,108	$73,813	$75,706	$75,000	$75,000	$75,000
Signing bonus	$10,000	$10,472	$8,818	$10,000	$10,000	$6,000
Other guaranteed compensation	$13,361	$13,671	$12,188	$10,000	$11,750	$10,000

Three of the Most Famous Graduates of M.B.A. Program

James Turley (class of 1978) Global Chairman and CEO, Ernst & Young

Keith Anderson (class of 1983) Founding Partner and Managing Director, BlackRock

Doug Foshee (class of 1992) President and CEO, El Paso Energy

UNIVERSITY OF ROCHESTER

(SIMON GRADUATE SCHOOL OF BUSINESS ADMINISTRATION)

Rochester's Simon School is bucking the age trend in M.B.A. programs. Increasingly, business schools have admitted older students with at least four or five years of work experience, but the Simon School is encouraging people to apply either straight out of college or after only a year or two in the workplace. It calls its new initiative the 4-2 program, urging students with strong academic, leadership, and communication skills to progress into the M.B.A. program after finishing their undergraduate studies.

In addition to the standard two-year M.B.A. program, the Simon School offers the 3-2 program, enabling Rochester undergraduates to earn both a bachelor's degree and an M.B.A. in five years rather than six. There's also an accelerated option for students with extensive work experience. They can complete the M.B.A. degree in 15 months by skipping the usual M.B.A. summer internship.

Students also can participate in the Simon School's joint-degree program, which has a medical and scientific focus. They receive an M.B.A. along with an advanced degree in biotechnology, anesthesiology, or public health. There's a combined five-year M.D./M.B.A. option, as well.

Named for former U.S. Treasury Secretary William E. Simon, the school promotes itself as the M.B.A. program "where thinkers become leaders." The school is best known for its fi-

ROCHESTER ON ROCHESTER

(Data provided by the William E. Simon Graduate School of Business Administration at the University of Rochester)

Business school website: http://www.simon.rochester.edu
Business school e-mail: admissions@simon.rochester.edu
Private institution
M.B.A. enrollment: 561
Full-time: 342
Part-time: 163
Executive program: 56

ADMISSIONS DIRECTOR:
Pamela Black-Colton
Assistant Dean for Admissions and Administration
305 Schlegel Hall
Rochester, NY 14627
585-275-3533 (voice)
585-271-3907 (fax)
E-mail:
admissions@simon.rochester.edu

APPLICATION DEADLINES:
Fall 2006: 12/1/2005, 2/1/2006, 4/1/2006, 6/1/2006
Winter 2007: 8/1/2006, 10/15/2006
Annual tuition: $34,710
Annual room and board: $6,500

nancial and analytical focus, and about half its graduates take jobs in financial services and investment banking.

International diversity is another hallmark of the Simon School, with nearly half its M.B.A. candidates coming from foreign countries. The school runs an intensive language and cultural immersion program during the summer to help sharpen international students' discussion and presentation skills. International students also visit companies and attend sporting and theater events to become more attuned to American business and culture.

In the latest *Wall Street Journal*/Harris Interactive survey, recruiters gave Rochester its highest ratings for students' analytical and problem-solving skills, their willingness to relocate, and the faculty's expertise. Rochester was rated lowest for students' communication and interpersonal skills and their prior work experience.

School Rankings

■ Regional ranking in the recruiter survey: 17 of 47 schools ranked

Recognition for Excellence in an Academic Concentration

■ With 79 nominations, Rochester ranked No. 10 among business schools that recruiters in *The Wall Street Journal*/Harris Interactive survey cited for excellence in finance.

THE RECRUITERS SPEAK

Rochester's most impressive features

"Leadership potential"

"Finance theory and application"

"Integrated, strategic thinking"

Rochester's major shortcomings

"Some students are too young"

"English skills of international students"

"Students lack swagger"

How Rochester can increase its appeal

"Don't recruit any students without experience"

"Get senior managers into your classrooms"

"Hire a top PR company"

FALL 2004 INCOMING M.B.A. CLASS

	Total	Full-Time Only
Number of applicants	880	793
Number of offers extended	359	295
Number of students who accepted offer	N/A	N/A
Number of students who enrolled	177	114

GMAT score: 665 (mean); 660 (median)
Years of full-time work experience: 4.2 (mean); N/A (median)
Undergraduate GPA: 3.4 (mean); N/A (median)

Demographic Profile of Full-Time Students

Male: 73%
Female: 27%
Minorities: 36%
U.S. citizens/residents: 51%
Foreign nationals: 49%

Class of 2004 Most Popular Academic Concentrations (% of Students)

Finance 78%
Competitive and organizational strategy 46%
Accounting 43%

CLASS OF 2004 EMPLOYMENT DATA

Industries Hiring Full-Time Graduates (% Hired)

Computer/technology/Internet/dot-com: 9.7%
Consumer products and services: 8.1%
Financial services/investment banking: 47.6%
Government: 1%
Management consulting: 16.5%
Nonprofit: 1.6%
Pharmaceutical/biotechnology/health-care products and services: 8.1%
Telecommunications: 4%
Travel and transportation: 2.4%
Other professional services (accounting, advertising, etc.): 1%

Position/Job Function (% Hired)

Consulting: 18.5%
Finance/accounting: 61.3%
General management: 6.5%
Marketing/sales: 7.3%
Operations/production/logistics: 2.4%
Other: 4%

Top Recruiters (Number of Full-Time Class of 2004 Graduates Hired)

Citigroup: 8
Deloitte & Touche: 5
Johnson & Johnson: 4
PricewaterhouseCoopers: 4
General Electric: 3
M&T Bank: 3
Moody's Investors Service: 3
Goodyear Tire & Rubber: 3
UBS: 3
Barclays Capital: 2

Percentage of Job-Seeking Full-Time Graduates Who:	All Students	Citizens/Residents	Foreign Nationals
Received offers prior to or within 3 months of graduation	92%	93%	90%
Accepted offers prior to or within 3 months of graduation	89%	89%	87%

Overall Compensation	MEAN			MEDIAN		
	All Students	Citizens/Residents	Foreign Nationals	All Students	Citizens/Residents	Foreign Nationals
Annual base salary	$77,995	$75,621	$82,477	$80,000	$79,200	$85,000
Signing bonus	$13,214	$12,695	$13,948	$12,500	$10,000	$13,000
Other guaranteed compensation	$22,030	$21,641	$22,855	$17,000	$15,000	$18,000

Three of the Most Famous Graduates of M.B.A. Program

Karen Smith Pilkington (class of 1988) President, Greater Asian Region, Eastman Kodak

Lance Drummond (class of 1985) Senior Vice President, Bank of America

Robert Keegan (class of 1972) President and CEO, Goodyear Tire & Rubber

MARSHALL
SCHOOL OF
BUSINESS

UNIVERSITY OF SOUTHERN CALIFORNIA (MARSHALL SCHOOL OF BUSINESS)

Under the leadership of its new dean, Yash Gupta, the Marshall School offers a variety of master's programs in Los Angeles, including full-time, part-time and executive-M.B.A. degrees, as well as specialized degrees in such areas as business taxation and medical management. There's also an intensive one-year international M.B.A. degree for midcareer managers that emphasizes business issues in Asia and the Americas.

USC's Marshall School prides itself on having developed an entrepreneurship program and global focus long before they became commonplace in M.B.A. programs. It takes credit for establishing in the early 1970s what it calls "the nation's first fully integrated M.B.A. program in entrepreneurship." It has since been expanded and endowed as the Lloyd Greif Center for Entrepreneurial Studies.

Another first, the school says, was its requirement in 1997 that all first-year M.B.A. students travel abroad, the focus of its Pacific Rim Education Program (PRIME). Four years later, Marshall extended its international reach by becoming the first business school invited to Havana to meet with Cuban authorities and learn about their international business interests. And in 2004, USC exported its executive-M.B.A. program to Shanghai in collaboration with Jiao Tong University.

USC students can specialize in a variety of fields, including the business of entertainment, health-care advisory services, the business of education, general marketing, corporate finance, real-estate finance, and retail e-business. To strengthen interpersonal communication skills, the Marshall School established a Business Communication department to teach students the art of business speaking and writing, as well as to guide them in developing logical persuasion skills

In *The Wall Street Journal*/Harris Interactive survey, recruiters gave students their highest scores for fit with the corporate culture, analytical and problem-solving skills, strategic thinking, and ability to work well in teams. USC received the lowest ratings for students' international knowledge, past work experience, and willingness to relocate for a job.

School Rankings

- National ranking in the recruiter survey: 10 of 19 schools ranked
- Ranking by consumer-products-industry recruiters: 5th place

Recognition for Excellence in Academic Concentrations

- With 61 nominations, USC ranked No. 9 among business schools that recruiters in *The Wall Street Journal*/Harris Interactive survey cited for excellence in accounting.
- With 71 nominations, USC ranked No. 9 for excellence in entrepreneurship.

FALL 2004 INCOMING M.B.A. CLASS

	Total	Full-Time Only
Number of applicants	2,690	1,693
Number of offers extended	1,310	621
Number of students who accepted offer	979	303
Number of students who enrolled	734	275

GMAT score: 685 (mean); 690 (median);
Years of full-time work experience: 5 (mean); 5 (median)
Undergraduate GPA: 3.3 (mean); 3.3 (median)

USC ON USC

(Data provided by the Marshall School of Business at the University of Southern California)

Business school website: http://www.marshall.usc.edu
Business school e-mail: mary-kay.demetriou@marshall.usc.edu
Private institution
M.B.A. enrollment: 1,588
Full-time: 600
Part-time: 792
Executive program: 196

ADMISSIONS DIRECTOR:
Keith Vaughn
Director, M.B.A. Admissions
JKP 308
University of Southern California
Los Angeles, CA 90089
213-740-8936 (voice)
213-749-8520 (fax)
E-mail:
marshallmba@marshall.usc.edu

APPLICATION DEADLINES:
Fall 2006: 12/1/2005, 1/15/2006, 2/15/2006, 4/1/2006
Annual tuition: $37,558
Annual room and board: $16,000

Demographic Profile of Full-Time Students

Male: 75%
Female: 25%
Minorities: 23%
U.S. citizens: 78%
Foreign nationals: 22%

Class of 2004 Most Popular Academic Concentrations (% of Students)

Finance 29%
Marketing 21%
Real estate and entrepreneurship 10% each

CLASS OF 2004 EMPLOYMENT DATA

Industries Hiring Full-Time Graduates (% Hired)

Computer/technology/Internet/dot-com: 6%
Consumer products and services: 16%
Energy and utilities: 1%
Financial services/investment banking: 19%
Government: 1%
Management consulting: 6%
Manufacturing: 7%
Media/entertainment: 10%
Nonprofit: 1%
Pharmaceutical/biotechnology/health-care products and services: 6%
Real estate: 12%
Telecommunications: 3%
Other professional services (accounting, advertising, etc.): 12%

THE RECRUITERS SPEAK

USC's most impressive features

"Smart, good communicators"

"Entrepreneurial"

"Knowledge of real estate"

USC's major shortcomings

"God's-gift-to-the-business-world mentality"

"Unwillingness to relocate outside California"

"Fraternity-like students"

How USC can increase its appeal

"Provide more outreach to new employers"

"Teach students to do their homework on recruiting companies"

"Better organization of career-placement office"

Position/Job Function *(% Hired)*

Consulting: 14%
Finance/accounting: 37%
General management: 5%
Human resources: 1%
Information technology/management information systems: 1%
Marketing/sales: 36%
Operations/production/logistics: 3%
Other: 3%

Top Recruiters *(Number of Full-Time Class of 2004 Graduates Hired)*

Wells Fargo: 9
Deloitte: 7
Walt Disney: 6
Mattel: 5
Toyota: 4
Procter & Gamble: 4
KPMG: 4
SBC Communications: 3
Matsushita Avionics Systems: 3
Bank of America: 3

Percentage of Job-Seeking Full-Time Graduates Who:	All Students	Citizens/Residents	Foreign Nationals
Received offers prior to or within 3 months of graduation	82%	85%	68%
Accepted offers prior to or within 3 months of graduation	73%	77%	55%

Overall Compensation	MEAN			MEDIAN		
	All Students	Citizens/ Residents	Foreign Nationals	All Students	Citizens/ Residents	Foreign Nationals
Annual base salary	$75,029	$76,326	$67,429	$75,000	$78,000	$66,000
Signing bonus	$12,388	$13,118	$7,188	$10,000	$12,400	$7,000
Other guaranteed compensation	$13,810	$14,372	$8,008	$10,000	$10,000	$8,250

Three of the Most Famous Graduates of M.B.A. Program

Bradford D. Duea (class of 1993) President, Napster Division of Roxio

J. Terrence Lanni (class of 1967) Chairman and CEO, MGM Mirage

Yang-Ho Cho (class of 1979) Chairman and CEO, Korean Air Lines

SOUTHERN METHODIST UNIVERSITY (COX SCHOOL OF BUSINESS)

Leadership skills receive high priority at SMU's Cox School and its Business Leadership Center. Managers from J.C. Penney, Accenture, EDS, and other companies teach courses on such topics as motivating and developing people, resolving conflict, and improving communication and interpersonal skills. Among the recent seminar offerings: "Dynamics of Effective Listening," "CQ: The Confidence Quotient," "Heart-Centered Leadership," and "Influencing the Media." Some Cox students have even visited the theme parks at Walt Disney World and kept daily diaries analyzing the company's service culture and leadership style.

To increase students' international business exposure, SMU sends all its first-year M.B.A. students abroad for two weeks of meetings with business executives and political leaders in Asia, Europe, or Latin America. They learn how marketing approaches vary among cultures, and how governments and trade regulations affect economies.

In addition to the full-time program, SMU offers both part-time and executive-M.B.A. degrees, as well as a joint M.B.A./J.D. Albert Niemi, the dean of the Cox School, believes the trend will increasingly be toward more part-time executive students, and the school is opening a new executive-education center to meet expected demand.

To increase the number of minority students, the Cox School recently created the position of director of diversity. Steve Den-

SMU ON SMU

(Data provided by the Cox School
of Business at Southern
Methodist University)

Business school website:
http://www.cox.smu.edu
Business school e-mail:
mbainfo@mail.cox.smu.edu
Private institution
M.B.A. enrollment: 953
Full-time: 169
Part-time: 616
Executive program: 168

ADMISSIONS DIRECTOR:
Arrion Rathsack
Director, M.B.A. Admissions
P.O. Box 750333
Dallas, TX 75275
214-768-1214 (voice)
214-768-3956 (fax)
E-mail:
mbainfo@mail.cox.smu.edu

APPLICATION DEADLINES:
Fall 2006: 4/30/2006
Annual tuition: $30,055
Annual room and board: $10,000

son, a citizen of the Chickasaw Nation, was named to the position following his groundbreaking efforts to attract more Native Americans to SMU's M.B.A. program. The school also has joined Management Leadership for Tomorrow, an organization that helps minority students through the Graduate Management Admission Test and M.B.A. application process.

Recruiters in the latest *Wall Street Journal*/Harris Interactive survey gave SMU its highest grades for value for the money invested in the recruiting effort, chemistry or good feelings about the school, and likelihood of recruiting stars. Recruiters gave SMU its lowest scores for students' international knowledge and experience and awareness of corporate citizenship issues.

School Rankings

- Regional ranking in the recruiter survey: 20 of 47 schools ranked

FALL 2004 INCOMING M.B.A. CLASS

	Total	Full-Time Only
Number of applicants	660	336
Number of offers extended	419	153
Number of students who accepted offer	286	69
Number of students who enrolled	272	69

GMAT score: 661 (mean); 665 (median)
Years of full-time work experience: 5 (mean); 4.3 (median)
Undergraduate GPA: 3.3 (mean); 3.3 (median)

THE RECRUITERS SPEAK

SMU's most impressive features

"Well-rounded, students present themselves well"

"Financial capabilities"

"Friendly"

SMU's major shortcomings

"Unwillingness to leave the Dallas-Fort Worth area"

"Too small, too Texas"

"Students expect the C-suite immediately"

How SMU can increase its appeal

"Sharper work experience"

"Improve interpersonal training"

"Prepare students better for interviews"

Demographic Profile of Full-Time Students

Male: 75%
Female: 25%
Minorities: 20%
U.S. citizens/residents: 83%
Foreign nationals: 17%

Class of 2004 Most Popular Academic Concentrations (% of Students)

Finance 45%
Marketing 21%
General management 11%

CLASS OF 2004 EMPLOYMENT DATA

Industries Hiring Full-Time Graduates (% Hired)

Computer/technology/Internet/dot-com: 4%
Consumer products and services: 5%
Financial services/investment banking: 29%
Industrial products and services: 1%
Management consulting: 9%
Manufacturing: 1%
Media/entertainment: 3%
Petroleum/energy: 1%
Real estate: 4%
Telecommunications: 6%
Travel and transportation: 8%
Other professional services (accounting, advertising, etc.): 29%

Position/Job Function (% Hired)

Consulting: 3%
Finance/accounting: 49%
General management: 4%
Human resources: 1%
Marketing/sales: 23%
Operations/production/logistics: 4%
Other: 16%

Top Recruiters (Number of Full-Time Class of 2004 Graduates Hired)

American Airlines: 6
Wells Fargo: 4

Bank of America: 2
Lehman Brothers: 2
FTI Consulting: 2
Texas Instruments: 2
Sabre Holdings: 2
Dean Foods: 2
Bank of Texas: 2
Frito-Lay: 2

Percentage of Job-Seeking Full-Time Graduates Who:	All Students	Citizens/Residents	Foreign Nationals
Received offers prior to or within 3 months of graduation	79%	82%	65%
Accepted offers prior to or within 3 months of graduation	73%	76%	59%

	MEAN			MEDIAN		
Overall Compensation	All Students	Citizens/Residents	Foreign Nationals	All Students	Citizens/Residents	Foreign Nationals
Annual base salary	$71,235	$71,100	$72,007	$72,000	$72,000	$67,500
Signing bonus	$9,485	$9,790	$6,333	$9,250	$10,000	$5,000
Other guaranteed compensation	$11,818	$11,606	$15,000	$8,000	$8,000	$15,000

Three of the Most Famous Graduates of M.B.A. Program

James H. MacNaughton (class of 1973) Managing Director, Rothschild

Ruth Ann Marshall (class of 1980) President, Americas, MasterCard International

F. Thaddeus Arroyo (class of 1989) Chief Information Officer, Cingular Wireless

STANFORD UNIVERSITY

STANFORD
GRADUATE SCHOOL OF BUSINESS

Founded in 1925 by Stanford alumnus and future U.S. President Herbert Hoover, Stanford became the first graduate business school west of the Mississippi River. Hoover hoped to halt the trend of talented students heading east for their degree.

Today, Stanford does indeed attract many of the brightest M.B.A. students, who achieve an average score of 711 on the Graduate Management Admission Test. However, Stanford officials stress that they don't focus on GMATs alone, but rather look at other factors such as applicants' previous work experience, integrity, and initiative.

Stanford promotes its relatively intimate atmosphere compared with Harvard, Wharton, and other larger rivals. Although Stanford often receives 5,000 applications, it enrolls only about 370 M.B.A. students a year.

While the school states that its mission continues to be the education of general managers, it has become increasingly linked with Silicon Valley because of its location and focus on technology and entrepreneurship. Although Stanford doesn't offer formal majors, students can earn academic certificates in public management or global management.

In addition, second-year students can participate in small seminars on such subjects as corruption; finance, behavioral economics and sports betting; and successes and failures of online market mechanisms. There's also the opportunity for

STANFORD ON STANFORD

(Data provided by the Stanford Graduate School of Business)

Business school website:
http://www.gsb.stanford.edu
Business school e-mail:
mba@gsb.stanford.edu
Private institution
M.B.A. enrollment: 753
Full-time: 753

ADMISSIONS DIRECTOR:
Derrick Bolton
Assistant Dean and Director of
M.B.A. Admissions
Stanford Graduate School of
Business
518 Memorial Way
Stanford University
Stanford, CA 94305
650-723-2766 (voice)
650-725-6750 (fax)
E-mail: mba@gsb.stanford.edu

APPLICATION DEADLINES:
Fall 2006: October 2005, January
2006, March 2006
Annual tuition and fees: $41,340
Annual room and board: $16,180

independent-study courses. Recent topics have included "Understanding the Impact and Mobility of Status Across Industries" and "Business Opportunities in the Online Wholesale Diamond Market."

Visiting lecturers are common at Stanford; in fact, some jointly teach courses. A former San Francisco 49ers coach has taught in a sports management class, while an award-winning documentary filmmaker has teamed with a professor in a class about working in the movie and television business.

Stanford doesn't award executive-M.B.A. degrees but does offer midcareer managers a jump-start to their careers with its 10-month Sloan master's program. The school says the demanding program is designed to deepen students' "command of all disciplines required for success as a general manager."

Recruiters in the latest *Wall Street Journal*/Harris Interactive ranking gave Stanford its top scores for students' strategic thinking, leadership potential, and analytical and problem-solving skills. Stanford's lowest ratings: students' willingness to relocate for a job, value for the money invested in the recruiting effort, and the career-services office.

School Rankings

- National ranking in the recruiter survey: 15 of 19 schools ranked
- International ranking: 18 of 20 schools ranked

THE RECRUITERS SPEAK

Stanford's most impressive features

"Smart and savvy leaders"

"Creativity, entrepreneurial bent"

"Graduates are dynamic and energetic"

Stanford's major shortcomings

"Stars are present, but egos abound"

"Too focused on California jobs post-M.B.A."

"Too tech-centric"

How Stanford can increase its appeal

"Become more recruiter-friendly"

"Admit more work superstars vs. academic all-stars"

"More humility and realistic expectations of job"

Recognition for Excellence in Academic Concentrations

- With 430 nominations, Stanford ranked No. 1 among business schools that recruiters in *The Wall Street Journal*/Harris Interactive survey cited for excellence in entrepreneurship.
- With 190 nominations, Stanford ranked No. 2 for excellence in strategy.
- With 168 nominations, Stanford ranked No. 3 for excellence in information technology.
- With 46 nominations, Stanford ranked No. 8 for excellence in operations management.

Special Recognition

- Good source for recruiting women: 3rd most nominated school, 73 nominations.
- Good source for recruiting minorities: 6th most nominated school, 45 nominations.
- Good source for recruiting graduates with high ethical standards: 9th most nominated school, 61 nominations.

FALL 2004 INCOMING M.B.A. CLASS

	Full-Time Only
Number of applicants	4,697
Number of offers extended	N/A
Number of students who accepted offer	N/A
Number of students who enrolled	371

GMAT score: 711 (mean); 710 (median)
Years of full-time work experience: 4 (mean); 4 (median)
Undergraduate GPA: 3.5 (mean); 3.5 (median)

Demographic Profile of Full-Time Students

Male: 65%
Female: 35%
Minorities: 24%
U.S. citizens/residents: 71%
Foreign nationals: 29%

Class of 2004 Most Popular Academic Concentrations (% of Students)

General management 100%
Global management 28%
Public management 25%

CLASS OF 2004 EMPLOYMENT DATA

Industries Hiring Full-Time Graduates (% Hired)

Computer/technology/Internet/dot-com: 16%
Consumer products and services: 9%
Energy and utilities: 2%
Financial services/investment banking: 32%
Management consulting: 18%
Manufacturing: 1%
Media/entertainment: 4%
Nonprofit: 4%
Pharmaceutical/biotechnology/health-care products/services: 4%
Real estate: 4%
Telecommunications: 1%
Travel and transportation: 1%
Other professional services (accounting, advertising, etc.): 4%

Percentage of Job-Seeking Full-Time Graduates Who:	All Students	Citizens/Residents	Foreign Nationals
Received offers prior to or within 3 months of graduation	94%	95%	93%
Accepted offers prior to or within 3 months of graduation	91%	92%	86%

Overall Compensation	MEAN			MEDIAN		
	All Students	Citizens/ Residents	Foreign Nationals	All Students	Citizens/ Residents	Foreign Nationals
Annual base salary	$100,400	$101,100	$97,900	$100,000	$98,800	$100,000
Signing bonus	$16,100	$15,400	$18,000	$15,000	$15,000	$15,000
Other guaranteed compensation	$38,100	$39,700	$33,100	$25,000	$25,000	$25,000

Position/Job Function *(% Hired)*

Consulting: 19%
Finance/accounting: 31%
General management: 15%
Marketing/sales: 15%
Operations/production/logistics: 2%
Other: 18%

Top Recruiters *(Number of Full-Time Class of 2004 Graduates Hired)*

McKinsey: N/A
Bain:
Boston Consulting Group:
Yahoo!:
Gap:
Genentech:
Morgan Stanley:
Amazon.com:
Deutsche Bank:
General Mills:

Three of the Most Famous Graduates of M.B.A. Program

Henry A. McKinnell (class of 1967) Chairman and CEO, Pfizer

Phil Knight (class of 1962) Founder and Chairman, Nike

Charles Schwab (class of 1961) Founder, Chairman and CEO, Charles Schwab & Co.

TECNOLOGICO DE MONTERREY (EGADE)

Tecnologico de Monterrey's EGADE business school is based in Monterrey, Mexico, but its reach extends much farther through exchange and joint-degree programs with schools in the Americas, Asia, and Europe.

EGADE's M.B.A. program has been steadily enhancing its international profile. Accredited by AACSB International in the U.S. and by EQUIS in Europe, it draws well over half its full-time students from more than 20 foreign countries.

In partnership with the business school at the University of North Carolina in Charlotte, EGADE offers an M.B.A. in global business and strategy on both a full-time and a part-time basis. EGADE has also joined with four business schools in the U.S., China, Brazil, and the Netherlands to offer an international executive-M.B.A. program. Managers spend most of their time at their home school, but travel around the world for other parts of the OneMBA program.

EGADE uses a team-teaching approach in its M.B.A. classes, with an academic expert in the field of study working alongside a top manager with practical experience in international companies. In addition to the traditional M.B.A. degree and its global programs, EGADE offers master's degrees in finance, marketing, and manufacturing leadership.

Recruiters in the latest *Wall Street Journal*/Harris Interactive ranking gave EGADE its highest scores for students' analytical and problem-solving skills, leadership potential, and fit with the corporate culture. The school received its lowest scores for students' past work experience, the career-services office, and the core curriculum.

School Rankings

- Regional ranking in the recruiter survey: 9 of 47 schools ranked

FALL 2004 INCOMING M.B.A. CLASS

	Total	Full-Time Only
Number of applicants	295	133
Number of offers extended	225	105
Number of students who accepted offer	N/A	N/A
Number of students who enrolled	170	83

GMAT score: 611 (mean); 609 (median)
Years of full-time work experience: 3.8 (mean); 2.8 (median)
Undergraduate GPA: N/A

Demographic Profile of Full-Time Students

Male: 79%
Female: 21%
Mexican citizens/residents: 40%
Foreign nationals: 60%

Class of 2004 Most Popular Academic Concentrations (% of Students)

General management 53%
Finance 15%
Strategy 10%

EGADE ON EGADE

(Data provided by EGADE at
Tecnologico de Monterrey)

Business school website:
http://www.egade.itesm.mx
Business school e-mail:
admisiones.egade@itesm.mx
Private institution
M.B.A. enrollment: 785
Full-time: 141
Part-time: 558
Executive program: 86

ADMISSIONS DIRECTOR:
Leticia Sierra
Director of Admissions and
Academic Services
Av. Fundadores y Rufino Tamayo
Col. Valle Oriente
Garza García, Nuevo León
Mexico 66269
52-81-8625-6000 (voice)
52-81-8625-6208 (fax)
E-mail: Leticia.sierra@itesm.mx

APPLICATION DEADLINES:
Fall 2006: 8/11/2006
Annual tuition: $15,882
Annual room and board: $12,000

CLASS OF 2004 EMPLOYMENT DATA

Industries Hiring Full-Time Graduates (% Hired)

Consumer products and services: 20%
Financial services/investment banking: 30%
Government: 5%
Management consulting: 15%
Telecommunications: 5%
Other: 25%

Position/Job Function (% Hired)

Consulting: 25%
Finance/accounting: 20%
General management: 5%
Information technology/management information systems: 5%
Marketing/sales: 35%
Operations/production/logistics: 10%

Top Recruiters

N/A

THE RECRUITERS SPEAK

EGADE's most impressive features

"Technical expertise"

"Leadership"

"Analytical skills"

EGADE's major shortcomings

"Lack of student work experience"

"Theoretical teachers"

"Graduates are not well-rounded"

How EGADE can increase its appeal

"Focus on careers, not only salary"

"Connect with the rest of Latin America"

"Encourage work experience before studying for master's"

Percentage of Job-Seeking Full-Time Graduates Who:	All Students	Citizens/Residents	Foreign Nationals
Received offers prior to or within 3 months of graduation	90%	75%	94%
Accepted offers prior to or within 3 months of graduation	48%	75%	41%

Overall Compensation	MEAN			MEDIAN		
	All Students	Citizens/ Residents	Foreign Nationals	All Students	Citizens/ Residents	Foreign Nationals
Annual base salary	$43,194	$43,194	$41,507	$38,476	$38,476	$36,571
Signing bonus	N/A	N/A	N/A	N/A	N/A	N/A
Other guaranteed compensation	$4,897	$8,333	$3,523	$3,809	$8,333	$3,428

Three of the Most Famous Graduates of M.B.A. Program

Fernando Canales Clariond (class of 1973) Minister of Economy of the Mexican government

Eugenio Clariond (class of 1972) CEO, IMSA Industrial Group

José Antonio Fernández (class of 1979) CEO, FEMSA Industrial Group

UNIVERSITY OF TENNESSEE

The University of Tennessee, responding to students' concerns about the cost of an M.B.A. degree in both dollars and time, has compressed its program into 17 months, including a summer internship. The school's primary academic concentrations include finance, marketing, operations management, and logistics and transportation.

Tennessee established its M.B.A. program in 1966 and has restructured it twice since then. First, in 1991, it moved to make the M.B.A. more relevant to the corporate world by breaking from the traditional model of teaching basic skills in isolation from one another and focusing more on the interrelationships among various business functions. More emphasis was also placed on "real-world applications" and less on theory.

Then in 2001, it shortened the program to reduce the length of time students must drop out of the work force. It also adopted an approach it calls "integrated value chain management" to focus on management of relationships, the supply chain, resources, and information. The school describes its perspective this way: "Especially in today's business environment, competitive advantage comes from working with rather than competing against other organizations."

In addition to the full-time program, Tennessee offers a 16-month weekend M.B.A. degree for working professionals, a one-year executive M.B.A. for senior managers with 14 years of experience on average, and two specialized one-year, part-time M.B.A. degrees targeted at physicians and aerospace managers.

Recruiters in *The Wall Street Journal*/Harris Interactive survey rated Tennessee highest for students' ability to work well in teams, their personal ethics and integrity, and the school's core curriculum. The lowest scores: students' international knowledge and past work experience.

School Rankings

- Regional ranking in the recruiter survey: 23 of 47 schools ranked

FALL 2004 INCOMING M.B.A. CLASS

	Full-Time Only
Number of applicants	230
Number of offers extended	103
Number of students who accepted offer	64
Number of students who enrolled	64

GMAT score: 600 (mean); 600 (median)
Years of full-time work experience: 3.2 (mean); 2.3 (median)
Undergraduate GPA: 3.25 (mean); 3.3 (median)

Demographic Profile of Full-Time Students

Male: 66%
Female: 34%
Minorities: 5%
U.S. citizens/residents: 83%
Foreign nationals: 17%

Class of 2004 Most Popular Academic Concentrations (% of Students)

Finance 37%
Marketing 36%
Logistics 21%

TENNESSEE ON TENNESSEE

(Data provided by the University of Tennessee College of Business Administration)

Business school website:
http://mba.utk.edu
Business school e-mail:
mba@utk.edu
Public institution
M.B.A. enrollment: 291
Full-time: 140
Executive program: 151

ADMISSIONS DIRECTOR:
Donna Potts
M.B.A. Admissions Director
527 Stokely Management Center
Knoxville, TN 37996
865-974-5033 (voice)
865-974-3826 (fax)
E-mail: mba@utk.edu

APPLICATION DEADLINES:
Fall 2006: 2/1/2006
Annual tuition: $6,376 (in-state);
$16,156 (out-of-state)
Annual room and board: $12,500

CLASS OF 2004 EMPLOYMENT DATA

Industries Hiring Full-Time Graduates (% Hired)

Computer/technology/Internet/dot-com: 3%
Consumer products and services: 28%
Energy and utilities: 4%
Financial services/investment banking: 12%
Government: 6%
Industrial products and services: 6%
Management consulting: 3%
Manufacturing: 7%
Nonprofit: 4%
Pharmaceutical/biotechnology/health-care products and services: 10%
Real estate: 3%
Telecommunications: 2%
Travel and transportation: 9%
Other professional services (accounting, advertising, etc.): 3%

Position/Job Function (% Hired)

Consulting: 6%
Finance/accounting: 17%
General management: 20%
Marketing/sales: 22%
Operations/production/logistics: 30%
Other: 5%

Top Recruiters (Number of Full-Time Class of 2004 Graduates Hired)

Schneider National: 3
Jewelry Television: 2
BB&T: 2

THE RECRUITERS SPEAK

Tennessee's most impressive features

"Supply-chain knowledge"

"Practical approach to business"

"Heavy emphasis on performing in team-based environment"

Tennessee's major shortcomings

"Large variance in skill background of students"

"Small class size"

"Lack of work experience"

How Tennessee can increase its appeal

"Improve students' knowledge of accounting and finance"

"Attract more top-tier students"

"Prepare students better for interview process"

Eli Lily: 2
Home Depot: 2
Iasis Healthcare: 2
IMTI: 2
Sun Trust Bank: 2
Williams-Sonoma: 2
Procter & Gamble: 1

Percentage of Job-Seeking Full-Time Graduates Who:	All Students	Citizens/Residents	Foreign Nationals
Received offers prior to or within 3 months of graduation	77%	79%	50%
Accepted offers prior to or within 3 months of graduation	69%	71%	50%

	MEAN			MEDIAN		
Overall Compensation	All Students	Citizens/Residents	Foreign Nationals	All Students	Citizens/Residents	Foreign Nationals
Annual base salary	$55,400	$55,300	$57,000	$55,000	$55,000	$56,000
Signing bonus	$7,800	$7,800	$5,000	$5,500	$5,500	$5,000
Other guaranteed compensation	$14,500	$14,500	N/A	$10,000	$10,000	N/A

Three of the Most Famous Graduates of M.B.A. Program

Kevin Clayton (class of 1989) CEO, Clayton Homes

Scott Parrish (class of 1991) Senior Vice President and CFO, Alcon Entertainment

Bob Hall (class of 1979) Co-Founder and President, Jewelry Television

UNIVERSITY OF TEXAS AT AUSTIN (MCCOMBS SCHOOL OF BUSINESS)

The McCombs School, already one of the leading M.B.A. programs among state universities, has ambitions to become America's best public business school. In a detailed strategic plan, Texas declares that by 2010 it intends to strengthen its finance, marketing, and management programs to match its prowess in accounting and information systems. It also plans to enhance its academic research, increase student diversity, strengthen its alumni network, and build more partnerships with companies.

Dean George Gau has been especially concerned that the school's past focus on entrepreneurship, globalization, and technology hasn't matched the M.B.A. placement market. Of those three, only technology proved to be an important placement area for students who found jobs in information-management consulting. What the school's recruiters want most are students with outstanding finance and marketing skills.

Texas has begun to differentiate itself in the finance field with programs in energy finance, private equity, and real-estate finance. But Dean Gau believes the school still needs to become more innovative in marketing and management.

By 2010, Texas plans to add 10 faculty members at the graduate level and 30 at the undergraduate level. To improve the quality of its programs before more professors come on board, it has decided to reduce the size of each full-time M.B.A. class to about 340 from the previous 405.

The strategic plan, of course, will require more money from a variety of sources, including tuition. Students will need to pay more to help cover expected annual increases of $2 million to $3.2 million in the school's instruction and operations budget.

The McCombs School is expanding its presence within Texas, which it hopes will strengthen its ties with local companies. Having already established a part-time M.B.A. program in Dallas, it entered the Houston market in 2005. The Houston M.B.A. is off to a strong start with about 100 students, double what the school originally expected for its first class.

In The Wall Street Journal/Harris Interactive recruiter survey, Texas was rated highest for students' leadership potential, ability to work well in teams, and analytical and problem-solving skills. The school received its lowest scores for students' international knowledge and experience, the career-services office, and faculty expertise.

School Rankings
- Regional ranking in the recruiter survey: 35 of 47 schools ranked
- Ranking by energy and industrial-products-industry recruiters: 7th place

Recognition for Excellence in Academic Concentrations
- With 133 nominations, Texas ranked No. 3 among business schools that recruiters in The Wall Street Journal/Harris Interactive survey cited for excellence in accounting.
- With 61 nominations, Texas ranked No. 6 for excellence in information technology.

TEXAS ON TEXAS

(Data provided by the McCombs
School of Business at the
University of Texas at Austin)

Business school website:
http://www.mccombs.utexas.edu
Business school e-mail:
McCombsMBA@mccombs.
utexas.edu
Public institution
M.B.A. enrollment: 1,301
Full-time: 705
Part-time: 230
Executive program: 366

ADMISSIONS DIRECTOR:
Tina Mabley
Director of Admissions, M.B.A.
Program
McCombs School of Business
1 University Station, B6004
Austin, TX 78712
512-232-6122 (voice)
512-471-4131 (fax)
E-mail: McCombsMBA@
mccombs.utexas.edu

APPLICATION DEADLINES:
Fall 2006: 4/15/2006
Annual tuition: $18,872 (in-state);
$35,730 (out-of-state)
Annual room and board: $12,980

FALL 2004 INCOMING M.B.A. CLASS

	Total	Full-Time Only
Number of applicants	2,116	1,647
Number of offers extended	1,022	708
Number of students who accepted offer	645	379
Number of students who enrolled	592	318

GMAT score: 670 (mean); 680 (median)
Years of full-time work experience: 5.1 (mean); 4.9 (median)
Undergraduate GPA: 3.4 (mean); 3.4 (median)

Demographic Profile of Full-Time Students

Male: 80%
Female: 20%
Minorities: 18%
U.S. citizens/residents: 74%
Foreign nationals: 26%

Class of 2004 Most Popular Academic Concentrations (% of Students)

Finance N/A
Marketing N/A
General management N/A

CLASS OF 2004 EMPLOYMENT DATA

Industries Hiring Full-Time Graduates (% Hired)

Computer/technology/Internet/dot-com: 15%
Consumer products and services: 11%

THE RECRUITERS SPEAK

Texas's most impressive features

"Strong on entrepreneurial skills"

"Accounting program"

"Collaborative spirit of the students"

Texas's major shortcomings

"Not all are stars; a lot fall through the cracks"

"Most grads like to remain local"

"Lack of interpersonal/consulting skills"

How Texas can increase its appeal

"Work on more real-world projects"

"Aggressively recruit Hispanic-Americans"

"More user-friendly recruiting"

Energy and utilities: 1%
Financial services/investment banking: 23%
Industrial products and services: 2%
Management consulting: 11%
Media/entertainment: 2%
Nonprofit: 2%
Petroleum/energy: 3%
Pharmaceutical/biotechnology/health-care products and services:
6%
Real estate: 9%
Telecommunications: 4%
Travel and transportation: 3%
Other professional services (accounting, advertising, etc.): 4%
Other: 4%

Position/Job Function (% Hired)

Consulting: 13%
Finance/accounting: 40%
General management: 11%
Information technology/management information systems: 3%
Marketing/sales: 23%
Operations/production/logistics: 6%
Other: 4%

Percentage of Job-Seeking Full-Time Graduates Who:	All Students	Citizens/Residents	Foreign Nationals
Received offers prior to or within 3 months of graduation	87%	89%	76%
Accepted offers prior to or within 3 months of graduation	83%	85%	74%

Overall Compensation	MEAN			MEDIAN		
	All Students	Citizens/ Residents	Foreign Nationals	All Students	Citizens/ Residents	Foreign Nationals
Annual base salary	$77,403	$78,862	$71,141	$80,000	$80,000	$75,000
Signing bonus	$12,281	$12,863	$10,150	$10,000	$10,000	$10,000
Other guaranteed compensation	$13,983	$14,641	$10,795	$10,000	$10,000	$8,600

Top Recruiters *(Number of Full-Time Class of 2004 Graduates Hired)*

Dell: 21
Deloitte Consulting: 9
Frito-Lay: 6
Johnson & Johnson: 6
UBS: 6
Citigroup: 5
HEB: 5
IBM: 5
American Airlines: 4
SBC Communications: 4

Three of the Most Famous Graduates of M.B.A. Program

William R. Johnson (class of 1974) Chairman, President and CEO, H.J. Heinz

James Mulva (class of 1969) President and CEO, ConocoPhillips

Gerard Arpey (class of 1982) Chairman, President and CEO, AMR

TEXAS A&M UNIVERSITY

(MAYS GRADUATE SCHOOL OF
BUSINESS)

Texas A&M promotes its full-time, fast-track M.B.A. degree as a way for students to reduce the opportunity costs of lost wages and start earning a return on their investment more quickly. Students who begin the full-time M.B.A. program in August can finish by December of the next year, even while managing to squeeze in a summer internship.

Alternatively, students can stick around longer to take more specialized courses in subjects like e-commerce and real estate, work toward a certificate in entrepreneurship, supply-chain management, or international business, or earn a dual M.B.A./master's degree in information systems.

The M.B.A. program, which was restructured a few years ago, includes a student consulting project and the "Tech-Transfer Challenge," in which student teams concoct commercialization plans for new technologies. With its location in America's oil patch, Texas A&M also has created the Reliant Energy Securities and Commodities Trading Center, where students can observe financial transactions firsthand.

Beyond the campus in College Station, Texas A&M provides "enrichment opportunities," including overseas study, a three-week "Aggies on Wall Street" program for meeting with investment and banking executives, and a visit to Washington, Ď.C., to observe the connection between business and public policy making.

TEXAS A&M ON TEXAS A&M

(Data provided by the Mays Business School at Texas A&M University)

Business school website: http://mba.tamu.edu
Business school e-mail: MaysMBA@tamu.edu
Public institution
M.B.A. enrollment: 231
Full-time: 144
Executive program: 87

ADMISSIONS DIRECTOR:
Carroll Scherer
M.B.A. Program Director
4117 TAMU/3003 Wehner Building
College Station, TX 77843
979-845-4714 (voice)
979-862-2393 (fax)
E-mail: cscherer@mays.tamu.edu

APPLICATION DEADLINES:
Fall 2006: 1/15/2006 (international), 5/31/2006 (domestic)
Annual tuition: $3,600 (in-state); $14,616 (out-of-state)
Annual room and board: $9,306

In the Houston area, Texas A&M also offers an 18-month executive-M.B.A. program focused on "how organizations create and sustain value." With an average age of 39, students typically have 17 years of work experience, including a decade of significant managerial responsibility.

Recruiters in *The Wall Street Journal*/Harris Interactive survey rated Texas A&M highest for its core curriculum, past success with graduates they have hired, the career-services center, and value for the money invested in the recruiting effort. The school received its lowest scores for students' international knowledge and experience, their strategic thinking, and faculty expertise.

School Rankings

- Regional ranking in the recruiter survey: 28 of 47 schools ranked

FALL 2004 INCOMING M.B.A. CLASS

	Full-Time Only
Number of applicants	348
Number of offers extended	124
Number of students who accepted offer	70
Number of students who enrolled	70

THE RECRUITERS SPEAK

Texas A&M's most impressive features

"Realistic expectations"

"Familiarity with the energy industry"

"Practical kids who want to work"

Texas A&M's major shortcomings

"Insufficient diversity"

"Lack of executive communication/presence training"

"Students have limited life experiences"

How Texas A&M can increase its appeal

"Polish interview skills"

"More focus on leadership skill training"

"Recruit more students from outside Texas"

GMAT score: 637 (mean); 635 (median)
Years of full-time work experience: 4.6 (mean); 4 (median)
Undergraduate GPA: 3.3 (mean); 3.3 (median)

Demographic Profile of Full-Time Students

Male: 78%
Female: 22%
Minorities: 8%
U.S. citizens/residents: 80%
Foreign nationals: 20%

Class of 2004 Most Popular Academic Concentrations (% of Students)

Finance 50%
Marketing 20%
Information systems 5%

CLASS OF 2004 EMPLOYMENT DATA

Industries Hiring Full-Time Graduates (% Hired)

Computer/technology/Internet/dot-com: 10%
Consumer products and services: 6%
Energy and utilities: 3%
Financial services/investment banking: 14%
Government: 5%
Industrial products and services: 12%
Management consulting: 7%
Manufacturing: 14%
Petroleum/energy: 5%
Pharmaceutical/biotechnology/health-care products and services:
3%
Real estate: 4%
Telecommunications: 5%
Other professional services (accounting, advertising, etc.): 3%
Other: 9%

Position/Job Function (% Hired)

Consulting: 7%
Finance/accounting: 37%
General management: 11%
Human resources: 6%
Information technology/management information systems: 7%

Marketing/sales: 21%
Operations/production/logistics: 11%

Top Recruiters *(Number of Full-Time Class of 2004 Graduates Hired)*

Hewlett-Packard: 3
General Electric: 2
Citigroup: 2
SBC Communications: 2
Deloitte & Touche: 2
Chevron: 2
World Savings: 2
CIA: 2
Exxon Mobil: 1
Procter & Gamble: 1

Percentage of Job-Seeking Full-Time Graduates Who:	All Students	Citizens/Residents	Foreign Nationals
Received offers prior to or within 3 months of graduation	95%	98%	85%
Accepted offers prior to or within 3 months of graduation	95%	98%	85%

	MEAN			MEDIAN		
Overall Compensation	All Students	Citizens/ Residents	Foreign Nationals	All Students	Citizens/ Residents	Foreign Nationals
Annual base salary	$77,153	$78,450	$71,315	$76,000	$76,950	$72,000
Signing bonus	$5,979	$6,332	$2,625	$5,000	$5,000	$2,250
Other guaranteed compensation	$4,748	$4,802	$3,500	$4,250	$5,000	$3,500

Three of the Most Famous Graduates of M.B.A. Program

Don Davis (class of 1963) Chairman and CEO, Rockwell Automation

H. Andrew Hansen (class of 2002) CEO, Heart Surgery Center of the Southwest

Karl Hielscher (class of 2002) President and CEO, METL-Span

TEXAS CHRISTIAN UNIVERSITY (NEELEY SCHOOL OF BUSINESS)

The Neeley School offers a range of M.B.A. programs, from the standard two-year, full-time degree to an accelerated 12-month option for students with an academic background in business. For people who want to continue working, there are both part-time and executive-M.B.A. options.

The Neeley School and the education school have created a three-year combination M.B.A./Ed.D. to train students to work for school districts or educational foundations and agencies. Texas Christian believes the dual degree will produce more educators who are proficient business managers and help reduce the shortage of leaders in education, especially public-school superintendents.

The business school includes a Center for Professional Communication because it has long realized the importance of "soft skills" to recruiters. In *The Wall Street Journal*/Harris Interactive survey, recruiters list communication and interpersonal skills as the most important attribute they look for in prospective employees. The center at Texas Christian offers students workshops and individual coaching in business writing, intercultural communication, effective presentations, and listening skills.

The Neeley School has invested heavily in entrepreneurship education since 2000, when it launched the program for both graduate and undergraduate students. "Entrepreneurship is maybe one of the most important ways we can inject indepen-

TEXAS CHRISTIAN ON TEXAS CHRISTIAN

(Data provided by the Neeley School of Business at Texas Christian University)

Business school website:
http://www.neeley.tcu.edu
Business school e-mail:
mbainfo@tcu.edu
Private institution
M.B.A. enrollment: 342
Full-time: 100
Part-time: 198
Executive program: 44

ADMISSIONS DIRECTOR:
Peggy Conway
M.B.A. Admissions Director
2900 Lubbock St.
Fort Worth, TX 76129
817-257-7531 (voice)
817-257-6431 (fax)
E-mail: p.conway@tcu.edu

APPLICATION DEADLINES:
Fall 2006: 4/30/2006
Annual tuition: $22,200
Annual room and board:
$7,000–$10,000

dence back into people, show them a way to strike out on their own and depend on themselves for getting ahead," Steve Smith, a "jack-of-all trades entrepreneur," said after he donated $10.5 million toward construction of the school's new Steve and Sarah Smith Entrepreneurs Hall.

Although Texas Christian was founded by a Christian denomination, it now operates independently and doesn't include religious content in the M.B.A. curriculum.

One of the smallest full-time programs in the *Journal* survey, Texas Christian received its highest scores for students' teamwork abilities, personal ethics and integrity, the core curriculum, and the career-services offices. Its lowest ratings: students' international knowledge and past work experience.

School Rankings

- Regional ranking in recruiter survey: 18 of 47 schools ranked

FALL 2004 INCOMING M.B.A. CLASS

	Full-Time Only
Number of applicants	111
Number of offers extended	81
Number of students who accepted offer	N/A
Number of students who enrolled	45

THE RECRUITERS SPEAK

Texas Christian's most impressive features	Texas Christian's major shortcomings	How Texas Christian can increase its appeal
"Well-rounded students willing to pay their dues"	"Uneven quality"	"Increase technical skills of the students"
"Trained to work in teams"	"Lack of real-world business knowledge"	"Raise the entry bar, set reputation for quality"
"Reasonably priced hard workers"	"Lack of sophistication"	"Reach beyond the Fort Worth business community"

GMAT score: 602 (mean); 600 (median)
Years of full-time work experience: 4.1 (mean); 3.7 (median)
Undergraduate GPA: 3.3 (mean); 3.3 (median)

Demographic Profile of Full-Time Students

Male: 69%
Female: 31%
Minorities: 7%
U.S. citizens/residents: 78%
Foreign nationals: 22%

Class of 2004 Most Popular Academic Concentrations

N/A

CLASS OF 2004 EMPLOYMENT DATA

Industries Hiring Full-Time Graduates (% Hired)

Financial services/investment banking: 20.5%
Management consulting: 15.8%
Manufacturing: 11.4%
Other professional services (accounting, advertising, etc.): 52.3%

Position/Job Function (% Hired)

Consulting: 17.8%
Finance/accounting: 26.7%
Marketing/sales: 37.8%
Operations/production/logistics: 11%
Other: 6.7%

Top Recruiters (Number of Full-Time Class of 2004 Graduates Hired)

Jet Powered Group: 3
Sabre Holdings: 2
Textron/Bell Helicopter: 2
Texas Health Resources: 2
Alcon Labs: 1
American Airlines: 1
Wells Fargo: 1
Bank of America Securities: 1
PepsiCo: 1
RadioShack: 1

Percentage of Job-Seeking Full-Time Graduates Who:	All Students	Citizens/Residents	Foreign Nationals
Received offers prior to or within 3 months of graduation	89%	98%	66%
Accepted offers prior to or within 3 months of graduation	83%	89%	66%

	MEAN			MEDIAN		
Overall Compensation	All Students	Citizens/ Residents	Foreign Nationals	All Students	Citizens/ Residents	Foreign Nationals
Annual base salary	$59,075	$61,133	$46,726	$60,000	$60,250	$43,000
Signing bonus	$6,107	$5,038	$20,000	$4,000	$3,000	$20,000
Other guaranteed compensation	$15,500	N/A	N/A	$15,750	N/A	N/A

Three of the Most Famous Graduates of M.B.A. Program

Gordon England (class of 1975) Secretary of the U.S. Navy

John Roach (class of 1965) Former CEO, Tandy

Robert McCann (class of 1982) Vice Chairman of Wealth Management, Merrill Lynch

THUNDERBIRD
(GARVIN SCHOOL OF
INTERNATIONAL MANAGEMENT)

Thunderbird is a rare bird: a business school focusing exclusively on international management and drawing nearly half its full-time M.B.A. students from abroad. The school was founded just after World War II by Lt. Gen. Barton Kyle Yount, commanding general of the U.S. Army Air Training Command, on Thunderbird Field No. 1, a former pilot-training center near Phoenix. He sensed early on that the business world would become increasingly global and specialized training was needed.

Thunderbird has thrived. The school's graduates, referred to as "T-birds," now number more than 35,000 and have nested in 135 countries.

In its full-time M.B.A. program, Thunderbird offers two tracks: a four-trimester program that includes study of a second language along with international management courses, and a one-year program recommended for applicants who are multilingual and have worked abroad.

M.B.A. students can choose from a variety of options for study in other countries. Thunderbird is a partner with foreign business schools in both student-exchange and dual-degree programs; it operates its own campus in France, as well as facilities in Japan, China, and Russia. Thunderbird also offers a variety of executive-M.B.A. degrees at the main campus in Arizona and at several foreign locations.

THUNDERBIRD ON THUNDERBIRD

(Data provided by Thunderbird, the Garvin School of International Management)

Business school website:
http://www.thunderbird.edu
Business school e-mail:
admissions@thunderbird.edu
Private institution
M.B.A. enrollment: 941
Full-time: 777
Executive program: 164

ADMISSIONS DIRECTOR:
Judy Johnson
Associate Vice President of Admissions
15249 N. 59th Avenue
Glendale, AZ 85306
602-978-7131 (voice)
602-439-5432 (fax)
E-mail: admissions@thunderbird.edu

APPLICATION DEADLINES:
Fall 2006: rolling admissions
Annual tuition: $29,300
Annual room and board:
$6,558–$13,952

Thunderbird officials, believing the school should be "a force for social reconstruction," helped create an entrepreneurship program in 2005 to assist Afghan women in rebuilding their country's economy. Called the Artemis Project after the Greek goddess known as a protector of women and children, it brought 15 women to Thunderbird and to Phoenix-area businesses for two weeks of training and mentoring.

The school's administration has become more international with the selection in 2004 of the first non-U.S. citizen as president: Angel Cabrera, formerly dean of the Instituto de Empresa business school in Madrid. Thunderbird also added the Garvin name to the school in 2004, following a $60 million gift from alumnus Samuel Garvin, founder of Continental Promotion Group, and his wife, Rita.

Recruiters in the latest *Wall Street Journal*/Harris Interactive ranking gave Thunderbird its most positive ratings for students' international knowledge and experience, leadership potential, and teamwork abilities. Thunderbird's lowest ratings were for its core curriculum, career-services office, and students' previous work experience.

School Rankings

- Regional ranking in the recruiter survey: 4 of 47 schools ranked
- International ranking: 7 of 20 schools ranked
- Ranking by financial-services-industry recruiters: 3rd place

THE RECRUITERS SPEAK

Thunderbird's most impressive features

"The intercultural richness of the students"

"Strategic-thinking ability"

"Leadership skills"

Thunderbird's major shortcomings

"Looking for the home-run job right off the bat"

"Lack of real-world experience"

"Oral communication skills of some foreign students"

How Thunderbird can increase its appeal

"Improve business focus of career-services office"

"Only apply for jobs where there is a fit"

"Increase quantitative skills"

Recognition for Excellence in an Academic Concentration

■ With 649 nominations, Thunderbird ranked No. 1 among business schools that recruiters in *The Wall Street Journal*/Harris Interactive survey cited for excellence in international business.

FALL 2004 INCOMING M.B.A. CLASS

	Full-Time Only
Number of applicants	867
Number of offers extended	711
Number of students who accepted offer	462
Number of students who enrolled	457

GMAT score: 596 (mean); 590 (median)
Years of full-time work experience: 4.7 (mean); 4 (median)
Undergraduate GPA: 3.3 (mean); 3.4 (median)

Demographic Profile of Full-Time Students

Male: 74%
Female: 26%
Minorities: 14%
U.S. citizens/residents: 57%
Foreign nationals: 43%

Class of 2004 Most Popular Academic Concentrations (% of Students)

International business N/A
Global finance N/A
Global marketing N/A

CLASS OF 2004 EMPLOYMENT DATA

Industries Hiring Full-Time Graduates (% Hired)

Financial services/investment banking: 17%
Government: 3%
Manufacturing: 46%
Nonprofit: 3%

Other professional services (accounting, advertising, etc.): 23%
Other: 8%

Position/Job Function (% Hired)

Consulting: 9%
Finance/accounting: 23%
General management: 11%
Human resources: 2%
Information technology/management information systems: 1%
Marketing/sales: 42%
Operations/production/logistics: 7%
Other: 5%

Top Recruiters (Number of Full-Time Class of 2004 Graduates Hired)

Citigroup: 10
Samsung: 8
Johnson & Johnson: 7
Intel: 7
Hilti: 5
IBM: 5
American Express: 4
DaimlerChrysler: 4

Percentage of Job-Seeking Full-Time Graduates Who:	All Students	Citizens/Residents	Foreign Nationals
Received offers prior to or within 3 months of graduation	54%	54%	54%
Accepted offers prior to or within 3 months of graduation	43%	44%	42%

	MEAN			MEDIAN		
Overall Compensation	All Students	Citizens/Residents	Foreign Nationals	All Students	Citizens/Residents	Foreign Nationals
Annual base salary	$66,676	$67,972	$64,317	$66,500	$69,300	$60,000
Signing bonus	$8,652	$7,828	$10,203	$7,500	$10,000	$5,000
Other guaranteed compensation	$9,940	$10,320	$8,952	$8,000	$8,000	$8,000

Ernst & Young: 4
Honeywell: 4

Three of the Most Famous Graduates of M.B.A. Program

Sam Garvin (class of 1988) Founder, Continental Promotion Group

William Perez (class of 1970) CEO, Nike

Mark Emkes (class of 1976) CEO, Bridgestone/Firestone

UNIVERSITY OF UTAH
(ECCLES SCHOOL OF BUSINESS)

Located at the foot of the Wasatch Mountains, the University of Utah's business school offers a complete portfolio of M.B.A. degrees—full-time, part-time evening for working students, and weekend executive for more experienced managers. It also offers master's degrees in finance, accounting, and statistics, as well as a combined M.B.A. and master's of architecture and a joint M.B.A./law program.

The M.B.A. programs allow students to choose from the following "emphases": accounting, e-business, entrepreneurship and emerging business, finance, health-services administration, information systems, international business, marketing, and product management.

But the Eccles School strives to go beyond the traditional curriculum. According to Dean Jack Brittain, the school's goal is "to graduate people who can talk to recruiters about the projects they have done in real companies, not just the courses on their transcripts." M.B.A. students take courses organized around company projects and are paired with alumni mentors, including some CEOs.

Utah's business school traces its origins to 1896, when it was part of the economics and sociology department. It became a separate school in 1917 and awarded its first M.B.A. degrees 40 years later. The school isn't named for a modern-day businessman, but rather for a frontier industrialist who founded 48 businesses in the West during the latter part of the 19th century. The David Eccles name was adopted in 1991 after Mr. Eccles' youngest daughter established a $15 million endowment.

In *The Wall Street Journal*/Harris Interactive survey, Utah was rated most positively for students' teamwork abilities, personal ethics and integrity, and value for the money invested in the recruiting effort. Its lowest scores: students' international knowledge, past work experience, and willingness to relocate for a job.

School Rankings

- Regional ranking in the recruiter survey: 26 of 47 schools ranked

FALL 2004 INCOMING M.B.A. CLASS

	Total	Full-Time Only
Number of applicants	492	209
Number of offers extended	328	106
Number of students who accepted offer	252	71
Number of students who enrolled	210	56

GMAT score: 616 (mean); 600 (median)
Years of full-time work experience: 3.58 (mean); 2.34 (median)
Undergraduate GPA: 3.4 (mean); 3.33 (median)

Demographic Profile of Full-Time Students

Male: 67%
Female: 33%
Minorities: 3%
U.S. citizens/residents: 77%
Foreign nationals: 23%

Class of 2004 Most Popular Academic Concentrations (% of Students)

Finance 35%
Accounting 18%
Marketing 13%

UTAH ON UTAH

(Data provided by the David Eccles School of Business at the University of Utah)

Business school website:
http://www.business.utah.edu
Business school email:
information@business.utah.edu
Public institution
M.B.A. enrollment: 556
Full-time: 110
Part-time: 330
Executive program: 116

ADMISSIONS DIRECTOR:
Helen L. Anderson
Admissions Specialist
1645 E. Campus Center Drive
University of Utah
Salt Lake City, UT 84112
801-585-7366 (voice)
801-581-3666 (fax)
E-mail: Helen.anderson@
business.utah.edu

APPLICATION DEADLINE:
Fall 2006: 2/15/2006
Annual tuition: $9,042 (in-state);
$20,385 (out-of-state)
Annual room and board: $11,310

CLASS OF 2004 EMPLOYMENT DATA

Industries Hiring Full-Time Graduates (% Hired)

Computer/technology/Internet/dot-com: 6%
Consumer products and services: 2%
Financial services/investment banking: 12%
Government: 10%
Management consulting: 2%
Manufacturing: 10%
Pharmaceutical/biotechnology/health-care products and services: 16%
Real estate: 4%
Telecommunications: 2%
Travel and transportation: 4%
Other professional services (accounting, advertising, etc.): 21%
Other: 11%

Position/Job Function (% Hired)

Consulting: 8%
Finance/accounting: 51%
General management: 17%
Information technology/management information systems: 6%
Marketing/sales: 8%
Operations/production/logistics: 4%
Other: 6%

Top Recruiters (Number of Full-Time Class of 2004 Graduates Hired)

Phase II Consulting: 3
KPMG: 3
Omniture: 2
Zions Bank: 2

THE RECRUITERS SPEAK

Utah's most impressive features

"Work ethic, commitment"

"Integrity"

"Well-rounded students"

Utah's major shortcomings

"Limited exposure to business culture outside Utah"

"Depth of talent"

"Class size is too small"

How Utah can increase its appeal

"Invest more money in the career-services department"

"Teach more analytical skills"

"Raise standards to get in"

ATK Thiokol: 2
PricewaterhouseCoopers: 2
Ford Motor: 1
Gallup Organization: 1
RSM Equico: 1
Deloitte: 1

Percentage of Job-Seeking Full-Time Graduates Who:	All Students	Citizens/Residents	Foreign Nationals
Received offers prior to or within 3 months of graduation	91%	94%	72%
Accepted offers prior to or within 3 months of graduation	91%	94%	72%

	MEAN			MEDIAN		
Overall Compensation	All Students	Citizens/Residents	Foreign Nationals	All Students	Citizens/Residents	Foreign Nationals
Annual base salary	$51,188	$51,534	$48,353	$45,000	$45,000	$48,465
Signing bonus	$2,000	$2,000	N/A	$3,863	$3,863	N/A
Other guaranteed compensation	$11,083	$11,083	N/A	$10,000	$10,000	N/A

Three of the Most Famous Graduates of M.B.A. Program

Pierre Lassonde (class of 1973) President, Franco-Nevada and Euro-Nevada Mining

Teresa Beck (class of 1993) Former President, American Stores

Jerry Atkin (class of 1972) President and CEO, Skywest Airlines

VANDERBILT
Owen Graduate School of Management

VANDERBILT UNIVERSITY (OWEN GRADUATE SCHOOL OF MANAGEMENT)

The Owen Graduate School of Management is in the midst of change, as new Dean Jim Bradford takes charge and the school continues its rebranding campaign to create a stronger tie with Vanderbilt's heritage.

Second-year marketing students were involved in creating a new logo and the slogan, "Discover this place. Shape your world." As part of the image campaign, the school also has given each student a wallet-size "promise card," which states the school's responsibility to all its stakeholders—students, faculty, alumni, and the business community.

Vanderbilt's business school opened its doors in 1969 to 10 students and 10 faculty members in a former funeral home and has grown to nearly 400 full-time M.B.A. students today. But with a 10-to-1 student-to-faculty ratio, it still strives to maintain small classes and a collegial environment.

The Owen School offers M.B.A. concentrations in finance, accounting, marketing, information technology, general management, strategy, operations, and human and organizational performance. The school also remains committed to electronic retailing. It developed its first course in e-commerce more than 10 years ago and recently established the Sloan Center for Internet Retailing, which studies the way companies connect with customers on the Internet and how they integrate offline and online sales and marketing functions.

Owen also offers an executive M.B.A. and a new nine-month master's degree in quantitative financial analysis.

Vanderbilt tumbled 19 places to No. 21 in the latest *Wall Street Journal*/Harris Interactive Regional ranking, with recruiters noting the uneven quality of students. The school received its lowest scores for students' international knowledge and experience, the core curriculum, and faculty expertise. Recruiters gave the Owen School top grades for students' teamwork skills, personal ethics and integrity, and leadership potential.

School Rankings
- Regional ranking in the recruiter survey: 21 of 47 schools ranked

FALL 2004 INCOMING M.B.A. CLASS

	Full-Time Only
Number of applicants	615
Number of offers extended	421
Number of students who accepted offer	210
Number of students who enrolled	178

GMAT score: 622 (mean); 620 (median)
Years of full-time work experience: 5.1 (mean); 5 (median);
Undergraduate GPA: 3.18 (mean); 3.2 (median)

Demographic Profile of Full-Time Students

Male: 80%
Female: 20%
Minorities: 21%
U.S. citizens: 72%
Foreign nationals: 28%

Class of 2004 Most Popular Academic Concentrations (% of Students)

Finance 41%
Marketing 21%
Consulting 11%

VANDERBILT ON VANDERBILT

(Data provided by the Owen Graduate School of Management at Vanderbilt University)

Business school website: http://www.owen.vanderbilt.edu
Business school e-mail: N/A
Private institution
M.B.A. enrollment: 481
Full-time: 387
Executive program: 94

ADMISSIONS DIRECTOR:
Melinda M. Allen
Assistant Dean, Admissions and Career Management
401 21st Avenue South
136 Management Hall
Nashville, Tennessee 37203
615-322-4067 (voice)
615-343-4661 (fax)
E-mail: melinda.allen@owen.vanderbilt.edu

APPLICATION DEADLINES:
Fall 2006: 11/30/2005, 1/15/2006, 3/1/2006
Annual tuition: $33,840
Annual room and board: $11,750

CLASS OF 2004 EMPLOYMENT DATA

Industries Hiring Full-Time Graduates (% Hired)

Computer/technology/Internet/dot-com: 4%
Consumer products and services: 11%
Financial services/investment banking: 30%
Government: 3%
Industrial products and services: 3%
Management consulting: 9%
Media/entertainment: 6%
Nonprofit: 3%
Pharmaceutical/biotechnology/health-care products and services: 10%
Real estate: 7%
Telecommunications: 3%
Travel and transportation: 2%
Other professional services (accounting, advertising, etc.): 2%
Other: 7%

Position/Job Function (% Hired)

Consulting: 11%
Finance/accounting: 41%
General management: 9%
Human resources: 6%
Marketing/sales: 21%
Operations/production/logistics: 5%
Other: 7%

Top Recruiters (Number of Full-Time Class of 2004 Graduates Hired)

Citigroup: 5
Emerson: 4

THE RECRUITERS SPEAK

Vanderbilt's most impressive features

"Collegial attitude"

"Students are down to earth"

"Hungry students"

Vanderbilt's major shortcomings

"Students overestimate value at the point of hire"

"Lacks deep talent pool"

"Limited reputation"

How Vanderbilt can increase its appeal

"Bring students to major cities to visit corporations"

"Enhance practical experiences while in school"

"Get students to value spending time in the trenches"

Harrah's Entertainment: 3
Hospital Corporation of America: 3
Morgan Stanley: 3
Johnson & Johnson: 3
Smith & Nephew: 3
Samsung: 3
UBS: 3

Percentage of Job-Seeking Full-Time Graduates Who:	All Students	Citizens/Residents	Foreign Nationals
Received offers prior to or within 3 months of graduation	91%	93%	85%
Accepted offers prior to or within 3 months of graduation	86%	88%	79%

Overall Compensation	MEAN			MEDIAN		
	All Students	Citizens/Residents	Foreign Nationals	All Students	Citizens/Residents	Foreign Nationals
Annual base salary	$74,311	$75,845	$66,756	$75,000	$75,000	$75,000
Signing bonus	$11,301	$11,063	$12,361	$10,000	$7,500	$10,000
Other guaranteed compensation	$18,243	$16,110	$30,333	$10,000	$10,000	$15,000

Three of the Most Famous Graduates of M.B.A. Program

David Kloeppel (Class of 1996) Executive Vice President and CFO, Gaylord Entertainment

Doug Parker (class of 1986) Chairman, President and CEO, America West Airlines

David Farr (class of 1981) Chairman and CEO, Emerson

UNIVERSITY OF VIRGINIA (DARDEN GRADUATE SCHOOL OF BUSINESS ADMINISTRATION)

Founded a half-century ago, Virginia's Darden School takes a strong general-management approach, using case studies as its primary teaching method. After graduation, more than half its M.B.A. students typically move into management consulting and financial services, with about 25% taking general-management positions.

Some students choose to combine their M.B.A. with degrees in law, nursing, engineering, government or foreign affairs, and East Asian studies. For international experience, students can participate in exchange programs with 11 foreign business schools for a quarter or a semester, or spend a week abroad as part of the school's "global business experiences."

The Darden School has long embraced entrepreneurship, starting with its first small-business classes back in 1961. Today, its "new entrepreneurial economy" curriculum includes about two dozen courses taught by professors and adjunct faculty members with experience as small-business owners and venture capitalists. Through the Darden Progressive Incubator, students also can gain firsthand experience leading new-business ventures to the point of start-up—or abandonment.

In recent years, Darden has boosted its full-time M.B.A. enrollment to about 310 students per class from 250, as part of a strategy to increase its "critical mass." Starting in 2006, the school plans to add even more students by offering its first executive-M.B.A. degree. It considered an executive program for a decade before finally acting. The impetus was the changing demands of the workplace, which make it harder for many people to leave the job market for two years to pursue a full-time M.B.A..

Darden established a reputation for teaching ethics long before the post-Enron call for more ethics instruction in business schools. It was among the first schools to require students to take an ethics course, and its Olsson Center for Applied Ethics dates back to 1966. It also offers elective courses such as "Business Ethics Through Literature" and "Leadership, Values, and Ethics."

More recently, Darden worked with the Business Roundtable, an organization of CEOs, to create an Institute for Corporate Ethics to try to restore public trust in corporate America. The institute will develop educational programs on ethics and corporate governance, including some Web-based materials that will be widely available to managers and the public.

In the latest *Wall Street Journal*/Harris Interactive survey, recruiters gave Darden its top ratings for students' ability to work well in teams, personal ethics and integrity, and analytical and problem-solving skills. Recruiters graded Darden lowest for students' international knowledge and experience and value for the money invested in the recruiting effort.

School Rankings

- National ranking in the recruiter survey: 11 of 19 schools ranked

Recognition for Excellence in Academic Concentrations

- With 76 nominations, Virginia ranked No. 8 among business schools that recruiters in *The Wall Street Journal*/Harris Interactive survey cited for excellence in strategy.
- With 63 nominations, Virginia ranked No. 10 for excellence in entrepreneurship.

VIRGINIA ON VIRGINIA

(Data provided by the Darden Graduate School of Business Administration at the University of Virginia)

Business school website:
http://www.darden.virginia.edu
Business school e-mail:
darden@virginia.edu
Public institution
M.B.A. enrollment: 630
Full-time: 630

ADMISSIONS DIRECTOR:
Dawna Clarke
Director of Admissions
P.O. Box 6550
Charlottesville, VA 22906
434-924-7281 (voice)
434-243-5033 (fax)
E-mail: darden@virginia.edu

APPLICATION DEADLINES:
Fall 2006: October 2005,
December 2005, January 2006,
March 2006
Annual tuition: $32,300
(in-state); $37,300 (out-of-state)
Annual room and board: $13,627

Special Recognition

- Good source for recruiting graduates with high ethical standards: 5th most nominated school, 92 nominations.

FALL 2004 INCOMING M.B.A. CLASS

	Full-Time Only
Number of applicants	2,110
Number of offers extended	792
Number of students who accepted offer	305
Number of students who enrolled	305

GMAT score: 680 (mean); 690 (median)
Years of full-time work experience: 4 (mean); 4 (median)
Undergraduate GPA: 3.3 (mean); 3.3 (median)

Profile of Full-Time Students

Male: 74%
Female: 26%
Minorities: 15%
U.S. citizens/residents: 73%
Foreign nationals: 27%

Class of 2004 Most Popular Academic Concentrations

N/A

THE RECRUITERS SPEAK

Virginia's most impressive features

"Superior general-management focus"

"Ethics"

"Strength of faculty"

Virginia's major shortcomings

"Difficult to get to the school for recruiting"

"Weak link between faculty and recruiters"

"Strong focus on case studies is creating a gap in practical skills"

How Virginia can increase its appeal

"More emphasis on small to mid-size recruiters"

"Stimulate interest in finance among female students"

"Help students tap into what they are passionate about"

CLASS OF 2004 EMPLOYMENT DATA

Industries Hiring Full-Time Graduates (% Hired)

Financial services/investment banking: 33%
Management consulting: 16%
Manufacturing: 31%
Other: 20%

Position/Job Function (% Hired)

Consulting: 16%
Finance/accounting: 38%
General management: 25%
Marketing/sales: 16%
Operations/production/logistics: 2%
Other: 3%

Top Recruiters (Number of Full-Time Class of 2004 Graduates Hired)

Citigroup: 8
McKinsey: 7
Lehman Brothers: 6

Percentage of Job-Seeking Full-Time Graduates Who:	All Students	Citizens/Residents	Foreign Nationals
Received offers prior to or within 3 months of graduation	88%	90%	82%
Accepted offers prior to or within 3 months of graduation	84%	85%	81%

	MEAN			MEDIAN		
Overall Compensation	All Students	Citizens/ Residents	Foreign Nationals	All Students	Citizens/ Residents	Foreign Nationals
Annual base salary	$84,882	$85,712	$82,227	$85,000	$85,000	$82,000
Signing bonus	$15,457	$15,436	$15,529	$12,250	$14,000	$12,000
Other guaranteed compensation	$17,811	$17,452	$18,545	$12,000	$13,000	$10,000

Boston Consulting Group: 6
General Electric: 5
Pfizer: 5
Booz Allen Hamilton: 4
Capital One Financial: 4
Bank of America: 3
Cargill: 3

Three of the Most Famous Graduates of M.B.A. Program

George David (class of 1967) Chairman and CEO, United Technologies

Steven S. Reinemund (class of 1978) Chairman and CEO, PepsiCo

Douglas R. Lebda (class of 1998) Founder and former CEO, Lending Tree

WAKE FOREST UNIVERSITY (BABCOCK GRADUATE SCHOOL OF MANAGEMENT)

Wake Forest promotes itself as one of the most personalized, team-oriented M.B.A. programs. The "3/38 Plan" in its full-time M.B.A. program features three sections of approximately 38 students each and is intended to increase interaction among classmates and professors.

Like a growing number of business schools, Wake Forest takes an interdisciplinary approach to teaching. As students progress through the curriculum, they are challenged to solve problems by drawing on their knowledge of finance, information technology, and other functions. The goal is to avoid silo-like thinking and instead produce graduates who understand how decisions made in one part of a company's operations affect other areas.

As for career focus, finance and accounting are the main choices of students at the Babcock School, followed by marketing and sales. Wake Forest, which relies heavily on the case method of instruction, also has developed academic concentrations in operations management, entrepreneurship, consulting, and information-technology management.

In addition to full-time, part-time and executive-M.B.A. programs at the main campus in Winston-Salem, the Babcock School offers a two-year M.B.A. degree in Charlotte, where working professionals attend evening or Saturday-morning classes.

WAKE FOREST ON WAKE FOREST

(Data provided by the Babcock
Graduate School of Management
at Wake Forest University)

Business school website:
http://www.mba.wfu.edu
Business school e-mail:
admissions@mba.wfu.edu
Private institution
M.B.A. enrollment: 556
Full-time: 217
Part-time: 244
Executive program: 95

ADMISSIONS DIRECTOR:
Stacy Owen
Director of Full-Time Admissions
P.O. Box 7659
Winston-Salem, NC 27109
336-758-5422 (voice)
336-758-5830 (fax)
E-mail:
admissions@mba.wfu.edu

APPLICATION DEADLINES:
Fall 2006: 11/1/2005, 2/1/2006,
4/1/2006
Annual tuition: $29,500
Annual room and board: $5,600

Beyond the classroom, Wake Forest stages what it calls the oldest marketing-case competition in the U.S. In the M.B.A. Marketing Summit, students from eight schools compete by developing a marketing plan for such sponsoring companies as Coca-Cola, GlaxoSmithKline and Heineken. In the 15th competition this year, Wake Forest placed second behind the University of Texas at Austin.

In another creative contest, teams of M.B.A. students from schools around the country participate in the Babcock Elevator Competition, during which they try to parlay a two-minute elevator ride with a venture capitalist into funding for their business concepts.

In the latest *Wall Street Journal*/Harris Interactive Regional ranking, Wake Forest climbed 10 places to No. 7. Recruiters gave their highest ratings for chemistry or good feelings about the school and its students, graduates' personal ethics and integrity, their teamwork abilities, and fit with the corporate culture. Graduates received their lowest ratings for international knowledge and past work experience.

School Rankings

- Regional ranking in the recruiter survey: 7 of 47 schools ranked
- Ranking by financial-services-industry recruiters: 9th place

THE RECRUITERS SPEAK

Wake Forest's most impressive features

"Down-to-earth and excellent work ethic"

"Values-driven"

"Emphasis on teamwork, interaction with local businesses"

Wake Forest's major shortcomings

"Limited work experience"

"Unwillingness to relocate outside the Carolinas"

"Not enough diversity"

How Wake Forest can increase its appeal

"Focus more on building analytical skills"

"Set realistic salary expectations"

"Prepare students better for interviewing"

FALL 2004 INCOMING M.B.A. CLASS

	Total	Full-Time Only
Number of applicants	664	417
Number of offers extended	454	252
Number of students who accepted offer	319	131
Number of students who enrolled	303	115

GMAT score: 630 (mean); 640 (median)
Years of full-time work experience: 4 (mean); 3.3 (median)
Undergraduate GPA: 3.2 (mean); 3.2 (median)

Demographic Profile of Full-Time Students

Male: 71%
Female: 29%
Minorities: 13%
U.S. citizens/residents: 77%
Foreign nationals: 23%

Class of 2004 Most Popular Academic Concentrations (% of Students)

Finance 48%
Marketing 19%
Operations 16%

CLASS OF 2004 EMPLOYMENT DATA

Industries Hiring Full-Time Graduates (% Hired)

Computer/technology/Internet/dot-com: 6%
Consumer products and services: 21%
Financial services/investment banking: 23%
Industrial products and services: 5%
Management consulting: 15%
Manufacturing: 1%
Media/entertainment: 1%
Nonprofit: 1%
Pharmaceutical/biotechnology/health-care products and services: 2%
Real estate: 1%
Telecommunications: 2%

Travel and transportation: 2%
Other professional services (accounting, advertising, etc.): 20%

Position/Job Function *(% Hired)*

Consulting: 11%
Finance/accounting: 38%
General management: 9%
Marketing/sales: 25%
Operations/production/logistics: 17%

Top Recruiters *(Number of Full-Time Class of 2004 Graduates Hired)*

Lowe's: 5
Wachovia: 4
Philip Morris: 3
Ernst & Young: 3
Bank of America: 2
Sara Lee: 2
Booz Allen Hamilton: 2
General Electric: 2
Intel: 2
BearingPoint: 2

Percentage of Job-Seeking Full-Time Graduates Who:	All Students	Citizens/Residents	Foreign Nationals
Received offers prior to or within 3 months of graduation	92%	96%	83%
Accepted offers prior to or within 3 months of graduation	89%	92%	79%

	MEAN			MEDIAN		
Overall Compensation	All Students	Citizens/ Residents	Foreign Nationals	All Students	Citizens/ Residents	Foreign Nationals
Annual base salary	$70,135	$71,076	$66,706	$70,000	$72,000	$65,000
Signing bonus	$7,778	$9,316	$6,278	$5,000	$8,160	$5,000
Other guaranteed compensation	$7,625	$9,853	$7,879	$6,750	$7,800	$5,000

Three of the Most Famous Graduates of M.B.A. Program

Charles Ergen (class of 1976) CEO, EchoStar Communications

G. Kennedy Thompson (class of 1976) President and CEO, Wachovia

John Medica (class of 1983) Senior Vice President and General Manager, Dell

UNIVERSITY OF WASHINGTON

The University of Washington tailors its M.B.A. programs to Seattle's technology-driven and entrepreneurial business climate. The full-time program's core curriculum is steeped in technology issues. For example, an accounting class might focus on a regional Internet software company and invite the chief financial officer to speak and answer questions, while an ethics class might include executives from local biotech companies in a panel discussion on genetic engineering. The school also has developed a part-time, 18-month technology-management M.B.A. aimed at people already working in tech fields.

M.B.A.s have access to Washington's center for technology entrepreneurship, which includes a new-venture creation lab for studying the market potential of the university's emerging technologies. Business-school students and faculty work with colleagues from bioengineering, chemistry, electrical engineering, and other university departments.

Given the school's location on the Pacific gateway to America, international business figures prominently in the M.B.A. programs. Students can earn a certificate in global business by taking certain international management courses, studying abroad, learning a foreign language, obtaining an international internship, or participating in study tours to such countries as China, Singapore, Brazil, Sweden, and South Africa.

Washington offers three executive-M.B.A. degrees. One is local, for people living in the Puget Sound region, while the North American executive program is promoted to executives who travel frequently or live outside the area. The global degree is aimed at Korean managers, with students splitting their time between the Washington campus and Yonsei University in Seoul.

In *The Wall Street Journal*/Harris Interactive survey, recruiters rated Washington highest for students' teamwork abilities, personal ethics and integrity, and analytical and problem-solving skills. The school's lowest scores: students' international knowledge and experience and their willingness to relocate for a job.

School Rankings
■ Regional ranking in the recruiter survey: 36 of 47 schools ranked

FALL 2004 INCOMING M.B.A. CLASS

	Total	Full-Time Only
Number of applicants	863	633
Number of offers extended	414	258
Number of students who accepted offer	234	99
Number of students who enrolled	228	99

GMAT score: 677 (mean); 680 (median);
Years of full-time work experience: 5.2 (mean); 4.3 (median)
Undergraduate GPA: 3.45 (mean); 3.5 (median)

Demographic Profile of Full-Time Students
Male: 73%
Female: 27%
Minorities: 21%
U.S. citizens/residents: 72%
Foreign nationals: 28%

**UNIVERSITY OF
WASHINGTON ON
UNIVERSITY OF
WASHINGTON**

(Data provided by the University
of Washington Business School)

Business school website:
http://depts.washington.edu/
bschool
Business school e-mail:
mba@u.washington.edu
Public institution
M.B.A. enrollment: 529
Full-time: 225
Part-time: 151
Executive program: 153

ADMISSIONS DIRECTOR:
Sunni Bannon
Director of Admissions
Box 353200, Mackenzie Hall 110
University of Washington
Seattle, WA 98195
206-543-4661 (voice)
206-616-7351 (fax)
E-mail: mba@u.washington.edu

APPLICATION DEADLINE:
Fall 2006: 11/15/2005, 1/15/2006,
3/15/2006 (domestic only)
Annual tuition: $14,780 (in-state);
$24,720 (out-of-state)
Annual room and board: $10,338

Class of 2004 Most Popular Academic Concentrations (% of Students)

Marketing 38%
Finance 29%
General management 15%

CLASS OF 2004 EMPLOYMENT DATA

Industries Hiring Full-Time Graduates (% Hired)

Computer/technology/Internet/dot-com: 25%
Consumer products and services: 4%
Financial services/investment banking: 18%
Government: 3%
Management consulting: 11%
Manufacturing: 8%
Nonprofit: 3%
Pharmaceutical/biotechnology/health-care products and services:
6%
Real estate: 1%
Telecommunications: 4%
Travel and transportation: 4%
Other professional services (accounting, advertising, etc.): 13%

Position/Job Function (% Hired)

Consulting: 11%
Finance/accounting: 30%
General management: 14%
Human resources: 1%
Marketing/sales: 37%
Operations/production/logistics: 6%
Other: 1%

THE RECRUITERS SPEAK

**Washington's most impressive
features**

"Driven students"

"Integrity and ethics"

"Well-rounded students with high
potential"

**Washington's major
shortcomings**

"High variability of students—some
great, some not"

"Students are too Northwest-
centered in their career search"

"Too theoretical"

**How Washington can increase
its appeal**

"Screen out the low-performers
during admissions"

"Teach students more about
consulting"

"Raise the work-experience bar"

Top Recruiters *(Number of Full-Time Class of 2004 Graduates Hired)*

Microsoft: 5
PACCAR: 5
Accenture: 3
Amazon.com: 3
Hitachi Consulting: 3
Planar: 3
Washington Mutual: 3
Wells Fargo Bank: 3
Alaska Airlines: 2
Intel: 2

Percentage of Job-Seeking Full-Time Graduates Who:	All Students	Citizens/Residents	Foreign Nationals
Received offers prior to or within 3 months of graduation	97%	98%	95%
Accepted offers prior to or within 3 months of graduation	97%	98%	95%

	MEAN			MEDIAN		
Overall Compensation	All Students	Citizens/Residents	Foreign Nationals	All Students	Citizens/Residents	Foreign Nationals
Annual base salary	$72,241	$73,254	$68,660	$75,000	$75,000	$75,000
Signing bonus	$13,327	$12,826	$15,080	$10,831	$10,000	$13,739
Other guaranteed compensation	$14,511	$16,284	$9,699	$10,000	$10,000	$10,000

Three of the Most Famous Graduates of M.B.A. Program

Charles Lillis (class of 1968) Former CEO, Media One Group

Dan Nordstrom (class of 1989) CEO, Nordstrom.com

William Ayer (class of 1978) CEO, Alaska Airlines

WASHINGTON UNIVERSITY (OLIN SCHOOL OF BUSINESS)

Washington University's Olin School began awarding M.B.A. degrees more than 50 years ago and today offers a broad menu of full-time, part-time, and executive programs. In 2002, it went global, creating an executive-M.B.A. degree in Shanghai, China, with Fudan University. M.B.A.s also can earn a dual degree in architecture, biomedical engineering, East Asian studies, health administration, law, or social work.

The Olin School is a strong believer in the value of real-world experiences. Through its Center for Experiential Learning, students do management consulting for such clients as Anheuser-Busch, Apple Computer, and Enterprise Rent-a-Car, as well as work with local nonprofit agencies on business problems. They also apply "total quality management" techniques to the St. Louis public schools, resulting in improved classroom behavior, less after-lunch tardiness, and higher student test scores.

The center provides students with international opportunities, too. For instance, in spring 2005, students could travel to China to learn about currency and banking issues, to Chile and Peru to study economic development and the business culture, or to Greece and Turkey to focus on European integration and the business climate.

Entrepreneurship programs offer another chance for practical experience. M.B.A.s map out business plans in the "hatchery," sometimes collaborating with students and researchers from other parts of Washington University. Recent projects have included a basket-selling venture to aid developing economies, a technology for diabetes therapy, and a program to help needy students prepare for college and the SAT.

The practical focus of the M.B.A. curriculum extends even to career planning. Realizing that the M.B.A. student's "eye is on the prize," the Olin School requires students to take its "Managing Your Career Strategy" course in the first semester. The goal is to help students realistically assess their strengths, develop job-search skills, and plan their course of study for the next three semesters.

In the latest *Wall Street Journal*/Harris Interactive survey, recruiters gave students their highest ratings for teamwork skills, personal ethics and integrity, and fit with the corporate culture. Washington received its lowest scores for students' international knowledge, previous work experience, and the core curriculum.

School Rankings

■ Regional ranking in the recruiter survey: 25 of 47 schools ranked

FALL 2004 INCOMING M.B.A. CLASS

	Total	Full-Time Only
Number of applicants	879	692
Number of offers extended	507	373
Number of students who accepted offer	307	172
Number of students who enrolled	266	141

GMAT score: 649 (mean); 650 (median)
Years of full-time work experience: 4.7 (mean); 4.1 (median)
Undergraduate GPA: 3.19 (mean); 3.2 (median)

WASHINGTON UNIVERSITY ON WASHINGTON UNIVERSITY

(Data provided by the John M. Olin School of Business at Washington University)

Business school website:
http://www.olin.wustl.edu
Business school e-mail:
mba@olin.wustl.edu
Private institution
M.B.A. enrollment: 899
Full-time: 275
Part-time: 357
Executive program: 267

ADMISSIONS DIRECTOR:
Brad Pearson
Director of M.B.A. Admissions
and Financial Aid
Campus Box 1133
1 Brookings Drive
Saint Louis, MO 63130
888-622-5115 (voice)
314-935-6309 (fax)
E-mail: pearson@wustl.edu

APPLICATION DEADLINES:
Fall 2006: November 2005, May
2006
Annual tuition: $34,500
Annual room and board: $13,372

Demographic Profile of Full-Time Students

Male: 77%
Female: 23%
Minorities: 16%
U.S. citizens/residents: 64%
Foreign nationals: 36%

Class of 2004 Most Popular Academic Concentrations

N/A

CLASS OF 2004 EMPLOYMENT DATA

Industries Hiring Full-Time Graduates (% Hired)

Computer/technology/Internet/dot-com: 6%
Consumer products and services: 20%
Energy and utilities: 3%
Financial services/investment banking: 22%
Industrial products and services: 6%
Management consulting: 12%
Media/entertainment: 4%
Pharmaceutical/biotechnology/health-care products and services: 8%
Real estate: 1%
Telecommunications: 1%
Travel and transportation: 4%
Other: 13%

Position/Job Function (% Hired)

Consulting: 21%
Finance/accounting: 34%
General management: 8%
Human resources: 3%

THE RECRUITERS SPEAK

Washington's most impressive features

"Quiet leaders"

"Good communication skills"

"Finance and operations programs are solid"

Washington's major shortcomings

"Limited depth of experience"

"Smaller school, hence smaller candidate pool"

"Lacks national reputation"

How Washington can increase its appeal

"Market the school more aggressively"

"Continued focus on experiential leadership"

"More students with finance-related backgrounds"

Marketing/sales: 23%
Operations/production/logistics: 6%
Other: 5%

Top Recruiters *(Number of Full-Time Class of 2004 Graduates Hired)*

Citigroup: 6
Guidant: 5
Anheuser-Busch: 3
IBM: 3
Masterfoods USA: 3
Kraft: 2
3M: 2
Credit Suisse First Boston: 2
Deloitte Consulting: 2
Emerson: 2

Percentage of Job-Seeking Full-Time Graduates Who:	All Students	Citizens/Residents	Foreign Nationals
Received offers prior to or within 3 months of graduation	84%	86%	78%
Accepted offers prior to or within 3 months of graduation	80%	82%	76%

	MEAN			MEDIAN		
Overall Compensation	All Students	Citizens/ Residents	Foreign Nationals	All Students	Citizens/ Residents	Foreign Nationals
Annual base salary	$78,691	$78,511	$79,200	$80,000	$80,000	$80,000
Signing bonus	$9,444	$9,735	$8,571	$10,000	$10,000	$8,750
Other guaranteed compensation	$7,339	$6,174	$10,250	$5,500	$4,650	$8,000

Three of the Most Famous Graduates of M.B.A. Program

William J. Shaw (class of 1972) President and COO, Marriott
International

W. Patrick McGinnis (class of 1972) President and CEO, Nestlé,
Purina Petcare

James H. Hance Jr. (class of 1968) Vice Chairman, Bank of America

UNIVERSITY OF WESTERN ONTARIO
(IVEY SCHOOL OF BUSINESS)

Western Ontario's Ivey School, considered by some recruiters and academics to be the Harvard of Canada, offers a general-management program. Students take foundation courses in strategy, marketing, finance, and other subjects in the first year. During the second year, student teams perform client field projects, working with such companies as IBM, Estée Lauder, and General Motors on problems or opportunities and making a final report with recommendations to senior management.

Although they receive a general-management education, Ivey students can specialize in certain areas such as biotech management, finance, entrepreneurship, and the business and culture of China. Upon graduation, most Ivey students pursue careers in consulting, finance, or accounting.

Ivey continues to emphasize the case-study method, which dates back to 1922, when two classics-scholars-turned-administrators saw growing demand for a liberal-arts education that prepared students for a business career. They searched for an academic model and finally settled on Harvard's case method of analyzing problems and opportunities that real companies had faced.

Located midway between Toronto and Detroit, Ivey offers an executive-M.B.A. program in three locations: the main campus in London, Ontario; Mississauga (the western end of greater Toronto); and Hong Kong. Ivey notes that it was the first North

American business school to open a permanent campus in Hong Kong.

These days, Ivey attracts more recruiters—both Canadian and American. But in the crowded M.B.A. market, the school still faces challenges in increasing its visibility and building an even stronger international reputation.

Recruiters in *The Wall Street Journal*/Harris Interactive survey gave Ivey its most positive ratings for students' communication and interpersonal skills, personal ethics and integrity, analytical and problem-solving abilities, and willingness to relocate. Ivey received its lowest scores for the career-services office and students' international knowledge, past work experience, and awareness of corporate social responsibility issues.

School Rankings

- Regional ranking in the recruiter survey: 43 of 47 schools ranked
- International ranking: 6 of 20 schools ranked
- Ranking by financial-services-industry recruiters: 9th place

FALL 2004 INCOMING M.B.A. CLASS

	Total	Full-Time Only
Number of applicants	605	580
Number of offers extended	365	348
Number of students who accepted offer	219	203
Number of students who enrolled	205	189

GMAT score: 647 (mean); 650 (median)
Years of full-time work experience: 5.6 (mean); 5 (median)
Undergraduate GPA: N/A

Demographic Profile of Full-Time Students

Male: 75%
Female: 25%

WESTERN ONTARIO ON WESTERN ONTARIO

(Data provided by the Richard Ivey School of Business at the University of Western Ontario)

Business school website:
http://www.ivey.ca
Business school e-mail:
mba@ivey.ca
Public institution
M.B.A. enrollment: 666
Full-time: 441
Part-time: 16
Executive program: 209

ADMISSIONS DIRECTOR:
Scott Walker
Director, M.B.A. Program Services
Richard Ivey School of Business
University of Western Ontario
1151 Richmond Street North
London, ON
Canada N6A 3K7
519-661-3795 (voice)
519-661-3431 (fax)
E-mail: swalker@ivey.ca

APPLICATION DEADLINES:
Fall 2006: 10/1/2005, 12/1/2005, 3/1/2006, 4/1/2006, 5/1/2006
Annual tuition: $23,333 (domestic); $25,000 (international)
Annual room and board: $16,600

Canadian citizens/residents: 43%
Foreign nationals: 57%

Class of 2004 Most Popular Academic Concentrations

N/A

CLASS OF 2004 EMPLOYMENT DATA

Industries Hiring Full-Time Graduates (% Hired)

Computer/technology/Internet/dot-com: 3%
Consumer products and services: 6%
Energy and utilities: 1%
Financial services/investment banking: 35%
Government: 1%
Management consulting: 16%
Manufacturing: 2%
Pharmaceutical/biotechnology/health-care products and services: 9%
Telecommunications: 9%
Travel and transportation: 2%
Other professional services (accounting, advertising, etc.): 11%
Other: 5%

Position/Job Function (% Hired)

Consulting: 29%
Finance/accounting: 32%
General management: 5%
Information technology/management information systems: 2%
Marketing/sales: 19%
Operations/production/logistics: 4%
Other: 9%

THE RECRUITERS SPEAK

Western Ontario's most impressive features	Western Ontario's major shortcomings	How Western Ontario can increase its appeal
"Case-method learning process"	"Lack of stars"	"More proactive career services"
"Good judgment, street-smart"	"Students have the 'what are you going to do for me?' attitude"	"Build stronger brand equity in the U.S."
"Strategy and finance"	"Too focused on banking and consulting"	"Increase students' French language capability"

Top Recruiters *(Number of Full-Time Class of 2004 Graduates Hired)*

Royal Bank of Canada: 12
Johnson & Johnson: 9
Scotiabank: 9
Canadian Imperial Bank of Commerce: 7
IBM: 7
Toronto Dominion Bank: 7
BMO Nesbitt Burns: 5
Deloitte: 5
Accenture: 4
A.T. Kearney: 4
Merrill Lynch: 4

Percentage of Job-Seeking Full-Time Graduates Who:	All Students	Citizens/Residents	Foreign Nationals
Received offers prior to or within 3 months of graduation	76%	N/A	N/A
Accepted offers prior to or within 3 months of graduation	76%	N/A	N/A

Overall Compensation (U.S. dollars)	MEAN			MEDIAN		
	All Students	Citizens/ Residents	Foreign Nationals	All Students	Citizens/ Residents	Foreign Nationals
Annual base salary	$67,917	N/A	N/A	$62,500	N/A	N/A
Signing bonus	$9,792	N/A	N/A	$6,250	N/A	N/A
Other guaranteed compensation	$14,583	N/A	N/A	$10,417	N/A	N/A

Three of the Most Famous Graduates of M.B.A. Program

E. Scott Beattie (class of 1986) Chairman and CEO, Elizabeth Arden

Arkadi R. Kuhlmann (class of 1972) Chairman, President and CEO, ING Direct USA

Henry K. S. Cheng (class of 1972) Managing Director, New World Development

COLLEGE OF WILLIAM AND MARY

William and Mary, the second-oldest college in America, was one of the first schools oriented toward business, beginning with the use of Adam Smith's *Wealth of Nations* as a textbook in a political economy course in 1798. The formal study of business began in 1919, with a graduate degree program established in 1967. Today, students can choose from the full-time program in Williamsburg or the part-time evening M.B.A. in the more central location of Newport News. There are also two executive-M.B.A. options, one in Williamsburg and a newer program in Reston, near Washington, D.C.

The business school emphasizes its small, collegial environment and teamwork focus. It also promotes strong ties with business managers through its Executive Partners mentoring program. When they begin their M.B.A., students are assigned to a mentor, often a retired corporate executive, who provides guidance on ethics, leadership, career development, and other matters during their two-year stint.

The school characterizes the first year of its full-time M.B.A. program as the "mastery year," when students are expected to gain command of basic business skills. During the second half—the "acceleration year"—students choose a "career acceleration module" in corporate finance, marketing, entrepreneurship, or operations and information-technology management. The modules combine classroom learning with seminars, panels, corporate visits, and a field consultancy project. During the project, student teams research and propose solutions to actual business problems.

William and Mary provides opportunities for global study, including exchange programs with schools in France, Norway, Germany, Mexico, and Costa Rica. Another alternative is the "European Business course," which offers an intensive one-week seminar in Paris that includes visits to such companies as L'Oréal and France Télécom.

In *The Wall Street Journal*/Harris Interactive survey, recruiters gave the highest ratings to William and Mary for students' personal ethics and integrity, teamwork abilities, leadership potential, and analytical and problem-solving skills. The lowest scores: the career-services center and students' international knowledge and experience.

School Rankings
- Regional ranking in the recruiter survey: 19 of 47 schools ranked

FALL 2004 INCOMING M.B.A. CLASS

	Total	Full-Time Only
Number of applicants	323	258
Number of offers extended	229	179
Number of students who accepted offer	111	63
Number of students who enrolled	111	63

GMAT score: 597 (mean); 600 (median)
Years of full-time work experience: 4.5 (mean) 4 (median)
Undergraduate GPA: N/A

Demographic Profile of Full-Time Students
Male: 71%
Female: 29%

WILLIAM AND MARY ON WILLIAM AND MARY

(Data provided by the College of William and Mary School of Business)

Business school website:
http://www.breakawayMBA.com
Business school e-mail:
admissions@business.wm.edu
Public institution
M.B.A. enrollment: 374
Full-time: 146
Part-time: 129
Executive program: 99

ADMISSIONS DIRECTOR:
Kathy Williams Pattison
Director of Admissions
College of William and Mary
School of Business
P.O. Box 8795
Williamsburg, VA 23185
757-221-2900 (voice)
757-221-2958 (fax)
E-mail: Kathy.Pattison@
business.wm.edu

APPLICATION DEADLINES:
Fall 2006: 5/15/2006
Annual tuition: $15,266 (in-state);
$27,938 (out-of-state)
Annual room and board: $8,330

Minorities: 5%
U.S. citizens/residents: 57%
Foreign nationals: 43%

Class of 2004 Most Popular Academic Concentrations (% of Students)

Finance 38%
Marketing 25%
Entrepreneurship 23%

CLASS OF 2004 EMPLOYMENT DATA

Industries Hiring Full-Time Graduates (% Hired)

Financial services/investment banking: 29.5%
Government: 6.9%
Management consulting: 20.5%
Manufacturing: 13.6%
Other: 29.5%

Position/Job Function (% Hired)

Consulting: 26%
Finance/accounting: 46%
General management: 8%
Information technology/management information systems: 2%
Marketing/sales: 16%
Other: 2%

Top Recruiters (Number of Full-Time Class of 2004 Graduates Hired)

Wachovia: 4
BB&T: 3
Trader Publishing: 3

THE RECRUITERS SPEAK

William and Mary's most impressive features

"Well-rounded students willing to work hard"

"Teamwork, not prima donnas"

"Integrity"

William and Mary's major shortcomings

"Lack of stars"

"Interviewing skills"

"Small size of the program"

How William and Mary can increase its appeal

"Increase M.B.A. program's visibility and recognition"

"More U.S. students"

"Better communication and presentation skills"

BearingPoint: 2
Booz Allen Hamilton: 2
Celerant: 2
Deloitte: 2
DuPont: 2
KPMG: 2
Merrill Lynch: 1

Percentage of Job-Seeking Full-Time Graduates Who:	All Students	Citizens/Residents	All Foreign Nationals
Received offers prior to or within 3 months of graduation	78%	83%	61%
Accepted offers prior to or within 3 months of graduation	72%	77%	56%

	MEAN			MEDIAN		
Overall Compensation	All Students	Citizens/ Residents	Foreign Nationals	All Students	Citizens/ Residents	Foreign Nationals
Annual base salary	$72,185	$71,224	$76,750	$70,000	$70,000	$76,000
Signing bonus	$6,692	$6,143	$9,000	$5,000	$5,000	$5,000
Other guaranteed compensation	$13,431	$15,325	$7,750	$10,000	$11,000	$7,500

Three of the Most Famous Graduates of M.B.A. Program

Gary M. Pfeiffer (class of 1974) Senior Vice President and CFO, DuPont

Daniel J. Ludeman (class of 1991) President and CEO, Wachovia Securities

C. Larry Pope (class of 1994) President and COO, Smithfield Foods

SCHOOL OF BUSINESS
University of Wisconsin-Madison

UNIVERSITY OF WISCONSIN-MADISON

The University of Wisconsin's business school, which offers full-time, part-time, and executive-M.B.A. degrees, has built a strong reputation for marketing research and brand management. It is home to the A.C. Nielsen Center for Marketing Research, which provides students access to computer labs with specialized software for research and statistics coursework. There's also the Center for Brand and Product Management, which the school says is the first such program in the U.S. And marketing figures into Wisconsin's center for supply-chain management, too.

Because of such centers, the business school attracts consumer-product and retail-industry recruiters such as General Mills, Philip Morris, and Best Buy. Nearly a quarter of its M.B.A. graduates end up taking marketing and sales positions.

But the largest share of students—about 40%—go into finance and accounting. Beyond basic finance and accounting classes, Wisconsin students can participate in two applied graduate programs. They can gain hands-on experience by managing multimillion-dollar investment portfolios in the applied security-analysis program, or they can work on consulting projects for such companies as 3M and Procter & Gamble in the applied corporate-finance program.

Among its notable accomplishments, the university says, was its creation in 1969 of the first arts administration program in

America. M.B.A. students take specialized courses in arts administration and nonprofit management, as well as work for such local organizations as the Madison's Children's Museum, the University Opera, and the Wisconsin Historical Society. They gain additional experience during the summer between their first and second year at such institutions as Lincoln Center and the Museum of Modern Art in New York.

Recruiters in *The Wall Street Journal*/Harris Interactive survey gave their highest ratings for students' fit with the corporate culture and for chemistry or good feelings about the school and its graduates. Wisconsin's lowest scores: students' international knowledge and experience and their leadership potential.

School Rankings
- Regional ranking in the recruiter survey: 34 of 47 schools ranked

FALL 2004 INCOMING M.B.A. CLASS

	Total	Full-Time Only
Number of applicants	629	524
Number of offers extended	250	170
Number of students who accepted offer	188	116
Number of students who enrolled	181	112

GMAT score: 658 (mean); 650 (median)
Years of full-time work experience: 4.4 (mean); 4 (median)
Undergraduate GPA: 3.38 (mean); 3.45 (median)

Demographic Profile of Full-Time Students
Male: 66%
Female: 34%
Minorities: 13%
U.S. citizens/residents: 75%
Foreign nationals: 25%

WISCONSIN ON WISCONSIN

(Data provided by the School of Business at University of Wisconsin-Madison)

Business school website:
http://www.bus.wisc.edu/mba/
Business school e-mail:
mba@bus.wisc.edu
Public institution
M.B.A. enrollment: 405
Full-time: 235
Part-time: 105
Executive program: 65

ADMISSIONS DIRECTOR:
Betsy Kacizak
Director of Admissions and
Financial Aid
3150 Grainger Hall
975 University Ave.
Madison, WI 53706
608-262-4000 (voice)
608-265-4192 (fax)
E-mail: mba@bus.wisc.edu

APPLICATION DEADLINE:
Fall 2006: April 2006
Annual tuition: $9,776 (in-state);
$25,214 (out-of-state)
Annual room and board: $9,230

Class of 2004 Most Popular Academic Concentrations (% of Students)

Finance 32%
Marketing 19%
Real estate 12%

CLASS OF 2004 EMPLOYMENT DATA

Industries Hiring Full-Time Graduates (% Hired)

Computer/technology/Internet/dot-com: 5%
Consumer products and services: 19%
Financial services/investment banking: 24%
Management consulting: 6%
Manufacturing: 12%
Nonprofit: 2%
Petroleum/energy: 1%
Pharmaceutical/biotechnology/health-care products and services: 13%
Real estate: 16%
Other professional services (accounting, advertising, etc.): 2%

Position/Job Function (% Hired)

Consulting: 6%
Finance/accounting: 38%
General management: 5%
Human resources: 2%
Information technology/management information systems: 2%
Marketing/sales: 22%
Operations/production/logistics: 14%
Other: 11%

THE RECRUITERS SPEAK

Wisconsin's most impressive features

"Market-research capabilities"

"Supply-chain program"

"Outstanding brand-management students"

Wisconsin's major shortcomings

"Narrow focus—can they lead?"

"Little prior management experience"

"Students unprepared for interviews"

How Wisconsin can increase its appeal

"Larger program—more students from which to choose"

"Improve communication and leadership skills"

"Invite more companies to talk to students about opportunities"

Top Recruiters *(Number of Full-Time Class of 2004 Graduates Hired)*

Abbott Laboratories: 4
CUNA Mutual Group: 4
Guidant: 4
Best Buy: 3
General Mills: 3
Philip Morris: 3
Bucyrus: 2
Charter Communications: 2
Credit Suisse First Boston: 2
Hewlett-Packard: 2

Percentage of Job-Seeking Full-Time Graduates Who:	All Students	Citizens/Residents	Foreign Nationals
Received offers prior to or within 3 months of graduation	82%	85%	75%
Accepted offers prior to or within 3 months of graduation	82%	85%	75%

	MEAN			MEDIAN		
Overall Compensation	All Students	Citizens/ Residents	Foreign Nationals	All Students	Citizens/ Residents	Foreign Nationals
Annual base salary	$72,720	$73,918	$67,264	$73,000	$75,000	$71,500
Signing bonus	$9,666	$9,785	$9,200	$10,000	$10,000	$6,500
Other guaranteed compensation	$17,636	$19,600	$6,835	$10,000	$12,500	$6,835

Three of the Most Famous Graduates of M.B.A. Program

Lynn Beasley (class of 1982) President and COO, R.J. Reynolds Tobacco

Tadashi Okamura (class of 1973) President and CEO, Toshiba

Aaron Kennedy (class of 1989) Founder, Chairman, and CEO, Noodles & Co.

YALE UNIVERSITY

Yale's 29-year-old M.B.A. program, the youngest in the Ivy League, sets as its mission "to educate leaders for business and society" and has developed a powerful reputation for nonprofit and public-sector management. Yale also emphasizes the growing importance of corporate citizenship. It was cited by the Aspen Institute and the World Resources Institute as one of six business schools "on the cutting edge" of incorporating social and environmental responsibility into their M.B.A. programs.

In addition to its public and nonprofit specializations, Yale offers concentrations in finance, strategy, marketing, leadership, and operations management, with the largest share of its graduates landing jobs in finance and accounting. The school's many elective courses go well beyond bread-and-butter business skills and deal with such provocative topics as "Emotionality and Irrationality in Management" and "Succeeding Without Selling Your Soul."

Some M.B.A. students take advantage of other parts of the prestigious university, earning an M.B.A. along with a degree in law, drama, divinity, forestry and environmental studies, medicine, nursing, public health, architecture, international relations, East Asian studies, or Russian and East European studies.

For the first time, Yale is branching out from its full-time program to offer an executive-M.B.A. degree. Starting in 2005, the

22-month program will focus specifically on health-care management and be marketed to managers in hospitals, the insurance industry, and drug and biotech companies, as well as to people involved in policy and regulation.

The management school has established a growing array of research centers on corporate governance, environment management, finance, chief executive leadership, social enterprise, and, most recently, customer insights. The customer insights center, which will probe customer behavior, is undertaking its first major research project in partnership with IBM to study "the difference between selling products and selling solutions."

In the latest *Wall Street Journal*/Harris Interactive survey, recruiters rated Yale M.B.A. graduates as strongest in personal ethics and integrity, well-rounded qualities, awareness of corporate citizenship issues, teamwork abilities, and communication and interpersonal skills. Yale received the lowest ratings for the career-services office, the core curriculum, students' international knowledge, and their past work experience.

School Rankings
- National ranking in the recruiter survey: 5 of 19 schools ranked
- Ranking by financial-services-industry recruiters: 2nd place

Recognition for Excellence in Academic Concentrations
- With 109 nominations, Yale ranked No. 6 among business schools that recruiters in *The Wall Street Journal*/Harris Interactive survey cited for excellence in strategy.
- With 98 nominations, Yale ranked No. 8 for excellence in finance.

Special Recognition
- Good source for recruiting graduates with high ethical standards: the most nominated school, 131 nominations.
- Good source for recruiting women: 6th most nominated school, 61 nominations.

YALE ON YALE

(Data provided by the Yale School of Management)

Business school website:
http://mba.yale.edu
Business school e-mail:
mba.admissions@yale.edu
Private institution
M.B.A. enrollment: 468
Full-time: 468

ADMISSIONS DIRECTOR:
Anne Coyle
Director of Admissions
135 Prospect Street
P.O. Box 208200
New Haven, CT 06520
203-432-5932 (voice)
203-432-7004 (fax)
E-mail:
mba.admissions@yale.edu

APPLICATION DEADLINE:
Fall 2006: October 2005, January 2006, March 2006
Annual tuition: $36,800
Annual room and board: $12,500

FALL 2004 INCOMING M.B.A. CLASS

	Full-Time Only
Number of applicants	1,998
Number of offers extended	511
Number of students who accepted offer	215
Number of students who enrolled	215

GMAT score: 696 (mean); 700 (median)
Years of full-time work experience: 4 (mean); 4 (median)
Undergraduate GPA: 3.5 (mean); 3.5 (median)

Demographic Profile of Full-Time Students

Male: 68%
Female: 32%
Minorities: 31%
U.S. citizens/residents: 77%
Foreign nationals: 23%

Class of 2004 Most Popular Academic Concentrations (% of Students)

Finance 48%
Strategy 24%
Marketing 13%

CLASS OF 2004 EMPLOYMENT DATA

Industries Hiring Full-Time Graduates (% Hired)

Computer/technology/Internet/dot-com: 5.3%
Consumer products and services: 4.7%

THE RECRUITERS SPEAK

Yale's most impressive features

"Social responsibility"

"Students who think outside the box"

"Strong leadership potential—future stars"

Yale's major shortcomings

"Offbeat—fewer students have industry backgrounds"

"Students expect Yale degree is enough to impress"

"Too many career-switchers"

How Yale can increase its appeal

"Better interview prep for students"

"Improve facilities"

"Work closer with the larger university"

Energy and utilities: 4.1%
Financial services/investment banking: 39.1%
Government: 3.6%
Industrial products and services: 1.2%
Management consulting: 7.7%
Manufacturing: 8.3%
Media/entertainment: 2.4%
Nonprofit: 3%
Pharmaceutical/biotechnology/health-care products and services: 7.1%
Real estate: 2.4%
Other professional services (accounting, advertising, etc.): 4.1%
Other: 7%

Position/Job Function (% Hired)

Consulting: 8%
Finance/accounting: 47%
General management: 10%
Information technology/management information systems: 1%
Marketing/sales: 13%
Operations/production/logistics: 2%
Other: 19%

Percentage of Job-Seeking Full-Time Graduates Who:	All Students	Citizens/Residents	Foreign Nationals
Received offers prior to or within 3 months of graduation	86%	89%	83%
Accepted offers prior to or within 3 months of graduation	81%	83%	76%

	MEAN			MEDIAN		
Overall Compensation	All Students	Citizens/ Residents	Foreign Nationals	All Students	Citizens/ Residents	Foreign Nationals
Annual base salary	$83,700	$84,784	$81,921	$85,000	$85,000	$85,000
Signing bonus	$16,061	$15,671	$16,881	$15,000	$15,000	$15,000
Other guaranteed compensation	$20,318	$19,345	$22,993	$15,000	$15,000	$12,133

Top Recruiters *(Number of Full-Time Class of 2004 Graduates Hired)*

McKinsey: 7
IBM: 6
Bank of America: 5
Citigroup: 5
Lehman Brothers: 5
Standard & Poor's: 5
General Electric: 4
Credit Suisse First Boston: 3
Fitch Ratings: 3
Merrill Lynch: 3
Hoffmann-La Roche: 3
UBS Investment Bank: 3

Three of the Most Famous Graduates of M.B.A. Program

John Thornton (class of 1980) Former President and Co-COO, Goldman Sachs

Indra Nooyi (class of 1980) President and CFO, PepsiCo

Nancy Peretsman (class of 1979) Managing Director, Allen & Co.

YORK UNIVERSITY

(SCHULICH SCHOOL OF

BUSINESS)

Schulich
Canada's Global Business School™
York University, Toronto

York's Schulich School trains its M.B.A. students to be strong generalists, but also offers an array of academic specialties, from finance and international business to e-business and health-industry management. About 40% of Schulich's recent graduates have pursued careers in financial services.

The Toronto school also produces managers for nonprofit and government organizations, with academic specializations in arts and media administration, public management, and nonprofit management and leadership. Schulich students also can focus on "business and sustainability," an academic program for which the school receives wide recognition. The Aspen Institute and the World Resources Institute have honored York as one of the top business schools in the world teaching about social and environmental responsibility.

M.B.A.s can participate in several special projects, including the six-month global leadership program. Students work with fellow M.B.A.s at other schools to help foreign companies plot a market-entry strategy for North America or to help Canadian firms develop an international marketing plan. They visit the assigned company, analyze its competitive position, and present final recommendations to management in Toronto.

Schulich offers a variety of degrees beyond the full-time and part-time M.B.A. Students can receive an International M.B.A. degree or participate in joint M.B.A. programs, including a master's of fine arts combination. There's also a joint degree with

YORK ON YORK

(Data provided by the Schulich
School of Business at York
University)

Business school website:
http://www.schulich.yorku.ca
Business school e-mail:
intladmissions@schulich.
yorku.ca
Public institution
M.B.A. enrollment: 1,298
Full-time: 617
Part-time: 600
Executive program: 81

ADMISSIONS DIRECTOR:
Charmaine Courtis
Executive Director, Student
Services & International Relations
4700 Keele Street
Toronto, Ontario
Canada M3J 1P3
416-736-5059 (voice)
416-650-8174 (fax)
E-mail: intladmissions@schulich.
yorku.ca

APPLICATION DEADLINES:
Fall 2006: 2/1/2006 (interna-
tional); 5/1/2006 (domestic)
Annual tuition: $16,800 (domes-
tic); $21,000 (international)
Annual room and board: $10,000

Université Laval in Quebec City to prepare managers for the bilingual, bicultural business environment in Canada. And Schulich and Northwestern University's Kellogg School of Management have designed an executive-M.B.A. program together.

Recruiters in The Wall Street Journal/Harris Interactive survey gave York its highest grades for students' ability to work well in teams and past success with graduates they have hired. York received the lowest ratings for the core curriculum, students' work experience, and their communication and interpersonal skills.

School Rankings

- Regional ranking in the recruiter survey: 46 of 47 schools ranked
- International ranking: 15 of 20 schools ranked

Recognition for Excellence in an Academic Concentration

- With 60 nominations, York ranked No. 10 among business schools that recruiters in The Wall Street Journal/Harris Interactive survey cited for excellence in international business.

FALL 2004 INCOMING M.B.A. CLASS

	Total	Full-Time Only
Number of applicants	1,234	986
Number of offers extended	690	554
Number of students who accepted offer	384	275
Number of students who enrolled	369	262

THE RECRUITERS SPEAK

York's most impressive features

"Global focus"

"Leadership attributes"

"Diverse student body"

York's major shortcomings

"Must dig through a lot of chaff to find the quality"

"International students need better English skills"

"Lack of preparedness for interviews"

How York can increase its appeal

"Increase efficiency in the career-services office"

"Raise entrance standards"

"More rigorous mathematical program"

GMAT score: 660 (mean); 650 (median)
Years of full-time work experience: 6 (mean); 5 (median)
Undergraduate GPA: 3.3 (mean); 3.3 (median)

Demographic Profile of Full-Time Students

Male: 63%
Female: 37%
Canadian citizens/residents: 52%
Foreign nationals: 48%

Class of 2004 Most Popular Academic Concentrations (% of Students)

Finance 33%
Marketing 18%
International business 13%

CLASS OF 2004 EMPLOYMENT DATA

Industries Hiring Full-Time Graduates (% Hired)

Computer/technology/Internet/dot-com: 11%
Consumer products and services: 13%
Energy and utilities: 2%
Financial services/investment banking: 41%
Industrial products and services: 2%
Management consulting: 9%
Manufacturing: 3%
Media/entertainment: 2%
Nonprofit: 1%
Petroleum/energy: 2%
Pharmaceutical/biotechnology/health-care products and services:
5%
Real estate: 2%
Telecommunications: 3%
Travel and transportation: 1%
Other professional services (accounting, advertising, etc.): 3%

Position/Job Function (% Hired)

Consulting: 13%
Finance/accounting: 38%
General management: 11%
Human resources: 1%
Information technology/management information systems: 5%

Marketing/sales: 28%
Operations/production/logistics: 4%

Top Recruiters *(Number of Full-Time Class of 2004 Graduates Hired)*

CIBC Group: 18
TD Financial Group: 15
Scotiabank: 7
IBM: 6
Royal Bank Financial Group: 6
Deloitte & Touche: 5
L'Oréal: 5
PricewaterhouseCoopers: 4
General Mills: 4
American Express: 4

Percentage of Job-Seeking Full-Time Graduates Who:	All Students	Citizens/Residents	Foreign Nationals
Received offers prior to or within 3 months of graduation	90%	N/A	N/A
Accepted offers prior to or within 3 months of graduation	88%	N/A	N/A

Overall Compensation	MEAN			MEDIAN		
	All Students	Citizens/Residents	Foreign Nationals	All Students	Citizens/Residents	Foreign Nationals
Annual base salary	$69,000	N/A	N/A	$59,580	N/A	N/A
Signing bonus	$4,615	N/A	N/A	$4,200	N/A	N/A
Other guaranteed compensation	$5,650	N/A	N/A	$3,360	N/A	N/A

Three of the Most Famous Graduates of M.B.A. Program

John Hunkin (class of 1969) President and CEO, Canadian Imperial Bank of Commerce

Paul Tsaparis (class of 1984) President and CEO, Hewlett-Packard Canada

Richard Waugh (class of 1974) President and CEO, Scotiabank

PART III.

WHICH M.B.A.?

CAN THE FULL-TIME DEGREE REGAIN ITS LUSTER?

The full-time M.B.A. degree, long the crown jewel of business schools, has lost its luster.

Applications to full-time programs plummeted over the past couple of years as both professors and M.B.A. graduates questioned the degree's cost and its value in the workplace. The big unanswered question: Will the full-time M.B.A. ever sparkle as brightly as it once did? Or has it become an overpriced commodity?

For now, it's still unclear whether the drop in full-time applications is merely cyclical or a harbinger of a longer-term shift. Daphne Atkinson, vice president of industry relations at the Graduate Management Admission Council, takes the cyclical perspective. "I'm cautiously optimistic that it's a short-term trend," she says. "I think it will be a slow build and that it simply wouldn't be reasonable to expect a complete reversal immediately. But as the job market improves and there's more choice for M.B.A.s, that will lead to happier grads and more positive word-of-mouth marketing."

She doesn't anticipate another application surge like the one after the Sept. 11, 2001, terrorist attacks in New York and Washington, but rather an eventual rebound to more normal levels. "I don't expect to see the highwater mark of 2001–2002 again in my lifetime," she adds. "A lot of people in the mix then really didn't belong because they didn't have the career focus of an ideal M.B.A. candidate. Some were just refugees from a tanking economy."

Looking toward 2010, the council is optimistic that applications for all types of M.B.A. programs will grow as demographics become more favorable in some regions of the world. Population statistics show an expected increase in the number of people in the primary M.B.A. age range—25 to 29 years old—in both the U.S. and Asia. However, the council says, the business-school-age population is expected to decline further in Western Europe.

Already, the graduate council sees encouraging signs in the slowing decline of the number of people taking its Graduate Management Admission Test. About 52,500 tests were taken in the first quarter of 2005, 1.5% fewer than in the year-earlier quarter—but still much smaller than the 9.7% decline from the first quarter of 2003 to 2004.

In surveying schools about their full-time programs in early 2005, the council found that 23% of full-time programs reported an increase in applications, compared with 16% in early 2004. At the same time, fewer schools experienced a decline—69% in 2005 vs. 74% in 2004.

Both part-time and executive-M.B.A. programs, which allow students to continue working, have fared better. Preliminary results showed applications in 2005 increased at 69% of executive-M.B.A. programs and at 32% of part-time programs. "The balance is clearly tipping more to programs that reduce the opportunity costs of going to business school," says Albert Niemi, dean of the Cox School of Business at Southern Methodist University. "It's easy to come out of school with $100,000 in debt from a full-time program, so you've mortgaged your future for the next decade."

Since 1997, full-time M.B.A. enrollment at the Cox School has fallen to 169 from 270, while part-time enrollment has grown to about 600 from 449, and executive-M.B.A. candidates have risen to 168 from 115. Betting on that trend, the school recently completed construction of an $18.6 million executive-education center. SMU also may develop specialized master's degrees in finance and management for those students who don't aspire to be CEO and don't really need an M.B.A. "Some people don't need a smorgasbord of courses and the full tool kit of management skills," says Dean Niemi. "Maybe they just want a good job in finance."

Cost is clearly one of the most significant challenges facing the full-time degree. Tuition increases continue to outpace the U.S. inflation rate, and tuition rose briskly at major business schools even when jobs were harder to come by and M.B.A. compensation slid. "We have to be sensitive to the fact that some people spent $60,000 for tuition and didn't get as good a job as they had given up to come to business school," says Robert Dolan, dean of the University of Michigan's Ross School of Business.

Even though the M.B.A. job market has improved considerably, many people still don't feel they can afford to quit secure positions and take on big student loans. Part-time and executive-M.B.A. programs seem to be better alternatives because not only can students keep working, but they also may qualify for some financial aid from their employers.

Tuition has been climbing 5% to 8% a year at many schools, with some two-year programs now starting to break the $40,000-a-year mark: Stanford University M.B.A.s will be paying $41,340 in tuition for the 2005–2006 school year, while the University of Pennsylvania's Wharton School is charging $40,458. Add other school expenses and housing costs, and the bill far exceeds $100,000.

Some schools are trying to ease the sting with more-generous scholarship programs. About 80% of full-time M.B.A. students at the Cox School at SMU, for example, received some degree of scholarship support in 2004. The Cox School's tuition for the 2005–2006 school year is about $30,000, up 5% from the previous year. "We're all concerned about pricing ourselves out of the market," says Dean Niemi. "But compared with some schools, we're still a relative bargain."

It hasn't helped that M.B.A. programs have come under fire from their own professors. Attacking the M.B.A. degree has almost become sport in the academic world, with a new antagonist emerging every few months.

The most recent assault came in a 2005 *Harvard Business Review* article in which Warren Bennis and James O'Toole, professors at the University of Southern California, declared that, "Instead of measuring themselves in terms of the competence of their graduates or by how well their faculties understand important drivers of business performance, [business schools] measure themselves almost solely by the rigor of their scientific research," much of which is less and less relevant to managers and executives. They added that, "Today it is possible to find tenured professors of management who have never set foot inside a real business, except as customers."

The most provocative critic certainly is Henry Mintzberg, a management professor at McGill University in Montreal, who weighed in with the 2004 book *Managers Not MBAs*, a scathing attack on the traditional full-time M.B.A. "M.B.A. programs not only fail to develop managers," he wrote, "but give their students a false impression of managing that, when put into practice, is undermining our organizations and our societies." He proposed that perhaps "no one should be allowed out of a conventional M.B.A. program without having a skull and crossbones stamped firmly on his or her forehead, over the words 'Warning: NOT prepared to manage!' "

Jeffrey Pfeffer, a professor at Stanford University's Graduate School of Business and one of the early critics of M.B.A. education, believes his 2002 article "The End of Business Schools?

Less Success Than Meets the Eye" and those that followed have prompted some schools to re-examine their curriculum and teaching methods. His article sparked much controversy with its contention that, "There is little evidence that mastery of the knowledge acquired in business schools enhances people's careers, or that even attaining the M.B.A. credential itself has much effect on graduates' salaries or career attainment."

He believes one of "the big problems in the typical M.B.A. classroom is that case discussions make students too passive." But now, he says, he is starting to see "more experiential programs in areas such as leadership and more ongoing team projects throughout the school year."

Some schools have indeed altered their strategies. The University of Michigan increasingly tries to connect theory with practice. For example, all first-year students participate in teams on "multidisciplinary action projects," which may involve a corporate assignment, an entrepreneurial venture, an international opportunity, or something more experimental. Some students also manage the $3 million Wolverine Venture Fund, while others apply for "dare to dream" grants to refine their own new-business concepts.

The College of William & Mary's M.B.A. program is trying to link more closely with the business world, too. It is drafting current and former business leaders to coach M.B.A.s and help the faculty teach and structure their courses. "We don't want to turn the business school into a trade school," says Jim Oliver, associate dean. "At the same time, it's important for business and business schools to work together so we can deliver what they need and students can hit the ground running."

With the decline in full-time applications, some schools are concluding that they need to be creative in the paths they offer toward the M.B.A. degree. Columbia University developed a bicoastal executive-M.B.A. program with the University of California at Berkeley and an international executive-M.B.A.

degree with London Business School. In addition, it offers an accelerated 16-month M.B.A. option that allows students to return to the workplace sooner.

"I still think there is great value to the longer two-year format," says Laura Tyson, dean of London Business School, "but we also have to give people more choice and flexibility."

Indiana University's Kelley School of Business has created yet another M.B.A. variation: a hybrid that allows students to spend eight months in residence on campus followed by an internship and then online courses. Students can either stay with their intern employer or return to their previous company while they finish the M.B.A. degree online. "We believe this type of program is the next wave," says Daniel Smith, interim dean of the Kelley School. "A lot of companies want their high-potential employees in an M.B.A. program, but don't want to lose them for two years."

Some school administrators and students maintain that part-time and executive programs will never be the equals of full-time programs. They argue that the full-time M.B.A. is a much more intense professional-development experience that's as much about clubs, guest speakers, close interaction with peers and faculty, and networking with alumni, as it is about the basic curriculum.

"I definitely wanted an M.B.A. that meant something," says Laurie Schrager, a recent graduate of Dartmouth College's Tuck School of Business. "I didn't want the stigma of being just a part-timer." She immersed herself in the Tuck School and the local Hanover, N.H., community by getting involved in the school's technology club and its women-in-business organization, developing a business plan for a women's athletic-gear store, and volunteering as a ski instructor for children.

"As a full-time student," Ms. Schrager says, "I had time to network with classmates and alumni, hear professors present their research, and go to coffee or dinner with visiting executive speakers. There are so many hidden benefits to a full-time education."

Tuck, the No. 1 school in this year's *Wall Street Journal/Harris Interactive* National ranking, actually is bucking the trend with an expected 5% increase in applications for the fall 2005 class, following two years of decline. "I believe there's a flight to quality, and that quality will win out," says Dean Paul Danos. "The schools below the top tier could continue to have problems with applications."

Dean Danos believes the full-time degree can "give people a new lease on life" through a major career switch. "The big motivation," he says, "for most of our students is changing their lives. That's not the same motivation for part-time students."

Dartmouth is one of the few remaining schools that offer only a full-time M.B.A. program. Aware of growth in the executive-M.B.A. market, it has considered adding an executive-degree

THE PRICE OF ADMISSION

These business schools in *The Wall Street Journal/Harris* Interactive rankings reported the highest annual tuition charges for full-time, two-year M.B.A. programs.

Rank	College	Tuition
1	Stanford University	$41,340
2	University of Pennsylvania (Wharton)	$40,458
3	Northwestern University (Kellogg)	$38,844
4	Carnegie Mellon University (Tepper)	$38,800
	University of Chicago	$38,800
6	Dartmouth College (Tuck)	$38,400
7	Columbia University	$38,290
8	London Business School	$38,000
9	University of Southern California (Marshall)	$37,558
10	Harvard University	$37,500
	Duke University (Fuqua)	$37,500

program for senior managers, but realizes that to attract enough students, it would have to be offered in more populous areas like Boston or New York rather than at its picturesque but remote New Hampshire campus.

Meanwhile, the application drop is forcing some full-time programs to reduce their class sizes to keep academic admissions requirements high. But if applications decline much more, schools may be tempted to let their quality standards slip and admit less qualified students in order to stabilize enrollment and tuition revenue. That's the big fear of David Wilson, president of the Graduate Management Admission Council. "What causes me the greatest heartburn is the possible devaluation of the M.B.A. degree by lowering admissions standards," he says. "Students learn as much from their peers as from professors, so they don't want to be sitting next to a dolt." Once quality starts slipping, he adds, "schools lose alumni support and recruiters don't return to campus. It's a very unpleasant scenario."

AN M.B.A. ON THE SIDE: THE RISE OF THE PART-TIME PROGRAM

An M.B.A. on the side—that's the approach more young students are taking as they return to school part-time while holding onto their day jobs.

Over the past few years, M.B.A. students have become more risk-averse. After seeing some full-time M.B.A.s sink $100,000 into their education and graduate jobless or to low-paying positions, many prospective students have gotten cold feet. If they have a secure job, they are much less likely to give it up and gamble that a full-time degree will ensure them a better position.

"I really didn't want to give up the nice income I had built up over seven years," says Matthew Barnes, who enrolled as a part-time student at the Cox School of Business at Southern Methodist University while continuing to work for Pegasus Solutions Inc., a Dallas company that provides technology systems to the travel industry. He did consider full-time programs at SMU, Texas Christian University, and the University of Texas at Austin, but he and his wife recently had their first child and bought their first home, making it even harder to give up a full-time salary. While Mr. Barnes acknowledges that "it's a lot of late hours and a very fine balance between school and work," he says that both his professors and supervisors have been very flexible when his two worlds conflict.

The big question for business schools is whether Mr. Barnes represents the future. Or will the improving job market prompt more students to stop working and return to school full-time? So far at least, application trends indicate part-time programs remain more popular. The Graduate Management Admission Council, which surveyed business schools in early 2005, said preliminary data showed applications were up at 32% of part-time programs, compared with an application increase at 23% of full-time programs. At the same time, nearly 70% of full-time programs showed an application decline, while 48% of part-time programs had fewer applicants. Some schools are starting part-time programs to capitalize on the changing market. In August 2005, for example, Georgetown University's McDonough School of Business planned to admit its first part-time class of evening students. "We're trying to be flexible in our formats to adjust to the changing market," says Reena Aggarwal, professor and former interim dean. "People's risk-tolerance has gone down so we need to give them more choices that allow them to keep their jobs." Georgetown intends to use the same faculty and keep the same international-business focus in the evening program as in its daytime classes. It also hopes to promote interaction between full-time and part-time students who will take some of the same electives.

"We have said we want to own Washington," she adds, "and that means having a full portfolio of M.B.A. options." Indeed, the University of Maryland opened two part-time M.B.A. programs in Washington a few years ago, and George Washington University also offers working students a part-time option.

Another new part-time program is taking shape at the University of Illinois at Urbana-Champaign. With a steep decline in full-time applications and in the size of its full-time program, Illinois decided its faculty could take on a part-time program when local companies called the school seeking an M.B.A. program for their young managers. Its first part-time class of about 50 students is expected to start in January 2006, with a program similar to the full-time counterpart, including a focus on teamwork and real-world projects.

"We have to be responsive to the marketplace," says Mary Miller, associate dean of the M.B.A. program. "This young generation now in its 20s likes choices. We saw that in marketing products to them when they were teenagers."

Flexibility is one of the key selling points for part-time programs. Typically, students finish a part-time M.B.A. in three years, but many schools allow more time. At New York University's Stern School of Business, students can choose to finish the degree in as few as two years or as many as six. They also have the option of taking classes in the evening or only on weekends and can start the degree in either September or January.

Of course, prospective students also must weigh whether the tradeoffs of a part-time program are worth it. The part-time M.B.A. degree doesn't enjoy the same cachet as a full-time program. "The focus isn't there—there's too much going on in a student's life to drink in what is being taught," said a corporate recruiter who participated in *The Wall Street Journal*/Harris Interactive survey "Many go part-time just to get the three letters—M.B.A.—behind their name."

Part-timers sometimes do feel like second-class citizens. After all, they see their full-time counterparts participating in enriching extracurricular activities and interacting more with fellow students, alumni, and professors. Indeed, that's what recruiters criticize most when they compare part-time and full-time degrees. In the *Journal* survey, about one-third of recruiters indicated that part-time programs are less effective than full-time programs in building M.B.A. students' skills. One survey respondent even said he sees little difference between part-time M.B.A. students and business undergraduates.

"If someone was asking me if they should pursue a part-time or full-time program, I'd strongly encourage them toward the full-time program even though it may stretch family time and resources," says Michael Peterson, a survey respondent who is strategy-planning manager at the OnStar division of General

Motors Corp. "It's harder as a part-time student to take full advantage of all the extracurricular opportunities an M.B.A. program can offer. The book and classroom learning is a big part of the education, of course, but the additional experiences really add to the program and help make it relevant and applicable for students."

Some programs are attempting to reduce the part-time stigma. Many schools, including SMU's Cox School, even avoid using the part-time label; instead, they call their evening and weekend programs "M.B.A.s for working professionals." The Cox School also is trying to make part-timers' experience more like that of their full-time counterparts by encouraging camaraderie in study teams and giving part-timers an opportunity to study abroad during their vacations from work.

Similarly, the Olin School of Business at Washington University in St. Louis promotes collaboration among part-timers from the start of their M.B.A. program. Each entering class is required to take the same core courses during their first year and students are broken into small study groups that share responsibility for projects, papers, and presentations. The Olin School believes this "cohort" approach is at least partly responsible for its completion rate of more than 90% for part-time students, compared with only about 55% at many other schools.

"The moral support and social pressure the cohorts create is a huge motivation for many students to stay on top of their work and complete their classes successfully," says Joe Fox, associate dean and director of Olin's M.B.A. programs. "One former student said that if it weren't for her group, she would have dropped out of the program after she had a baby. Instead, her peers kept on top of her and encouraged her to continue her studies."

Beyond the financial and flexible-scheduling benefits, there are other advantages to working and attending school at the same time. So Yun Maryn, a part-time M.B.A. student at the University of Maryland, says she has learned to balance time much better and has become a more effective manager at British Telecommunications' media and broadcast division. "You gain knowledge and tools to apply to the workplace right away," she says. "Due to the massive quantity of subject material we go through, I can't help wondering if some of the full-time students tend to forget what they have learned once they return to the workplace."

Ms. Maryn says she has applied leadership and teamwork lessons to improve communication with her staff and to reassess her own managerial style. In team meetings, some employees have reacted positively to her academic applications by opening up and sharing their views. But other people considered her team-building exercises "too textbook" and didn't respond as positively. "There are some things that I have learned recently in school," she says, "that I wish I knew a year ago because it would have helped me in my interviewing and hiring practices and in performance management."

Students who plan to stay with their current employer are probably the best candidates for part-time programs. When making a major career switch, students often choose a full-time program for its intensity and for the opportunity to land a summer internship and gain experience in their new area of interest. Without that summer internship in a new job function, students are much less appealing to most recruiters.

Even so, a growing number of part-timers are heading back to school hoping to use their new degree as a ticket out of their current job. They have long been envious of the intensive coaching full-time students receive during their job search, as well as their easy access to recruiters and alumni networks. Now, more schools are hiring staffers focused exclusively on part-time placement to provide job leads and advice on networking, writing résumés, and making a good impression in interviews.

Several major schools, including the Anderson School at the University of California at Los Angeles and the University of

Chicago Graduate School of Business, have started allowing part-time students to interview with recruiters who visit the campus—the activity many part-timers covet most.

As soon as he became associate dean for career initiatives at the Anderson School last year, Eric Mokover was "almost accosted," he says, by part-time students. He heard "loud and clear" that the students needed help and wasted little time boosting career services for them. "Fewer of them are sponsored by their companies today, and many are looking to switch careers," says Mr. Mokover. "We realized things have changed, so we had to change, too."

Now, part-time students can try to snag interviews with recruiters as long as they attend workshops on résumé and interview preparation first. UCLA even organized its first All-Anderson Networking Event, bringing together students from all of its M.B.A. programs to trade contacts and schmooze about career issues. "We try very hard to be one school," Mr. Mokover says. "We're not a good community if we get into full-time vs. executive vs. part-time M.B.A.s."

But that's exactly how some part-timers view the situation at NYU's Stern School. Stern created a five-person Career Center for Working Professionals that's open in the evening and on Saturdays to provide career counseling, a database of job postings, networking events, mock-interview programs, and seminars on such topics as job loss and switching careers. But Stern also decided to bar part-timers from seeking interviews with campus recruiters who are in the market primarily for full-time students. That riles some part-timers, who feel cheated. They contend that they enrolled at Stern believing they could sign up for interviews with all on-campus recruiters.

The critics insist on remaining anonymous because, as one put it, they don't want recruiters to view them as troublemakers. "When several classmates and I started to look for post-M.B.A. employment, we were literally stopped at the registration desk for on-campus interviews," a Stern part-timer says. "One lady was so upset that she practically broke down in tears right there and then."

Gary Fraser, associate dean of student affairs at Stern, has heard the students' complaints and understands their perspective. But he's not backing down. He says the policy was changed because "hundreds of part-time students went through the interviewing process but with poor placement results." He stresses that the change certainly "was not meant to punish the part-time students." NYU found, Mr. Fraser says, that part-timers weren't a good match for many recruiters who were looking for younger, less experienced full-time students. "Some of Stern's part-time students with seven years' experience were applying for jobs requiring only four years," he says. "They were too qualified."

Opening on-campus recruiting to part-timers also can be a delicate matter because some students receive tuition assistance from employers, who understandably don't expect them to be out looking for a better job on the company's dime. Some schools try to keep such recruitment under the radar, calling their services "professional development" rather than "placement." Other schools are more vigilant because they don't want to alienate companies that are sponsoring part-time students and may also be recruiting full-time graduates. They require students receiving tuition assistance to obtain written permission from their current employers before interviewing with other companies.

"We used to e-mail job postings to part-time students, but one supervisor who was in the same class with his subordinate complained to us that he did not appreciate it," one career-services director confides. "So we quit promoting our services very heavily to part-timers."

THE BIGGEST PART-TIME PROGRAMS
The 20 largest part-time M.B.A. programs offered by the schools in the *Wall Street Journal/Harris* Interactive rankings.

New York University Stern School of Business

TOTAL ENROLLMENT	1,689
PROGRAM AND FORMATS	COMBINATION— EVENING AND WEEKEND
STARTING MONTHS	September and January
APPLICATION DEADLINE	Spring 2006: Sept. 1, 2005 Fall 2006: April 1, 2006
AVERAGE NUMBER OF MONTHS TO COMPLETE DEGREE	36
MAXIMUM NUMBER OF MONTHS TO COMPLETE DEGREE	72
TUITION	$78,000* *Estimated average for 60 credits

STUDENTS

Average GMAT	671
Average years of students' prior full-time work experience	5
Average Age	28

DEMOGRAPHICS

Male	68%
Female	32%
Citizens/Permanent Residents of Country in Which School is Located	88%
Foreign Nationals	12%
Minority Citizens/Permanent Residents (Black, Hispanic, Asian, other)	24%
ABILITY TO SWITCH FROM PART-TIME TO FULL-TIME PROGRAM	NO
ACCESS TO CAREER SERVICES	YES
ACCESS TO RECRUITERS	NO

University of Minnesota Carlson School of Management

TOTAL ENROLLMENT	1,623
PROGRAM AND FORMATS	COMBINATION— EVENING AND WEEKEND
STARTING MONTHS	September or January
APPLICATION DEADLINE	Spring 2006: Oct. 1, 2005 Fall 2006: May 1, 2006
AVERAGE NUMBER OF MONTHS TO COMPLETE DEGREE	42
MAXIMUM NUMBER OF MONTHS TO COMPLETE DEGREE	84
TUITION	$44,000 to $52,000* *depending on credits required

STUDENTS

Average GMAT	612
Average years of students' prior full-time work experience	6.4
Average Age	29.4

DEMOGRAPHICS

Male	66%
Female	34%
Citizens/Permanent Residents of Country in Which School is Located	95%
Foreign Nationals	5%
Minority Citizens/Permanent Residents (Black, Hispanic, Asian, other)	12%
ABILITY TO SWITCH FROM PART-TIME TO FULL-TIME PROGRAM	NO
ACCESS TO CAREER SERVICES	YES
ACCESS TO RECRUITERS	YES

AN M.B.A. ON THE SIDE

University of Chicago Graduate School of Business

TOTAL ENROLLMENT	1,433
PROGRAM AND FORMATS	EVENING AND WEEKEND
STARTING MONTHS	January, March, June, September (Evening); September (Weekend)
APPLICATION DEADLINE	Winter 2006: Oct. 21, 2005 (Evening); Fall 2006: June 10, 2006 (Weekend) Spring 2006: Jan. 20, 2006 (Evening) Summer 2006: April 21, 2006 (Evening) Fall 2006: July 14, 2006 (Evening)
AVERAGE NUMBER OF MONTHS TO COMPLETE DEGREE	30
MAXIMUM NUMBER OF MONTHS TO COMPLETE DEGREE	60
TUITION	$77,600* *Estimate based on 20 courses

STUDENTS	
Average GMAT	n/a
Average years of students' prior full-time work experience	6
Average Age	30
DEMOGRAPHICS	
Male	76% (Evening); 81% (Weekend)
Female	24% (Evening); 19% (Weekend)
Citizens/Permanent Residents of Country in Which School is Located	91% (Evening); 85% (Weekend)
Foreign Nationals	9% (Evening); 15% (Weekend)
Minority Citizens/Permanent Residents (Black, Hispanic, Asian, other)	26% (Evening); 24% (Weekend)
ABILITY TO SWITCH FROM PART-TIME TO FULL-TIME PROGRAM	YES
ACCESS TO CAREER SERVICES	YES
ACCESS TO RECRUITERS	YES

Fordham University

TOTAL ENROLLMENT	1,249
PROGRAM AND FORMATS	COMBINATION— EVENING AND WEEKEND
STARTING MONTHS	September, January and April
APPLICATION DEADLINE	Spring 2006: Nov. 1, 2005 Fall 2006: June 1, 2006
AVERAGE NUMBER OF MONTHS TO COMPLETE DEGREE	36
MAXIMUM NUMBER OF MONTHS TO COMPLETE DEGREE	72
TUITION	$53,130
STUDENTS	
Average GMAT	575
Average years of students' prior full-time work experience	5
Average Age	28

DEMOGRAPHICS	
Male	63%
Female	37%
Citizens/Permanent Residents of Country in Which School is Located	97%
Foreign Nationals	3%
Minority Citizens/Permanent Residents (Black, Hispanic, Asian, other)	12%
ABILITY TO SWITCH FROM PART-TIME TO FULL-TIME PROGRAM	YES
ACCESS TO CAREER SERVICES	YES
ACCESS TO RECRUITERS	YES

Northwestern University Kellogg School of Management

TOTAL ENROLLMENT	1,200	**DEMOGRAPHICS**	
PROGRAM AND FORMATS	EVENING	Male	68%
STARTING MONTHS	September, January, March and June	Female	32%
APPLICATION DEADLINE	Winter 2006: Oct. 21, 2005 Spring 2006: Jan. 20, 2006	Citizens/Permanent Residents of Country in Which School is Located	82%
		Foreign Nationals	18%
AVERAGE NUMBER OF MONTHS TO COMPLETE DEGREE	36	Minority Citizens/Permanent Residents (Black, Hispanic, Asian, other)	12%
MAXIMUM NUMBER OF MONTHS TO COMPLETE DEGREE	60	**ABILITY TO SWITCH FROM PART-TIME TO FULL-TIME PROGRAM**	YES*
TUITION	$72,744	*After the completion of 10 courses	
STUDENTS		**ACCESS TO CAREER SERVICES**	YES**
Average GMAT	690	**Career coaching available during last year of study.	
Average years of students' prior full-time work experience	7	**ACCESS TO RECRUITERS**	YES***
Average Age	29	***Restricted to students in final year of study who haven't received employer tuition assistance or who have employer's permission.	

University of Maryland Smith School of Business

TOTAL ENROLLMENT	1,019	**DEMOGRAPHICS**	
PROGRAM AND FORMATS	EVENING, WEEKEND, AND COMBINATION	Male	72%
		Female	28%
STARTING MONTHS	August	Citizens/Permanent Residents of Country in Which School is Located	88%
APPLICATION DEADLINE	Fall 2006: June 2006	Foreign Nationals	12%
AVERAGE NUMBER OF MONTHS TO COMPLETE DEGREE	31	Minority Citizens/Permanent Residents (Black, Hispanic, Asian, other)	27%
MAXIMUM NUMBER OF MONTHS TO COMPLETE DEGREE	60	**ABILITY TO SWITCH FROM PART-TIME TO FULL-TIME PROGRAM**	NO
TUITION	$43,362* *based on 54 credits	**ACCESS TO CAREER SERVICES**	YES
STUDENTS		**ACCESS TO RECRUITERS**	YES
Average GMAT	607		
Average years of students' prior full-time work experience	6.4		
Average Age	28		

University of Michigan Ross School of Business

TOTAL ENROLLMENT	914	**DEMOGRAPHICS**	
PROGRAM AND FORMATS	EVENING	Male	77%
STARTING MONTHS	September or January	Female	23%
APPLICATION DEADLINE	Winter 2006: Oct. 1, 2005 Fall 2006: May 1, 2006	Citizens/Permanent Residents of Country in Which School is Located	85%
AVERAGE NUMBER OF MONTHS TO COMPLETE DEGREE	48	Foreign Nationals	15%
MAXIMUM NUMBER OF MONTHS TO COMPLETE DEGREE	120	Minority Citizens/Permanent Residents (Black, Hispanic, Asian, other)	26%
TUITION	$72,000	**ABILITY TO SWITCH FROM PART-TIME TO FULL-TIME PROGRAM**	YES*
STUDENTS		*after completion of core classes	
Average GMAT	656	**ACCESS TO CAREER SERVICES**	N/A
Average years of students' prior full-time work experience	7	**ACCESS TO RECRUITERS**	YES**
Average Age	30	**not full access to on-campus internship recruiting resources	

University of Southern California Marshall School of Business

TOTAL ENROLLMENT	792	**DEMOGRAPHICS**	
PROGRAM AND FORMATS	EVENINGS plus 8 weekends over 3 years	Male	71%
		Female	29%
STARTING MONTHS	August	Citizens/Permanent Residents of Country in Which School is Located	97%
APPLICATION DEADLINE	Fall 2006: May 1, 2006	Foreign Nationals	3%
AVERAGE NUMBER OF MONTHS TO COMPLETE DEGREE	33	Minority Citizens/Permanent Residents (Black, Hispanic, Asian, other)	50%
MAXIMUM NUMBER OF MONTHS TO COMPLETE DEGREE	60	**ABILITY TO SWITCH FROM PART-TIME TO FULL-TIME PROGRAM**	NO
TUITION	$67,617	**ACCESS TO CAREER SERVICES**	YES
STUDENTS		**ACCESS TO RECRUITERS**	YES
Average GMAT	627		
Average years of students' prior full-time work experience	5.8		
Average Age	30		

University of Iowa Tippie School of Management

TOTAL ENROLLMENT		746
PROGRAM AND FORMATS		COMBINATION— EVENING AND WEEKEND
STARTING MONTHS		August, January
APPLICATION DEADLINE		Spring 2006: Dec. 15, 2005 Fall 2006: July 15, 2006
AVERAGE NUMBER OF MONTHS TO COMPLETE DEGREE		42
MAXIMUM NUMBER OF MONTHS TO COMPLETE DEGREE		120
TUITION		$19,890
STUDENTS		
Average GMAT		573
Average years of students' prior full-time work experience		8
Average Age		31

DEMOGRAPHICS

Male	66%
Female	34%
Citizens/Permanent Residents of Country in Which School is Located	95%
Foreign Nationals	5%
Minority Citizens/Permanent Residents (Black, Hispanic, Asian, other)	9%
ABILITY TO SWITCH FROM PART-TIME TO FULL-TIME PROGRAM	NO
ACCESS TO CAREER SERVICES	YES*
	*During final 12 months
ACCESS TO RECRUITERS	YES**
	**During final 12 months

University of California, Berkeley, Haas School of Business

TOTAL ENROLLMENT		657
PROGRAM AND FORMATS		COMBINATION— EVENING AND WEEKEND
STARTING MONTHS		August
APPLICATION DEADLINE		Fall 2006: Nov. 15, 2005; March 1, 2006 (subject to change)
AVERAGE NUMBER OF MONTHS TO COMPLETE DEGREE		30-36
MAXIMUM NUMBER OF MONTHS TO COMPLETE DEGREE		84
TUITION		$75,600
STUDENTS		
Average GMAT		680
Average years of students' prior full-time work experience		7.8 years
Average Age		32

DEMOGRAPHICS

Male	73%
Female	27%
Citizens/Permanent Residents of Country in Which School is Located	89%
Foreign Nationals	11%
Minority Citizens/Permanent Residents (Black, Hispanic, Asian, other)	41%
ABILITY TO SWITCH FROM PART-TIME TO FULL-TIME PROGRAM	YES*
	*Only after first year and completion of core classes, on a space-available basis
ACCESS TO CAREER SERVICES	YES
ACCESS TO RECRUITERS	YES

George Washington University School of Business

		DEMOGRAPHICS	
TOTAL ENROLLMENT	638	Male	55%
PROGRAM AND FORMATS	COMBINATION—EVENING AND WEEKEND	Female	45%
STARTING MONTHS	September or January	Citizens/Permanent Residents of Country in Which School is Located	n/a
APPLICATION DEADLINE	Spring 2006: Nov. 30, 2005 Fall 2006: May 31, 2006	Foreign Nationals	n/a
AVERAGE NUMBER OF MONTHS TO COMPLETE DEGREE	30	Minority Citizens/Permanent Residents (Black, Hispanic, Asian, other)	35%
MAXIMUM NUMBER OF MONTHS TO COMPLETE DEGREE	60	**ABILITY TO SWITCH FROM PART-TIME TO FULL-TIME PROGRAM**	NO*
TUITION	$44,400	*Students can enroll for 9 or more credit hours (full-time)	
STUDENTS			
Average GMAT	580	**ACCESS TO CAREER SERVICES**	YES
Average years of students' prior full-time work experience	5.5	**ACCESS TO RECRUITERS**	YES
Average Age	31		

Southern Methodist University Cox School of Business

		DEMOGRAPHICS	
TOTAL ENROLLMENT	616	Male	73%
PROGRAM AND FORMATS	COMBINATION—EVENING AND WEEKEND	Female	27%
STARTING MONTHS	August or January	Citizens/Permanent Residents of Country in Which School is Located	97%
APPLICATION DEADLINE	Spring 2006: Nov.1, 2005 Fall 2006: May 15, 2006	Foreign Nationals	3%
AVERAGE NUMBER OF MONTHS TO COMPLETE DEGREE	24	Minority Citizens/Permanent Residents (Black, Hispanic, Asian, other)	22%
MAXIMUM NUMBER OF MONTHS TO COMPLETE DEGREE	72	**ABILITY TO SWITCH FROM PART-TIME TO FULL-TIME PROGRAM**	NO
TUITION	$69,900	**ACCESS TO CAREER SERVICES**	YES*
STUDENTS		*Restricted to students who are fully self-funded, have employer approval or are unemployed; also must be within one year of graduation and must have completed career management course.	
Average GMAT	612		
Average years of students' prior full-time work experience	5.7		
Average Age	28	**ACCESS TO RECRUITERS**	YES

York University Schulich School of Business

TOTAL ENROLLMENT	600	**DEMOGRAPHICS**	
PROGRAM AND FORMATS	EVENING, WEEKEND, AND COMBINATION	Male	70%
		Female	30%
STARTING MONTHS	January or September	Citizens/Permanent Residents of Country in Which School is Located	80%
APPLICATION DEADLINE	Winter 2006: Oct. 15, 2005 Fall 2006: May 1, 2006	Foreign Nationals	20%
AVERAGE NUMBER OF MONTHS TO COMPLETE DEGREE	40	Minority Citizens/Permanent Residents (Black, Hispanic, Asian, other)	n/a
MAXIMUM NUMBER OF MONTHS TO COMPLETE DEGREE	72	**ABILITY TO SWITCH FROM PART-TIME TO FULL-TIME PROGRAM**	YES
TUITION	$40,000	**ACCESS TO CAREER SERVICES**	YES
STUDENTS		**ACCESS TO RECRUITERS**	YES
Average GMAT	665		
Average years of students' prior full-time work experience	7		
Average Age	31		

University of California, Los Angeles, Anderson School

TOTAL ENROLLMENT	594	**DEMOGRAPHICS**	
PROGRAM AND FORMATS	COMBINATION— EVENING AND WEEKEND	Male	76%
		Female	24%
STARTING MONTHS	September	Citizens/Permanent Residents of Country in Which School is Located	100%
APPLICATION DEADLINE	Fall 2006: May 1, 2006	Foreign Nationals	0%
AVERAGE NUMBER OF MONTHS TO COMPLETE DEGREE	33	Minority Citizens/Permanent Residents (Black, Hispanic, Asian, other)	32%
MAXIMUM NUMBER OF MONTHS TO COMPLETE DEGREE	60	**ABILITY TO SWITCH FROM PART-TIME TO FULL-TIME PROGRAM**	NO
TUITION	$76,500* *subject to annual change	**ACCESS TO CAREER SERVICES**	YES
STUDENTS		**ACCESS TO RECRUITERS**	YES
Average GMAT	661		
Average years of students' prior full-time work experience	5.9		
Average Age	29		

University of Florida Warrington College of Business

TOTAL ENROLLMENT	576		**DEMOGRAPHICS**	
PROGRAM AND FORMATS	WEEKEND		Male	75%
STARTING MONTHS	N/A		Female	25%
APPLICATION DEADLINE	Spring 2006: Dec. 1, 2005 Fall 2006: July 1, 2006		Citizens/Permanent Residents of Country in Which School is Located	94%
AVERAGE NUMBER OF MONTHS TO COMPLETE DEGREE	24		Foreign Nationals	6%
MAXIMUM NUMBER OF MONTHS TO COMPLETE DEGREE	15		Minority Citizens/Permanent Residents (Black, Hispanic, Asian, other)	22%
TUITION	$29,750		**ABILITY TO SWITCH FROM PART-TIME TO FULL-TIME PROGRAM**	NO
STUDENTS			**ACCESS TO CAREER SERVICES**	YES*
Average GMAT	602		*limited availability for students with no employer funding	
Average years of students' prior full-time work experience	7		**ACCESS TO RECRUITERS**	NO
Average Age	31			

Tecnologico de Monterrey EGADE (Monterrey Campus)

TOTAL ENROLLMENT	558		**STUDENTS**	
PROGRAM AND FORMATS	EVENING, WEEKEND, AND COMBINATION MBA specialized in global business and strategy (E); MBA specialized in global e-management (W); MBA (C)		Average GMAT	598(E); 590(W); 587(C)
			Average years of students' prior full-time work experience	3.8(E); 10(W); 7(C)
			Average Age	27(E); 33(W); 29(C)
STARTING MONTHS	January (E); January or September (W); January, April and September (C)		**DEMOGRAPHICS**	
			Male	58%(E); 73%(W); 76%(C)
APPLICATION DEADLINE	Winter 2006: October 2005 (E); Spring 2006: February 2006 (E); Fall 2006: July 2006 (E)		Female	42%(E); 27%(W); 24%(C)
			Citizens/Permanent Residents of Country in Which School is Located	83%(E); 91%(W); 96%(C)
			Foreign students	17%(E); 9%(W); 4%(C)
AVERAGE NUMBER OF MONTHS TO COMPLETE DEGREE	30(E); 18(W); 36(C)		Minority Citizens/Permanent Residents (Black, Hispanic, Asian, other)	n/a (All)
MAXIMUM NUMBER OF MONTHS TO COMPLETE DEGREE	30(E); 18(W); 36(C)		**ABILITY TO SWITCH FROM PART-TIME TO FULL-TIME PROGRAM**	YES(E); NO(W); YES(C)
TUITION	$30,000(E); $30,000(W); $26,000 to $30,000(C)		**ACCESS TO CAREER SERVICES**	YES (All)
			ACCESS TO RECRUITERS	YES (All)

Arizona State University Carey School of Business

TOTAL ENROLLMENT	476	**DEMOGRAPHICS**	
PROGRAM AND FORMATS	EVENING	*Male*	75%
STARTING MONTHS	Fall	*Female*	25%
APPLICATION DEADLINE	Fall 2006: May 1, 2006; rolling deadline thereafter	*Citizens/Permanent Residents of Country in Which School is Located*	86%
		Foreign Nationals	14%
AVERAGE NUMBER OF MONTHS TO COMPLETE DEGREE	22	*Minority Citizens/Permanent Residents (Black, Hispanic, Asian, other)*	13%
MAXIMUM NUMBER OF MONTHS TO COMPLETE DEGREE	96	**ABILITY TO SWITCH FROM PART-TIME TO FULL-TIME PROGRAM**	NO
TUITION	$37,283	**ACCESS TO CAREER SERVICES**	YES
STUDENTS		**ACCESS TO RECRUITERS**	YES
Average GMAT	594		
Average years of students' prior full-time work experience	6.25		
Average Age	30		

University of California, Irvine, Merage School of Business

TOTAL ENROLLMENT	476	**DEMOGRAPHICS**	
PROGRAM AND FORMATS	COMBINATION— EVENING AND WEEKEND	*Male*	71%
		Female	29%
STARTING MONTHS	March or September	*Citizens/Permanent Residents of Country in Which School is Located*	92%
APPLICATION DEADLINE	Spring 2006: January 2006 Fall 2006: July 2006	*Foreign Nationals*	8%
AVERAGE NUMBER OF MONTHS TO COMPLETE DEGREE	31	*Minority Citizens/Permanent Residents (Black, Hispanic, Asian, other)*	38%
MAXIMUM NUMBER OF MONTHS TO COMPLETE DEGREE	33	**ABILITY TO SWITCH FROM PART-TIME TO FULL-TIME PROGRAM**	YES
TUITION	$63,900	**ACCESS TO CAREER SERVICES**	YES
STUDENTS		**ACCESS TO RECRUITERS**	YES
Average GMAT	580		
Average years of students' prior full-time work experience	6.2		
Average Age	29.7		

University of Pittsburgh Katz Graduate School of Business

TOTAL ENROLLMENT	466
PROGRAM AND FORMATS	EVENING
STARTING MONTHS	September, January and April
APPLICATION DEADLINE	Winter 2006: Nov. 1, 2005
	Spring 2006: March 1, 2006
	Fall 2006: July 1, 2006
AVERAGE NUMBER OF MONTHS TO COMPLETE DEGREE	36
MAXIMUM NUMBER OF MONTHS TO COMPLETE DEGREE	72
TUITION	$37,357 (in-state)
	$66,780 (out of state)

STUDENTS

Average GMAT	559
Average years of students' prior full-time work experience	4
Average Age	29

DEMOGRAPHICS

Male	69%
Female	31%
Citizens/Permanent Residents of Country in Which School is Located	97%
Foreign Nationals	3%
Minority Citizens/Permanent Residents (Black, Hispanic, Asian, other)	8%
ABILITY TO SWITCH FROM PART-TIME TO FULL-TIME PROGRAM	NO
ACCESS TO CAREER SERVICES	YES
ACCESS TO RECRUITERS	YES

Boston University School of Management

TOTAL ENROLLMENT	385
PROGRAM AND FORMATS	EVENING
STARTING MONTHS	September
APPLICATION DEADLINE	Fall 2006: June 1, 2006
AVERAGE NUMBER OF MONTHS TO COMPLETE DEGREE	41
MAXIMUM NUMBER OF MONTHS TO COMPLETE DEGREE	72
TUITION	$60,928

STUDENTS

Average GMAT	574
Average years of students' prior full-time work experience	5
Average Age	28

DEMOGRAPHICS

Male	64%
Female	36%
Citizens/Permanent Residents of Country in Which School is Located	78%
Foreign Nationals	22%
Minority Citizens/Permanent Residents (Black, Hispanic, Asian, other)	15%
ABILITY TO SWITCH FROM PART-TIME TO FULL-TIME PROGRAM	YES
ACCESS TO CAREER SERVICES	YES
ACCESS TO RECRUITERS	YES

THE BOOMING EXECUTIVE-M.B.A. MARKET

It takes a savvy consumer to navigate the fast-growing executive-M.B.A. market.

Betting on continued enrollment growth, business schools are adding new degrees at a rapid-fire clip. The good news is that potential applicants enjoy more choice than ever. The bad news: Quality and price vary greatly. So it's critical that prospective students shop carefully for the executive program that best suits their needs and pocketbooks, especially if their company is paying little or none of the bill.

The business schools at Northwestern University, Yale University, University of California at Davis, and University of Maryland, to cite just a few, all recently started new executive-M.B.A. programs. The University of Virginia's Darden Graduate School of Business Administration is developing its first executive degree. And Cornell University, in partnership with Queen's School of Business in Kingston, Ontario, has started offering students an alternative way to earn an executive degree. The "Cornell Boardroom Executive M.B.A." will bring the classroom into the workplace through interactive video-conferences.

The explosion of programs in such a short time is striking: According to the Executive MBA Council, 24% of programs were created just in the last five years, and 40% during the 1990s. The council has 212 member schools offering more than 300 programs.

The flurry of new programs is understandable as schools try to tap into the most robust part of the M.B.A. market. Two-year executive programs, which typically attract people who are older and more experienced than full-time students, have been the only real sweet spot lately. Even though fewer companies these days are picking up the full tab when their executives return to business school, interest in the weekend and evening programs remains relatively strong. That's at least partly because students can keep their jobs and salaries during the two-year programs.

When the Graduate Management Admission Council surveyed schools in early 2005, preliminary data showed that 69% of executive-M.B.A. programs were seeing an increase in applications, compared with only 23% of full-time and 32% of part-time programs.

Still, the executive-M.B.A. market could face a shakeout of lesser-quality programs. "It is a very competitive market today, especially as schools move into new geographic territory and challenge existing programs," says Penny Oslund, director of executive-M.B.A. programs at the University of North Carolina at Chapel Hill, which offers three executive degrees. When North Carolina designed its evening executive program, it was aimed primarily at the local Research Triangle region. Now, its weekend M.B.A. attracts people from the entire Eastern seaboard, and its OneMBA program, an alliance with four foreign business schools, draws a global mix of applicants.

Already, some markets are getting pretty crowded. The University of California at Davis is entering the San Francisco market and notes that Bay Area residents will now be able to choose from 10 executive-M.B.A. programs. UC Davis says its competitive edge will be its "strategic" location near a cluster of software and telecommunications companies about 35 miles east of the city. Even so, the school is sure to face aggressive marketing from the established players, such as Wharton West, and will need to make a compelling case for its M.B.A. brand.

Nowhere are things hotter than in Houston, where the University of Texas at Austin recently introduced a weekend M.B.A. program, open to working professionals with either a little or a lot of work experience. But it is still expected to attract more seasoned executives who might otherwise have chosen one of the more established weekend executive-M.B.A. programs offered by Rice University, Tulane University, Texas A&M University, and the University of Houston.

So upset was Rice that it challenged UT's invasion of its hometown market in advertisements and in a formal protest to the state of Texas. Rice complained to the Texas Higher Education Coordinating Board that UT faculty could better serve the state by improving the school's undergraduate business program rather than wasting their time driving from Austin to Houston. But the board refused to get involved because the UT program won't receive state financial support.

"There's no market need for the University of Texas to come into Houston," says Gilbert Whitaker, the recently retired dean of Rice's Jones Graduate School of Management. "The M.B.A. programs in Houston aren't full; every one of them could use more students." But the University of Texas contends that it "needs to be where the market is" and that its many Houston alumni wanted their alma mater to set up a local branch.

Aware of saturation in places like Houston, some business school officials say they are scouting for "underserved markets," both in the U.S. and abroad. Asia and Eastern Europe are particularly ripe targets. A consortium of European business schools developed an executive-M.B.A. program in St. Petersburg, Russia, in association with the management school at St. Petersburg State University. The University of Maryland is adding an executive M.B.A. in Shanghai to complement its two-year-old Beijing program; it also is launching a dual-degree executive program with the Graduate School of Business Administration Zurich in Switzerland.

Duke University's Fuqua School of Business, which offered three executive-M.B.A. degrees, recently teamed up with Frankfurt University in Germany to start a fourth. "We'll probably be looking to Asia for another program," says Dan Nagy, associate dean for executive-M.B.A. admissions at Fuqua. "We must get a call a week from China about a potential partnership." For Fuqua, expansion is helping to increase its brand awareness around the globe.

Some schools are offering more specialized executive degrees to stand out from the competition. Northwestern's Kellogg School of Management is targeting Latin American executives in Miami, while Yale is making its entry into the market with a degree tailored for health-care executives. Duke also is adding a health-sector management concentration to its weekend program in Durham, N.C.

Even if student demand eventually cools, executive-M.B.A. degrees will remain tempting to budget-conscious deans. Because they charge higher tuition and fees, executive programs are typically self-sufficient and often generate a surplus. Full-time programs, on the other hand, usually must be subsidized by philanthropic gifts, state funding in the case of public universities, and other income sources.

To prospective executive-M.B.A. students, all this variety may look enticing. But it's important that customers make sure they're getting their money's worth. First and foremost, applicants should measure the quality of the executive degree based on whether the school's full-time professors or adjunct faculty are teaching the classes and how closely the course content matches that of the full-time program. Then there's the question of whom you'll be sitting next to in class. "The experience level of other students is critical," says George Bobinski, associate dean of the School of Management at Binghamton University in New York State, which offers two executive programs. "You learn so much from interaction with your fellow students."

It's also important that the program's structure fits your lifestyle. Will you be able to spend a full week on campus if necessary? Is there an international residency that must be factored into your work schedule?

Executive-M.B.A. students who are paying their own tuition and hoping the degree will be a passport to a new career should find out whether schools offer career services and access to corporate recruiters. "Career services are becoming a bigger and bigger issue as more students are self-sponsored," says Duke's Mr. Nagy. "We'll even open the door to career services for company-sponsored students if they get a letter from their employer saying it's OK."

Price, of course, is an important consideration. The Executive MBA Council estimates that the total program cost in North America averages about $47,000, but top-ranked schools charge significantly more. While full-time tuition these days is far from cheap at the most prestigious M.B.A. programs, the price for an executive M.B.A. at the same schools can run well into six figures, including weekend room-and-board expenses.

Among the priciest: the executive M.B.A. programs offered by the Wharton School in San Francisco and Philadelphia—at about $138,000 and $128,000, respectively, and Columbia University's three programs, which cost between $115,000 and $124,000. In addition to its New York executive-M.B.A. program, Columbia has entered the West Coast market in a bi-coastal venture with the University of California at Berkeley and has created a presence in Europe in partnership with London Business School.

Top schools like Columbia promise the same faculty and curriculum as their full-time programs offer. But others seem to skimp, with more online content and less face-to-face interaction. Indeed, executive M.B.A.s still suffer somewhat from perceptions that they are watered-down versions of the traditional full-time degree.

M.B.A. Lite—that's what some people still call the executive degree. In *The Wall Street Journal*/Harris Interactive survey, some recruiters said they believe that executive degrees are just moneymakers for schools and that they lack the value of a full-time degree. About 30% said they consider executive programs less effective in building skills. One survey respondent characterized studying for an executive degree as more like "surfing, not deep-diving." Another recruiter stated that "the depth of knowledge is not there" and that graduates end up with "a Swiss cheese diploma."

Sensitive to that stigma, some schools have started to avoid the popular E.M.B.A. label and instead advertise their "M.B.A. program for executives." It may seem like a piddling change, but in marketing, perception is everything.

Michael Fenlon, associate dean for the executive-M.B.A. programs at Columbia, believes the degree's image is improving in more substantive ways. "Perceptions of the executive M.B.A. have clearly been changing as people recognize its unique value—the real-time application of learning," he says. "Students will discuss how they applied the tools they learned in the previous class, how they sometimes did a deal differently. At Columbia, they are interacting with and learning from some very experienced and diverse people who may include a U.N. weapons inspector, a neurosurgeon, and executives from companies like Goldman Sachs and Accenture."

THE BIGGEST E.M.B.A. PROGRAMS

The 10 largest executive M.B.A. programs offered by the schools in *The Wall Street Journal*/Harris Interactive rankings.

Columbia University Business School

■ Total enrollment: 600

Program and Formats	EMBA—NY	EMBA—Global	Berkeley-Columbia EMBA
Class Schedule	Alternate Fridays/Saturdays	First year: 3–4 consecutive days per month in London & NY; second year: London Business School or Columbia.	3–4 consecutive day terms at Berkeley and Columbia
Residential requirement	Two 1 week periods, off-site	1 week	1 week
Online coursework	—	—	—
STARTING MONTHS	September and January	May	May
Application deadline	Winter 2006: Oct. 15, 2005 Fall 2006: June 1, 2006	Spring 2006: February 2006	Spring 2006: February 2006
Length of program	20 months	20 months	19 months
TUITION	$120,195	$115,000	$124,000
STUDENTS			
Average GMAT	n/a	—	—
Average number of years of prior full-time work experience	10	—	—
Average Age	33	—	—
DEMOGRAPHICS			
Male	83%	—	—
Female	17%	—	—
Citizens/Permanent Residents of Country in Which School is Located	81%	—	—
Foreign Nationals	19%	—	—
Minority Citizens/Permanent Residents (Black, Hispanic, Asian, other)	31%	—	—
PERCENTAGE SPONSORED BY EMPLOYERS	100%	—	—
PERCENTAGE WHOSE EMPLOYERS PAY FULL COST	60%	—	—
PERCENTAGE WHOSE EMPLOYERS PAY PARTIAL COST	10%	—	—

Program and Formats	EMBA—NY	EMBA—Global	Berkeley-Columbia EMBA
TOP FIVE COMPANIES SENDING PARTICIPANTS OVER LAST THREE YEARS			
1	J.P. Morgan Chase	—	—
2	Ernst & Young	—	—
3	General Electric	—	—
4	IBM	—	—
5	Deutsche Bank	—	—
	Goldman Sachs	—	—
ACCESS TO CAREER SERVICES	YES*	—	—
ACCESS TO RECRUITERS	YES*	—	—
	*Only for students approved for career services; i.e. self-employed, unemployed, and those receiving employer permission		

University of Miami School of Business

- Total enrollment: 508

Program and Formats	EMBA	Health Administration Program
Class Schedule	Monday evenings & Saturday mornings, or all-day Saturday	—
Residential requirement	—	One week
Online coursework	—	—
STARTING MONTHS	August and January	—
Application deadline	Spring 2006: Jan. 1, 2006 Fall 2006: July 1, 2006	—
Length of program	23 months	—
TUITION	$57,984	—

Program and Formats	EMBA	Health Administration Program
STUDENTS		
Average GMAT	Not required for admission	—
Average number of years of prior full-time work experience	9	—
Average Age	35	—
DEMOGRAPHICS		
Male	64%	—
Female	36%	—
Citizens/Permanent Residents of Country in Which School is Located	92%	—
Foreign Nationals	8%	—
Minority Citizens/Permanent Residents (Black, Hispanic, Asian, other)	63%	—
PERCENTAGE SPONSORED BY EMPLOYERS	49%	—
PERCENTAGE WHOSE EMPLOYERS PAY FULL COST	n/a	—
PERCENTAGE WHOSE EMPLOYERS PAY PARTIAL COST	n/a	—
TOP FIVE COMPANIES SENDING PARTICIPANTS OVER LAST THREE YEARS		
1	Motorola	—
2	Sony	—
3	Commerce Bank	—
4	Hewlett-Packard	—
5	Carrier Interamerica	—
ACCESS TO CAREER SERVICES	YES	—
ACCESS TO RECRUITERS	YES* *Upon graduation or during program if they are not supported by their company.	—

Duke University/Fuqua School of Business

■ Total enrollment: 486

Program and Formats	Cross Continent	Weekend Executive	Global Executive
Class Schedule	During residencies	Every other Friday and Saturday	During residencies
Residential requirement	Eight 1-week residencies on Durham, N.C., campus, Europe and Asia	—	Five 2-week residencies on Durham campus, Europe, Asia and South America
Online coursework	6 weeks of Internet course work per term	—	10–12 weeks of Internet course work per term
STARTING MONTHS	July	February	May
Application deadline	Spring 2006: Sept. 30, 2005; Dec. 15, 2005; March 31, 2006	Winter 2006: April 15, 2005; July 15, 2005; Oct. 31, 2005	Spring 2006: Aug. 15, 2005; Nov. 15, 2005; Feb. 15, 2006
Length of program	20 months	20 months	19 months
TUITION	$86,900	$83,900	$111,200
STUDENTS			
Average GMAT	643	645	Not required
Average number of years of prior full-time work experience	6	11	13
Average Age	30	34	39
DEMOGRAPHICS	EMBA	—	—
Male	70%	—	—
Female	30%	—	—
Citizens/Permanent Residents of Country in Which School is Located	65%	—	—
Foreign Nationals	35%	—	—
Minority Citizens/Permanent Residents (Black, Hispanic, Asian, other)	34%	—	—
PERCENTAGE SPONSORED BY EMPLOYERS	72%	91%	70%
PERCENTAGE WHOSE EMPLOYERS PAY FULL COST	21%	33%	30%
PERCENTAGE WHOSE EMPLOYERS PAY PARTIAL COST	51%	58%	40%

Program and Formats	Cross Continent	Weekend Executive	Global Executive
TOP FIVE COMPANIES SENDING PARTICIPANTS OVER LAST THREE YEARS			
1	IBM	—	—
2	Capital One	—	—
3	Duke University Medical Center	—	—
4	Wachovia	—	—
5	Bank of America	—	—
ACCESS TO CAREER SERVICES	YES*	*For students who are 100% self-sponsored or who gain permission from their sponsoring company	
ACCESS TO RECRUITERS	NO**	**Not for on-campus recruiting but do have access through database and résumé book	

University of Chicago Graduate School of Business (1 program—3 campuses in Chicago, London and Singapore)

■ Total enrollment: 481

Program and Formats	International EMBA/ Chicago	International EMBA/ London	International EMBA/ Singapore
Class Schedule	Friday and Saturday every other week	Classes in one-week modules	Classes in one-week modules
Residential requirement	4 week-long sessions	—	—
Online coursework	—	—	—
STARTING MONTHS	June	June	June
Application deadline	Summer 2006: Dec. 1, 2005, Feb. 1, 2006, and May 1, 2006	—	—
Length of program	20 months	20 months	20 months
TUITION	$107,000	$99,000	$89,500
STUDENTS			
Average GMAT	—	—	—

Program and Formats	International EMBA/ Chicago	International EMBA/ London	International EMBA/ Singapore
Average number of years of prior full-time work experience	12	—	—
Average Age	35	—	—
DEMOGRAPHICS			
Male	84%	—	—
Female	16%	—	—
Citizens/Permanent Residents of Country in Which School is Located	—	—	—
Foreign Nationals	—	—	—
Minority Citizens/Permanent Residents (Black, Hispanic, Asian, other)	—	—	—
PERCENTAGE SPONSORED BY EMPLOYERS	—	—	—
PERCENTAGE WHOSE EMPLOYERS PAY FULL COST	—	—	—
PERCENTAGE WHOSE EMPLOYERS PAY PARTIAL COST	—	—	—
TOP FIVE COMPANIES SENDING PARTICIPANTS OVER LAST THREE YEARS			
1	—	—	—
2	—	—	—
3	—	—	—
4	—	—	—
5	—	—	—
ACCESS TO CAREER SERVICES	YES	—	—
ACCESS TO RECRUITERS	NO	—	—

Northwestern University/Kellogg School of Management

■ Total enrollment: 400

Program and Formats	North American Programs (NAP)	Regional Program
Class Schedule	Bimonthly weekend classes; September program, Friday-Saturday-Sunday; January program, Friday-Saturday	Once-a-week class day on alternating Fridays and Saturdays
Residential requirement	September program, two weeks; January program, four weeks	Two weeks
Online coursework		
STARTING MONTHS	September and January	—
Application deadline	Rolling admissions Winter 2006: Nov. 15, 2005; Fall 2006: July 1, 2006	—
Length of program	Two academic years	—
TUITION	$120,000	$108,000
STUDENTS		
Average GMAT	Not required, but admissions committee may request the GMAT; expected average score of 650	—
Average number of years of prior full-time work experience	14	—
Average Age	36.6	—
DEMOGRAPHICS		
Male	81%	—
Female	19%	—
Citizens/Permanent Residents of Country in Which School is Located	85%	—
Foreign Nationals	15%	—
Minority Citizens/Permanent Residents (Black, Hispanic, Asian, other)	29%	—
PERCENTAGE SPONSORED BY EMPLOYERS	95.6%	—
PERCENTAGE WHOSE EMPLOYERS PAY FULL COST	89.75%	—
PERCENTAGE WHOSE EMPLOYERS PAY PARTIAL COST	5.85%	—

Program and Formats	North American Programs (NAP)	Regional Program
TOP FIVE COMPANIES SENDING PARTICIPANTS OVER LAST THREE YEARS		
1	General Electric	—
2	ABN AMRO	—
3	Deere	—
4	Harley-Davidson	—
5	Motorola	—
ACCESS TO CAREER SERVICES	YES	—
ACCESS TO RECRUITERS	NO	—

IPADE School of Management

- Total enrollment: 370

Program and Formats	Master in Business Administration for Experienced Executives (MEDEX)
Class Schedule	Twice weekly
Residential requirement	—
Online coursework	—
STARTING MONTHS	September
Application deadline	Fall 2006: July 2006
Length of program	24 months
TUITION	$45,000
STUDENTS	
Average GMAT	n/a
Average number of years of prior full-time work experience	10
Average Age	33
DEMOGRAPHICS	
Male	84%
Female	16%
Citizens/Permanent Residents of Country in Which School is Located	94%
Foreign Nationals	6%

Program and Formats	Master in Business
Minority Citizens/Permanent Residents (Black, Hispanic, Asian, other)	n/a
PERCENTAGE SPONSORED BY EMPLOYERS	70%
PERCENTAGE WHOSE EMPLOYERS PAY FULL COST	70%
PERCENTAGE WHOSE EMPLOYERS PAY PARTIAL COST	30%
TOP FIVE COMPANIES SENDING PARTICIPANTS OVER LAST THREE YEARS	
1	HSBC
2	Grupo Banamex—Citibank (Accival)
3	CEMEX
4	Hewlett-Packard
5	Grupo Salinas (TV Azteca—Elektra)
ACCESS TO CAREER SERVICES	NO
ACCESS TO RECRUITERS	NO

University of Texas, McCombs School of Business

- Total enrollment: 366

Program and Formats	Texas MBA at DFW	Option II EMBA— Austin	EMBA in Mexico City	Texas MBA at Houston
Class Schedule	Alternate weekends, Friday and Saturday	Alternate weekends, Friday and Saturday, plus week-long executive seminars	Alternate weekends, Friday and Saturday, at Tecnologico de Monterrey campus	Alternate weekends, Friday and Saturday
Residential requirement	—	—	3 one-week executive seminars: two in Austin, one at an international location	—
Online coursework				
STARTING MONTHS	August	August	August	August
Application deadline	Fall 2006: June 15, 2006	Fall 2006: June 15, 2006	Fall 2006: June 1, 2006	Fall 2006: Priority deadline, March 31, 2006
Length of program	22 months	22 months	22 months	22 months

Program and Formats	Texas MBA at DFW	Option II EMBA—Austin	EMBA in Mexico City	Texas MBA at Houston
TUITION	$68,500	$59,400	$47,000	$68,500
STUDENTS				
Average GMAT	602	659	641	650
Average number of years of prior full-time work experience	8	11	6.1	6
Average Age	33	36	29.5	30
DEMOGRAPHICS				
Male	86%	87%	86%	70%
Female	14%	13%	14%	30%
Citizens/Permanent Residents of Country in Which School is Located	82%	78%	2%	92%
Foreign Nationals	18%	22%	98%	8%
Minority Citizens/ Permanent Residents (Black, Hispanic, Asian, other)	40%	36%	n/a	36%
PERCENTAGE SPONSORED BY EMPLOYERS	n/a	64%	60%	50%
PERCENTAGE WHOSE EMPLOYERS PAY FULL COST	n/a	18%	30%	n/a
PERCENTAGE WHOSE EMPLOYERS PAY PARTIAL COST	n/a	46%	30%	n/a
TOP FIVE COMPANIES SENDING PARTICI-PANTS OVER LAST THREE YEARS				
1	Texas Instruments	Dell	General Electric	ExxonMobil
2	Frito-Lay	IBM	Motorola	Hewlett-Packard
3	Honeywell	AMD	Deloitte & Touche	Texas Instruments
4	Sematech	Hewlett-Packard	Grupo Elektra	AIG
5	Verizon	Valero Energy, Dow Chemical, Emerson Process Management	Procter and Gamble de Mexico	Dow Chemical
ACCESS TO CAREER SERVICES	YES*	YES	NO	YES*

Program and Formats	Texas MBA at DFW	Option II EMBA— Austin	EMBA in Mexico City	Texas MBA at Houston
ACCESS TO RECRUITERS	YES* *Must meet sponsorship requirement, complete disclosure form and attend workshop series	YES	NO	YES* *Must meet sponsorship requirement; complete a disclosure form and attend workshop series.

University of North Carolina at Chapel Hill, Kenan-Flagler Business School

- Total enrollment: 314

Program and Formats	Weekend	Evening	OneMBA
Class Schedule	Twice monthly, Friday-Saturday, plus 2 immersion weeks	2 evenings a week	1 weekend per month
Residential requirement	—	—	4 week-long sessions in U.S., Europe, Latin America and Asia
Online coursework	—	—	—
STARTING MONTHS	January	August	September
Application deadline	September	April	June
Length of program	20 months	24 months	21 months
TUITION	$64,000	$51,000	$74,000
STUDENTS			
Average GMAT	N/A	N/A	N/A
Average number of years of prior full-time work experience	11	9	12
Average Age	34	33	35
DEMOGRAPHICS			
Male	87%	83%	76%*
Female	13%	17%	24*
Citizens/Permanent Residents of Country in Which School is Located	83%	71%	60%*

Program and Formats	Weekend	Evening	OneMBA
Foreign Nationals	17%	29%	40%*
Minority Citizens/Permanent Residents (Black, Hispanic, Asian, other)	12%	20%	15%*
PERCENTAGE SPONSORED BY EMPLOYERS	64%	56%	82%
PERCENTAGE WHOSE EMPLOYERS PAY FULL COST	31%	17%	41%
PERCENTAGE WHOSE EMPLOYERS PAY PARTIAL COST	33%	39%	41%
TOP FIVE COMPANIES SENDING PARTICIPANTS OVER LAST THREE YEARS			
1	IBM	IBM	America Online
2	Capital One	Cisco	FedEx
3	Progress Energy	GlaxoSmithKline	Exxon
4	Bank of America	General Electric	NII Holdings
5	Cisco	Progress Energy/Sony Ericsson/Novo Nordisk	IBM
ACCESS TO CAREER SERVICES	YES	—	—
ACCESS TO RECRUITERS	NO	—	—

*UNC students only

London Business School

■ Total enrollment: 298

Program and Formats	EMBA
Class Schedule	Fridays and Saturdays of alternate weeks
Residential requirement	1 week, plus 2 week-long residential field trips
Online coursework	
STARTING MONTHS	January and September
Application deadline	Winter 2006: September 2005 Fall 2006: May 2006
Length of program	Maximum 20 months
TUITION	$75,600
STUDENTS	
Average GMAT	657
Average number of years of prior full-time work experience	9
Average Age	33
DEMOGRAPHICS	
Male	82%
Female	18%
Citizens/Permanent Residents of Country in Which School is Located	30%
Foreign Nationals	70%
Minority Citizens/Permanent Residents (Black, Hispanic, Asian, other)	n/a
PERCENTAGE SPONSORED BY EMPLOYERS	58%
PERCENTAGE WHOSE EMPLOYERS PAY FULL COST	57%
PERCENTAGE WHOSE EMPLOYERS PAY PARTIAL COST	43%
TOP FIVE COMPANIES SENDING PARTICIPANTS OVER LAST THREE YEARS	
1	PricewaterhouseCoopers
2	Royal Dutch/Shell Group
3	Citigroup
4	General Electric
5	O2
ACCESS TO CAREER SERVICES	YES
ACCESS TO RECRUITERS	NO

Instituto de Empresa

- Total enrollment: 286

Program and Formats	EMBA
Class Schedule	Face-to-face or online
Residential requirement	—
Online coursework	Yes
STARTING MONTHS	October
Application deadline	Rolling admissions
Length of program	10 months
TUITION	$36,500
STUDENTS	
Average GMAT	675
Average number of years of prior full-time work experience3	7
Average Age	35
DEMOGRAPHICS	
Male	62%
Female	38%
Citizens/Permanent Residents of Country in Which School is Located	69%
Foreign Nationals	31%
Minority Citizens/Permanent Residents (Black, Hispanic, Asian, other)	n/a
PERCENTAGE SPONSORED BY EMPLOYERS	40%
PERCENTAGE WHOSE EMPLOYERS PAY FULL COST	50%
PERCENTAGE WHOSE EMPLOYERS PAY PARTIAL COST	50%
TOP FIVE COMPANIES SENDING PARTICIPANTS OVER LAST THREE YEARS	
1	Telefonica
2	Endesa
3	Accenture
4	Iberdrola
5	Bayer
ACCESS TO CAREER SERVICES	YES
ACCESS TO RECRUITERS	YES

THE ONLINE M.B.A.: A BLENDED APPROACH

Business degrees come in more shapes and sizes all the time, and one of the newest concoctions is the "blended M.B.A."

That's the term increasingly being used to describe programs that include a heavy dose of "distance learning" over the Internet. More schools, including online-education pioneer University of Phoenix, are promoting such programs, which mix Internet instruction with traditional teaching in a bricks-and-mortar classroom setting.

"The blended approach provides the best of all possible worlds and is our fastest-growing program," says Laura Palmer Noone, president of Apollo Group Inc.'s University of Phoenix, which began offering its FlexNet option about three years ago. FlexNet students take the first and last sessions of a course in classrooms and the rest online.

Dr. Palmer Noone expects both blended and completely online programs to become even more popular as computer-literate teenagers reach their mid-20s and think about pursuing an M.B.A. degree. "They've been playing games with *Sesame Street*'s Elmo on computers since they were babies," she says. "This type of learning will be second nature to them."

That may be true, but is an online format the best way to earn an M.B.A.? Although more online-M.B.A. degrees are being awarded every year to working adults, they are still considered an incomplete education by many people, including corporate recruiters. While students certainly gain useful knowledge, there is a vigorous debate over the value of learning in front of a computer screen compared to the classroom. That explains why the blended approach is gaining momentum.

Most online-M.B.A. students receive their degrees from for-profit schools, such as the University of Phoenix that aren't accredited by AACSB International the major business-school accreditation organization. Without such accreditation, considered a hallmark of academic quality, schools don't qualify to participate in *The Wall Street Journal*/Harris Interactive recruiter survey.

However, a small but growing number of accredited schools in the *Journal* rankings, such as Duke University, Indiana University, Thunderbird, Pennsylvania State University, Arizona State University, and the University of Florida, offer M.B.A. programs with a strong online component.

"The reputation of the school in general and the quality of the teachers are critical issues for prospective students," says Richard Magjuka, faculty chairman of Indiana University's Kelley Direct online program, which uses only full-time members of the Kelley School of Business faculty.

Kelley Direct, which requires students to spend two weeks in residence, one in Indianapolis and one in Bloomington, is growing fast, with more than 900 students today, up from 14 when it started in 1999. In addition to M.B.A. degrees, Kelly Direct also offers master's degrees in finance, supply-chain management, and strategic management, and creates special degree programs for employees of such companies as General Motors Corp., Deere & Co., and United Technologies Corp.

Duke's Fuqua School of Business is one of the most ardent proponents of the blended approach, though it requires more classroom time than most schools. "Interacting in a face-to-face fashion is critical," says John Gallagher, associate dean for executive-M.B.A. programs. "People communicate and do team-building when they're together with the other students and the faculty. That immersion with the entire group allows the distance portion to function well." According to Dr. Gallagher, Duke's Global Executive and Cross-Continent M.B.A. programs are about a 50-50 split of Internet and classroom teaching.

Duke is sensitive about being linked with online-M.B.A. programs with lower academic standards and even tends to avoid using the word "online." Instead, it describes its programs as "Internet mediated" or "Internet enabled."

Duke's euphemistic approach to online learning is understandable. While the North Carolina school is certainly a respected institution, some marketers of online degrees clearly amount to little more than diploma mills. Spam e-mails promise people they'll earn more money if they "get a business degree FAST," and a recent Associated Press article even reported on a bogus operation that awarded an M.B.A. to a cat. Given such abuses, GetEducated.com, an online-degree clearinghouse, established a "diploma mill police" service to help prospective students weed out disreputable e-M.B.A. programs.

Convenience, of course, is the primary marketing focus for online programs. For at least a sizable chunk of the program, students can work at their own pace in the comfort of their own home. If they move to another city in the middle of the program, it usually means little disruption. In promoting the flexibility of its online degrees, the University of Phoenix tells prospective students: "Imagine no long commute, no waiting in lines to register, no separate trips to buy books, and no babysitter to pay. Never again will you have to use the phrase, 'No, I can't. I have a class.' " A promotional e-mail for another online program depicts a woman working on her laptop with her two adoring children by her side and declares, "Online education is the best way to get your degree and not sacrifice social, family, or work commitments."

Some schools also play up the speed of their online and blended options. For example, Babson College's "fast-track M.B.A.," which combines Internet and classroom teaching, allows part-time students to finish the degree in 26 months, 10 months sooner than in the traditional part-time evening program. "It's a dynamic marketplace, forcing us to be more aggressive in giving working professionals greater value and variety," says Mark Rice, dean of Babson's Olin Graduate School of Business, who expects to develop an even faster fast-track blended program by 2006. "People's expectations are changing," he adds. "There's greater conflict between the desire for the M.B.A. degree and the stress over the time and cost involved."

Global reach is another selling point for the blended format. In September 2005, Thunderbird's Garvin School of International Management plans to launch its 21-month Global M.B.A. On-Demand, which it describes as "accessible anytime, anywhere." About 75% of the coursework is Internet-based and the rest takes place in the classroom, including seminars in the U.S., France, and China. "The University of Phoenix is serious competition for traditional business schools," says Angel Cabrera, Thunderbird's president. "We have to find new models for our degree programs."

Some schools note that they don't award a different M.B.A. degree to online students. That means that unless a student points out the program's format on a résumé or in an interview, it may not be apparent to recruiters that much of the coursework was completed on the Internet. Such evasiveness may prove beneficial, judging from recruiters' reactions to on-line-M.B.A. degrees, which received a failing grade from most respondents in The Wall Street Journal survey. About 80% said they consider online programs less effective than full-time programs in building M.B.A. skills. In fact, more than a third said online programs are "not at all effective."

The recruiters were savage in their critiques of online-M.B.A. degrees. "Come on," one recruiter said, "anyone in the world can do an online M.B.A. It's a commodity." Another said he had been asked to teach courses in online programs for which he felt unqualified, leading him to conclude that they are "scams." Recruiters question the admissions standards at some programs that don't require students to take the Graduate Management Admission Test. They also complain that even in most blended programs, students have too little personal contact with teachers and peers to develop critical communication and teamwork skills.

"The value of interacting in dynamic, difficult team situations with a peer set of highly motivated, intelligent, aspiring, successful individuals is lost in the online setting," says Brad Nichol, a consultant in New Jersey. To him, at least half of the value of his M.B.A. came from the high-quality international network he built. "My network was constructed on a continual basis in the classroom, in professor's offices, in the pub, on the sports field, and on group trips," he says. "I don't believe this is possible to achieve to the same degree online."

Solitary learning at a computer is indeed at odds with the trend in M.B.A. education toward more contact with other students, professors, and business executives. Business schools also are incorporating more practical content into the curriculum, such as consulting projects for companies that require time and personal interaction.

"As a full-time M.B.A. student, my analysis and strategy skills were tested many times in business-case competitions," says Todd Wodzinski, a market-development manager for Dow Chemical Co.'s automotive business. "I felt like I had gained a true gut feel for what worked and didn't work in the business world. I also gained valuable experience leading teams full of different personalities from different cultures."

But he finds that colleagues and acquaintances who went the online route often have more trouble delivering "real-world results" when they can't depend on a textbook for the answer. "While they have mechanically gone through the motions of earning the M.B.A.," he says, "they lack the personal transformation that happens when immersed in a full-time, on-campus program. Online-degree earners tend to stay in the mindset of their previous job."

Given such comments, it's hardly surprising that some top-ranked business schools still shy away from online programs, fearful of harming their reputations. But Dean Rice of Babson College believes many schools and recruiters lack awareness of the benefits of e-learning. For example, an online discussion wouldn't seem to measure up to a lively classroom debate. But Dr. Rice argues that discussions on the Internet can actually be more fruitful "because loudmouths can't dominate the way they do in a classroom where thoughtful people don't get a word in edgewise."

"Online M.B.A.s may not have the same market power and cachet right now as other types of degrees," says Dr. Rice. "But I predict that 10 years from now, there will be top managers at companies who did an online program and who will be able to say it worked for them."

PART IV.

DIVERSITY IN M.B.A. PROGRAMS

THE EMPLOYMENT OUTLOOK FOR FOREIGN STUDENTS

Juan Hernandez, a newly minted M.B.A. from the University of California at Berkeley, has certainly learned the power of personal connections and corporate brand names in America.

From the time he arrived from Uruguay to start his M.B.A. program in 2003, he realized the many challenges a foreign national faced in the bleak U.S. job market. He started his search for an internship right away but encountered one dead-end after another. "I really struggled," Mr. Hernandez recalls, "as companies said their policies simply wouldn't allow them to interview an international student."

Eventually, he managed to parlay relationships he had established with Coca-Cola Co. in his previous banking job in Uruguay to win an internship for summer 2004. It wasn't in the U.S. as he had hoped, but in the company's Latin American division in Costa Rica. No matter. He figured it still might lead to a full-time job with Coke's U.S. operations after graduation.

Unfortunately, that scenario never played out. Mr. Hernandez says he could have returned to Coke's Latin American operations, but thanks at least partly to the Coke internship, he got a job offer as a senior financial analyst at Gap Inc. in San Francisco, just across the bay from Berkeley. "Putting a big name like Coca-Cola on my résumé opened many doors," he says. "A major obstacle for me had been trying to explain or demonstrate that my previous work experience in Uruguay was relevant."

Mr. Hernandez is one of the lucky international M.B.A. students who found their dream jobs in America in 2005. Even as the U.S. job market improves and more business schools provide specialized placement services, foreign nationals still must hustle to land a position. "The situation for international students is still more difficult than it is for domestic students," says Abby Scott, director of M.B.A. career services at Berkeley. "They continue to be excluded from certain job postings."

When the M.B.A. Career Services Council surveyed business schools in spring 2005, it found that more than a third had seen a decrease in the number of employers willing to hire international students for positions in the U.S. Only 19% saw an increase; the rest reported no change from 2003 and 2004.

As always, the primary obstacle for foreign M.B.A. graduates is finding a company that will sponsor them for an H-1B work visa. Many U.S. companies flatly refuse to hire foreign students as long as there are qualified American applicants. They object to the expense and paperwork of the H-1B process. What's more, a "hire-Americans-first" attitude has taken hold more strongly since September 11, 2001.

In *The Wall Street Journal*/Harris Interactive survey of corporate recruiters, about one-third of the respondents said they wouldn't hire a qualified foreign national who needed sponsorship for an H-1B visa. About 38% said they would recruit such a student, and 29% said they don't know.

In addition, companies worry that foreign students will stay only a couple of years and then return to their home countries. There also are concerns about international students' interpersonal and communication styles. Michael Couger, a survey respondent and manager at a software-consulting firm, says he has observed some international graduates "who have an overly non-confrontational style that tends to avoid issues and have an inability to say 'no' when resources do not exist to accomplish a task." Some foreign students, he adds, also may not appear confident enough to clients because they are uncomfortable with their English skills. "Because these issues are often difficult to observe during an interview process," Mr. Couger says, "I believe that many companies may be more inclined to pass over an otherwise qualified international candidate."

Multinational companies often are more willing to hire international students if they can assign them to offices in their home countries. But many foreign graduates want to work in the U.S. for at least a few years, both to gain experience and to earn a higher salary. They often are burdened with large student loans that would take much longer to pay off at the lower compensation they would receive in their homelands.

"Part of the dream for international students is to work in the U.S. before going home," says Terri Gregos, assistant dean and director of career services at the University of Pittsburgh's Katz Graduate School of Business. "It's like a ticket for success when they return home to their families."

The job market challenges, as well as potential complications in securing student visas, are scaring some international applicants away from U.S. M.B.A. programs. But they should realize that perseverance often does pay off, as in Mr. Hernandez's case. Clearly, networking with corporate contacts, alumni, and fellow classmates can prove very beneficial.

For example, Niccolo Reiser, an M.B.A. student from the U.K. at the University of Virginia's Darden Graduate School of Business Administration, "leveraged" contacts from his classmates for internship leads and eventually received a summer job offer from General Electric Co., whose hiring manager was a Darden alumnus. Although foreign M.B.A.s can work between their first and second year of classes on their student visas, he still encountered opposition from some recruiters.

Mr. Reiser understood the value of networking, but he nevertheless found it a bit awkward. "Personally, I felt a little uncomfortable with the process of contacting alumni in order to develop job leads," he says. "The subtext of your communication with alumni is that you want a job. Perhaps my discomfort with this process says more about my personality than about my culture."

Mr. Reiser isn't alone in his feelings. In fact, to prepare foreign students for networking, Emory University's Goizueta Business School requires them to have at least two "informational interviews" with people in their home country before coming to campus. Ideally, some of the contacts will be American executives working in their home countries who could facilitate connections with U.S. headquarters.

"Most U.S. students at least have family, friends, a former job, and an undergraduate school to start from," says Tom Key, senior associate director of business development at the Goizueta School. "Most international students have none of that—at least that's what they think. We try to get them thinking early about the contacts they might have to help them gain some confidence."

Helen Shu, a recent Goizueta graduate, learned quickly that "it's all about relationships." Cultivating contacts paid off for her, but she faced some nerve-racking moments along the way. As graduation approached in spring 2004, the job market looked hopeless. Ms. Shu's cold calls were leading nowhere. After researching companies and contacting alumni, she would phone a corporate contact whose first question was always, "Do you need to be sponsored for a visa?" When she replied "yes," that was the end of the conversation—no questions about her education, work experience, or specialized skills.

But she persisted. "Networking applies to everyone you know," she remembers thinking, "even your professors." And indeed, one of her professors stepped in at the last minute and used his connections with senior managers at UPS to get her an interview. She was hired into a training program at UPS that would eventually lead to a job back in her home country of China. But she changed her mind about going home and used connections developed in business school to switch to an international trading company willing to sponsor her and hire her for a position in Atlanta. "UPS saw me as valuable because of my local market knowledge in China," Ms. Shu says. "But I decided to stay in America longer to get more experience and make myself more marketable in the future."

More business schools, especially those with a high percentage of foreign nationals, are coaching students like Ms. Shu on job-search strategies and even offering companies incentives to sponsor their graduates. The University of Pittsburgh's Katz School has started a program called "Katzport" that provides employers with free legal services to sponsor Katz students for H-1B visas. "This gives small and midsize companies the opportunity to consider our international students if they're intimidated by the cost and paperwork involved in securing a work visa," says Ms. Gregos, the assistant dean at the Katz

THE MOST INTERNATIONALLY DIVERSE BUSINESS SCHOOLS IN AMERICA

These U.S. business schools in *The Wall Street Journal*/Harris Interactive rankings reported the largest percentage of foreign-national M.B.A. students.

Rank	University (Business School)	% Foreign Nationals
1.	University of Illinois, Urbana-Champaign	54%
2.	University of Rochester (Simon)	49%
3.	University of Pittsburgh (Katz)	48%
4.	University at Buffalo/SUNY	43%
	Thunderbird (Garvin)	43%
	College of William & Mary	43%
7.	University of Arizona (Eller)	41%
8.	University of Iowa (Tippie)	39%
	University of Maryland (Smith)	39%
10.	Georgetown University (McDonough)	38%
	Purdue University (Krannert)	38%

School. "We're trying to demystify the visa process for employers by providing immigration attorneys who will lead them through the process." She attributes three "success stories" so far to Katzport.

Other schools have stepped up training in English, public speaking, American culture, and even etiquette. They are counseling foreign students to be flexible about job functions and to be willing to relocate anywhere in the U.S. Students are wise to pursue companies more likely to sponsor them, such as technology firms, consultancies, and banks, and to be aware that some industries, such as consumer-products, tend to be more resistant. Career-services directors also tell them to never passively accept a company's refusal to interview them.

"We always advise students that companies may have a corporatewide policy against hiring international students but will still allow certain departments to make an exception," says Mr. Key of Emory. "Alumni also may be able to go to bat for them and get them in the door. Of course, we always temper such comments with the warning that they never want to become a pest."

Recently, the University of Rochester's Simon Graduate School of Business Administration called on alumni who once faced the same hurdles as foreign nationals themselves. The school flew about 10 alumni into Rochester from such companies as Verizon and Johnson & Johnson for a daylong workshop during which they described their personal trials and eventual successes in the job market. Students practiced cold calls and received feedback from the alumni. There was even a mock "happy hour" to polish the students' socializing skills.

Ipek Tunca, the Simon School graduate who organized the "Opening Opportunities' Door in the U.S." program, recalled her own long job search, which resulted in a position as a senior marketing manager for Microsoft Corp. "I approached my search with an 'it's my job to convince companies why they should take a risk and hire me' approach vs. playing victim," says Ms. Tunca, who came to the Simon School from Turkey. "I had to get over certain cultural aspects like feeling comfortable with praising yourself or thinking about networking as an opportunity rather than as desperation."

Ms. Tunca and the other alumni helped bolster the confidence of Julio Castillo, a Spanish student at the Simon School, who has found many companies unwilling to even accept his résumé. As the number of recruiters coming to campus slowed by late spring 2005, Mr. Castillo reached out more than ever to Rochester's alumni. "When I apply for a job either through the recruiting system of Simon or Web sites, I try to find an alumnus to reiterate my interest in the company and the specific position," he says. "What I notice is that international alumni are more receptive to help me since they passed through the same circumstances and better understand the process."

THE STRUGGLE TO ATTRACT MORE WOMEN M.B.A. STUDENTS

Meg Booth Powell hit the jackpot when she applied to business school. To her surprise, she won admission to all three of her top choices—Harvard, Stanford, and Duke. She chose Stanford University and found that its M.B.A. program gave her the grounding she needed in business basics, enhanced her leadership skills, and, most important, bolstered her self-confidence.

She also happily found Stanford collegial and nonsexist. "Gender really wasn't on the radar screen for me there," she says. But getting an M.B.A. degree, nevertheless, often affects men and women differently. In Ms. Booth Powell's case, the M.B.A. degree has altered her plans to start a family—at least for now. "Before business school, I always thought I would have children, but now I'm not sure," says the 29-year-old M.B.A., who also holds a doctorate of pharmacy and plans to return to her former employer, Eli Lilly & Co., as a marketing manager.

Guest speakers at Stanford related stories about needing two nannies and a personal assistant to cope, and about not having set foot in a gym for 10 years. That made Ms. Booth Powell realize just how demanding it can be to combine a high-powered job and family life. "My husband and I have decided to wait five years and talk about it again," she says. "I have invested in myself, and I know that it can take 10 years to establish yourself before you feel you can take a maternity leave. Then you're in your late 30s and infertility can be a problem."

Such are the tradeoffs that women consider either before they seek an M.B.A. degree or after they graduate. Although women like Ms. Booth Powell say they can't imagine not having the degree, many prospective female students remain ambivalent. It's the typical timeline for an M.B.A. degree that most discourages some women from applying to business school. M.B.A. students tend to be about 27 years old, creating what one business-school official calls "a biological collision." As they near 30, women who are focusing on marriage and children worry about how an M.B.A. will affect their plans.

Medical and law schools attract more women in part because they can enter right after college, while most business schools seek applicants with at least four or five years of work experience. Some schools are starting to be more flexible to encourage younger women to apply, but it's too early to detect any measurable impact on enrollment data.

Female M.B.A. enrollment grew nicely during the 1980s and 1990s, but has since leveled off at 25% to 30% at many schools. In its surveys of prospective students, the Graduate Management Admission Council found that women were significantly more likely than men to list the following potential reservations about attending business school: it might be intimidating or too stressful; it might force them to postpone marriage, children, or other personal plans; it might require more experience than they felt they had; and it might severely limit available time for people who are important in their lives.

Being married only complicates the equation. It's critical, of course, to have a supportive husband willing to follow his wife to business school. In Ms. Booth Powell's case, her husband joined her in Stanford's M.B.A. program. For Paige Darby, who left her marketing job at American Airlines in Texas and headed to Northwestern University's Kellogg School of Management, the timing was right for her husband to pack up and move, too. "My husband was ready for a change so he quit his job and joined me in the Chicago area," she says. "But I know a lot of women who don't come to business school because of the guy. They won't risk hurting their husband's career or won't even break up with a boyfriend if they're just dating."

Now, Ms. Darby and her husband are returning to Texas, where she has landed a job in brand management at Dell Inc. "The M.B.A. program was certainly well worth it; I view my new degree as a way to push the glass ceiling away," she says. "I knew I needed an M.B.A. because I didn't want anyone ever telling me I was not qualified to move up the corporate ladder."

Despite success stories like Ms. Booth Powell and Ms. Darby, business schools still find the M.B.A. a hard sell to women. While they can't change the work/family conflicts that are inherent in many managerial and executive jobs, the schools do promote the M.B.A. as a way to narrow the salary gap between men and women, and as a versatile degree that can be useful whether women become investment bankers, doctors, or art-gallery directors.

There's quite a large salary gap to bridge. In a survey of 2005 graduates, the Graduate Management Admission Council found that men accepted jobs with salaries averaging $93,066, compared with $84,356 for women. That difference partly reflects the fact that some women are avoiding high-paying, high-stress careers in fields like investment banking. In the survey, 29% of female respondents said they sought jobs in the less intense field of sales and marketing, compared with 19% of men. Another 4% of women were interested in human-resource positions, compared with only 1% of men.

Corporate America's battered reputation isn't helping admissions directors in their marketing pitches to women. "More women may be deciding business isn't the environment they want to be in," says Nicole Chestang, chief operating officer of the Graduate Management Admission Council. "Martha Stewart and the other corporate scandals aren't a very positive example for young women. The climate of a company and ethics matter a great deal to many women."

Indeed, the graduate council's survey found that women were more likely to cite "achieving something you personally value," a company's "high ethical standards," and "positive organizational climate" as important in their career choices, while men gave more weight to salaries and opportunity for advancement.

Other research by the graduate council has revealed gender differences in graduates' learning experiences. Recent female alumnae were much more likely than men to wish they had learned more about analyzing statistical data, conducting financial analyses, preparing budgets, and doing cost-benefit analyses. In fact, some women are so concerned about their quantitative abilities that they don't even apply to business schools.

The Forte Foundation, a nonprofit organization of schools and corporations that encourages women to consider business careers, is starting to grapple with that issue by urging undergraduate women to take the Graduate Management Admission Test when math knowledge is still fresh. They also can determine early on whether they need to enroll in a remedial math class and then retake the entrance exam. "The differences in GMAT scores for men and women are notable," says Elissa Ellis, executive director of Forte. "There's definitely room for improvement in women's quantitative results."

The University of Chicago is also very concerned about women's math insecurities and their perception that Chicago's graduate business school is just for "quant jocks." That belief so discouraged women that Chicago admitted a class of only about 22% women as recently as 2001. The percentage has since fluctuated, with a fall 2004 class of 26% women. In 2005, the school is hoping for a class of about 30% women. "We're changing our communications to be clearer about what

Chicago is really about," says Stacey Kole, deputy dean for the full-time M.B.A. program. "We're demystifying the quant image and telling students they can come to Chicago without taking a heavy quantitative load. They can be very flexible and take a basic microeconomics course or more advanced mathematics."

In *The Wall Street Journal*/Harris Interactive survey, recruiters still don't view Chicago as one of the prime sources of female talent. It didn't make the list of the 10 schools that recruiters named most often when asked which they consider best for hiring women graduates. Columbia University topped the list, with Northwestern a close second.

Columbia is so appealing to recruiters partly because there's a relatively large selection of female graduates—36% of the class of 2006 students are women. That consistently high percentage reflects the school's strong commitment to diversity. After Andrea Henderson was admitted to Columbia Business School a couple of years ago, she was astounded by the number of calls she received from school officials and student-run organizations offering advice and help. "That type of outreach made me feel that it must be symptomatic of the kind of support I'd receive as a student," says Ms. Henderson, a single mother who was hired as a program director for an education company after receiving her M.B.A. in 2005. "I tell women thinking about business school to check out the number of women students, because that indicates how much support to expect from classmates and how responsive the professors will be to women."

What else do women look for when they evaluate different M.B.A. programs? They are no different than men in applying to certain schools because of reputation, academic specialties, and location. But women also look for clues that a school will make them feel comfortable. Many are drawn to M.B.A. programs with a collegiate, team-oriented environment like Northwestern, Yale University, and the University of California at Berkeley. But that certainly isn't universal, given the large number of women at schools with a more competitive culture like Harvard University and Columbia.

Financial aid also affects women's choice of schools. "I think it's clear that women are very sensitive to getting scholarships," says Laura Tyson, dean of London Business School. "They tend to come into M.B.A. programs from jobs that paid lower salaries than what men earned." London Business School has been increasing the number of scholarships for women, including new ones from the Citigroup Foundation and one created in partnership with Saatchi & Saatchi and Spencer Stuart. In Madrid, Instituto de Empresa is expanding its scholarship program as it sets the very ambitious goal of a 50-50 gender split by 2007. That would be a striking change from the current 64% to 36% male advantage.

The presence of women in leadership positions, such as president of the student body, editor of the school newspaper, or head of the consulting club, is another important considera-

TOP SCHOOLS FOR RECRUITING WOMEN

Recruiters named these schools most often when asked which M.B.A. programs are best for hiring women graduates. The list is based on total nominations in *The Wall Street Journal*/Harris Interactive survey in both 2004 and 2005.

Rank	University (Business School)	Number of Nominations
1	Columbia University	123
2	Northwestern University (Kellogg)	116
3	Stanford University	73
4	University of Michigan (Ross)	67
5	University of California, Berkeley (Haas)	64
6	Yale University	61
7	Duke University (Fuqua)	58
8	Harvard University	55
9	New York University (Stern)	47
9	University of Pennsylvania (Wharton)	47

tion for some M.B.A. applicants. So is the number of power-ful alumnae who can provide job connections. And active women's organizations on campus can be an important draw-ing card. For example, the Columbia Women in Business or-ganization hosts one of the school's premier events, an annual conference that attracts stellar graduates like Sallie Kraw-check, chief financial officer and head of strategy at Citigroup Inc., and features seminars on such topics as "Broads on Boards: Making an Impact Through Corporate Governance" and "How to Win in the Workplace: Mastering Assertive Com-munication."

Applicants also judge business schools by the number of women on the faculty and in the administration—usually a small number. Women account for less than 15% of business-school professors, 28% of associate professors, and 31% of as-sistant professors, according to AACSB International, the organization that accredits business schools. It estimates that about 15% of business-school deans are women, a growing proportion but clearly still very much a minority.

Some women are impressed when female role models are in-cluded in the curriculum. More schools are adding case studies involving women managers and executives in marketing, strat-egy, and other courses. Corus Entertainment Inc. donated $2 million to the Ivey School of Business at the University of West-ern Ontario to establish a chair for teaching about women in management. And at Stanford University, students can take the course "Women and Work," which covers such subjects as earnings discrimination, time management and work/family conflicts, and the economic value of stay-at-home moms.

Some M.B.A. graduates believe that business schools, not just companies, need to help women cope better with the demands of their personal lives. Students with children say they would appreciate a day-care center near the business school, as well as more sensitive student-team members who understand that they may have to be home in time to fix dinner.

At some schools today, it isn't unusual to see students sitting in a lounge playing with a baby while the child's mother attends a lecture. Ms. Henderson, the Columbia M.B.A. graduate, took her young son Roland to some classes and let him help with homework. Every day, he would watch CNBC to let his mom know how the Dow Jones Industrial Average and other stock-market indexes closed.

Many of her professors were supportive, allowing her to make up early morning classes she couldn't attend because of child-care responsibilities. And her study group accepted that she had to leave by 10 p.m. to get home to Roland. "I wasn't viewed as a mother dragging the group down," she says.

Still, Ms. Henderson believes Columbia could increase its appeal to mothers by offering more child-care assistance. "We started a dialogue with Columbia," she says, "about doing something more organized to support mothers, like creating a child-care co-op and providing women with more information about schools and nannies in New York City."

MINORITIES IN M.B.A. PROGRAMS

As an M.B.A. student at Harvard Business School in 1992, John Rice gazed around the classroom one day and was struck by the dearth of minorities. That observation proved to be an important turning point for the young African-American man. He not only was disturbed by the colorless picture he saw, but he also felt challenged to understand it—and perhaps even change it.

Before long, he had developed an independent study project with one of his management professors to analyze the reasons for the minority shortage. He tried to interest some of his fellow minority classmates and friends in launching a program to deal with the problem, but no one stepped up to join him. "That bothered me and also motivated me to try to do something about the problem in the near term," he says, "rather than wait several years until I had made it to the senior levels and was better situated to give back."

So with seed funding from a few corporate backers, Mr. Rice launched Management Leadership for Tomorrow (MLT) in 1994 as a nonprofit career-mentoring program matching college students with M.B.A.s. MLT was initially a side project for Mr. Rice, who worked first for Walt Disney Co. and later for the National Basketball Association.

By 2001, MLT had grown to nearly 300 participants, but Mr. Rice realized that his organization's "strategy wasn't robust or measurable enough to move the needle at M.B.A. programs."

More research was needed, so MLT brought in Boston Consulting Group to study the minority M.B.A. pipeline to identify the "choke points" along the way. What resulted was a more extensive M.B.A. preparation program in 2002 that is gaining many supporters from academia and corporate America. Both business schools and corporate diversity managers believe MLT has successfully tapped into the most fundamental causes of the minority shortage in the classroom and the boardroom.

Although the schools have courted minorities over the past decade through marketing programs and scholarships, they weren't connecting early enough with prospective students. Mr. Rice's strategy: groom minority M.B.A. hopefuls long before they're ready to begin the application process. "With so much competition in M.B.A. programs, it's important that minorities be extremely well-prepared and super-qualified," says Mr. Rice, who now works full-time on MLT. "We need to teach them how to package their strengths—and their weaknesses—in the best way possible."

For starters, MLT connects high-potential college juniors with corporate managers for skill development and personal coaching to help them land internships and full-time jobs in preparation for an M.B.A. program. When the time comes to apply to a graduate business school, MLT participants receive help in brushing up on math and language skills for the Graduate Management Admission Test (GMAT), writing persuasive and lively application essays, and practicing mock admission interviews. "It's an intensive process over the course of a year," Mr. Rice says. "It's almost like training to be a professional athlete."

Some minority students shy away from M.B.A. programs because they believe their GMAT scores aren't up to par. Indeed, the Boston Consulting Group study found that only 18% of blacks and 35% of Hispanics score more than 500 points out of a possible 800 on the GMAT, compared with more than 60% of whites and Asians who exceed 500. Mr. Rice says MLT's goal is to boost scores into the 600s, putting applicants "into the game at the most selective schools."

Ramsey Jay Jr., who recently received his M.B.A. from the Tuck School of Business at Dartmouth College and plans to work for Morgan Stanley's private-wealth-management division, received tutoring on critical-reasoning and reading-comprehension skills, helping to boost his GMAT score. He also was coached on how to make his application more compelling. For example, he wasn't sure how to explain his transfer from the University of Southern California to California State University, Fresno, after he was injured and lost his athletic scholarship at USC. "I was advised to articulate what I learned from the experience and how I turned a setback into a success," he says. "In essence, MLT gave me a blueprint for perfecting my application."

MLT also alerts prospective students to scholarships and financial aid from such organizations as the Toigo Foundation, which promotes diversity in the finance industry, and the Consortium for Graduate Study in Management, which annually awards more than 350 minority fellowships funded by companies and member schools. Such information might motivate minority applicants from low-income families, who are reluctant to quit a secure job and take on student loans.

According to AACSB International, the organization that accredits business schools, only about 5.3% of U.S. M.B.A. students are African American; 5.2% Hispanic American, and less than 1% Native American. Not only are minority students in short supply, but professors of color also are scarce. The AACSB estimates that only 3.6% of business-school professors are black, 1.8% Hispanic, and less than 1% Native American. It used to be worse. According to the PhD Project, an organization dedicated to increasing diversity in business schools, the number of minority faculty has grown to 672 from fewer than 300 in 1994, with an additional 422 individuals in doctoral programs.

Clearly, progress is slow. Many experts on minority issues consider perception to be a root cause of the minority shortage. The most talented minority youth simply don't see business as an appealing career choice and often opt for law or medicine. The Boston Consulting Group study estimated that only 7% of students in what it considers the top 20 M.B.A. programs are minorities, compared with 15% at the best medical schools and 14% at the major law schools.

MLT believes that soon it will start to make a dent in the enrollment data. The pilot class from its M.B.A. prep program totaled about 40. But the latest group entering business school in fall 2005 has grown to nearly 100, and another 175 plan to apply for 2006 admission.

Kumi Walker, an M.B.A. student at Stanford University's Graduate School of Business, is one of MLT's recent successes. He had applied to Harvard and the University of Pennsylvania's Wharton School without success before approaching MLT. Because it receives far more applications than it can accept, MLT takes only people it considers to be promising M.B.A. prospects. Fortunately for Mr. Walker, he showed the potential to benefit from the prep program.

His MLT coach proved most valuable in helping him craft a better application and present himself well in interviews. "My coach challenged me to dig much deeper than I did the first time into who I am, what I want out of my career, and why the M.B.A. fits in," says Mr. Walker, who previously worked as an analyst at Goldman Sachs Group Inc. "That led to much stronger application essays, interviews, and more career-life clarity and confidence." After his MLT prep work, he says, he successfully applied to Harvard, Wharton, Stanford, and Columbia University and received scholarship offers from all four.

Michelle Wonsley, an MLT graduate who was admitted to Cornell University's Johnson Graduate School of Management on a full-tuition scholarship in 2005, increased her GMAT score by 170 points and learned to communicate her story in record time. "There was a speed networking exercise that forced me to get my elevator pitch down to about 15 seconds," she says. "It allowed me to present myself very quickly and clearly to others when asked about my desire to attend business school and the career path I would pursue in human resources."

Ms. Wonsley was also accepted at Dartmouth and the University of Virginia, but she chose Cornell both because of its program in industrial and labor relations and its clear commitment to diversity. "One of the things that attracted me to Cornell was its office dedicated solely to recruiting and nurturing the talents of women and minority M.B.A. candidates," she says. "Efforts like that are what let applicants know that a school is serious about making them a part of the community. Otherwise, it's all rhetoric."

Students say that one of MLT's best features is the feedback they receive from seasoned admissions directors at some of the major business schools. They also build relationships with admission representatives before applying so that when school officials later read applications, they can connect a name with a face.

For instance, admissions officials from the Yale School of Management spend five weekends a year meeting with MLT participants, who account for more than 10% of its minority applications. "Because of the counseling they receive from their coaches, MLT participants come into the application season having already addressed many of the common troubles that applicants face," says Nicole Lindsay, associate director of admissions and student affairs. "They are asking higher-level questions and generally have a better sense of the value of the M.B.A. and its importance to their careers."

Another MLT fan is Ana Duarte McCarthy, director of global work-force diversity and college relations at Citigroup Inc. She strongly believes that an individual's vision of a future career is shaped at an early age. "MLT provides diverse youth, many of whom are the first in their families to attend college or graduate school, with information on the world of financial services, and, more importantly, informs them that financial services are accessible to them," she says. "I am a Dominican, first generation, and my father is a doctor. So I wanted to study medicine. No one in my family worked in financial services and it was clearly not on my radar."

Citigroup, along with PepsiCo Inc. and Booz Allen Hamilton, has developed "boot camps" for MLT participants just prior to the start of their M.B.A. studies. The three-day seminars include a simulated investment-banking exercise, leadership training, and presentations by senior corporate executives. As a result of the boot camp, Citigroup hired 11 MLT students as summer interns in finance and corporate and investment banking.

There's no question that much of corporate America is in the market for more minority M.B.A. graduates. "Every recruiter I

TOP SCHOOLS FOR RECRUITING MINORITIES

Recruiters named these schools most often when asked which M.B.A. programs are best for hiring minority graduates. The list is based on total nominations in *The Wall Street Journal*/Harris Interactive survey in both 2004 and 2005.

Rank	University (Business School)	Number of Nominations
1	University of Michigan (Ross)	113
2	Howard University	105
3	Columbia University	67
4	Harvard University	55
5	University of California, Berkeley (Haas)	52
6	Stanford University	45
7	Clark Atlanta University	41
7	New York University (Stern)	41
9	University of Pennsylvania (Wharton)	40
10	Carnegie Mellon University (Tepper)	33

met with recently in New York asked me about diversity," says Rich Lyons, acting dean at the Haas School of Business at the University of California at Berkeley, one of MLT's partner schools. "They want to see larger incoming numbers for minorities at all the business schools." Unfortunately, he adds, Berkeley's minority initiatives have suffered from California's Proposition 209 and the state's prohibition against preferential treatment for minority applicants. "Our hands are tied behind our backs," he says. "We can offer scholarships to people who have overcome obstacles in their lives, but we can't target specific racial groups."

Some business schools are both partnering with MLT and developing their own minority-recruitment programs. The University of Texas at Austin, a partner with MLT, has also created Jump Start, which targets college seniors who are academically qualified but lack the required work experience for an M.B.A. degree. Such companies as Deloitte Consulting, PepsiCo's Frito-Lay, and J.P. Morgan Chase & Co. agree to provide the missing experience by hiring the students for three years. The McCombs School of Business at Texas then offers the students deferred admission based on completion of the job commitment. About 7% of the M.B.A. students at McCombs are black, Hispanic, or Native American.

Most schools focus heavily on blacks and Hispanics, but Southern Methodist University, one of MLT's newest allies, has distinguished itself by also actively recruiting Native Americans. Steve Denson, director of diversity at SMU's Cox School of Business, is a member of the Chickasaw Nation and has used his heritage to establish relationships on some Indian reservations. He hopes to persuade tribal leaders to send their children to business school so they can return home and run businesses on the reservations. So far, SMU's American Indian outreach has resulted in three graduates and seven current students.

The University of Michigan, another MLT partner, enjoys the strongest reputation for producing minority M.B.A. students.

In *The Wall Street Journal*/Harris Interactive survey, recruiters cite Michigan as the best school for hiring minority graduates. But that reputation is based more on past success than current enrollment.

In the 1980s and 1990s, Michigan produced a large crop of minority M.B.A. graduates and attracted the attention of many corporate recruiters. But as other schools have followed its lead, the competition for minority students has become much more intense, and Michigan is looking less diverse these days. When Asian Americans are included, Michigan's minority enrollment represents about a quarter of the total. But only about 11% of the M.B.A. students are black, Hispanic, or Native American. That's down from more than 20% in the early 1990s, school officials say, but up from a dismal 6% in 2003.

David Wooten, an African American alumnus and assistant professor of marketing, says the drop to 6% "was a real wake-up call." Michigan has since become more aggressive in reaching out to minorities both through organizations like MLT and its own students and alumni network. "Our minority alumni were very concerned about the numbers, and they have worked with the faculty and admissions staff on recruiting," says Dr. Wooten. "The good news is that because of Michigan's history, we have a lot of minority alumni to mobilize to help get the numbers back up."

PART V.

HOW TO GET HIRED

THE M.B.A. JOB-MARKET OUTLOOK

After a prolonged slump that left many M.B.A. graduates unemployed, the job market is finally firing on all cylinders again.

Financial-services and management-consulting companies, the traditional drivers of M.B.A. hiring, flocked back to campuses during the 2004–2005 school year, dangling richer paychecks and signing bonuses. And companies that hadn't retrenched as much as banks and consultants also stepped up hiring, leading to the most robust recruiting season since the severe downturn began in 2001.

"The recovery seems to be solid," says Maury Hanigan, a New York consultant who works with companies on their campus recruiting programs. "Companies are no longer as tentative as they set up fall interview schedules at business schools; they feel confident they will need more people by the time students graduate."

In a survey of business-school placement directors, the M.B.A. Career Services Council found that nearly 75% expected the job market to improve further in the second half of 2005, while about a quarter of respondents anticipated that it would remain the same. No one believed it would weaken.

Boston Consulting Group Inc. certainly fits that prognosis. It is on track to hire a record number of M.B.A.s in 2006, according to Kermit King, head of North American recruiting. "We continued to hire substantial numbers even during the downturn," he says, "because we are looking to build talent over many years and take a perspective beyond a couple of years."

Some consulting firms and technology companies damaged their relationships with M.B.A. students in 2001 and 2002, when business soured and they rescinded job offers. Companies that didn't renege believe they are benefiting now. "There was no bait-and-switch in our hiring," says Mr. King, "and I'd like to think that is strengthening our reputation on campus."

It still isn't easy for career switchers, however. Companies continue to seek M.B.A.s with experience in the job functions for which they're hiring. "It's rare to see companies willing to hire someone without demonstrated functional experience," says Ms. Hanigan. "So it's going to continue to be hard for a financial analyst to move into, say, luxury-products marketing. That would have been much more doable in the late '90s, when competition for talent was so heated."

Many business schools reported significantly more recruiter traffic even into late spring. That's because some companies continue to hire on a "just-in-time" basis when they need to fill a position rather than in anticipation of expected growth. It's difficult "to project the number of high-tech companies hiring this year because many in that industry tend to do just-in-time hiring," says Andy Chan, the M.B.A. career-management director at Stanford University's Graduate School of Business. Even so, the number of companies recruiting on campus in January to March 2005 was up 24% for both full-time jobs and summer internships.

The nearby Haas School of Business at the University of California at Berkeley reported a 35% increase in the number of interviews on campus, with a variety of industries, including real-estate development, hedge funds, and technology, hiring more M.B.A.s. Among the school's new recruiters in 2005: Amazon.com, IBM Consulting, and the Nestlé PowerBar business.

"Companies not only need more people to get the work done today," says Abby Scott, Berkeley's director of M.B.A. career services, "but they also realize they need to develop some bench strength for future leadership." To increase its reach in the expanding job market, Berkeley has stationed a career-services employee in New York City. "We want to build our momentum," Ms. Scott says, "and send more students to Wall Street."

Wall Street recruiters were certainly back in force at New York University's Stern School of Business in 2005. "Banking and consulting are our lead horses," says Gary Fraser, associate dean of student affairs. By spring, about three-quarters of Stern M.B.A.s had received job offers—and the rest weren't panicking. "The stress level of students has gone down dramatically," says Mr. Fraser. "Students are looking for what's right for them and don't feel pressured as they did in past years."

After several years of reduced compensation, M.B.A.s appear to be back in the money. In The Wall Street Journal/Harris Interactive survey, about 45% of recruiters said starting salaries were higher in 2005 than the year before. The largest share of recruiters—about 55%—said they would pay starting salaries of between $75,000 and $100,000. About one-fifth planned to offer $50,000 to $75,000, while about 13% were in the $100,000 to $125,000 range.

"Compensation is increasing, but you don't see the big bonuses that really pushed up packages during the dot-com era; no one is talking about instant wealth like they used to," says Ms. Hanigan. "Companies want to make sure salaries are competitive, but it's not a bidding war."

Still, salaries are growing at a nice clip at Dartmouth College's Tuck School of Business, where consulting and investment banking are particularly hot again. According to Richard McNulty, Tuck's career-development director, consulting firms have raised starting salaries to the $110,000-to-$120,000 range from $100,000 to $110,000 in 2004 and signing bonuses to $15,000 to $30,000 from $10,000 to $20,000, while investment banking salaries have increased to an average of $95,000 from $85,000 and signing bonuses, to $30,000-plus from $25,000. "Financial services came back pretty strong in 2004 and consulting was brewing a little," Mr. McNulty says. "Now in 2005, consulting is back, too. So it's a double punch, with the right hand and the left hand swinging."

Of course, M.B.A.s run the risk of limiting their choices if they gravitate too much to those two industries. When banking and consulting firms cut back hiring a few years ago, "we pounded the pavement and established relationships in marketing and health care," says Mr. McNulty. "Now, with both financial services and consulting back strong, it's harder to maintain those new relationships. Biotech and pharmaceutical companies have their eye on some of the same students now going to Goldman Sachs and McKinsey."

Although M.B.A.s are in demand again, they shouldn't become too complacent. In the *Journal* survey, recruiters complain as much as ever about graduates' shortcomings. In particular, they criticize M.B.A.s for weak communication and leadership abilities, arrogance and unrealistic expectations about compensation and job responsibilities, and inadequate work experience. They also are scrutinizing students more than ever for personal ethics and integrity.

Where do M.B.A.s most want to work these days? When it comes to their dream jobs, their choices aren't very surprising. M.B.A.s clearly aim for the companies that are hiring the most and paying the most. In a 2005 survey that asked students to name their "ideal" employers, consulting and financial-services companies received by far the highest popularity scores. Such companies as Bain & Co., Boston Consulting Group, Booz Allen Hamilton Inc., and Bank of America gained in popularity, knocking some corporate icons—BMW, Coca-

Cola Co., and IBM—out of the top 10 in an annual ranking compiled by Universum Communications, a research and consulting firm that surveyed more than 4,700 M.B.A.s at 50 U.S. schools.

McKinsey, the consulting firm that is well-known as a training ground for CEOs, has ranked No. 1 in the Universum study of ideal M.B.A. employers for 10 straight years. The firm expected to hire some 600 M.B.A.s for 2005, 2% to 3% more than a year earlier. A spokesman notes, however, that M.B.A.s represent a shrinking share of new hires as McKinsey increasingly recruits for specialized talent at medical and law schools.

The survey found that for their first post-M.B.A. job, men on average expect a salary of $89,933 and signing bonus of

SCHOOLS WITH THE MOST HIGHLY PAID GRADUATES

These business schools in *The Wall Street Journal*/Harris Interactive rankings reported the highest average salaries for their class of 2004 full-time M.B.A. graduates.

Rank	University (Business School)
1	IMD: $123,000 annual base salary, $23,000 signing bonus
2	Insead: $103,300 annual base salary, $20,000 signing bonus
3	London Business School: $101,831 annual base salary, $23,765 signing bonus
4	Stanford University: $100,400 annual base salary, $16,100 signing bonus
5	Harvard University: $99,848 annual base salary, $17,358 signing bonus
6	Massachusetts Institute of Technology (Sloan): $94,131 annual base salary, $14,451 signing bonus
7	University of Pennsylvania (Wharton): $92,986 annual base salary, $16,803 signing bonus
8	Dartmouth College (Tuck): $91,900 annual base salary, $16,500 signing bonus
9	HEC, Paris: $91,534 annual base salary, $16,482 signing bonus
10	Northwestern University (Kellogg): $91,390 annual base salary, $14,380 signing bonus

$18,028, while women look to earn $81,962, with a $15,415 signing bonus. Five years after graduation, salary expectations soar, with men hoping for $184,352, and women, $155,909.

Some M.B.A.s are drawn to multinationals such as Johnson & Johnson, General Electric Co. and Procter & Gamble Co., the highest-ranked companies outside consulting and financial services. Image also matters to some students who aspire to work for companies with a reputation for style and innovation. Apple Computer Inc., for example, rose to 15th place from 31st last year in the Universum study, leaping ahead of Microsoft Corp. and Dell Inc. Although BMW fell seven spots to No. 13, the German auto maker still far outranks other car companies.

Women and men expressed somewhat different employer preferences. Female M.B.A.s include more consumer-product marketers and retailers at the top of their wish lists. Male M.B.A.s are intensely focused on consulting and financial services, but they also find some technology companies alluring.

A small but growing number of students are thinking beyond traditional M.B.A. recruiters. While Wall Street and Silicon Valley have long been meccas for job-hunting M.B.A.s, a hot new destination is the glitzy Las Vegas Strip. In 2005, student clubs at both Harvard Business School and Columbia University made their first pilgrimages to Las Vegas, while M.B.A.s at the Massachusetts Institute of Technology made a repeat visit.

The casino business is becoming more a numbers game as casinos adopt sophisticated financial and marketing strategies, such as database-driven customer-loyalty programs. When M.B.A.s came calling in Las Vegas, they met with executives from Las Vegas Sands Corp., MGM Mirage, and Harrah's Entertainment Inc., took back-of-the-house tours of the casino-hotels, restaurants, nightclubs and theaters, and attended cocktail receptions with B-school alumni in the gambling industry.

The Las Vegas treks are just one sign of how M.B.A. students are testing the waters in industries that haven't traditionally recruited more than a few graduates. Columbia students, for example, expanded their retailing club to include the fast-growing luxury-goods sector and have attracted the attention of such companies as Chanel Inc. and Polo Ralph Lauren Corp. Columbia M.B.A.s also are targeting entertainment and media companies and recently ventured to Los Angeles to connect with Walt Disney, Paramount Pictures, and other studios.

Some students say quality of life trumps lofty salaries. "I might make less money in the hospitality industry, but I want to have fun in my job and feel passionate about it," says Erica Pergament, a Columbia M.B.A. graduate who interned in 2004 in marketing at the MGM Grand in Las Vegas. Some M.B.A.s "are no longer as willing to take a job at an investment bank where they're practically a slave. We want to work for companies where we can get excited about the product we're selling."

But she's still in the minority. Universum Communications also asked M.B.A.s which factors most influence their decision to accept or reject a job offer. Not surprisingly, compensation package was the top pick, followed closely by "challenging role." Next in importance: corporate culture, a clear path for advancement, and work-life balance. "To me, work-life balance is not all that important so long as compensation is high to make up for it," says Sean Hazlett, a Harvard M.B.A. student, who participated in the Universum survey and aspires to be a vice president at a prominent investment bank. "I spent the last five years in the Army and my family is fully aware of how it can cope with a terrible work-life balance and low paycheck to match. My children will thank me when I pay for their college education."

A DEARTH OF COMMUNICATION AND LEADERSHIP SKILLS

For Chris Aisenbrey, director of global university relations at Whirlpool Corp., it's a daunting challenge these days to hire literate M.B.A. students who can write a coherent letter or memo. Too often, what he gets from job applicants are collections of rambling thoughts littered with misspellings and grammatical gaffes.

Blame it on e-mail and instant messaging. Mr. Aisenbrey and other recruiters bemoan the fact that technology has eroded M.B.A. students' ability to communicate clearly and professionally. "It is staggering the frequency of typos, grammatical errors, and poorly constructed thoughts we see in e-mails that serve as letters of introduction," says Mr. Aisenbrey. "We still see a tremendous amount of e-mail from students who are writing to the recruiter like they are sending a message to a friend asking what they are doing that evening."

These days, the recruiter's ideal target is the student who shows promise as an articulate leader, but such M.B.A.s are proving to be all too rare. Of all the complaints recruiters register about M.B.A. students in *The Wall Street Journal*/Harris Interactive survey, inferior communication skills top the list. Close behind are criticisms of leadership ability.

Recruiters say they can count on students from any of the major business schools to bring solid knowledge of accounting, marketing, strategy, and other business fundamentals. What distinguishes the most sought-after schools and M.B.A.

graduates are the "soft skills" of communication and leadership that happen to be among the hardest to teach.

Recruiters worry most about declining writing and oral-presentation skills because even M.B.A. graduates who don't demonstrate the leadership potential to win a spot in the executive suite still must be able to communicate to succeed. "The situation will only get worse," Mr. Aisenbrey fears, "because business schools are not emphasizing communications skills enough right now."

Some recruiters stress the importance of communicating financial information in a concise, persuasive manner. "We all work in an environment of data overload, and we value people who can tell a story when presenting financials that engages the audience," says Kelle Vela, purchasing controller at Ford Motor Co. She says it's sometimes hard to assess communication skills when interviewing M.B.A.s, but that Ford's case-based process tends to work well. A business case is deliberately structured so there isn't a right or wrong answer. Success, Ms. Vela says, is based on the job candidate's ability to identify the key information, perform an appropriate analysis, and present and defend the analysis in one-on-one discussions and in a group setting.

Recruiters in the survey say they would encourage M.B.A. students to take advantage of as many public-speaking opportunities as possible to become more comfortable and polished. "Students seem to think a better grade is assigned based on the number of slides in a presentation," says one recruiter. "In real life, you have 10 minutes to present to management. If you can't get the whole story in that time on two or three slides, you're dead in your career."

Whirlpool is so concerned about communications skills that it recently introduced a new assessment measure to its M.B.A. recruiting program. To evaluate students' ability to communicate in a dynamic manner, the appliance maker's recruiters now ask job candidates to deliver a 10-minute oral presentation of their résumé. Some students make quite elaborate presentations, using PowerPoint or overhead projectors, and go well beyond the printed résumé to reveal their personalities and accomplishments. But, Mr. Aisenbrey says, "We see a lot of candidates who simply regurgitate their résumé in chronological order. This is a simple case of candidates not understanding the audience and what message they want to deliver."

As part of his interviews with M.B.A. students, Darren Whissen, a financial-services recruiter in California, provides an executive summary of a fictitious company and asks them to write about 500 words recommending whether to invest in the business. At worst, he receives "sub-seventh-grade-level" responses with spelling and grammar errors. "More often than not," he says, "I find M.B.A. writing samples have a casual tone lacking the professionalism necessary to communicate with sophisticated investors. I have found that many seemingly qualified candidates are unable to write even the simplest of arguments. No matter how strong one's financial model is, if one cannot write a logical, compelling story, then investors are going to look elsewhere. And in my business, that means death."

Effective communications skills are a prerequisite, of course, for an outstanding business leader. But leadership also means having vision, inspiring and motivating people, taking risks, and driving change in an organization. What's more, integrity is an increasingly important element of leadership in these days of seemingly endless corporate scandals. (See related essay on page 454.)

Students may indeed get by on their technical and quantitative skills in the first few years on the job, but leadership skills quickly distinguish the stars. To Grant Bauserman, a recruiter and manufacturing manager, leadership is the great "differentiator" among M.B.A.s. "The top schools do a great job of developing managers," he says. "What is needed are more leaders."

Mr. Bauserman is frustrated with students who believe it's enough "to be the smartest person in the room." What they don't understand is that they need to focus less on themselves and more on their team and business goals. "Personal leadership," he says, "is listening more than talking, being more inspiring than demanding, spending more time looking forward than being reactive, and maintaining self-control and high ethical standards."

Maria Corral, manager of succession management at Chiquita Brands International Inc., the banana producer, believes schools are far too preoccupied with technical expertise at a time when leadership and accountability are more critical than ever. "Strong financial skills or marketing knowledge is important," she says, "but they're not the soul of leadership." When she recruits M.B.A.s, she is seeking "bench strength" for the future and looks for people who will be "passionate about results but equally passionate about values" and who can cope well with ambiguity.

Recruiters advise business schools to require students to take more leadership and communications courses. Some M.B.A. programs already are listening to such feedback, but they find that it's no easy task to strengthen communication and leadership abilities among M.B.A.s. For one thing, some professors find it hard to convince know-it-all M.B.A.s that it's as important to write clearly as it is to master number-crunching skills. Many students prefer to focus on finance, marketing, and other business functions, and balk at what they consider remedial instruction. But the painful truth is that many M.B.A.s do need remedial help.

"Budding M.B.A.s tend to be overly confident," says Shirley Maxey, who has long taught business-communication classes at the University of Southern California's Marshall School of Business. "Our biggest single problem is convincing them they don't have the skills needed to communicate well in a corporate environment."

Seth Christensen, an M.B.A. alumnus of the University of Oregon, says he is sympathetic to the schools because he and his classmates often failed to appreciate their communications lessons. He says he'll never forget the time his finance professor marked down his team's first case study because even though the technical answer was correct, the tone of the paper was so arrogant that the chances were nil that a real management team would ever implement the recommendations. "You can't just know the right answer," Mr. Christensen says. "You also must have the tool set to persuade those who do not have your same perspective or level of education."

Some schools are offering more specialized communications courses. For example, New York University's Stern School of Business has added a series of "advanced topics in management communication," including a class about persuasion strategies for financial-services executives and another focusing on the challenges of cross-cultural communication.

The Kenan-Flagler Business School at the University of North Carolina is so committed to turning out more articulate graduates that it split its M.B.A. class into small groups of just 10 students for the required management-communication class. That way they receive more individual attention and have more opportunities to make oral presentations. Professors had found that students didn't master written and oral skills well enough in larger groups of 75.

"We're trying to get students to move beyond the academic tone of a business case write-up and write for the business world rather than for a business professor," says Heidi Schultz, the professor who directs Kenan-Flagler's management communication program. The major flaws she sees when students begin the class include long, passive sentences, weak verbs, inappropriate tone, and sloppy organization. She and other professors provide sentence-streamlining tips, lessons on creating PowerPoint slides that enhance rather than detract from speeches, and "corporate storytelling" techniques for communicating abstract concepts.

Business school professors find that leadership isn't as easily taught as communications. It's a lifelong process of studying how other leaders behave, becoming self-aware, practicing leadership styles, and learning from mistakes. And to some extent, leadership is an inborn trait. How many times have you heard the cliché, "He's a born leader"?

But some schools believe there's plenty of leadership development that can occur during an M.B.A. program. For one thing, more schools are putting students through self-assessment exercises to discern their leadership assets and weaknesses. As with communications, students also require a high degree of personalized training in leadership classes.

To that end, the Terry College of Business at the University of Georgia revised its entire full-time M.B.A. curriculum to add a strong leadership spin in 2004. The leadership program includes a variety of courses and projects, but the most important element is executive coaching. All students are assigned to an executive coach, who helps them write a personal development plan and provides regular feedback on their progress. "Business schools talk a lot about leadership, but it's mostly lip service," says George Benson, dean of the Terry College. "Our personalized leadership training through individual coaches sets us apart from most other M.B.A. programs."

But leadership training is a long-established tradition at some schools. The University of Chicago takes credit for pioneering "experiential" leadership development in 1989, when it launched its Leadership Effectiveness and Development Program (LEAD) in response to critical feedback from corporate executives and recruiters. The school continues to listen to its corporate contacts, adjusting the program based on their needs and adding sections on such topics as ethics and power and influence in organizations.

The LEAD program is varied—an outdoor retreat involving rope courses and wall climbing, role-playing exercises, lessons on conflict-management strategies, "Audience Captivation Training" seminars on presentation skills, and the capstone All-Star Challenge competition. In the competition, senior corporate executives judge student teams on their ability to communicate and motivate people.

Newer leadership initiatives include Duke University's Fuqua/ Coach K Center of Leadership and Ethics to support academic research and develop new leadership electives for M.B.A. students. Duke basketball coach Mike Krzyzewski (Coach K) joined the center and the Fuqua School of Business faculty as an executive-in-residence, teaching and writing about ethics and leadership during the off-season.

"Faculty used to think leadership was sort of mumbo jumbo, what with all those books about it that you see in airport bookstores," says Robert Joss, dean of the Stanford University Graduate School of Business. "But there's a growing recognition that leadership is something that we can teach well and help students develop in themselves."

Stanford offers a growing roster of courses, including "The Paths to Power" and "High-Performance Leadership." It also has created a Center for Leadership Development and Research and a program that focuses on greater self-awareness through leadership assessments, business simulations, teamwork, and personal coaching. "Our graduates rarely work by themselves in trying to change organizations, whether as team leaders, supervisors, or CEOs," says Dean Joss. "So we in M.B.A. programs have to keep asking ourselves: How can we better prepare them to lead?"

HIGHER STANDARDS OF INTEGRITY

CEOs aren't the only ones being held to higher standards of integrity these days. So are M.B.A. applicants and graduates. They are being scrutinized more closely than ever by both business-school admissions officers and corporate recruiters.

At the front end, more schools are checking the accuracy of applications to weed out cheats. The Wharton School at the University of Pennsylvania hires an outside firm to do background checks on every admitted student. If a dishonest student manages to escape detection at that stage, he isn't necessarily home-free. Wharton recently expelled a second-year second-semester student after it belatedly discovered falsified material in the individual's application.

"Our policy is zero tolerance," declares Patrick Harker, Wharton's dean. "Cheating—from padding résumés to falsifying recommendations—is more pervasive in the admissions process than ever before. If people come in as cheaters, it is hard to change them, and sorting them out from the start is not as simple as it used to be."

Wharton isn't alone in taking a hard line on students deemed to be unethical. In early 2005, Harvard Business School and the Sloan School of Management at the Massachusetts Institute of Technology decided to reject applications from hackers who managed to sneak a peek at confidential admissions information on a Web site called ApplyYourself.

"This behavior is unethical at best—a serious breach of trust that cannot be countered by rationalization," said Kim Clark, dean at the time of Harvard Business School, following complaints that the school overreacted by denying admission to applicants who had gained unauthorized access to ApplyYourself. "Our mission is to educate principled leaders who make a difference in the world. To achieve that, a person must have many skills and qualities, including the highest standards of integrity, sound judgment, and a strong moral compass and intuitive sense of what is right and wrong. Those who have broken into this Web site have failed to pass that test."

Once they near the finish line of their M.B.A. program, students are in for another round of scrutiny by recruiters. Companies hope to avoid hiring M.B.A.s who end up doing a perp walk. Some of the most notorious figures in the fraud at Enron Corp. and the other corporate scandals received their M.B.A. degrees from such prestigious schools as Harvard and Northwestern University's Kellogg School of Management.

Indeed, the public has been pinning some of the blame for corporate malfeasance on business schools. Critics believe that schools not only neglected ethics lessons, but that they also encouraged students to go to practically any lengths to increase corporate profits and shareholder value. In a recent Harris Interactive public opinion survey of how companies can repair their scandal-tainted reputations, there was clearly an M.B.A. backlash: "Fire all of the M.B.A.s under 35," one respondent said, while another commented, "Listen to common sense and not some off-the-wall M.B.A."

Given such sentiments, recruiters certainly are going to be more alert to M.B.A. students' moral character. "We look for very high ethical standards, and it is that area that disqualifies more candidates than any other factor," says Chris Lanser, director of virtual manufacturing at Direct Supply Inc., a healthcare company in Milwaukee, Wis. Many people, he adds, "self-disqualify by not being honest on résumés or other employment documents."

In *The Wall Street Journal*/Harris Interactive recruiter survey, 74% of respondents rated personal integrity and knowledge about corporate ethics as "very important," while 24% said they are "somewhat important." As one survey respondent put it: "Integrity is the cornerstone of our recruiting process. We check job candidates' references and background much more thoroughly now."

Some recruiters say separating the saints from the sinners comes down to a gut feeling, but others are asking more ethics-related questions. They also are using second-round interviews and social events to better size up students. "We incorporate questions about ethics into our behavioral interviews because it's too difficult to assess ethics from a résumé or to predict someone's ethical nature from the fact that they've had an ethics class," says Bryan Benoit, managing director at Standard & Poor's Corporate Value Consulting in Houston.

Here are some of the ways other recruiters say they try to select virtuous M.B.A.s:

—"We watch students' body language when they are faced with challenging questions."
—"We want to see that they have been involved in community activities."
—"If the student shows an interest in my company's ethical standards, that makes a big impression."
—"We have become more sensitive about distinguishing the sheep from the goats and look to schools with religious ties that tend to attract students with a strong ethical orientation."
—"We want students who are looking to make a positive impact on the world, as well as earn a personal financial reward. We are no longer looking for the stereotypical M.B.A. out only for himself."

—"We are more careful of the hot shots. We want less aggressive and more people-oriented students."

—"We want honest answers and humility."

Some recruiters believe business schools still don't sufficiently emphasize integrity and take enough responsibility for turning out so many "win-at-any-cost" graduates. In fact, many schools are still grappling with how to teach ethics more effectively. "Ethics isn't getting a whole lot more substantive attention at many schools," says Craig Smith, associate dean at London Business School, which requires both full-time and executive-M.B.A. students to study ethics. "It's often just an elective offering at best, arguably preaching to the converted."

Despite the new climate of corporate accountability, some M.B.A. students and professors bristle at ethics requirements. Faculty members resent being forced to squeeze ethics lessons into an already jam-packed syllabus, while students grumble that ethics classes tend to be preachy and philosophical. At Carnegie Mellon University in Pittsburgh, some students even objected recently to a required ethics course because they believed it didn't matter to corporate recruiters and wouldn't help them land jobs. They were obviously mistaken, but it seems recruiters need to convey the importance of ethics more clearly to Carnegie Mellon's M.B.A.s during the interview process. "Students have to start realizing that they must be part of improving the business world's image," says Kenneth Dunn, dean of Carnegie Mellon's Tepper School of Business.

Some professors find that international students in particular balk at ethics lessons. "Business ethics is a harder sell for many foreign students, especially from developing countries, because they have seen all this corruption around them and it's so far off their radar screen," says David Vogel, a business-ethics professor at the Haas School of Business at the University of California at Berkeley. "But I think it's very useful for American business students to hear foreign students' take on ethics."

Some professors are troubled to see M.B.A. students separating their personal and professional values. Bob Adler, who teaches ethics at the University of North Carolina's Kenan-Flagler Business School, asked his M.B.A. students for their reaction to the statement: "Some types of behavior that might be viewed as unethical in a friendship or personal relationship are perfectly proper in a business setting." The result: 60% agreed with it. "But my perspective is that you really can't separate your personal and professional life," says Prof. Adler. "So in class, we discuss why a person should be good and what it takes to be good. Can you be a nice guy at home but cheat consumers on your job?"

To be sure, some students do value ethics and good corporate citizenship. Professors at Stanford University and the University of California at Santa Barbara surveyed M.B.A. students from 11 North American and European schools and found that virtually all of them—more than 97%—say they would be willing to accept reduced compensation to work for an organization with a better reputation for ethics and social responsibility. How much less? On average, they say they are willing to give up 14% of their expected income.

"Everyone thinks they know that M.B.A.s are avaricious and greedy," says Stanford professor David Montgomery, "and while no one is claiming they are perfect, it turns out that M.B.A.s are willing to forgo a significant percent of their income to be more moral."

There is still much debate about the best format for teaching ethics. Some schools make it a required course, others believe an elective is good enough, and still others attempt to integrate ethics into all basic business courses, from finance to marketing. Maybe the best solution, given the sorry state of corporate America's reputation, is all three.

Columbia University's M.B.A. program undoubtedly concocted one of the most ambitious ethics courses. It also proved to be one of the thorniest. What went wrong? Clearly, the course's novel but rather convoluted structure proved to be a major flaw. Columbia devised a separate course that included a final exam and grade, but had many of the class sessions taught within other required "core" courses, such as finance, operations, and economics.

"When a professor said it was time for the ethics module, it felt very forced and students didn't participate very much," says Matt Wang, a recent Columbia graduate. "A lot of students were also upset about being graded on a curve. If you received a low grade, you felt you would be viewed as a bad person." (Aware of such concerns, Columbia ended up switching to a pass/fail grading system.)

Columbia's revamped program—"The Individual, Business and Society: Tradeoffs, Choices and Accountability"—is no longer a separate course with its own final and grade. But the school still requires professors in the basic courses to weave in ethics content, such as fair pricing policies in marketing and the boundaries of "earnings management" in accounting. "We still believe in putting ethics in the context of our core courses," says Paul Glasserman, senior vice dean. "When I teach managerial statistics, for example, I deal with the misleading ways information can be represented." The revised ethics program also features guest lecturers and panel discussions.

There was even a modern morality play of sorts performed for Columbia's M.B.A. students. Actors presented "Scenes from the Slippery Slope," in which an investment banker is pressured to falsify expense accounts to conceal his boss's extramarital affair. At pivotal points in the minidrama, students were called on to advise the ethically challenged young man.

Olivia Ralston, editor in chief of Columbia Business School's *Bottom Line* newspaper, finds that ethics lessons still "feel too compartmentalized" and that "some professors present ethics as something the administration is requiring rather than something we should take seriously the entire semester and in our careers." She gives Columbia's special events mixed reviews: a panel on the Sarbanes-Oxley corporate-accountability law "bored" her, but a discussion of a case involving racism in the workplace proved "provocative."

Columbia deserves credit for persevering to integrate ethics throughout the M.B.A. program. And it appears to be on the right track with its broader approach of blending ethics with social responsibility and corporate governance. "The problem with ethics is that it's such a loaded word," says Dr. Glasserman. "What we want to give students are strategies for protecting their integrity in the workplace. We aren't trying to teach them right from wrong."

Harvard Business School's new required course, "Leadership and Corporate Accountability," also places ethics within a larger framework and appears to be off to a good start. Using the school's trademark case-study format, the course includes sections on personal values and leadership, governance issues,

TOP SCHOOLS FOR RECRUITING STUDENTS WITH INTEGRITY

Recruiters named these schools most often when asked which M.B.A. programs are best for hiring graduates with strong ethical standards. The list is based on total nominations in *The Wall Street Journal*/Harris Interactive survey in both 2004 and 2005.

Rank	University (Business School)	Number of Nominations
1	Yale University	131
2	Brigham Young University (Marriott)	127
3	Dartmouth College (Tuck)	122
4	University of Denver (Daniels)	101
5	University of Virginia (Darden)	92
6	University of California, Berkeley (Haas)	72
7	IPADE	70
8	University of Notre Dame (Mendoza)	67
9	Stanford University	61
10	Carnegie Mellon University (Tepper)	51
10	ESADE	51
10	University of Michigan (Ross)	51

and the legal, ethical, and economic responsibilities of companies to their stakeholders. "The course works well," says Harvard M.B.A. Julian Flannery, "because instead of a lot of philosophical musings, it focuses on how to apply ethics lessons in the real world." Among the cases: Enron's collapse, WorldCom's recovery strategy, and the Tylenol poisonings.

Lynn Paine, the lead professor for the class, believes a stand-alone course is essential because "ethics discussion too easily gets crowded out" of other management courses. "The integration model sounds good," she says, "but many faculty members have no training in ethics and the law and don't know how to incorporate them well." The Wharton School recently launched a doctoral program in ethics and legal studies, but it will take time to produce a significant crop of new ethics scholars.

"The odd thing about ethics is that people assume anyone can teach it because everyone faces ethical issues in life," says Prof. Paine. "But just because you shop, that doesn't mean you can teach marketing."

THE IMPORTANCE OF ETHICS

M.B.A. recruiters in *The Wall Street Journal*/Harris Interactive survey were asked, "How important is it that job candidates display awareness or knowledge" in the following areas.

	Personal and Corporate Ethics	Corporate Governance	Corporate Social Responsibility	Diversity and Cultural Sensitivity	Globalization
Very important	73.6%	31.3%	32.3%	50.7%	33.2%
Somewhat important	23.5%	49.3%	51.4%	40%	44.7%
Not very important	2.5%	17.2%	14.3%	7.9%	17.5%
Not at all important	0.3%	2.3%	1.9%	1.4%	4.6%

(May not add to 100% due to rounding.)

A MATTER OF
EXPERIENCE

David Speicher is looking for a few good M.B.A.s who have made their share of mistakes.

To Mr. Speicher, head of human resources for a Philadelphia asset-management firm, the best M.B.A. students have made enough decisions and mistakes in their careers to have gained some valuable insight. "When someone makes one of those nausea-inducing errors in judgment," he explains, "he or she comes away with a blend of confidence and humility."

For example, he hired a student from the Goizueta Business School at Emory University in Atlanta who had worked nearly seven years as an accountant and an investment analyst before seeking an M.B.A. "I saw him as a candidate with a demonstrated work ethic and the maturity to introspectively explain what mistakes he'd made in the roles he'd held," says Mr. Speicher. "While he did not possess the ideal sales experience that I would have liked, these other points were too strong to ignore."

Hiring an M.B.A. graduate is an expensive proposition, and companies complain that too often they aren't immediately getting their money's worth from a green recruit. In *The Wall Street Journal*/Harris Interactive survey, recruiters frequently criticize M.B.A. students for lacking enough specialized, "relevant" experience. Most recruiters say they expect a minimum of four or five years' experience, preferably in their industries. Some are even hoping for six or seven years.

Both quantity and quality of experience are crucial. Recruiters are looking for students who have learned to cope with ambiguity, adversity, and conflict in the workplace. Some M.B.A.s believe "simply working two or three years entitles them to a leadership position immediately following graduation," says Jeff Rynbrandt, who does recruiting for Guidant Corp., a marketer of cardiovascular products. "To me, students need to have demonstrated success in their past job with positions of increasing responsibility and be able to articulate how their actions specifically contributed to those successes."

Recruiters also are wary of too much job-hopping—a red flag that students may have moved on because they weren't getting promoted. That's how Aaron Mitchell, a management consultant in Oakland, Calif., perceives people "who moved between five or six companies within a five-year period." Their résumés, he says, "are a common relic of the dot-com era, when the average tenure was less than a year." Even if an M.B.A. had advanced to a higher position at a new company, Mr. Mitchell finds it difficult to determine whether the applicant "demonstrated the motivation to move up through an organization."

But despite recruiters' concerns about adequate work experience, more business schools are admitting students either straight out of college or after only a year or two in the workplace. If they enforce a strict work-experience policy, business school officials say, they worry that they risk losing top-caliber undergraduates who might instead proceed to medical or law school.

Recruiters are noticing an increase in young M.B.A.s—and they find it troubling. Christopher O'Toole, a brand manager in Milwaukee, Wis., has seen more applicants recently with less than two years of work experience. "Their focus is not clear," he says. "I haven't been confident that they really know what they want to do because they haven't had a real job." Inexperienced students sometimes "have been oversold on what an M.B.A. can do for them," he adds, "and there may be some un-

A MATTER OF EXPERIENCE

realistic expectations. Jobs may sound interesting or sexy before you get into them, but once you have experience, you have a much better idea of what you want and what it really takes to succeed."

While 22-year-olds are still a fraction of most M.B.A. classes, school officials clearly don't see eye to eye with recruiters. "The schools see the talented people we've missed, but the recruiters don't," says Edward Snyder, dean of the University of Chicago Graduate School of Business. To try to ensure that it doesn't keep missing those great catches, Dean Snyder's school has established the GSB Scholars program. Chicago undergraduates can apply to the M.B.A. program in their senior year. If they are provisionally admitted, they must then get two to three years of "substantive" work experience before starting classes.

It used to be more common for students to head right into an M.B.A. program after college. But during the 1990s, experience levels began creeping up, and by the end of the decade, most M.B.A. students were about 28 years old with at least five years of work experience under their belts.

Some of the top-ranked schools have relaxed experience requirements, partly in hopes of attracting more minorities and women. "We believe that going younger will result in a more diverse class," Dean Snyder says. Women, in particular, have proved elusive for many top M.B.A. programs, partly because some get married and start to think about having children when they reach the magical M.B.A. age of 28.

Brit Dewey, managing director for M.B.A. admissions and financial aid at Harvard Business School, says women are quite interested in Harvard's "early career initiative," which encourages people to apply with zero to three years' work experience. Harvard's "early career" brochure declares "no minimum age or experience required" and features an eclectic list of young achievers throughout history, such as Wolfgang Amadeus Mozart, Bobby Fischer, Jane Austen, and Steve Jobs.

"We're looking for academic ability and leadership potential first and foremost," says Ms. Dewey. "Then we consider the quality of experience and maturity of the candidate, not the quantity of experience." She notes that Harvard looks closely at younger applicants who have started their own business, worked part-time, or participated in a co-op program while in college.

At the University of Rochester in New York state, M.B.A.s are increasingly youthful. Mark Zupan, dean of Rochester's Simon Graduate School of Business Administration, believes talented young students will represent a larger share of M.B.A.s, especially given the recent declines in applications to many full-time programs. These are "challenging" years for M.B.A. programs, says Dr. Zupan. "Anytime you face adversity, it causes you to think deeply about what you're basing your decisions on." In 2004, full-time applications to the Simon School fell more than 20%, which he calls "the most significant decline I've seen in my 17 years in this business." In fall 2004, the Simon School's entering M.B.A. class was 27 years old on average, two years younger than in 2003.

Dr. Zupan and other deans believe some recruiters will find younger graduates refreshing because they're more idealistic and less set in their ways. "Companies can train them more easily to fit their culture," he says. One of his young M.B.A. recruits is Tom Starin, who enrolled in fall 2004, a few months after earning his bachelor's degree in meteorology from Pennsylvania State University, with a minor in global business strategy. His only work experience was a series of summer internships with a small lens manufacturer.

Even so, Mr. Starin made a big impression on the Simon School's admissions officials and on Dean Zupan. Mr. Starin's high Graduate Management Admission Test score (710) certainly helped. But what really made the applicant stand out was his successful online baseball-card trading scheme. While at Penn State, he earned annual returns of $2,000 to $3,000 on an average investment of $3,000 to $4,000 a year in baseball cards. "In effect, I started my own little arbitrage business," Mr. Starin says. He bought cards of players once their teams were eliminated in post-season games and sold them at times of peak excitement, such as opening day in the spring.

"This guy is going to be a winner," says Dean Zupan. "He has entrepreneurial zeal, creativity and a can-do attitude." All of which, the dean believes, overcomes Mr. Starin's lack of traditional work experience.

Some schools fret that young M.B.A.s won't be able to contribute as much to classroom discussion because they have fewer work experiences to draw upon. Indeed, that worried Mr. Starin when he arrived at Simon. But, he says, he quickly overcame his "underdog mentality" and had little trouble "finding

SCHOOLS WITH THE MOST EXPERIENCED STUDENTS

These business schools in The Wall Street Journal/Harris Interactive rankings reported the highest average amount of previous work experience for their full-time M.B.A. students.

Rank	University (Business School)	
1.	IMD (Institute for Management Development)	7 years
2.	University of Pennsylvania (Wharton)	6.2
3.	York University (Schulich)	6
4.	University of Michigan (Ross)	5.8
5.	HEC Paris	5.7
6.	University of Western Ontario (Ivey)	5.6
7.	London Business School	5.5
8.	Massachusetts Institute of Technology (Sloan)	5.4
	University of California, Berkeley (Haas)	5.4
10.	Erasmus University (Rotterdam)	5.3
	Fordham University	5.3
	University of California, Davis	5.3

insightful experiences to bring to the table," including his baseball-card business.

But Mr. Starin may be an exception. Some business-school officials believe young students are less prepared than ever for management responsibilities because they have been sheltered by so-called helicopter parents, who hover protectively even after their children reach adulthood. "Even 27 is younger than it used to be," says Robert Joss, dean of the Stanford University Graduate School of Business. "Many are still not married and are getting support from their parents."

Dean Joss is interested in students who worked in teams, interacted with customers, and hired and fired people, rather than just dealt with numbers in an office. "We would love to see students with more operating experience," he says. "Many business-school applicants have never experienced angry customers or a production stoppage."

To attract more seasoned students, the University of North Carolina at Chapel Hill is sticking with high standards of four to six years. "We've decided to err on the high side and keep our experience level up," says Mindy Storrie, career-services director at North Carolina's Kenan-Flagler Business School. "There are some things you can't make up for if you haven't been in enough different situations, gone through a restructuring or two, and worked for several bosses with different management styles."

Both recruiters and career-services directors agree that younger M.B.A.s aren't likely to fetch as high a salary after graduation. Alan Ferrell, director of graduate career services at Purdue University's Krannert School of Management, estimates that about two-thirds of recruiters reduce salary and bonus offers for students who are light on experience.

Arthur Rowe, a manager at Deere & Co., recalls hiring a woman who went immediately into an M.B.A. program after receiving her bachelor's degree in business. "She interned with us in the summer between her first and second year of the M.B.A. program and we regard her very highly," he says. "But her salary offer was less than 10% above what we would have offered her if she'd only had the bachelor's degree."

THE RIGHT ATTITUDE

FedEx Corp. took a gentle swipe at M.B.A. prima donnas in a recent television commercial. It shows an M.B.A. on his first day on the job bristling at a request to handle a large package shipment. "I don't do shipping," the nattily dressed young man informs his colleague. She assures him that using FedEx.com is so easy anybody can do it. To which he smugly responds: "No, you don't understand. I have an M.B.A." The bemused co-worker quickly replies "Oh, you have an M.B.A. In that case, I'll have to show you how to do it." The horrified M.B.A. is speechless.

While viewers chuckled at the award-winning commercial, corporate recruiters found it all too realistic. M.B.A. arrogance is an unpleasant fact of life for most recruiters, who cite it as one of the chief shortcomings of many business schools and their graduates. Commenting on students at Duke University's Fuqua School of Business, one respondent to *The Wall Street Journal*/Harris Interactive recruiter survey declared, "Student egos are as high as their GMAT scores."

"Gentler and kinder" and "more humility" have become an annual refrain in the survey. Recruiters repeatedly urge students "to come back down to earth" and get over their grandiose expectations. Many students seem to believe that the degree guarantees an immediate six-figure salary and a fast track to the C-suite. "I suggest that students learn what they can in business school and then check their egos at the door when they start work," says Elizabeth Bock, a manager at Hartford

Financial Services Group Inc. "While some M.B.A.s have expectations that their careers will skyrocket, the reality is that it takes time to build a knowledge base, garner experience, and earn a reputation."

Some of the most prestigious schools, including Harvard, Stanford and France's INSEAD, clearly suffer in *The Wall Street Journal* ranking because their elitism rubs off on some of their students. "They seem to think the world owes them a living," says investment banker Mark Greenbaum, describing some Harvard M.B.A. students he has encountered.

Such attitudes are certainly no way to secure a job. Mr. Greenbaum believes students behave better in interviews with the companies they really aspire to join, and reserve their cocky attitude for their third or fourth choices. He recalls that when he recruited for a major Wall Street firm, he would visit prestigious schools such as Harvard and Wharton and sometimes "feel like we were just a back-up opportunity." But at other schools like the University of California at Los Angeles, he found M.B.A.s who were hungrier for great jobs and gave recruiters a better reception. "What some students don't realize," Mr. Greenbaum says, "is that we're screening out people who demonstrate a sense of entitlement and reluctance to do whatever it takes to get the work done."

The most extreme example of M.B.A. arrogance was the student who never showed up on the first day of work. "We must have been his safety net," Mr. Greenbaum says, "but he didn't even call to say he wasn't taking the job. It was very selfish and cheated other candidates who had really wanted the position."

Some recruiters resent students who seek interviews even though they lack the credentials for the job. Sanjay Thakkar, a finance manager for Johnson & Johnson's LifeScan business, recalls discouraging a student at Stanford University from interviewing with him after reading the M.B.A.'s résumé and deciding it wasn't a good match. Nevertheless, the M.B.A.

arrogantly insisted on an interview. "It turned out that our in-stincts were right—he was not a good fit for us," Mr. Thakkar says. "He did not have any previous experience in finance or ac-counting, and he could not answer simple accounting and fi-nance questions."

Equally irritating are students who demonstrate scant knowl-edge of the company they claim they'd like to work for. They spoil their chances for a job offer and also give their schools a black eye. "Students need to ask themselves what kind of im-pression they are making on prospective employers when they approach us without any preparation," says Mark Asher, a product manager and recruiter in San Jose, Calif. He com-plains that business schools' career centers should advise stu-dents against contacting alumni at companies before they even research the firms. "Doing company research beforehand seems like a simple step," he says, "but every year I am con-tacted by a flurry of uninformed students from many top busi-ness schools."

Ken Bayne, a recruiter for Guidant Corp., recalls that during a visit to the Sloan School of Management at the Massachusetts Institute of Technology, he grew increasingly frustrated as the majority of his morning interviewees seemed to be using Guidant as practice for consulting and investment banking in-terviews later in the day. Both McKinsey & Co. and Goldman Sachs Group Inc. recruiters were at Sloan the same day.

So during lunch Mr. Bayne assembled a short list of questions about Guidant that students couldn't bluff their way through but could be answered by anyone who had browsed the corpo-rate Web page for as little as five minutes. When he asked his afternoon interviewees the questions followed by the query, "So why do you want to work for Guidant?" he received a lot of "deer in the headlights" looks. "We didn't invite anyone back for second-round interviews," Mr. Bayne says, "but hopefully we made an impression about the importance of taking inter-views seriously."

Of course, most business schools discourage such rudeness. When the University of Chicago's Graduate School of Business gathered job-search advice from its alumni to pass on to M.B.A.s, it urged students to "avoid hubris" and "keep the ego in check" when meeting recruiters. Although graduates may be armed with an elite M.B.A. degree, the school and its alumni advised that "you still have much to learn to be an effective professional—and employers know it."

At New York University's Stern School of Business, M.B.A. students are frequently coached on interviewing and networking strategies. "We tell our students they're great, but we temper the message," says Gary Fraser, associate dean of student affairs. "There's a fine line between confidence and cockiness." During orientation, for example, second-year students put on a skit for the first-year class in which they demonstrate the right and wrong ways to network with corporate recruiters. Among the tips: Don't cut in before the recruiter finishes his sentence and don't glibly drop off your résumé and say you have to run.

"We talk a lot about personal interactions and this sense of entitlement some M.B.A.s feel," says Mr. Fraser. "We try to impart to students their responsibility in representing the school. We tell them that every interaction they have with corporate representatives reflects on NYU Stern." That message appears to be getting through to many students. Although some recruiters in The Wall Street Journal survey complain about arrogance and aggressiveness when rating NYU, the school receives less criticism than some of its competitors.

Beyond being personally offended by snobbish behavior, recruiters say students who can't relate well to other employees are a liability to their businesses. Recruiters are seeking M.B.A.s who can work well with employees from the highest to the lowest levels of an organization. Too often, they say, M.B.A.s are so full of themselves that they don't treat fellow employees with the proper respect. One recruiter in the survey noted that, "Many M.B.A.s seem unable to tone down the attitude and integrate into the organization, respecting other people's past experience."

John Krotzer, a marketing manager in Massachusetts, has observed M.B.A. recruits clashing with lower-level manufacturing employees. "I have seen too often," he says, "graduates coming out on the shop floor and talking down to blue-collar employees, getting upset because they don't stay late to finish things important to the M.B.A., and getting frustrated in general that the priorities of the shop-floor employee are quite different than those of the M.B.A."

He believes that just as business schools emphasize the importance of interacting with people of different races and nationalities, they need to help students learn to appreciate and work effectively with blue-collar and clerical employees. He finds that schools like Northwestern University and Dartmouth College produce more open-minded graduates because of their collegial cultures and teamwork focus.

"An M.B.A. doesn't need to become a beer drinker, NASCAR fan or deer hunter to interact on the shop floor," Mr. Krotzer says, "but he or she needs to appreciate the different things that drive lower-level employees and work within those differences. The fact is that factory-shop workers and back-office administrative staff play an incredibly important role in the success of the business."

Shannon McKeen, a recruiter who works in sales at Sara Lee Corp.'s apparel division, also finds that some M.B.A.s are "high maintenance" and "act as if certain work is beneath them." So she seeks students who demonstrate maturity. To her, that means the willingness to "go the extra mile." For example, she says, mature M.B.A.s will take the time to drive to a retail store and inspect a product on the shelf so they can make a better assessment of a packaging change.

More than once, Ms. McKeen has counseled M.B.A.s that the degree doesn't mean they can skip steps on the career ladder. At best, it means that they have developed skills in school that may allow them to move through the steps more rapidly. "Regardless of the degree," she says, "at the end of the day, results, consistent performance, and alignment with company objectives are what make for success."

APPENDIX

SURVEY METHODOLOGY

The Wall Street Journal/Harris Interactive Business School Year 5 Survey is based on the opinions and behavior of 3,267 M.B.A. recruiters who hire full-time business school graduates. All interviews were conducted online from Dec. 6, 2004, to March 9, 2005. The 3,267 recruiters, all of whom were asked to rate schools with which they had recent recruiting experience, provided a total of 4,938 school ratings. To qualify for a ranking, a school needed a minimum of 20 recruiter ratings (range = 21 to 137 ratings).

THE SCHOOLS

The universe of U.S. schools identified for inclusion in the survey was based on information from AACSB International, the major accrediting organization for business schools. This list continues to provide the best objective source of information about U.S. business schools. Due to the absence of objective lists, the universe of non-U.S. schools was created through discussions with experts in the field of M.B.A. recruiting.

Schools without traditional full-time programs and those that didn't graduate 50 candidates at full-time programs in 2004 were eliminated from the list of schools eligible to be rated. The final sample of business schools eligible for ranking included 186 U.S. schools and 79 non-U.S. schools. These schools were invited to submit lists and contact information of recruiters who recruit their students.

THE THREE RANKINGS

Among the list of 265 schools eligible to be ranked in the Year 5 survey, 76 received the minimum of 20 recruiter ratings required for the final ranking. As in Year 4, we are publishing three separate rankings:

National Ranking: includes 19 North American schools

Regional Ranking: includes 47 North American schools

International Ranking: includes 20 schools—9 European schools, 1 Central American school, 6 National schools, and 4 Regional schools.

Our goal in creating three rankings is to group schools according to the recruiters they share, based on where recruiters say they tend to recruit. To create the three groups, we conducted a multivariate analysis known as hierarchical clustering based on the schools that recruiters said they had had contact with since September 2003.

The analysis revealed one large cluster of 19 schools (National schools) that attracted 39% of the survey's 3,267 recruiters, and a mix of 11 smaller school clusters—47 schools in all (Regional schools)—that attracted 50% of recruiters. There was some overlap with 10% of recruiters (312) working with at least one school from both clusters. However, recruiters are more likely to recruit at another school within the same cluster than at a school in another cluster.

CHARACTERISTICS OF THE THREE RANKING CLUSTERS

Mass appeal—the number of recruiters who say they recruit at a particular school—is one of the most differentiating characteristics between the National and Regional clusters. For example, National school recruiters are more likely to recruit at four to 10 schools (46%) than Regional school recruiters (26%). Regional school recruiters are also more likely to recruit at a single school than are National school recruiters (36% vs. 15%). Regional recruiters also tend to recruit within a network of schools that, for the most part, are geographically close.

Other differentiating characteristics include enrollment, type of recruiting, starting salaries, geography, and whether the school is a public or private institution.

Schools in the National cluster tend to have more students (84% have 500+ students, vs. 9% of Regional schools). National school recruiters are more likely than their Regional counterparts to primarily recruit M.B.A. students (53% vs. 40%). Regional school recruiters are more likely than National recruiters to recruit a mix of both M.B.A. and non-M.B.A. students (50% vs. 42%).

National school recruiters are more likely than Regional recruiters to offer starting salaries of $100,000 or more (25% vs. 8%). A higher proportion of Regional school recruiters offer starting salaries of $75,000 or less (37% vs. 7%).

Approximately half of National school recruiters do most of their M.B.A. recruiting in the East. Regional school recruiters are more evenly distributed across the East (25%), South (25%), Midwest (23%), and West (22%).

The majority of National schools are private (74% vs. 26% public); more than half of Regional schools are public (57% vs. 43% private).

International schools represent those schools that have a more global recruiter reach, attracting recruiters from four or more countries (range = 4–20).

THE RECRUITERS

The Wall Street Journal and Harris Interactive contacted recruiters by e-mail and/or regular mail, using names and contact information provided by the business schools. Each recruiter was sent the online survey's Web address and a unique password to ensure that no recruiter could take the survey more than once.

Recruiters were asked to identify all schools with which he or she had recruiting experiences since September 2003. Recruiters identifying more than three schools were randomly assigned three of those schools to rate, so that the maximum number of schools rated by any one recruiter was three. Recruiters identifying three or fewer schools were asked to rate all schools identified; recruiters weren't required to rate all three schools. Overall, 63% of recruiters rated one school, 18% rated two schools, and 19% rated three schools.

As in previous years, business schools didn't have control over which schools recruiters chose to rate, nor could they prevent recruiters whose contact information they hadn't provided from rating them.

To ensure that only qualified recruiters participated in the survey, we conducted a detailed audit of the results. In some cases, the ratings provided by recruiters showed patterns that fell outside what is considered a normal range based on the distribution among all schools in the survey. Recruiters who provided unusual ratings were removed from the overall sample. Ratings from those who didn't qualify as a recruiter for the purposes of our survey were also removed from the final results. Schools whose ratings consequently dropped below the minimum of 20 required for ranking were then deemed ineligible for the final ranking.

Among the 3,267 recruiters, 76% were company employees or managers who engaged in M.B.A. recruiting, 19% were human-resources professionals, 2% were executive-search-firm recruiters, and 1% were independent consultants.

THE RANKING COMPONENTS

The ranking components for all schools measured in the Year 5 survey include three elements: perception of the school and its students (20 attributes), intended future supportive behavior toward that school, and mass appeal. For National and Regional schools, "mass appeal" is defined as the total number of respondents who recruit from that school. For International schools, "mass appeal" is defined as the number of countries in which the school's recruiters are based.

Each of these three components—perception, supportive behavior, and mass appeal—accounts for one-third of the overall current-year (Year 5) rank. The Year 5 ranking of schools that were ranked in Year 4 and remained within the same cluster is based on an average of the Year 5 and Year 4 rank. For schools that are new to the survey or moved between clusters, the ranking is based on Year 5 results only.

CALCULATING THE 2005 RANKINGS

To be ranked in *The Wall Street Journal*/Harris Interactive Survey, a school required a minimum of 20 recruiter ratings. In most cases, the school rankings in the 2005 survey are based on a combination of results from the current year (Year 5) and the previous year (Year 4).

STEP 1: CALCULATION OF CURRENT-YEAR RANKINGS

Each school ranking is based on three components, each accounting for one-third of the overall current-year results:

Perception: The perceptions of the school and its students on 20 attributes.

Supportive Behavior: The intended future supportive behavior toward the school based on two attributes.

Mass Appeal: The number of recruiters indicating that they recruit from the school.

Calculating Current-Year Perception

The current-year perception score consists of recruiter ratings on 20 attributes.

1. Each recruiter's rating (from 1 "poor performance, does not meet your needs" to 10 "excellent performance, meets your needs very well") on each of the 20 individual attributes was multiplied by the importance that recruiter gave that attribute (from "1," "not at all important," to "4," "very important").

2. For each recruiter, the sum across the 20 attributes (importance rating multiplied by the rating of the school on that attribute) was divided by the total possible score. The total possible score is the total number of attributes answered (maximum of 20).

3. A mean perception score was then calculated for each school. The total possible perception score a school could receive is 40.

Calculating Current-Year Supportive Behavior

The current-year supportive-behavior score consists of two attributes: "likelihood of recruiting from the school in the next two years" and "likelihood of making an offer to a student at the school in the next two years."

1. Each recruiter's rating (from 1 to 10) on each of the two individual attributes was tallied and divided by the total score possible. The total possible score is the total number of attributes answered (maximum of 2).

2. A mean supportive-behavior score was then calculated for each school. The total possible supportive-behavior score a school could receive is 10.

Calculating Current-Year Mass Appeal

For National and Regional schools, a school's mass-appeal score is the total number of participating recruiters who indicated they recruit from that school. For International schools, mass appeal is the number of countries in which recruiters for that school are based. In the case of a tie among the International schools, the school with the higher standard mass appeal—the number of recruiters who say they recruit at the school—received the higher rank.

CALCULATING THE OVERALL CURRENT YEAR (YEAR 5) RANK

All schools were assigned a rank for each of the three components—perception, supportive behavior, and mass appeal. The lowest possible rank for each component was equal to the number of schools in that cluster (19 for National schools, 47 for Regional schools, and 20 for International schools). The overall current-year (Year 5) rank is an average of the three ranks across the three components.

STEP 2: CALCULATION OF FINAL 2005 RANKS

The final rank for all schools measured in Year 4 and Year 5 and within the same cluster is based on the average of the current-year rank and the previous year's rank. In cases of ties, the school with the higher Year 5 rank received the higher overall final rank. The Year 5 rank for schools that received fewer than 20 ratings in the previous year was based on the current-year results only.

Interpreting the Results

The results of The Wall Street Journal/Harris Interactive Recruiter Year 5 Survey are based on a total sample of 3,267 recruiters. When reported results are based on the entire sample, differences of plus or minus three percentage points can be considered statistically different at the 95% confidence level. Ratings for each school, however, are based on smaller sample sizes (from 21 to 137). Though we believe the final sample of recruiters rating each school can be considered representative of recruiters for that school, the results based on these smaller sample sizes may prevent conclusions that include statements about statistically significant differences.

THE WALL STREET JOURNAL/HARRIS INTERACTIVE YEAR 5 BUSINESS SCHOOL SURVEY ATTRIBUTES

Business schools were rated on 20 attributes that influence a recruiter's decision to visit particular campuses and hire top talent, as well as two supportive-behavior attributes.

Below is a list of the attributes against which each school was measured.

Student and School Attributes

- Ability to work well within a team
- Analytical and problem-solving skills
- Awareness of corporate citizenship issues
- Career services office at that school
- Communication and interpersonal skills
- Content of the core curriculum
- Faculty expertise
- Fit with corporate culture
- Leadership potential
- Likelihood of recruiting stars
- Overall value for the money invested in the recruiting effort
- Personal ethics and integrity
- School chemistry—that is, the general like or dislike a recruiter has of the school overall
- Strategic thinking
- Student chemistry—that is, the general like or dislike a recruiter has of the student overall
- Students' average number of years of work experience
- Students' international knowledge and experience

- Success with past hires
- Well-roundedness
- Willingness of the school's students to relocate

Supportive Behavior
- Likelihood of extending an offer to a student at the school in the next 2 years
- Likelihood of making an effort to recruit at the school in the next 2 years

ABOUT THE AUTHOR

Ronald J. Alsop, a news editor and senior writer at *The Wall Street Journal*, is the author of the book *The 18 Immutable Laws of Corporate Reputation: Creating, Protecting, and Repairing Your Most Valuable Asset.* He also writes the M.B.A. Track column and articles about business education, corporate reputation, and marketing for the *Journal.* He previously served as the *Journal's* marketing columnist and as editor of its Marketplace page, and is the author of several other books, including *The Wall Street Journal on Marketing* and *The Wall Street Journal Almanac.* He is a frequent speaker at international conferences on corporate reputation and business education. A graduate of the Indiana University School of Journalism, he lives with his wife and son in Summit, New Jersey.

ABOUT HARRIS INTERACTIVE

Harris Interactive Inc. (*www.harrisinteractive.com*) is a Rochester, N.Y.-based global research and strategic-consulting company. Known for The Harris Poll and for pioneering Internet-based research methods, Harris Interactive conducts proprietary and public research through its U.S. and London offices, its wholly owned subsidiary Novatris in Paris, and through an independent global network of affiliate market research companies. To become a member of the Harris Poll Online and be invited to participate in future online surveys, go to *www.harrispollonline.com*.